Paul Bunyan, Two Old Men, and a Wizard

A Collection of Fantasy, Absurdist, and Theatrical
Plays from a Career in Theatre

Bob May

Skye Bridge Publishing
Asheville, NC

Paul Bunyan, Two Old Men, and a Wizard: A Collection of Fantasy, Absurdist, and Theatrical Plays from a Career in Theatre

Copyright © 2018 by Bob May

Paul Bunyan, Lumberjack Extraordinaire © 1985 by Bob May
The Way the World Turns © 1988 by Bob May
The Andrew is Dead Story © 1991 by Bob May
Go To... © 1992/2008 by Bob May
Are There Really Any Kings? © 1992/2013 by Bob May
9th Inning Wedding © 1994 by Bob May
The Clown, the Penguin, and the Princess © 1993/2016 by Bob May
For the Love of a Woman © 1994/2018
Table Stakes © 1994 by Bob May
Hindsight © 2000 by Bob May
Sleeping Beauty © 2008/2017 by Bob May
The True Story of the Pied Piper © 2005/2017 by Bob May
The White Cat With Crystal-Blue Eyes © 2009/2017 by Bob May
The Wizard of Bamboozlement © 2009/2017 by Bob May
Two Old Men © 2017 by Bob May

All rights, including the right of reproduction in whole or in part, in any form, are reserved.

Cover Art by Gustav Carlson
www.touristunknown.com

Skye Bridge Publishing
Asheville, NC
Contact: Publisher@SkyeBridgePublishing.com

ISBN: 978-0-692-17963-5

CAUTION: *Paul Bunyan, Two Old Men, and a Wizard: A Collection of Fantasy, Absurdist, and Theatrical Plays from a Career in Theatre* and the individual plays published therein are fully protected under the copyright laws of the United States of America and all other countries of the Berne and Universal Copyright Conventions and are subject to royalty. All rights are strictly reserved, including professional, amateur, motion picture, television, radio, recitation, lecturing, video or sound recording, all forms of mechanical or electronic reproduction, such as CD-ROM, CD-I, DVD information-storage-and-retrieval systems, public reading and foreign translation, and none of such rights can be exercised or used without written permission from the copyright owner.

All inquiries for licenses and permissions for stock and amateur uses for all plays should be addressed to bobmay1049@gmail.com.

Royalty of the required amount must be paid, whether the play is presented for charity or profit and whether or not admission is charged.

AUTHOR CREDIT: All groups or individuals receiving permission to produce these Works must give the author(s) credit in any and all advertisement and publicity relating to the production of this Work. The author's billing must appear directly below the title on a separate line where no other written matter appears. The name of the author(s) must be at least 50% as large as the title of the Work. No person or entity may receive larger or more prominent credit than that which is given to the author(s).

Contents

Foreword	v
Introduction	vii
Paul Bunyan, Lumberjack Extraordinaire	1
The Way the World Turns	35
AIDS: The <u>A</u>ndrew <u>I</u>s <u>D</u>ead <u>S</u>tory	63
Go To…	95
Are There Really Any Kings?	100
9th Inning Wedding	106
The Clown, the Penguin, and the Princess	124
For the Love of a Woman	189
Table Stakes	227
Hindsight	311
Sleeping Beauty	350
The True Story of the Pied Piper	385
The White Cat with the Crystal-Blue Eyes	411
The Wizard of Bamboozlement	445
Two Old Men	499
About the Author	581
Published Works	582

Foreword

I first met Bob May in 1987 when he cast me in a production of *Brighton Beach Memoirs*. He directed me in two more shows in two years and then invited me to become a student at Brainerd Community College, where he was teaching and directing.

Throughout the summer of 1989, when there wasn't a good role for me in Bob's summer stock, I kept running into Bob at the college, at the theater, and at parties. Every time, he would say, "I'm writing a play for you."

With about a week to go before becoming Bob's student, and—I hoped—his protégé, I called him and asked him for some details about this play he was writing for me. He told me it would be the first play in the academic year, that it would be called *Carl and the Witches*, and that I would be playing Carl. When I asked what it was about, he told me he didn't know.

A week later at auditions, Bob told me that Carl's name had changed to Beanie and the title of the play had changed to *Beanie and the Bamboozling Book Machine*. I was still to play Beanie. I asked if I could read a script. Bob said there wasn't one. I asked if I could help write the play. "I'm a writer," I said.

So that's how Bob and I came to collaborate on *Beanie and the Bamboozling Book Machine*.

From his successful careers as an actor and a director, Bob brings to playwriting a masterful knowledge of dramatic action and plot. I always learned a lot when Bob directed me. But I learned a whole bunch of different things in a different way when we collaborated as authors. I was studying English and Drama by day, and each night, I was getting a master class from Bob in showing and not telling. Bob was showing me that he was a writer who understands writing—especially playwriting—just as well as he understands dramatic action, blocking, beats, and units.

I've read every script Bob has written. What dazzles me, as I reread each of these scripts in preparation for writing this foreword, is how well Bob revises. Sometimes it's just a tweak to dialogue or bits of dramatic action. Sometimes it's a radical rewrite that always crystalizes the action and clarifies why the character has to do what she does, why the reader has to keep reading, why the audience member can't look away. In each of the revisions, the play gets better. I think part of what makes Bob so good at revising is just plain old stubbornness. But I think it also involves his skill as a teacher. Bob the teacher has given a note to Bob the writer, who has taken the note and improved the script.

As thrilling as it was to write two shows with Bob in which I got to play the leads, it was even more thrilling for him to write a new play for me. In *The Wizard of Bamboozlement* (*included in this collection*), I was playing the character of Beanie, now twenty years later. I saw twenty years of working, reading, and writing come to fruition.

I'm one of those actors who always thinks I can say something better than the writer. It was true when I played Polonius in *Hamlet* and when I played Andrew in *The Andrew Is Dead Story* (*also included in this collection*). But wait a damn minute! When I read *The Wizard of Bamboozlement*, I didn't want to change one word. I still don't. I think it's Bob's best play yet. I hope you do too.

—Cris Tibbets

Cristopher Tibbetts has worked as an actor, director, performance coach, and program facilitator at theaters and schools across the country. As a playwright, his original scripts for children and adults have been performed and published around the world. He lives in Minneapolis.

Introduction

The first play I can remember writing was in 1971, and it was called *America the Great*. It reflected the hippie love and peace dreams of the time. I will spare you and not include the script in this collection. I wrote several plays after that, but I don't remember the titles, nor do I have copies of them.

I began a successful career as a director after graduating from St. Cloud State (*MN*) University in 1972, and to date I've guided over 450 shows to opening night around the country. I was always writing, but it wasn't until 1985 that I started to take playwriting seriously.

Up until I graduated from the University of Nevada, Las Vegas, with a Masters of Fine Arts (*MFA*) in playwriting (*1994*), I always considered myself a director who wrote plays. After earning the degree, I now consider myself a playwright who also directs.

Twenty-five of my plays have been published, but this collection is not about those plays. The fifteen plays included in this collection (*Paul Bunyan, Two Old Men, and a Wizard: A Collection of Fantasy, Absurdist, and Theatrical Plays from a Career in Theatre*) are plays that have never been published or they have been published and the publisher is no longer in business.

The plays are a representation of my playwriting from 1985 to 2018. They have all been produced and appear in chronological order in the collection.

Each script has a unique production history.

Paul Bunyan, Lumberjack Extraordinaire was written in 1985 for the Brainerd (*MN*) Community College Theatre

Department to perform, at the time, the annual Paul Bunyan Festival. In researching Paul Bunyan, I found that he really didn't have any adversaries. Sowbelly Burke, who is mentioned in the play, came closest. Paul and Sowbelly would have contests to see who could clear an area in the forest the fastest. Sowbelly just didn't seem like a strong enough villain. Then I read an article that stated "In 1951, a Russian newspaper in Vladivostok claimed that the Russians were the ones who originated the great lumber hero whose name was really Paulski Bunyanovitch." So with a little imagination and a lot of dramatic license, the villain was born, a Russian B4 KGB agent, Boris Slimovitch.

The Way the World Turns was commissioned by the Brainerd (*MN*) Independent School District for a program called the Bright HERizons Program in 1988. Its aim was to illustrate the importance of an education to middle school girls. It has enjoyed a life of several productions around the country.

The Andrew is Dead Story was commissioned in 1990 for an AIDS Conference in Brainerd, MN, and later published by I. E. Clark, Inc. The script, cowritten with Cris Tibbitts, was edited and changed per the wishes of the publisher. The draft, included in this collection, is the original draft performed at the conference. Cris and I have always liked this draft more than the published version. *Andrew* was my second collaboration with Cris, the first being *Beanie and the Bamboozling Book Machine*, also written with Roy C. Booth and published by Samuel French, Inc.

Go To... began as a class project while in graduate school at UNLV. The original title was *Go to Jail, Do Not Pass Go, Do Not Collect Two Hundred Dollars or Let's Make a Deal*, but the head of playwriting, Dr. Jerry L. Crawford, kept referring to it as *Go To...*, and the name just stuck. The short play was originally produced by UNLV Theatre in 1992 and has had many productions since then. It was made into a short student film, *Pass Go*, at the University of Central Arkansas in 2004. The script was published by Heuer Publishing in 2006 and it was published in the literary journal, *The Exquisite Corpse* in January 2009. It has undergone five rewrites, with this draft being completed in 2015.

Are There Really Any Kings? was first written in 1992 as a class project while in the MFA Playwriting Program at UNLV. It has been rewritten four times, ending with this 2013 draft. A short film of the play was made at the University of Central Arkansas.

The play, *9th Inning Wedding*, was originally written as part of a larger piece titled *Full Circle* and was first presented by the Senior Theatre Program at the University of Nevada, Las Vegas, in 1993. It was published as a one-act play by I. E. Clark, Inc. in 1994. It, too, was made into a film at the University of Central Arkansas.

The first draft of *The Clown, the Penguin, and the Princess* was written in 1992. I wanted to write about the effects of alcohol on a family and how the disease moves from generation to generation. *C, P, and P* was the result. The script became my MFA thesis and was originally produced in 1994 at the University of Nevada, Las Vegas, under the direction of Davey Marlin-Jones. There was another production of the play at the University of Arkansas, Little Rock, in 1996. The script undertook a major rewrite in 2016 for this published version.

For the Love of a Woman began as a class project at UNLV. The assignment was to adapt the Edgar Alan Poe short story, *William Wilson*. My first draft was called *Guts*. It contained elements of film noir, so in a rewrite, I focused on those elements. After watching many the classic film noir movies, including *The Big Sleep* and *Double Indemnity*, I began the rewrite. And I changed the title to *For the Love of a Woman*. It was produced by the UNLV theatre in 1994. A third draft was written in 2018 to be included in this collection.

Table Stakes was my second UNLV MFA thesis play produced by the UNLV Theatre Department in 1994 under the direction of Davey Marlin-Jones. Living in and attending graduate school in Las Vegas was a unique experience. This is my tribute to the 24/7 city of lights.

Hindsight was commissioned by and performed by Clay County High School in Rector, Arkansas in 1998. Its roots were in three different script plots I had been working on. One plot took its genesis from the title *Three Sisters* by Chekhov. My title was *Five Sisters*. It centered around one young girl with a half sister and stepsister on her mother's side and a half sister and a stepsister on her father's side. The second plot involved coming up with ten titles of plays with a number in the title from 1–10; example, *Three Sisters* or *Ten Little Indians*. And the third was a plot that involved a relationship between an athlete and a theatre person. *Hindsight* was what was born of those three plots.

Sleeping Beauty was written for and performed by my company Children's Theatre to Go in Conway, Arkansas, in 2008. Seven drafts later in 2017, the draft included in this collection was written.

The True Story of the Pied Piper was originally written for and produced by Children's Theatre to Go, Conway, Arkansas, in 2005. Rewrites were completed in 2017.

The White Cat with Crystal-Blue Eyes. My musical collaborator Karen Owings's favorite children's tale as a child was *The White Cat*, so I adapted the story in 2009 with intentions of producing it at Children's Theatre to Go. The theatre closed before we could produce the adaptation. Meanwhile, Karen and I adapted my play into a musical with the book by me, music by Karen, and the lyrics by both of us. The musical had its premiere with the Young Players at the Royal Theatre in Benton, Arkansas, in 2011. Later that year, the musical enjoyed another production in Rector, Arkansas, at Clay County High School. The script of the nonmusical included in this collection was rewritten in 2017 to include many of the elements we discovered in writing the musical.

The Wizard of Bamboozlement. For years I'd been wanting to write a fourth sequel to my popular play *Beanie and the Bamboozling Book Machine*, with Beanie as an adult. He would have a young son who uses the twenty-year-old book machine. And after my cousin asked me to write a play that dealt with the issue of dyslexia, I found a reason Beanie Jr. would need to use the machine, and the two plots became *The Wizard of Bamboozlement*. Cris Tibbetts, the actor who played the original Beanie back in 1989, flew down from Minnesota to play the adult

Beanie in the 2009 premiere of the sequel at Children's Theatre to Go in Conway, Arkansas.

Two Old Men came about after I had committed to a 2017 academic year-end Creative Writing faculty reading at the University of Central Arkansas. I planned for the Dean of the College of Fine Arts and Communication, Terry Wright, and myself to read a short play I had written several years earlier called *Park Angels*. I searched everywhere for that script and couldn't find it. I remembered the script was set in a park in southern Florida and one of the two older men in it got into a verbal altercation with a young kid at the park. With that in mind, I planned to write a one-act script around twenty pages. I even named the two old men characters in the new script Terry and Bob. At the faculty reading, Terry and I read the first act of what eventually turned into this full-length play published in this collection. The first act was published in 2017 by *Cave Region Review-Journal*, North Arkansas College, Harrison, AR.

I owe a great deal of gratitude to my wife, Cathy, for always being there for me, even when I am holed up in my office for hours and hours working on a script.

Enjoy,
Bob May 2018

A Collection from a Career in Theatre

Paul Bunyan, Lumberjack Extraordinaire

---

or

WHO IS PAULSKI BUNYANOVITCH AND
WHY DO THEY CALL HIM BY THAT NAME?

or

PAUL'S PLUNGE, PAULINE'S FLIGHT,
BORIS'S BLUNDER, AND TESSIE'S TURNABOUT

a melodrama in one act
by Bob May

© 1985 by Bob May
All rights reserved

CAST OF CHARACTERS

TALL TIMBER TESSIE, the lumberjackess
CLEAR CLARENCE, the spirits pourer
BORIS SLIMEOVITCH, the villain
PAULINE PURE, the heroine
SHOT GUNDERSON, the woods boss
SOURDOUGH SAM, the camp cook
JOHNNY INKSLINGER, the bookkeeper
BACKWOOD BILL BARBER, the bull cook
PAUL BUNYAN, the hero

SYNOPSIS OF SCENES

Scene One: A small saloon in the timber country of Northern Minnesota, just after lunch
Scene Two: The Bunyan Loggin' Camp, late afternoon
Scene Three: The camp, later that evening.
Scene Four: In the tall timbers outside the logging camp, six a.m. the next day.
Scene Five: A clearing in the tall timbers, late afternoon.

The premiere of *Paul Bunyan, Lumberjack Extraordinaire*, was presented at the Paul Bunyan Festival in Brainerd, Minnesota, on September 20, 1985, by the Brainerd Community College Theatre Department produced by Bob Dryden, under the direction of Bob May, with set and costume design by James S. Erdahl, lighting design by Rob Rettig, sound design by Larry Gochberg, with the following cast:

Tall Timber Tessie—Julie Pundt
Clear Clarence—Dan Anderson
Boris Slimeovitch—Paul Johnson
Pauline Pure—Sandy Brown
Shot Gunderson—Matt Cooper
Sourdough Sam—Rob Marohn
Johnny Inkslinger—Roy C. Booth
Backwood Bill Barber—Dan Anderson
Paul Bunyan—Erik Paulson

SCENE ONE

(The scene is a saloon in the timber country of northern Minnesota, 1890, just after lunch. AT RISE: BORIS, the villain, is sitting upstage at a table with his back to the audience. CLEAR CLARENCE is behind the bar. TALL TIMBER TESSIE enters in a huff and crosses to the bar.)

TESSIE: Whiskey! Make it a double.
CLARENCE: What's eating you this time, Tessie?
TESSIE: Shut up! I want whiskey, not talk.
CLARENCE: (*As he pours*) Drink! When you want me, my ears are all yours.
TESSIE: (*She drinks*) More... (*CLARENCE starts to pour*) Just leave the bottle.
CLARENCE: Tessie...
TESSIE: ...and leave me alone. (*She drinks*) That damn Paul... (*CLARENCE looks over*) I'm not talking to you. (*CLARENCE looks away*) I clear an entire acre lot before breakfast and he doesn't say a thing to me. And after breakfast, I out cut all seven Elmers. His famous axmen! They're still pulling my wood chips out of their stinkin' beards. Before lunch, I filled his pipe. Do you know how long it takes to fill Paul's pipe? And not so much as a thank-you. And then for lunch...
CLARENCE: He eats a picnic lunch with Pauline.
TESSIE: Am I talking to you? (*Pause*) How'd you know that?
CLARENCE: (*Mocking her*) Are you talking to me?

TESSIE: (*Grabs the front of his shirt*) Just answer my question.
CLARENCE: Sourdough Sam just left. He said you'd be stormin' in here any minute.
TESSIE: He should stick to his flapjacks and stop flapping his big mouth.
CLARENCE: Listen, Tessie, you know Paul loves Pauline. It's a match made in heaven. This jealousy jig you're on is no good. So just stop it.
TESSIE: Who's jealous? As far as I'm concerned, Mr. Mighty Paul B. can take a drink standing up, in that new creek that was started near Itasca when Ole the blacksmith knocked over one of the water tanks.
CLARENCE: That little creek has turned into a major river. Why, it's been flooding people out as far south as New Orleans. They're calling it the Mighty Miss-hap. A writer livin' in St. Louis coined it the Mississippi.
TESSIE: My association with the Bunyan Logging Camp is finished.
CLARENCE: You know Paul likes you. He respects you. You're his only woman logger. A lumberjackess!
TESSIE: Watch it!
CLARENCE: He gave you your name, Tall Timber Tessie. Why, because of him, you're as famous as Annie Oakley or Belle Star.
TESSIE: Yeah… Well, he'll be sorry when I'm not swinging my ax for him anymore.

(*She sashays over to a table and sits. BORIS stands up and turns around. The audience "BOOS." He crosses to TESSIE.*)
BORIS: Are you not Tall Timber Tessie?
TESSIE: Tessie. Just Tessie! Now be a good fly and buzz off.
BORIS: May I please to buy you a drink?
TESSIE: (*Pointing to her bottle*) Are you blind as well as deaf? Go chop your jaw in some other forest.
BORIS: I could not help but overhear your conversation with Mr. Clarence, kind bartender man, about Paulski. I too have a, how you say, a beef with Mr. Bunyanovitch.
TESSIE: You're talkin' some mighty strange words, but I think the bark is clearing from my mind and the sap is beginning to run.
BORIS: May I please have a sit?
TESSIE: That log's been made into a chair with your name on it.
BORIS: My name is Boris Slimeovitch. I am Russian. B4 KGB. I am in this country to bring Paulski Bunyanovitch to his rightful home. Back to Motherland Russia where he was born.
TESSIE: Bunyanovitch?
BORIS: You call him Bunyan. Paul Bunyan.
TESSIE: So that big ox is not only a two-timer but a Red as well!
BORIS: Not Babe. Don't want Babe... just Paul! Babe can stay here in America.
TESSIE: With Pauline! How can I help?
BORIS: I need your help to get into the logging camp... to meet the other loggers... to gain their confidence and Paul's.

TESSIE: What's in it for me?
BORIS: You may come to Russia with us and be Paulski's wife.
TESSIE: But what if he won't marry me? He's stubborn. His head's as hard as an oak and thick as maple syrup.
BORIS: In Russia, you do what you are told.
TESSIE: I like it. (*They shake*) You got a deal. We'll seal it in tree sap when we get out of here.
BORIS: Good… Take me to the camp.
TESSIE: (*Yelling triumphantly to CLARENCE*) He'll be mine before the next shipment of Swedish snuff comes for his stupid working ants!

(*BORIS and TESSIE exit, laughing as the LIGHTS fade to black.*)

SCENE TWO

(*The Bunyan Logging Camp, later that afternoon. AT RISE: The camp is empty. PAULINE enters, the audience "Ahhhs."*)

PAULINE: The afternoons are so long when my big Paulie is working. But loggers will be loggers. An afternoon without knocking off a few acres, he'd be like a bear without honey. (*She lets out a squeal*) Ohhh! I'll bet he's hot… and sweaty… and thirsty. I'll take him a drink of refreshing cool water. She picks up a giant canteen)
(*BORIS and TESSIE enter. The audience "BOOS."*)

TESSIE: Well, if it isn't Miss Pauline. The heartthrob of Bunyan Logging Camp and the inspiration to millions of lonely loggers throughout the land.

BORIS: (*Aside to audience*) MICE!! Or is it, RATS!! A dilemma. She is too beautiful for words.

PAULINE: Tessie, we used to be friends. We can be again.

TESSIE: They say the giant redwoods of California can be chopped down. It just takes so long no one wants to do it.

PAULINE: Oh Tessie, you hurt me so. I'll pray for you.

TESSIE: You best save your prayers for Paul!

PAULINE: (*Alarmed*) What?

BORIS: (*Jumping in to change the subject*) Ah, Miss Pauline, your famous reputation is preceded only by your beauty. (*Aside to the audience*) And she is so beautiful! Calm down my beating heart. Russia may have Paul, but Pauline is mine! (*To PAULINE*) Please to let me introduce myself. Boris Slimeovitch, at your service. I have come a long way to chop the trees at Paul's feet and worship the ground you grace with yours.

PAULINE: Oh, Paul will be thrilled to hear that.

TESSIE: I bet he will.

PAULINE: Now, I must get this water to my big Paulie. Make yourself at home. Tessie knows the camp.

BORIS: (*As he kisses PAULINE's hand*) Until we meet again, my every heartbeat will say your name. Paul-ine. Paul-ine.

PAULINE: (*Aside to the audience*) OHHH! He's such a charmer. (*PAULINE flutters off. BORIS watches her.*)

TESSIE: (*Aside to the audience*) What's that woman got that I don't have? (*Pause*) I know… Paul! (*To BORIS*) Heya, Slime-o?

BORIS: It's Slimeovitch! (*He laughs and makes the audience boo him*) I hate it the way you Americans always shorten names.

TESSIE: What's with the goo-goo eyes over Miss Perfect Pauline?

BORIS: It is nothing. I was uh… uh… play acting. To win her favor.

TESSIE: So, what's the general game plan? How are we gonna kidnap that big ox…

BORIS: No ox. Not Babe. Don't want Babe… just Paul! Babe stay here in America.

TESSIE: I mean Paul, he's a big ox. Babe is a dumb ox. How do you plan to get him to Russia? He won't leave willingly. He loves these north woods as much as he loves Pauline Pure. And the lumberjacks! They'll protect him. They worship him.

BORIS: Little by little, I will whittle away Paulski's confidence, his strength, and his hold on his men. Soon the lumberjacks, Pauline, and the world will see him as a has-been, a braggart, and a giant fool. I will win the power he once had and the men will gladly give him to me. Like throwing away yesterday's garbage.

TESSIE: How do you plan to do all that?

BORIS: A secret Russian formula! (*He pulls out a bottle.*)

TESSIE: (*Scared*) What is it?

BORIS: Vodka! (*The voices of the lumberjacks are heard approaching the camp.*)
TESSIE: Here come the animals!
BORIS: Animals!! Not Babe. Don't want Babe… just… Paul. Babe stay here in America.
TESSIE: Yeah. Yeah… just Paul. I know. I know.
(*SHOT GUNDERSON, SOURDOUGH SAM, JOHNNY INKSLINGER and BACKWARD BILL BARBER enter. All are carrying axes and are all exhausted and angry from having to chop timbers.*)
JOHNNY: (*Upon seeing TESSIE*) Oh, Tall Timber… it's good to see ya. I'll never be able to hold a pen in these hands again. He's got me choppin' trees.
SAM: I'd much prefer sweatin' over a hot stove.
TESSIE: You mean Paul has all of you choppin' timbers?
SHOT: Had to since you walked out. The bet with Sowbelly Burke was we'd have the entire Brainerd Lakes area cleared and developed for resorts before nightfall tomorrow.
SAM: Are you back to chop or sulk?
TESSIE: Watch your big mouth! I'm back to chop and I brought along some help. Let me introduce Russia's leading lumberjack, Boris Slimeovitch.
(*All the men start laughing as BORIS steps forward.*)
SHOT: A lot of help he'll be.
JONNY: He's so little.
SAM: Hot Biscuit Slim is bigger than he is.
BILL: My ax is as tall.
BORIS: (*Aside to the audience*) They will not be laughing so hard this time tomorrow!

TESSIE: You 'jacks are a barrel of laughs. If that's the way you feel, we won't help ya. We'll put a wager on the Sowbelly Burke team.
SHOT: Now hold on, Tess. Don't start sproutin' new leaves. We're glad to have you back. And welcome... (*Holds out his hand to BORIS*)
BORIS: Slimeovitch, B., Russian lumberjack. Helped log off the entire Siberian Forest. In just four days. Now it is nothing but a frozen wasteland. Good for nothing but Gulags. (*They shake hands*)
SHOT: Shot Gunderson, woods boss.
BORIS: Shoot, I've heard of you, Shot. Knocked a wildcat out of the top of a thirty-foot bull pine with one squirt of tobacco juice.
TESSIE: Shot can swing a double-bitted ax in each hand and fell four trees at a time. (*Points to SAM*) And this is Sourdough Sam, the camp cook.
BORIS: (*As he shakes SOURDOUGH's hand*) Sourdough flapjacks for breakfast?
SAM: Yep! I invented 'em!
BORIS: And this must be Johnny Inkslinger.
JOHNNY: What gave me away?
BORIS: The ink ring around your collar.
TESSIE: Camp bookkeeper and sole owner and inventor of numbers and figures.
JOHNNY: Now about your pay.
BORIS: No want pay. Just the chance to work alongside all of you great men and the Mighty Paul Bunyan.
TESSIE: Speakin' of which... where is our fearless leader?

SHOT: Pauline and him stopped by Granny's Tub, on the Gull Lake Narrows.
TESSIE: You mean the Causeway?
SHOT: Yeah, to freshen up.
TESSIE: Cute! Probably another picnic.
JONNY: No, something about inventing a Channel Inn. The logs jammin' Granny's could filter into the Channel and we wouldn't have to wait for the spring floods to float them down to the mills.
BORIS: Such a genius. What a man, this Bunyan. The inventor of so many mighty things and the doer of much more.
SAM: Paul can do just about anything.
SHOT: He single-handedly logged both Dakotas in a day and a half, just to furnish grazin' land for the buffalo.
BILL: It wouldn't have even taken him that long, but he stopped to help Gutzon Borglum.
BORIS: Who?
BILL: The Polish critter who carved the faces of the three presidents on Mount Rushmore.
TESSIE: There are four faces, you idiot. Can't you even get a story straight?
BORIS: (*To the audience*) A dumb one! An easy mark. I'll butter him up and soon he'll be on my side! (*To BILL*) I'm sure this strong handsome lumberman is not an idiot. (*Holds out his hand*) I've not had the pleasure.
BILL: My name is William. Bill for short. Bill Barber.
TESSIE: Give him your full name. It's Backward Bill Barber, the bull cook. A good-for-nothing grunt who carries wood and water for Sourdough. He

also looks after the bunkhouse and the outhouse. Paul really must be hurtin' if he has him handlin' an ax.

BILL: I did my share.

TESSIE: Pauline does more. Right, guys? (*All the other men start to laugh at BILL*)

BORIS: (*To the audience*) It is too easy! (*To BILL*) Do not let them get to you. Why, back in Russia, my good friend and leader among all lumberjacks, Backwood-na-kov Billski, Barber of Siberia, he looked a lot like you and he could just look at a tree and it would fall out of fear.

BILL: Really? Why, that's even better than Paul. Paul at least has to holler at the tree. And I look just like him?

BORIS: (*To audience*) A dead ringer? (*To men*) And I was just as good a lumberman as he.

SHOT: That's a bunch of bark. There's no one anywhere, any place as good a lumberjack as Paul Bunyan. And I'll stake my life on that claim.

JOHNNY: Shot's right. There's only one person as great as Paul. And that's Paul himself.

SAM: I'd cook for the Czar if there is anyone better.

BILL: If Mr....?

BORIS: Slimeovitch. (*Looks at audience and makes them "boo" him*)

BILL: If Mr. Slimeovitch says there is, I believe him. Right, Tessie?

TESSIE: I don't know, Paul's mighty big and he has…

BORIS: …he has Pauline!

TESSIE: And he has some competition. If B. S. says there is someone bigger and better, I believe him.

(*All start arguing - BORIS, TESSIE, and BILL against SHOT, SAM, and JOHNNY. PAUL enters, the audience cheers. PAULINE enters, the audience "ahhhs."*)

PAUL: What's all the commotion? We could hear ya clear out to Wilson's Bay. Ain't that right, Pauline, my sugar plum.

PAULINE: That's right Paul, my peach. (*They kiss*)

PAUL: You're raisin' such a ruckus, you got the ole black bear growling off the walls of his den. We've got one Mad—den on our hands.

(*Author's Note: "Mad—den" refers to a resort in northern Minnesota called Madden's. It is a regional reference. The line may be changed to "We've got one mad bear on our hands." In the original production, Paul stepped forward and spoke directly to the audience, saying, "Mad—den, Madden's, get it? Madden's Resort?" He then went back into character for his next line.*)

PAUL: (*cont'd*) Now what's the problem? (*All talk at once*) Hold on. One at a time. Keep your 'spenders attached. Somebody has to explain this. (*Pointing to SHOT*) Shot, shoot!

TESSIE: You always ask him to explain. He always does the talking. Why?

PAUL: Tall Timber. I'm glad to see you're back.

TESSIE: Yeah! I bet.

PAULINE: I am.

TESSIE: Put a lid on it, Pauline. (*To PAUL*) Why do you always ask Shot to explain?

PAUL: Cause I like to say, Shot, shoot. I said it. I think I'll say it again. Shot, shoot. (*He giggles and says it again*) Shot, shoot. (*He continues to repeat this phrase, giggling more hysterically each time he says it. The effect should be comical.*)

PAULINE: (*Tapping PAUL on the shoulder to interrupt his giggling.*) Paul, you're doing it again, my big pear!

PAUL: (*Embarrassed and trying to hold back his laughter*) You're right, my little papaya. (*They kiss*) All right, I won't say you know what to Shot. I'll say… (*He thinks for a moment*) Tall Timber Tessie tell! (*He repeats this over and over, laughing each time he says it. PAULINE taps him on the shoulder. PAUL looks at her. She shakes her head "no." PAUL pulls himself together*) What's all this noise about?

TESSIE: Boris here says he—

PAUL: Boris?

TESSIE: Oh yeah, Paul, meet Boris. Boris, this is Paul.

PAUL: (*As they shake hands*) A pleasure.

BORIS: The pleasure is all mine. (*To the audience*) Right?

TESSIE: Anyway, Boris here says he knows a lumberjack back in Russia who can out cut, chop, slip, and log you.

PAUL: That could very well be. After all, I am only human.

PAULINE: Oh Paulie, really?

PAUL: Yes, my puddin' pie.

PAULINE: Oh, my puddin' pop. (*They kiss*)

TESSIE: Well, I guess he's not the greatest 'jack in the world after all. (*All begin to argue*)

SHOT: Hold on, hold everything. I think the only way to settle this is to have a little contest.

TESSIE: How are we gonna do that? Backwood-na-kov ain't here, he's back in the USSR. Shot, you've been swallowin' too much tobacco juice.
SHOT: Boris, here, said he was just as good.
SAM: That's right. I heard him say, "I was just as good as he."
JOHNNY: I heard it too!
SHOT: What do you say, Big Boris? Wanna have a little loggin' contest with Paul?
BILL: Come on, Boris. You can do it.
TESSIE: Put Paul in his place. (*All talking excitedly about the contest.*)
PAULINE: (*Trying to get their attention*) Yoo-hoo! Yoo-hoo! (*She shouts*) YOO-HOO! (*All look at her*) Is this really necessary?
JOHNNY: Pauline, an American legend has been challenged. The first folk hero to arise since Davy Crockett has been shamelessly slandered. The enrichment of our American culture and lives has been desecrated. And you ask, is this really necessary? I mean, really, Pauline, get a life!
PAULINE: Oh!
BORIS: I accept the challenge for Motherland Russia.
PAUL: I too accept, for God, mom, apple pie, and the American way… and Chevrolet.
ALL: What?
PAUL: I haven't invented them yet. I'm working on it.
SHOT: The challenge has been accepted by both parties. The contest will begin tomorrow morning at six a.m. sharp. The first man to fell three 30-foot jackpines is the greatest logger alive. May the best man win.

BORIS: (*To the audience*) He will.
SAM: Come, Paul, Hot Biscuit Slim has been preparing your supper. You'll need your strength.
PAULINE: And rest, Paulie.
PAUL: Thanks, my sweet pineapple.
PAULINE: You're welcome, my sweet pea! (*They kiss*)
(*PAUL, PAULINE, SHOT, SAM, and JOHNNY exit*)
TESSIE: Can you really beat him, Boris?
BILL: Of course he can.
BORIS: I need his canteen.
TESSIE and BILL: Why?
BORIS: Just get me that canteen. (*He exits, laughing*)
BILL: Where's he going?
TESSIE: I don't know. This scene must be over!
(*BLACKOUT*)

SCENE THREE

(*The camp, later that evening. AT RISE: BORIS enters, the audience "boos."*)

BORIS: (*Calling*) Tessie! Tall Timber Tessie?
TESSIE: (*As she enters*) Here I am, Babe.
BORIS: No! Not Babe. Don't want Babe... just Paul! Babe can stay here in America.
TESSIE: I know, I know, no Babe.
BORIS: Do you have it? The canteen?
TESSIE: Pauline has it. She uses the damn thing as a pillow.
BORIS: Ah, very interesting. A water pillow. (*BILL comes running in*)
BILL: She's up. Her nightly jaunt to the outhouse. She's comin' this way.

BORIS: You two, go get that canteen.
BILL: She has it with her.
TESSIE: Figures!
BORIS: I'll get it from her. You two hide. When I separate Pauline from the canteen, fill it with this.
BILL: What is it?
BORIS: Secret Russian formula.
BILL: What?
TESSIE and BORIS: Vodka!! (*All three laugh. TESSIE takes the bottle and hides behind wagon with BILL. BORIS hides behind a tree. PAULINE enters, audience "ahhhs." BORIS steps out.*)
BORIS: Miss Pauline, you are looking beautiful in the moonlight.
PAULINE: Oh! You startled me.
BORIS: Please for you to forgive me. It is I, Boris Slimeovitch… (*Looks at audience and makes them "boo," then turns to PAULINE and kisses her hand.*)… only wishing you greetings in the night. A night so beautiful as you are.
PAULINE: You say the sweetest things.
BORIS: It is easy when I look at a face as bright as the many stars that form halo above your head.
PAULINE: Yes. Oh, yes. You're so kind, please don't stop.
BORIS: (*Crosses to a tree stump and sits*) Please to have a sit with me. I have not yet begun. (*To audience*) Have I?
PAULINE: For just a moment. I must get my sleep for the contest in the morning. (*She puts the canteen down, starts to cross to him. TESSIE and BILL start toward the canteen. PAULINE changes her mind and*

goes back to the canteen. TESSIE and BILL scurry back into hiding.)
BORIS: (*He grunts in frustration, then says sweetly*) Wouldn't you rather sit over here? (*He taps tree stump seductively*)
PAULINE: (*Who is now sitting on her canteen*) Thank you, this is fine.
BORIS: But over here, I can whisper poetry. Poetry should always be whispered.
PAULINE: You're right. (*She gets up and takes the canteen with her, puts it down next to BORIS and sits on it again.*)
BORIS: (*To the audience*) Rats!
PAULINE: (*Screams and jumps on top of the canteen*) Where?
BORIS: Oh no, my precious. Nowhere. Do not be frightened. Your face is too fine and soft to be wrinkled with fear. Come to Boris. I will protect you.
PAULINE: Are you sure?
BORIS: There are no rats.
PAULINE: I mean my face. Does it really have a wrinkle?
BORIS: Only the soft wrinkle of a rose petal. Now come. (*She steps off the canteen. TESSIE and BILL start toward the canteen. PAULINE stops and returns to the canteen. TESSIE and BILL return to hiding.*)
PAULINE: I can't.
BORIS: Why?
PAULINE: It's Paul.
BORIS: I know, you love Paul.

PAULINE: No. I mean, yes, I do. I love Paul. It's just that I promised Paul I'd stay with his canteen. I wouldn't let it out of my sight.
BORIS: I don't understand.
PAULINE: If I tell you a secret, do you promise not to tell anyone?
BORIS: (*With a look to the audience*) Cross my heart.
PAULINE: It's a secret formula…
BORIS: He knows! (*To the audience*) Rats!
PAULINE: (*Screams and jumps on the canteen*) I knew it!
BORIS: There are no rats… What secret formula?
PAULINE: Oh, I couldn't tell you. You'll laugh at me. You'll think it's silly.
BORIS: How could I, Boris Slimeovitch… (*Looks at audience and makes them "boo"*)… think anything that lofts from those lovely lips could be silly?
PAULINE: You do say the nicest things.
BORIS: I try.
PAULINE: Well, all right! Paul thinks if I have his canteen in my possession the night before a contest, it brings him luck. He calls it his secret formula.
BORIS: Is this all? (*To the audience*) Wait till he tries my secret formula! (*To PAULINE*) Why, that is not silly. I think it's… well, it's… for lack of a better word, sweet.
PAULINE: Do you really think so?
BORIS: (*As he tries to pull her away from the canteen.*) Yes, my lovely. Now, come sit with me under the full moon and starlit night and let me recite

Russian. (*TESSIE and BILL, once again, go for the canteen.*)

PAULINE: But the canteen.

BORIS: It's safe. I'll keep an eye on it.

PAULINE: (*She breaks away and returns to the canteen.*) You sit here with me. (*TESSIE and BILL return to hiding.*)

BORIS: (*To the audience*) She's a stubborn one. But never fear, superior Russian intelligence. (*To PAULINE*) RATS!! RATS!! RATS!! RATS!! RATS!!

PAULINE: (*Screaming*) Where? Where? Where?

BORIS: On the canteen!

PAULINE: (*As she jumps into BORIS'S arms.*) Oh, save me! Save me! (*He carries her away from the canteen.*)

BORIS: (*As he says this, TESSIE and BILL come out of hiding and fill the canteen with vodka.*) You're safe. It's all right. Nothing's going to harm you. Relax. (*To TESSIE and BILL*) Will you two hurry up?

PAULINE: Pardon me?

BORIS: Just telling the rats to hurry up and get out of here. (*PAULINE starts to look around.*) No, no, don't look. They're almost done. I mean gone. (*TESSIE and BILL finish and return to hiding.*) There now, all gone. You're safe.

PAULINE: I don't know how to thank you, Boris.

BORIS: Believe me, you've done plenty.

PAULINE: (*Realizing she is in BORIS'S arms.*) Oh! I must be going now. To where I was going before you... I mean, before I... Oh, I don't know what I mean. Goodbye. (*She starts to leave.*)

BORIS: Miss Pauline, don't forget your canteen.

PAULINE: Paul's canteen. Oh, yes.

BORIS: Until tomorrow. My eyes will retain your image on them.
PAULINE: Yes… uh, yes… until tomorrow. (*She exits. TESSIE and BILL come out of hiding.*)
BORIS: Great success!
BILL: You really think you can beat Paul?
BORIS: There is no doubt whatsoever now. By tomorrow afternoon, Mighty Paul Bunyan will be a joke in the eyes of every lumberjack around the world. He'll be begging me to take him to Russia. Me! The man who out-logged Paul Bunyan!!

(*All three exit, laughing. The LIGHTS fade to black.*)

SCENE FOUR

(*In the tall timbers, outside the logging camp, at six a.m. the next morning. AT RISE: SHOT enters and crosses to center.*)

SHOT: Contestants take your starting positions. (*BORIS enters, audience "boos." PAUL enters, audience "cheers." PAULINE enters, audience "ahhhs." The rest of the characters then enter.*) This contest will determine who is the greatest lumberjack in the world. Mr. Paul Bunyan of the USA… (*PAUL steps forward and makes the audience "cheer."*)… or Comrade Boris Slimeovitch representing the USSR. (*BORIS steps forward and makes the audience "boo."*) The first man to fell three 30-foot jack pines and return here to do ten jumpin' jacks, five push-ups, eat a stack of Sourdough Sam's famous sourdough flapjacks, then jump through this hoop and ring this bell is the winner. Come to me and shake hands. (*They do so.*) May the best man win.

(*BORIS and PAUL cross back to their sides. everyone ad-libs encouragement to their man.*)

PAUL: Pauline, my pearl, did you keep my canteen safely with you?

PAULINE: Yes, Paul, my oyster, (*They kiss*) right here.

PAUL: Give me strength. (*He drinks*) Pauline, you done good. This is potent stuff. (*He drinks*) Whoa!

TESSIE: Good luck, Boris.

BORIS: Do you have water in my canteen?

TESSIE: The best water in the world. Brainerd pure water. No fluoride! (*BORIS drinks*)

SHOT: Lumberjacks to your marks. (*They cross to center, turn back-to-back and crouch down into sprinter's starting positions.*) Set?

PAUL: Set. (*He raises his hindquarters.*)

BORIS: Set. (*He raises his hindquarters.*)

SHOT: Let the contest begin. (*He rings the bell.*)

(*PAUL runs offstage, then returns to kiss PAULINE, then runs offstage again. Meanwhile, BORIS sits down to have a smoke.*)

BILL: What in the name of tree bark are you doin'?

BORIS: Never to fear.

(*Chopping is heard. SHOT, JOHNNY, SAM, and PAULINE shout encouragement to PAUL.*)

PAUL: (*From offstage*) TIMBER! (*The top of a tree falls on stage. PAUL enters.*) Give me something to drink, Pauline. Our secret formula, my pet.

PAULINE: Here, my pickle! (*They kiss*)

PAUL: (*Drinks some more, then moves his arm ala Jack Nicholson in Easy Rider and says*) Nick. Nick. Nick. Nick. Nick. (*Sees BORIS sitting*) What's he doin'?
SAM: Never mind him. Probably some form of Russian psych-out.
JOHNNY: According to my calculations, the first tree took 37 seconds. You should be done with the others in less than two minutes.
SHOT: Go get 'em, Paul.
(*PAUL takes another drink from the canteen and stumbles offstage.*)
PAULINE: Is he all right? He sure is walkin' funny.
TESSIE: Boris, ain't ya gonna start soon?
BORIS: Patience.
TESSIE: You better win this thing. Remember, you promised I could marry Paul. When we got to Russia.
BORIS: Yes. In Russia.
(*Chopping is heard offstage again. All shout encouragement to PAUL.*)
PAUL: (*From offstage*) Timber! (*He starts to giggle*) Look out below! (*Another tree falls on stage from offstage. PAUL then enters, laughing.*) More secret formula, Pauline, my pumpkin.
PAULINE: Of course, my peanut. (*They kiss*)
PAUL: (*He drinks*) Smoooooooth! (*To BORIS*) Come on, Big Bad Boris, show me what ya got.
BORIS: The time has come. (*To the audience*) Soon he'll be mine and Motherland Russia's! (*To PAUL*) A toast. (*BORIS holds up his canteen, PAUL holds up his*) To the greatest lumberjack. Whoever it might be. (*BORIS drinks*)

PAUL: Bottoms up! (*He drinks and is now very drunk*) Wonderful stuff. Let's go. (*PAUL starts offstage in the wrong direction. SHOT stops him and points him in the correct direction.*)
PAULINE: Paul, my pepperoni, are you all right?
PAUL: Fine, my potato. (*They kiss*) Couldn't be better. (*He exits. Chopping is heard.*)
BORIS: Now. (*He exits.*)
PAUL: (*From offstage*) TIMBER!
BORIS: (*From offstage, starts a chainsaw and we hear him yell*) TIMBER! TIMBER! TIMBER!
(*Two trees fall from BORIS'S side, then a tree from either side hit the stage at the same time. BORIS enters with a big smile on his face. PAUL crawls in, very drunk.*)
PAUL: More formula.
PAULINE: It's all gone.
SHOT: (*Helping PAUL to his feet*) Come on, Paul. It's dead even. Get up and beat this guy.

(*BORIS is leisurely doing his jumping jacks. PAUL is falling down drunk doing his. BORIS then does his push-ups. PAUL can barely do his. BORIS goes to eat his flapjacks, but he doesn't. He cheats. He hands them to TESSIE, who hands them to BILL, who hides them offstage. PAUL falls face down in his flapjacks. The end has come for PAUL. All the men start to cheer for the winner, BORIS. BORIS jumps through the hoop and rings the bell. PAULINE, meanwhile, has stood astonished, flabbergasted, and devastated by PAUL'S side.*)

SHOT: The winner and greatest lumberjack in the world. Boris Slimeovitch.
(*All carry BORIS offstage on their shoulders.*)

PAULINE: (*Who has remained behind*) Oh, dear! My Big Paulie is down. What should I do? I know! I'll fill his canteen with more water. (*She exits*)

PAUL: (*Pulls his face out of the flapjacks.*) I've lost. I've let my men, Pauline, and my country down. I'm a failure. It's to the woods for me, to hide my head in shame. No man will ever see my face again. I'll grow a beard to cover my face. (*He walks offstage with his head down.*)

(*BORIS enters. The audience "boos."*)

BORIS: I won. Now to take Paul to Russia. Paul? Paulski Bunyanovitch? He's gone. This wasn't supposed to happen. RATS! Now how will I ever get him to Motherland Russia?

(*PAULINE enters. The audience "ahhhs."*)

PAULINE: Paul? (*BORIS does a take to the audience with a big smile.*)

BORIS: (*To the audience*) Of course! (*To PAULINE*) Ah, Pauline, my fair lady. You are just as lovely in the sunlight as you are in the moonlight.

PAULINE: Don't waste your words on me. Where's Paul?

BORIS: He's gone. The agony of defeat has humiliated him. He must have gone deep in the tall timbers to hide. You must help me find him.

PAULINE: No, I must stay here. He's always told me to wait here if he's gone.

BORIS: You must come with me. (*To audience*) If not willingly, by force! (*To PAULINE*) Now, come.

PAULINE: NO! I won't go. I won't!

BORIS: (*As he grabs her hand*) You must come!

(*A stylized tug-of-war starts here, in the old-fashioned melodramatic manner.*)
PAULINE: NO!
BORIS: YES!
PAULINE: NO!
BORIS: YES!
PAULINE: NO!
BORIS: YES!
PAULINE: NO! NO!
BORIS: YES! YES! (*BORIS wins and starts to drag PAULINE off.*)
PAULINE: Help! Help!
BORIS: Scream all you want. I beg you, scream. I want them to hear you. You will be my bait, in the trap to capture Paul Bunyan and take him back to Russia. So scream. Scream.
PAULINE: Help! Help! (*BILL enters*)
BILL: Boris, my friend and comrade. What's goin' on?
BORIS: The idiot comes. Why?
PAULINE: Help me, Bill.
BILL: (*To PAULINE*) Hold on, Pauline. (*To BORIS*) I'm not an idiot. You said so. You said I was the spittin' image of Backwood-na-kov Billski. The greatest lumberjack in all the...
BORIS: And you fell for it.
PAULINE: Don't you see, Bill, he tricked you. Help me.
BILL: No, Boris wouldn't lie to me. Let me come with you.
BORIS: I don't want you. I want Paul.
PAULINE: Please, Bill, help me.
BILL: No, Pauline, I want to help Boris!

BORIS: Get away, you fool. (*He shoves BILL to the ground.*) I don't need you. You'd just get in the way. Tell the others to find Paulski Bunyanovitch and send him to me. Tell him to come, if he ever wants to see his precious Pauline again.
BILL: What are you going to do?
BORIS: I'll tie her to some railroad tracks or strap her to a conveyor belt in front of a giant circular saw.
BILL: But there aren't any railroad tracks or sawmills around here.
BORIS: Then I'll do something else a villain would do to a heroine! (*He starts to drag poor PAULINE off.*)
PAULINE: Help! Help!
BORIS: And tell Paulski to come alone.
PAULINE: (*As they exit*) Help! Help me! Someone, help me! Help! Help!
BILL: He called me an idiot. And a fool. (*SHOT, JOHNNY, SAM, and TESSIE enter.*)
SHOT: Bill, what's goin' on? Who's callin' for help?
BILL: Pauline.
TESSIE: Did she see another rat? (*She laughs*)
BILL: Boris took her.
SHOT: Where? Why?
BILL: He wants Paul. He's gonna hurt Pauline to get to Paul.
SHOT: What?
BILL: Oh, Shot, I think I done something bad. Paul didn't lose the contest. At least not fair and square. Tessie and me...
TESSIE: Watch your big mouth, Backward Bill Barber!

BILL: I can't help it, Tessie. These guys (*He points to the others*) are my friends. My only friends. And I should have known it all along.
TESSIE: Boris is too.
BILL: He lied to me. He only used me.
SHOT: Used you for what?
BILL: Tessie and me filled Paul's canteen with a secret Russian formula.
ALL BUT TESSIE: What?
BILL: Vodka!
JOHNNY: No wonder he lost.
SAM: I knew that no man could beat Paul.
SHOT: At least not fair and square.
BILL: I'm sorry. He tricked me. He buttered me up. And he did the same thing to you.
TESSIE: (*As she backs off*) No! No! He didn't. He promised me, Paul. He promised I could marry Paul. (*She runs off*)
SHOT: Forget her. We gotta find Paul.
BILL: Boris warned that Paul had better come alone.
SHOT: He'll go alone. But we gotta find him first. Johnny, you go west, young man, toward the village that's always being pillaged. Sam, you head east to that big Cros-Bee hive, where all the deer are in the woods. I'll hightail it south to the little falls on the Miss—hap.
BILL: What about me? I want to help.
SHOT: Okay, Bill. You go north through the hole in the day.
BILL: But no one's ever made it through and lived to tell about it.

SHOT: Let's hope you do. Men, I know this is a dangerous task. There's a lot of land we have to cover, but we must find Paul and find him soon. Pauline's life depends on it. Now, let's go. And men, God bless you. (*They all exit.*)

SCENE FIVE

(*A clearing in the tall timbers that afternoon. AT RISE: PAULINE is discovered tied to the top of a tall tree: The audience "Ahhhs." BORIS enters, the audience "Boos."*)

BORIS: Where is he? Your Paulski? It's been over five hours. He must not care about you. He doesn't love you.
PAULINE: Paul's love for me will never die.
BORIS: But you might, if he doesn't come soon. For I will take a chop to this tree every ten minutes until it falls and you along with it. Starting now. (*He picks up an ax and swings at the tree.*)
PAULINE: Oh, help!
BORIS: You see, he better come soon.
PAULINE: He will. He will. (*TESSIE enters*)
TESSIE: (*Mimicking PAULINE*) He won't. He won't.
PAULINE: Tessie, help me.
TESSIE: Button it up, Pauline. He won't come. He doesn't even know about your little predicament.
PAULINE: I refuse to believe you.
BORIS: How do you know?
TESSIE: I saw him. He's sulking with the squirrels over to Sauk Centre. He's still drunk. He's made

himself a fortress not far from here. He was so ripped on the vodka...

PAULINE: Paul doesn't drink!

TESSIE: Even the tallest tree has to fall one day.

PAULINE: Oh!

TESSIE: Anyway, he was so ripped he chopped down ten acres, built himself a fortress and hung himself a "Do Not Disturb" sign on it. I think I'll call it Fort Ripped-ly!

PAULINE: Tessie, go get my Paul. Tell him to save me.

TESSIE: Your Paul? HA! He'll be mine, very soon. Boris promised him to me. Come, Boris, let's leave this flower here to rot and go get Paul. There's no guards at the Fort. He's a sittin' woodchuck.

PAULINE: He lied, Tessie. You can't give the heart of another person away.

BORIS: Quiet!! (*He takes another chop at the tree.*)

PAULINE: Oh, help me, Tessie!

TESSIE: Did you lie, Boris? He'll still be mine, won't he?

BORIS: He can only belong to one.

PAULINE: I told you so, Tessie.

BORIS: And that one is Motherland Russia!

TESSIE: Why, you good for nothin'... (*She starts for BORIS. There is a struggle. During the struggle, TESSIE jumps on BORIS'S back. He spins her around. She falls off and is very dizzy. BORIS grabs her.*)

BORIS: (*To the audience*) Dizzy broad! (*He ties TESSIE to another tree.*) Let's hope your Paulie comes soon.

PAULINE: He will. He will.

TESSIE: Can it, Pauline. Let's just face it. We'll soon be choppin' tall trees for the king of 'jacks in the giant forest in the sky.
BORIS: That's right. And I've waited long enough. The time is up. (*He crosses to PAULINE's tree and takes another chop.*)
TESSIE: What an aspen I've been!
PAULINE: I do believe in miracles. I do believe in miracles. I do. I do. I do.
(*PAUL enters, the audience "cheers."*)
PAUL: And with just cause, you should, my pawpaw!
PAULINE: Paul, my pomegranate, you've come.
(*PAUL crosses for a kiss, but BORIS raises his ax threateningly.*)
PAUL: (*He crosses away*) Yes, my love, I've come.
PAULINE: How'd you know? How'd you find us?
PAUL: A hootpecker flew over ya, a bit ago, and came and told me.
BORIS: Who cares how you found us. You're here, and that's all that matters. Now, will you come back to Motherland Russia, your rightful birthplace and home, with me peacefully? Or do I have to persuade you by using your Pauline? (*He takes another chop at her tree.*)
PAULINE: Don't do it, Paul!
BORIS: Do it, Paul! (*He takes another chop.*)
PAULINE: Don't do it, Paul!
BORIS: Do it, Paul! (*He takes another chop*)
PAULINE: Don't do it, Paul!
BORIS: Do it, Paul! (*He raises his ax for another chop.*)
PAUL: (*Stopping him from taking the chop.*) All right, Boris. You win. You win. I'll...

TESSIE: No, Paul. Look out, Boris, here comes Babe!
BORIS: Babe!! No Babe. No want Babe… just… Paul. Babe stay here in America.

(BORIS has lost his concentration because he is looking around for BABE. This gives PAUL enough time to overpower BORIS and pin him to the ground.)

PAUL: Give up?
BORIS: Uncle-ski! Uncle-ski!
PAULINE: Paul, my hero!
(SHOT, JOHNNY, SAM and BILL ENTER.)
SHOT: We got here as fast as we could.
SAM: The hootpecker told us where you were.
BORIS: My, such a busy little bird.
JOHNNY: We'd given up hope. (*To PAULINE*) Pauline, I figured your number was the big zero.
PAUL: Help the women down. (*BILL and SAM help TESSIE and PAULINE out of the trees.*)
SHOT: What are we gonna do with him?
JOHNNY: Tie him to a log and let him float back to Russia.
ALL: (*Ad lib*) Yeah! Let's do that. That's a good idea.
BORIS: No, I defect. I defect. Never really liked Russia anyway. It was my job. They made me do these things. I'm sorry. You could always use another lumberjack. And I am good. After all, I did win contest.
BILL: But you cheated.
SAM: Send him back. Tarred and feathered.
ALL: (*Ad lib*) Right. After what he did. He's no good.

PAUL: No! After all, we here in America are supposed to be civilized. We are all man enough—
TESSIE: (*Clearing her throat*) Ahem.
PAUL: And woman enough to forgive. To err is human, to forgive, divine. I believe Boris when he says he is sorry.
BORIS: I do. I do. I am!
PAUL: And we could use another lumberjack. Remember, we still have a wager goin' on against Sowbelly Burke to have the Brainerd Lakes area cleared before sundown tonight.
PAULINE: That only gives us a couple of hours.
PAUL: Then we better get choppin'. Are you still with us, Tessie?
TESSIE: Always, Paul.
PAUL: Let's get to work. I have this vision of great things happening to this area when we get done with it. They'll remember us around here for a long time.
BORIS: They will build monument to you. Giant talking statue.
SAM: And festivals celebrating you.
SHOT: Let's stop gabbin' about it and get to work so they can do all these things.
(*All leave except PAUL, PAULINE, and BORIS.*)
BORIS: By the way, Paulski, where is Babe?
PAUL: On vacation. He went home to Lake Mooselookmeguntic to see his mom and dad.
PAULINE: No, Paul. Look! He's back!
BORIS: AHH! No. Not Babe. Don't want Babe... (*He gets an idea*) Send Babe to Russia! (*He runs off*)

PAULINE: Paul, did I say, you're my hero?
PAUL: Yes, you did. (*Crosses to BABE*) Babe, my ole buddy!
PAULINE: (*To audience*) Oh! (*She runs after PAUL.*)

END

A Collection from a Career in Theatre

THE WAY THE WORLD TURNS

a fantasy in one act
by
Bob May

© 1988/2004 by Bob May
All rights reserved

CAST OF CHARACTERS

ALICE
DOROTHY
BUTCH
JEANIE

The premiere of *The Way the World Turns* was presented at an AIDS Conference in Brainerd, Minnesota, in 1988, under the direction of Bob May, with set and costume design by James S. Erdahl, with the following cast:

Alice—Sandy Brown
Dorothy—Amy Roach (Borash)
Butch—Matt Cooper
Jeanie—Coral Stein

Author's note: The play has several scenes/locations, but it has been written so there should only be short breaks in the action, and even those breaks are part of the show, as the actors shift from one location to another. The shifts are part of the nightmare ALICE is going through. The setting can be very elaborate or as simple as five cubes (*18" square.*) The original production used only five cubes, a lamp, and various hand props.

(IN THE DARK melodramatic soap opera music is heard, maybe an organ. The music fades under a SOAP OPERA ANNOUNCER on tape.)

ANNOUNCER: Good afternoon, soap opera lovers, and welcome to another exciting episode of The Way the World Turns. In yesterday's story, we were saddened to see that the triplets born to Peter and Wendy Pan didn't save their marriage... it only drove Peter back to Neverland to play with the boys for the rest of his life and forced Wendy into the cruel reality of the work world. We last saw single Wendy being turned away by an unsympathetic Burger King manager. The always-dreaming Alice was not fairing much better. Her life was anything but the Wonderland she played in as a child. As yesterday's chilling episode came to its dramatic conclusion, we left Alice talking on the telephone with her childhood playmate and fantasy-friend, Dorothy. We were all hoping that Alice would get off the phone before her bossy husband, Butch, got home from his long exhausting job of managing the local Burger King.

And now the continuing saga of *The Way the World Turns...*

(*AT RISE: ALICE is discovered in her suburban home talking on the telephone to DOROTHY, who is in her home. All the movements and gestures made by both women should be very exaggerated as the same movements and gestures will be repeated in scene two.*)

ALICE: Dorothy, do you think we'll ever find it?
DOROTHY: I doubt it Alice... and the older I get, the more I know it will never exist.
ALICE: But you had it in Oz.
DOROTHY: No I didn't.
ALICE: Glenda was there. All I had in Wonderland was that wicked Queen of Hearts.
DOROTHY: You don't have to tell me about wicked.
ALICE: Wouldn't it be nice?
DOROTHY: Wonderful!
ALICE: To find a world that wasn't male dominated.
DOROTHY: Speaking of... won't that dominant husband of yours be home soon?
ALICE: (*Alarmed.*) What time is it?
DOROTHY: (*Looking at her watch.*) Five to five.
ALICE: I still have five minutes. If Butch is anything, he's punctual. Nothing ever changes. He won't be home till five.
(*BUTCH enters holding a steering wheel in his hands as he drives a make-believe car in front of the women from DL to DR. He makes car engine sounds, complete with squealing tires. He does not see the women and they do not see him.*)

BUTCH: This ought to give the little lady a shock. Home before five. Supper better be on the table. (*He is gone.*)
DOROTHY: Did you hear, channel nine is going to start airing I Dream of Jeanie in the afternoons?
ALICE: Those old reruns will never die.
DOROTHY: I'd love to have a magic lamp… I'd rub myself right out of this existence.
ALICE: (*Wishing it would happen to her.*) That only happens on TV.
DOROTHY: (*Hinting that they are getting a divorce.*) Have you heard about Peter and Wendy?
ALICE: Yes, that poor girl… and with three new babies.
(*BUTCH enters his home and slams an imaginary door.*)
BUTCH: Surprise, Alice… I'm home.
ALICE: Oh my goodness, Butch is home!
BUTCH: Where are my slippers and newspaper?
ALICE: Dorth… I gotta run.
BUTCH: Supper better be on the table.
DOROTHY: Okay, Alice… I have to feed Toto anyway. (*They both hang up phones.*) Come on, Toto… it's din-din time. (*She exits.*)
BUTCH: Where's my supper? You been on the phone gabbin' again with that lazy good for nothing from Oz. Get me a cold beer. (*ALICE gets him a can of beer. A SOUND effect of a baby crying is heard.*) And shut that baby up. (*ALICE runs down stage and mimes soothing a baby.*)
ALICE: Shhh… that's a good baby. Shh… (*A SOUND effect of a dog barking is heard.*)
BUTCH: Haven't you feed the dog yet?

(*ALICE runs to another part of the stage and mimes petting the dog.*)

ALICE: That's a good boy. You're a good dog.

BUTCH: (*As he sits in his easy chair.*) I've already asked once about my newspaper. (*ALICE runs and gets the newspaper from the kitchen and then runs back to BUTCH and hands it to him.*) Turn the lamp on. I can't read in the dark. I said turn on the lamp… what do you think… it's going to magically turn itself on?

ALICE: (*As she moves to turn the light on.*) I wish it were a magic lamp. (*She begins to rub the lampshade.*) I wish it were… I wish… I wish… I wish…

(*Suddenly there is a big puff of smoke and JEANIE is discovered next to the lamp.*)

JEANIE: Yes, Master… your wish is my command.

ALICE: Who are you?

JEANIE: My name is Jeanie. You are my master. Your wish is my command.

ALICE: This is a joke. Butch put you up to this.

JEANIE: I came from the lamp. You rubbed the lamp. (*ALICE looks to BUTCH.*) Don't worry about him; he can't hear a word we are saying. Your wish is my command.

ALICE: Then I wish—

JEANIE: Before you wish… think! I can only grant you three wishes.

ALICE: I still wish… that I had a normal marriage.

(*JEANIE nods her head and claps her hands twice. There is another cloud of smoke. A strobe light flashes as fast calliope music plays. JEANIE and BUTCH exit. ALICE pinwheels and spins back to her original position on the telephone.*

DOROTHY enters spinning to her original position on the telephone. The music and strobe light stop when they are in position. This scene is played exactly like the previous scene, with the same gestures and movements. The only thing that has changed is the characters attitudes; and the lines slightly.)

ALICE (*cont'd*): Dorothy, aren't you happy we found it?

DOROTHY: I couldn't ask for anything more, Alice… and the older I get, the more I know we did the right thing.

ALICE: You mean by going to Oz?

DOROTHY: That's right.

ALICE: The Wizard was there… And in Wonderland I had the Cheshire cat.

DOROTHY: You don't have to tell me about cats… I had a lion.

ALICE: Isn't it nice?

DOROTHY: Wonderful!

ALICE: All those men… they helped us out so much.

DOROTHY: Speaking of… shouldn't your wonderful husband be home soon?

ALICE: (*Still very happy.*): What time is it?

DOROTHY: (*Looks at her watch.*) Five to five.

ALICE: We can talk for another five minutes. Butch is very punctual… he won't be home before five.

(*BUTCH enters holding a steering wheel in his hands as he drives an imaginary car across the stage. This time the car sounds he makes are mellow, as if he were driving a nice quiet Chevy station wagon. He also carries a newspaper and a dozen roses. Again the women do not see him nor does he see them.*)

BUTCH: I can't wait to see my lady, my love. I'm right on time. Home by five on the nose. (*He is gone.*)
DOROTHY: Did you hear channel nine is going to start airing The Love Boat in the afternoons?
ALICE: Those old reruns will never die.
DOROTHY: I'd love to take one of those cruises... it would be right out of this world.
ALICE: Television is such a sweet reflection of life.
DOROTHY: Aren't you happy for Peter and Wendy?
ALICE: Yes, that lucky girl... three new babies.
(*BUTCH enters and shuts the imaginary door.*)
BUTCH: Alice, honey... I'm home.
ALICE: (*Into the phone.*) Butch is home... (*Calling to BUTCH.*) I'm on the phone, darling.
BUTCH: I picked up a paper and I brought you some roses.
ALICE: Dorth, I gotta run. He bought me flowers and that can mean only one thing.
BUTCH: Do you want to go out for dinner?
DOROTHY: Okay, Alice... Toto's hungry anyway. (*ALICE and DOROTHY hang up their phones.*) Here Toto, baby... din din time. Is filet mignon all right? (*DOROTHY exits. BUTCH hands ALICE the roses and kisses her.*)
BUTCH: Since you've been on the phone again, I know you haven't had time to cook supper, so let's go out. We can have a nice cold bottle of wine. (*A SOUND effect of a baby crying is heard. BUTCH walks DS and comforts an imaginary baby.*) And how's my little pumpkin? (*A SOUND effect of a barking dog is heard. BUTCH walks over and pets the imaginary dog.*) Hi, Sport... good dog. (*HE sits in his easy chair*

to read his paper.) Honey, would you like to read the gossip section? (*He hands ALICE a section of the paper. He notices the lamp isn't on so he jumps up.*) Here, sweetie, let me turn on the lamp for you. (*ALICE jumps up and blocks his way.*)
ALICE: No! Don't touch that lamp! (*ALICE sits BUTCH back in his chair and then sits on his lap.*)
BUTCH: Anything for you, sugar! (*He lets out a big sigh.*)
ALICE: Butch, is anything wrong?
BUTCH: (*Not telling the truth.*) Nothing… I'm so happy.
ALICE: Oh, darling… so am I. I couldn't ask for anything more. A loving husband and one point six adorable children in a beautiful two-bedroom prefab suburbia home surrounded by a white picket fence with a dog in the backyard and two cats in the front. Everything is perfect!
BUTCH: Well… not everything.
ALICE: What else could you possibly want?
BUTCH: A job.
ALICE: You have a wonderful job at Burger King.
BUTCH: (*A little bit of the old BUTCH is talking here.*) I thought I did. And I did up until about five minutes ago… but things are different now… things have changed. I left work early today to surprise you and make sure you had dinner on the table. (*As the new, loving BUTCH.*) But none of that seems to make any difference. (*Very happy.*) I lost my job… dinner's not ready and I don't care… I have you and I'm happy. (*He gives ALICE a big loving bear hug.*)
ALICE: But you have to work.

BUTCH: Why?

ALICE: Bills! How are we going to eat? Pay the mortgage?

BUTCH: Who cares? We have one another. (*BUTCH gives ALICE another bear hug. ALICE breaks free of the embrace.*)

ALICE: Just a second, honey... I think I know what happened. (*Shouting to the heavens.*) Jeanie! Jeanie! (*Runs to the lamp and starts to rub the shade.*) Come out of there. Darn you, Jeanie... come here!

(*In a cloud of smoke JEANIE appears. Although BUTCH is in the scene, he only talks to ALICE, he does not see JEANIE.*)

JEANIE: You rubbed... my wish is your command. I mean your wish is my command.

ALICE: What the Queen of Hearts happened? I wished for a normal marriage.

JEANIE: And I gave you one. Isn't Butch sweet?

ALICE: But he lost his job.

JEANIE: You asked for a normal marriage, not a perfect one. Husbands lose their jobs all the time.

ALICE: Then I wish for a... (*She shuts her eyes an begins to wish.*)

JEANIE: Uh uh... don't waste a wish. You only have two left.

ALICE: What am I supposed to do?

JEANIE: Go out and get a job, like millions of other housewives. You be the breadwinner.

ALICE: Why should I? Butch is the man, he's supposed to work. He can find another job.

JEANIE: He tried... no luck!

(*BUTCH, who has been reading the paper this entire time, suddenly jumps up and runs to ALICE. HE refers to the paper as though he has been searching the want ads for a job.*)

BUTCH: (*Whining.*) This whole town has something against young people. I can't find a job anywhere.

JEANIE: He should have finished high school.

BUTCH: Alice, honey… why don't you look for a job?

ALICE: Me?

JEANIE: Why not? You went to high school.

ALICE: Only for the social life and the boys.

BUTCH: We have to do something, baby. Little Butch needs food and clean diapers. I've been unemployed for over a month.

ALICE: A month? It's only been a few minutes.

JEANIE: Time does funny things when you are fooling with Jeanies.

ALICE: Then I'll just wish Butch gets another job and we have a perfect marriage.

JEANIE: That's two wishes… you'll be out of wishes and my job will be finished.

ALICE: You don't think I can do it.

JEANIE: You haven't tried.

BUTCH: (*Pleading.*) Alice, sweetie… you have to do something. Little Butch is starting to look like one of those starving African babies. (*The SOUND of a baby crying is heard.*)

JEANIE: It's decision time. (*The baby begins to wail.*)

BUTCH: Alice… please!

ALICE: (*To BUTCH.*) All right, I'll get a job. (*To JEANIE.*) I'll show you… I don't need your dumb ol' wish.

(*With a flash the strobe light comes on. Calliope music and smoke fill the stage. The actors move the cubes to form a desk and chair in an employment office. JEANIE and BUTCH exit. ALICE spins to stop behind a girl waiting in an employment line. The music and strobe stop. The lighting returns to normal. ALICE taps the girl on the shoulder.*)

ALICE (*cont'd*): Excuse me have you been here long? (*The girl turns around. It is DOROTHY.*) Dottie... what are you doing here?

DOROTHY: Don't ask me. One second I am watching The Love Boat with Toto and the next thing I know I'm standing in an employment line looking for a job.

ALICE: It's a long story.

DOROTHY: What am I doing here? I don't wanna work. You wanna go ahead of me? Go ahead.

ALICE: (*Frantic.*) Thanks, I need this job. Little Butch is in the hospital and— Wait a minute. What did I just say?

DOROTHY: (*Calmly repeating what ALICE just said.*) Little Butch is in the hospital and...

ALICE: It's all happening so fast. It isn't fair! (*Shouting to the heavens.*) Do you hear me, Jeanie... it isn't fair!

(*JEANIE enters with notepad and pencil. She sits behind the desk. She is the person in charge of hiring.*)

JEANIE: Next. (*With a smile to ALICE.*) Life isn't fair! (*The smile is gone. She is all business.*) Next! (*ALICE walks to the desk.*) Name?

ALICE: You know my name.

JEANIE: (*As she writes.*) Hmmmm! Doesn't take orders.

ALICE: Alice.

JEANIE: (*Asking for last name.*) What?
ALICE: (*Thinking JEANIE really heard and is playing games.*) You heard me.
JEANIE: That's a peculiar last name.
ALICE: That's not my last name.
JEANIE: Then what is it?
ALICE: (*Thinks for a moment.*): I don't know.
JEANIE: Hold on… are you a high school graduate? You have to be a high school graduate to apply.
ALICE: You know I am.
JEANIE: Then answer the questions. Last name?
ALICE: I can't remember.
JEANIE: Come on Alice, these questions aren't that hard.
ALICE: It's always just been Alice in Wonderland!
JEANIE: (*As she writes.*) Last name, Wonderland. Middle initial N. (*To ALICE.*) Past experience?
ALICE: I'm a mother. (*Pause. JEANIE gives ALICE a look.*) And I've traveled a lot.
JEANIE: (*As she writes.*) None. (*To ALICE.*) Do you type?
ALICE: A little.
JEANIE: How many words per minute?
ALICE: It depends on how many fingers I use and if I look at the keyboard.
JEANIE: Shorthand?
ALICE: No, I have large hands. I can reach three octaves on the piano.
JEANIE: (*As she rips up the application form.*) I hear the civic theatre is looking for a rehearsal accompanist. Next!

ALICE: Wait... you don't understand... what am I saying... of course you understand.
JEANIE: Next.
ALICE: I need this job.
JEANIE: I'm sorry Miss Wonderland. You're not qualified for this job. Next, please. (*DOROTHY steps up to the desk. ALICE backs away in a daze.*) Name?
DOROTHY: The name's Dorothy, but I don't want this job. I don't even know what I'm doing here. I was at home and the next thing I know, I'm here. (*Referring to ALICE.*) This is her fantasy, not mine.
JEANIE: Past experience?
(*ALICE pushes DOROTHY away from the desk and speaks to JEANIE.*)
ALICE: You're so uncaring... if you were a man I could deal with you. Ooooh... I wish you were a man!
(*JEANIE stands with a smile. SHE nods her head and claps her hands twice as she speaks.*)
JEANIE: Number two!
(*With a flash the strobe light comes on. Calliope music and smoke fill the stage. The actors move the cubes to form a counter at a Burger King at SL and ALICE's house with the table and lamp at SR. JEANIE and DOROTHY exit. ALICE spins to a stop by the counter. BUTCH is behind the counter complete with Burger King paper crown on his head. The music and strobe stop. The lighting returns to normal.*)
BUTCH: Welcome to Burger King... may I help you?
ALICE: (*Still in a daze, from things happening so quickly.*) I'd like to see the manager.
BUTCH: Alice... it's me. You know I'm the manager.

ALICE: Butch! What are you doing here? And Little Butch... what did you do with Little Butch?

BUTCH: Relax... Little Butch is fine. Dorothy is watching him.

ALICE: What are you doing here? You lost your job!

BUTCH: Don't ask me what's happening. Little Butch was just going into intensive care and then bang, he's okay and we're sitting in the living room and I get a call telling me I'm late for work... then bang, Dorothy's there, saying she'll sit Little Butch and boom, here I am.

ALICE: I'll try to explain later. Right now I'd like to apply for a job.

BUTCH: But, honey, I got my job back. You don't have to work now.

ALICE: Yes I do.

BUTCH: Why?

ALICE: It's turned into a quest. You don't think I can do it.

BUTCH: Sure I do.

ALICE: Don't patronize me. Are you going to hire me or not?

BUTCH: (*As pulls out an application form.*) Fill out this application.

ALICE: Can't you do that for me? You know all the information.

BUTCH: Fine. (*Reading from the application form.*) Name, address, phone... blah, blah, blah... I know all those answers. Can you do simple addition and subtraction?

ALICE: What for? You have computers... they do it all for you.

BUTCH: We had computers when I worked here before... but now we don't. Something odd is happening.
ALICE: (*Agreeing with him.*) I'm caught in some weird Twilight Zone ruled by a Jeanie with a strange sense of humor.
BUTCH: (*Still asking questions that are on the application.*) Did you have math in high school?
ALICE: The last math class I had was back in junior high... seventh grade, I think.
BUTCH: Do you remember anything from it?
ALICE: Now? I didn't think it was helping me then!
BUTCH: Everything you learn all the way through school is eventually used in life.
ALICE: (*Sarcastically.*) When did you become a philosopher? You didn't even graduate from high school.
BUTCH: That was earlier in the play. Now I'm a graduate from Harvard Law School. (*He produces a big diploma.*)
ALICE: Then why are you working at a Burger King?
BUTCH: I don't know! (*He yells to unseen employees and throws his paper crown to the floor.*) I quit. (*To ALICE.*) And I want a divorce. Goodbye.
ALICE: (*Panicking.*) You can't leave me... what about Little Butch?
BUTCH: Who's Little Butch?
ALICE: Our son.
BUTCH: We don't have any children.
ALICE: You were just talking about him. Intensive care! Dorothy is babysitting him now.

BUTCH: Are you on drugs? You should just say no... you know! My law partner will be in touch. (*BUTCH exits.*)

ALICE: (*Confusion and panic.*) A phone... where is my cell phone? (*ALICE digs threw her purse, finds her phone, and dials. The phone rings in ALICE's house. DOROTHY enters and answers.*)

DOROTHY: Hello... Wonderland and Oz residence.

ALICE: Dottie... it's Alice.

DOROTHY: Hey roomie!

ALICE: Is Little Butch all right?

DOROTHY: Who?

ALICE: My baby... Little Butch! Is he okay?

DOROTHY: Oh... just a minute I'll check. (*SHE puts the phone down, walks to an imaginary fireplace area, then returns to the phone.*) He's fine. He's curled up next to the fireplace with Toto.

ALICE: Are you crazy? Get him away from the fire and that filthy dog.

DOROTHY: I think it's great that a dog and a cat are such close friends.

ALICE: Little Butch is not a cat!

DOROTHY: I know you don't treat him like a cat... but he is.

ALICE: (*More to herself.*) Job hunting is so confusing.

DOROTHY: How's the job search going?

ALICE: Don't ask.

DOROTHY: Is everything all right?

ALICE: No... but I know how to fix it. Dottie, will you do me a favor?

DOROTHY: Anything for my roomy.

ALICE: I'm not your roommate... I am married.

DOROTHY: Sure you are... just like your cat is a baby.
ALICE: Go to the lamp on the side table and rub the shade.
DOROTHY: What for?
ALICE: (*Screaming.*) Just do it!
DOROTHY: Okay... okay! (*She puts down the phone down, walks to the lamp, rubs the shade slightly, walks back to the phone, picks it up, and talks.*) Now what?
ALICE: Did you rub it?
DOROTHY: Yes.
ALICE: You didn't rub it hard enough. Do it again. (*As DOROTHY goes to the lamp and rubs the shade, ALICE pleads to the heavens.*) Please work. Jeanie, please come.
(*In a cloud of smoke JEANIE appears next to DOROTHY.*)
JEANIE: Yes, master... your wish is my command.
DOROTHY: Really?
ALICE: (*Yelling into the phone.*) Dorothy...stay away from that Jeanie. She's mine.
JEANIE: (*To DOROTHY, pointing to the phone.*) Someone's yelling for you on the phone.
(*DOROTHY picks up the phone and speaks into it.*)
DOROTHY: That's a neat trick. Where did you get that lamp?
ALICE: Never mind. Put her on the phone.
(*DOROTHY gives the phone to JEANIE.*)
DOROTHY: It's for you. (*JEANIE takes the phone and talks into it.*)
JEANIE: Hello... Jeanie speaking. How may I help you?

ALICE: You know perfectly well how you can help me. Butch wants a divorce.
JEANIE: In today's society over one third of all marriages end in divorce.
ALICE: And what about my son?
JEANIE: If you have a son and you're getting divorced... hadn't you better get a job.
ALICE: That's what I called you for.
JEANIE: You didn't call me... this young lady did. And now she has three wishes coming.
DOROTHY: Holy Oz!
JEANIE: (*To DOROTHY.*) And you don't even have to click your heals together.
ALICE: You're not finished with me yet. Isn't there something in the Jeanie union rules that say you can't move on to the next master until you've finished with the first?
JEANIE: You're an intelligent girl. You shouldn't have any trouble finding a job.
ALICE: But I can't. I don't have any training.
JEANIE: You have a problem. What do you want from me?
ALICE: My husband and son back.
JEANIE: Then get a job. Choose the profession of your choice.
ALICE: But I'm a girl.
JEANIE: Woman can do anything they set their minds to. You want to be a judge, be a judge. You want to be a clerk, be a clerk. A cop, lawyer, newspaper reporter, astronaut... anything. You could even be President of the United States.
ALICE: But I need an education.

JEANIE: (*Agreeing.*) And the desire.
ALICE:: What am I going to do?
JEANIE: At least YOU have another chance.
ALICE: How?
JEANIE: You still have one more wish left.
ALICE: Then I wish I was a college graduate… first in my class… now working in the corporate world, making a very large salary.

(*JEANIE nods her head and claps her hands twice. In a flash the strobe light comes on. Calliope music and smoke fill the stage. The actors move the cubes to form a desk with a chair in an executive's office somewhere in the corporate world. DOROTHY and JEANIE exit. ALICE spins to the chair behind the desk and sits. The music and strobe stop. The lighting returns to normal. A buzzing sound is heard as ALICE is pushing a button, trying to call her secretary.*)

ALICE (*cont'd*): Where is my secretary? (*Pushes the button again. Buzzer sounds.*) Where is that girl?

(*BUTCH enters carrying a steno pad.*)
BUTCH: Yes, Ms. Wonderland?

(*ALICE is happy to see BUTCH. She runs to him and throws her arms around him.*)
ALICE: Butch! Oh, Butch… I love you and I don't want a divorce.
BUTCH: (*As he moves away from ALICE.*) Ms. Wonderland, is that anyway to talk to your secretary?
ALICE: My secretary? You're my husband. I love you. You want a divorce. I don't want one.
BUTCH: You're too late. I got my divorce.
ALICE: Butch! How could you?
BUTCH: But it wasn't from you, Ms. Wonderland.

ALICE: Stop all this. I am your wife. Please, call me Alice.
BUTCH: I couldn't do that Ms. Wonderland.
ALICE: All right... if we weren't married to me, whom did you divorce?
BUTCH: Dorothy.
ALICE: My friend, Dorothy?
BUTCH: (*Shaking his head yes.*) Your old roommate.
ALICE: (*To self, trying to stay sane.*) I hope I wake up from this nightmare soon. (*To BUTCH.*) I thought you were a lawyer? Why are you working as a secretary?
BUTCH: I was a lawyer... but Dorothy was a judge. She had me disbarred. This was the only job I could get.
ALICE: (*Talking more to herself than BUTCH.*) She must have used her first wish to become a judge.
BUTCH: (*Shaking his head yes.*) Throughout law school, that's all she dreamed about... becoming a judge.
ALICE: (*Still more to herself than BUTCH.*) If she hasn't used her other wishes, she'll soon be president.
BUTCH: She's running for congress now.
ALICE: Hindsight is great.
BUTCH: I beg your pardon.
ALICE: She's a shoe-in. That woman will not only be the first lady president, she'll be her own first lady.
BUTCH: Speaking of the President... the boss wants to see you.
ALICE: By the way, Butch... who is the boss? What's his name?
BUTCH: HIS name?

ALICE: Yes, what's HIS name? (*JEANIE enters.*)
JEANIE: HER name is Jeanie.
ALICE: Oh no… you're the boss?
JEANIE: I'm the boss.
ALICE: I thought I was finished with you. I used my three wishes.
JEANIE: One is never finished with an education. I'm with you for the rest of your life.
ALICE: (*Defiantly.*) I don't need you anymore. I'm successful now.
BUTCH: But it's not now!
JEANIE: Time just flies by… when you are having fun.
BUTCH: We are in the new millennium.
ALICE: So?
JEANIE: It's time to change jobs.
ALICE: I've only had this one for five minutes.
BUTCH: High tech is the culprit. Your job doesn't exist anymore.
ALICE: Be quiet… you're still my secretary.
BUTCH: Not anymore. I trained and studied for the future. I've advanced with the times. I've been promoted to vice president of this corporation.
JEANIE: He's right… because of foreign competition and automation, you don't have a job anymore. (*DOROTHY enters.*)
DOROTHY: Is this my new office?
ALICE: (*Sarcastically.*) I thought you were going to be the first woman president?
BUTCH: (*As saying that DOROTHY was the first woman president.*) Where have you been the past twenty years?
ALICE: (*Deflated.*) Looking for a job.

DOROTHY: I was sworn in as the Commander-and-Chief in (*fill in date as appropriate.*) Not only was I the first female President, but I was the first person to be elected from the Independent Party. I beat both the Democratic and Republican candidates.

JEANIE: Now she's my VP in charge of foreign affairs... and you're in her office.

ALICE: (*She hasn't any fire left.*) What am I supposed to do?

BUTCH: Find another job, you graduated first in your class.

ALICE: Another job?

JEANIE: In today's world, it is not unusual for a person to make eight to twelve career changes in their lifetime.

BUTCH: Look at all the jobs I've had in just the past half hour.

ALICE: Where did I go wrong?

JEANIE: Expecting life to be handed to you on a silver platter. You have to work for your place in society.

ALICE: I wish I were dead.

(*JEANIE nods her head and claps her hands twice. In a flash the strobe light comes on and Calliope music and smoke fill the stage. The actors move the cubes to form two pillars. JEANIE and BUTCH exit. DOROTHY and ALICE spin to the right of the pillars. The music and strobe stop. The lights return to normal.*)

ALICE: Wait a minute... I didn't have any wishes left.

DOROTHY: I forgot to tell you... I used my last wish to wish you would have one more wish.

ALICE: With friends like you, I don't need any enemies. What do we do now?

DOROTHY: How would I know? I've never been dead before.
ALICE: I only wished I were dead… not you. Why are you even here?
DOROTHY: I guess the playwright needed someone you could talk to… to further the plot.
ALICE: Where do you think we are?
DOROTHY: Well, I can tell you this… we ain't in Kansas.
ALICE: Then we have to be in heaven.
DOROTHY: (*Pointing to the pillars.*) Those must be the pearly gates. (*They walk to the pillars.*)
ALICE: Should I knock?
DOROTHY: Can't dance.
ALICE: Who do you think will answer?
DOROTHY: If we are in heaven… Saint Peter will.
(*ALICE knocks on one of the pillars. JEANIE enters.*)
ALICE: (*Upon seeing JEANIE.*) We're not in heaven.
JEANIE: Hi, girls. Isn't the weather lovely up here? Never changes… just like Hawaii.
ALICE: Are YOU Saint Peter?
JEANIE: Have I changed that much? Don't you remember me… I'm Jeanie.
ALICE: I know who you are.
JEANIE: I'm so happy… death does strange things to the mind.

(*The next six lines are said very rapidly, they almost overlap.*)

DOROTHY: So we really are dead?
JEANIE: (*Pointing to ALICE.*) She is… she wished it.
ALICE: Can I see Saint Peter?

JEANIE: (*Correcting her grammar.*) I don't know… can you?
DOROTHY: If I'm not dead… why am I here?
ALICE: May I see Saint Peter?
JEANIE: Girls… please… one at a time… please! (*To DOROTHY.*) You are not dead. The playwright just needed you here to open this scene and further the plot.
DOROTHY: Who is the playwright?
JEANIE: Why Saint Peter is… he writes down everything you do.
ALICE: (*Losing her patience.*) So, we both need to see Saint Peter.
JEANIE: I was just about to say that.
ALICE: So, get him… please.
JEANIE: (*Calling off through the pillars.*) Hey, Butch… got two young ones out here that want to see you.
ALICE: Butch?
JEANIE: (*Nodding her head, "Yes."*) Saint Peter's nickname.
(*BUTCH enters through the pillars.*)
ALICE: Don't tell me… another career change.
BUTCH: (*Pointing a finger upward.*) I'm going UP in the world.
ALICE: If you make another career change… don't try comedy.
BUTCH: So, what can I do for you?
ALICE: If you really are Saint Peter… I guess I want to be admitted past the gates.
(*BUTCH pulls out an application form and a pencil.*)
BUTCH: Past experience?
ALICE: What do you mean?

BUTCH: Did you work while you were down there?
ALICE: What does working down there have to do with getting in up here?
BUTCH: I have to know where to place you. What do you think we do up here? Sit around on clouds all day and play harps.
ALICE: I'll never get away from it. (*Pleading.*) Look, Butch, just let me in. For old time's sake... after all, we were married once... a long time ago... I think.
BUTCH: (*Not giving in.*) I didn't make up the rules.
ALICE: (*She explodes, having had enough of this nightmare.*) Then who did? Let me see the one who made up these stupid rules.
DOROTHY: I don't think you should have asked that.
ALICE: (*Still angry.*) Why not? I want some answers. Come on, Butch... where is he?
BUTCH: You're standing right in front of him.
ALICE: Who... YOU?
BUTCH: No, not me! Her! (*He points to JEANIE.*) Him is a Her or He is a SHE.
ALICE: (*Deflated.*) I should have known.
JEANIE: Welcome to the real Wonderland, Alice.
ALICE: I suppose after all the trouble I've given you throughout my life... there's no way I'm going to walk through those gates?
JEANIE: Getting past these gates is another problem you'll have to face. As for causing me trouble. You haven't caused me any. You've only hurt yourself.
ALICE: Why, cause I didn't get a job?
JEANIE: You had a job. You were a wife and mother, a good one. That's one hell of a job... (*Looking down.*) Pardon my French. (*Back to ALICE.*) You hurt

yourself by not being prepared to do anything BUT be a mother.
ALICE: I can see that now. But what can I do about it?
JEANIE: Make another wish.
ALICE: You've granted me all my wishes.
JEANIE: You forget who I am! (*ALICE looks at DOROTHY and BUTCH.*)
BUTCH: Do it, Alice.
DOROTHY: I'm game.
(*ALICE decides to give it a try.*)
ALICE: What's one more adventure.
JEANIE: (*Agreeing with ALICE.*) You only live once.
(*ALICE shuts her eyes and clenches her fists.*)
ALICE: I wish I could go back to my plain ordinary life… back to my teens… and still retain all this knowledge.

(*JEANIE nods her head and claps her hands twice. In a flash the strobe light comes on. Calliope music and smoke fill the stage. The actors move the cubes to the original position forming ALICE's house and DOROTHY's house. BUTCH and JEANIE exit. ALICE and DOROTHY spin to their homes and pick up the phones. The music and strobe stop. The lights return to normal. Things are almost the same. ALICE and DOROTHY are now thirteen-year-olds.*)

ALICE: Dorothy, I think we found it.
DOROTHY: I know we did, Alice. (*BUTCH enters. He is now a fourteen-year-old boy.*)
BUTCH: Hi, Mom, I'm home. (*Runs up to ALICE.*) Will you get off the phone… I have to make a very important phone call.

ALICE: Get out of my room. (*JEANIE enters.*)
JEANIE: Butch, leave your sister alone.
BUTCH: Ah, Mom, she's always on the phone talking to that dumb Dorothy.
JEANIE: Did you finish your paper route?
BUTCH: All done.
JEANIE: Homework?
BUTCH: I'll do it later.
JEANIE: You'll do it now, young man.
BUTCH: What about Alice?
JEANIE: Alice, off the phone. Time to set the table.
ALICE: (*Speaking into the phone.*) Dorth… gotta go. I'll call you later tonight.
DOROTHY: Great… catch you later. (*ALICE and DOROTHY hang up. As DOROTHY exits she shouts.*) Auntie Em… can I get a dog?
BUTCH: (*Referring to ALICE being off the phone.*) It's about time.
ALICE: You're just jealous you weren't talking to her.
BUTCH: Gross me out… no eighth grader would want to talk to a dumb seventh grader.
ALICE: You'll probably end up married to her one day.
BUTCH: No way.
JEANIE: That's enough, you two. Butch… the homework waits. (*BUTCH exits. JEANIE turns to ALICE.*) I suppose I don't even have to ask you?
ALICE: I did it right after school.
JEANIE: You're education will work for you in the future. I wish I had more.
ALICE: You're perfect the way you are. (*ALICE and JEANIE embrace.*) Thanks, Mom.

JEANIE: What for?
ALICE: For helping me make my wishes come true.

END

A Collection from a Career in Theatre

AIDS: The Andrew Is Dead Story

A play in one act
by Bob May
and
Cristopher Tibbetts

©1990 and 2008
by Bob May and Cristopher Tibbetts
All rights reserved

CAST OF CHARACTERS

ANDREW WATSON GREER
BOB
LOUISE
SARA
SAILOR 1
SAILOR 2
ANGELA
FAY, a counselor
RICHIE
TONY
SAM
THE REAL LOUISE

The play can be performed with as few as three men and three women with doubling as follows:

Male 1—Andrew
Male 2—Bob
Sailor 2
Male 3—Sailor 1
Richie
Tony
Sam
Female 1—Louise
Angela
Female 2—Sara
Faye
Female 3—Real Louise

Although the play has several different locations, the action is continuous. In the original production, stools were placed several feet apart in a line upstage. The actors never left the stage; when not in a scene, they sat on the stools and watched the action. The stools also formed everything from the car to the gravestone.

The premiere of *The Andrew Is Dead Story* was presented at an AIDS Conference in Brainerd, Minnesota, on April 9, 1990, under the direction of Bob May, with the following cast:

Andrew Watson Greer—Cristopher Tibbetts
Bob—Kevin Boyles
Louise —Amy Roach
Sara—Angie Ryappy
Sailor 1—Eric Peterson
Sailor 2—Kevin Boyles
Angela—Amy Roach
FAY, a counselor—Angie Ryappy

Richie—Eric Peterson
Tony—Eric Peterson
Sam—Eric Peterson
The Real Louise—Joan Lee-Clark

The play was previously published by I. E. Clark, Inc., and had several productions until released in 2004. This updated rewrite was completed for a Los Angeles production.

(The scene is a bare stage, holding only a few benches, chairs, or whatever forms the designer needs to carry out the action so as to permit the characters to appear and disappear easily. The play takes place in the mind of Andrew Watson Greer. Throughout the events, characters step from his memory for anything from a scene to a few lines. AT RISE: ANDREW steps forward, holding a book, and speaks to the audience.)

ANDREW: *(To audience)* Andrew Watson Greer. Born July 28, 1964. Died April 1, 1989. Of AIDS... Well, not technically AIDS. He died of congestive pneumonia. His white blood cell count was so low his body's natural immune system couldn't fight off a simple, common cold, which turned into pneumonia, and that's what he died of. I knew him well... for, you see, I am Andrew Watson Greer. I'm dead. And this book contains my life history. You might say it's sort of a biography. Everyone here has one. Where is here? I'm not sure. It's a cross between a holding cell in a local jail and a waiting room in a doctor's office. It doesn't matter. I'm here, and I'm dead. *(He opens the book.)* This book knows everything about me. It lists the date of every major event in my life. Like on January 14, 1965—I said my first word, "Mama." (*Beat; he muses fondly*) By now, you're all probably wondering: Since I died of AIDS, am I a homosexual? Yes. All my life. I think I've known I was gay since I was four. I used to always enjoy being around the boys more than the girls. There's nothing wrong with that—every boy goes through that. It's just that I felt different when I was with boys. From that first memory at four… through coming out… and through the rest of my life. But I'm from Glade, a small town of twelve thousand in south-central Florida, and growing up was hard enough there, without growing up in everybody's eyes as a faggot. And especially in Bob's eyes. (*BOB appears, ogling a centerfold.*) Bob was the quintessential, heterosexual, teenage, sex-always-on-the-mind maniac. And as his best friend, he expected me to be the same. I tried my best.

BOB: Have you seen this month's Playboy? The potteries on the Playmate of the Month are the finest jewels this side of the Nile. Look at 'em.

ANDREW: (*As he looks at the foldout*) Yeah, man, they're really… hot.

BOB: Hot? They're wonderful… Oh God, would I like to hold one of them. One would do! I'm not asking too much. Am I asking for too much, Andy? Wouldn't you love to feel one?

ANDREW: Sure. That'd be great.

BOB: Yeah, but we're not gonna get anything like this. I guess we'll just have to settle for Louise and Sara. Are you ready for the hot date this weekend?
ANDREW: Sure.
BOB: Fort Lauderdale, here we come! (*BOB exits, looking at the magazine.*)
ANDREW: (*To audience*) Glade is about an hour and half, two hours maybe, from Fort Lauderdale, and that's where all the kids went when they wanted to escape from Small Town, USA, and get crazy. That's where I first got it... I mean, contracted it... AIDS... in Fort Lauderdale. (*He looks in book.*) At least it says right here that I did. Only July 28, 1980. My sixteenth birthday. From a sailor. I didn't know it at the time. I guess I have to believe what the book says. But I'm getting ahead of myself. (*SOUND: A telephone RINGS. ANDREW picks up a receiver.*) Hello? (*BOB appears, holding a receiver.*)
BOB: (*Into phone*) Hey ding-dong! We're junior high graduates. We're high schoolers now. And you're sittin' on your butt at home on a warm June night? I copped a bottle of whiskey from my old man. I'll meet you at the park in five minutes. Be there! (*ANDREW and BOB hang up their receivers and walk to the park. BOB has a bottle of whiskey.*) Thought you'd never get here. Have a drink.
ANDREW: Thanks. And it only took me two minutes to get here. You know you can get anywhere in ten minutes in this Podunk town. Where are the girls?
BOB: At home, watching that stupid TV show... CHiPS... with whatshisname... uh... uh... Erik

Estrada. They'll be here when it's over. So tell me, Stud, have you made it with Louise yet?

ANDREW: None of your business.

BOB: I know you haven't if you're saying that.

ANDREW: You know, there's more to life than sleeping with a girl. I really like Louise.

BOB: I like Sara, too, but man, you don't know what you're missin'. It's the best feeling. You can't describe it. Go for it! Louise likes you, she'll do it. She told Sara she wants to. But she said you never try anything. What's wrong with you, man, are you queer?

ANDREW: Ha ha. Very funny. I just think there's something beautiful about saving sex until you've chosen a lifelong partner.

BOB: Isn't that sweet? So choose Louise as your "lifelong partner" and this weekend we'll both get it… on the beach. I'll teach you how.

ANDREW: Thanks, buddy. (*ANDREW turns back to the audience. Under the following, BOB, LOUISE, and SARA enter, and assemble the car. SARA is driving, BOB is beside her in the front seat; LOUISE is in the back, with an empty seat for ANDREW beside her.*) So on June 15, Bob and Sara and Louise and I took a road trip to Fort Lauderdale, where Bob had determined I would lose my virginity. Sara was the only one of us who was sixteen and old enough to drive, so she borrowed her father's Pontiac station wagon, and we headed east to the coast. Bob rode shotgun. Louise and I had the back to ourselves. Bob kept leaning over the seat, making tacky comments like "At least your woman ain't driving,"

and "Why don't you do something back there?"
(*ANDREW joins them in the car.*)

LOUISE: Bob, you're so gross!

BOB: Yeah, but look where it's gotten me.

SARA: Oh, Bob, shut up and light me a fag.

LOUISE: A fag?

ANDREW: A cigarette.

LOUISE: Oh yeah, let's smoke.

BOB: (*To LOUISE; as he lights cigarette and hands it to SARA*) Since when did you start smoking, Miss Virgin Queen?

ANDREW: Bob… Just shut up and give us a cigarette.

BOB: Aren't we there yet?

SARA: We've been here for the past ten minutes.

BOB: To the beach, to the beach!

SARA: It's a big beach. Where should we go? We can't stop here. Too many people.

BOB: Take the 17th Street Causeway past the port, to US 1, and head toward Dania Beach. There's supposed to be a great deserted beach there. Hey, Andrew, remember what I told you.

LOUISE: What? What did he tell you?

ANDREW: Nothing.

SARA: Okay, okay, we're here. Where do I turn?

BOB: Left, turn left.

SARA: Where to now?

BOB: Straight, just go straight.

SARA: Anything you say, baby.

BOB: I've been lookin' forward to this all week.

ANDREW: Looks like a lot of other people had the same idea, Bob.

SARA: Boy, there's a lot of cars out here.

LOUISE: And a lot of people.
BOB: A party! Somebody's probably throwing a beach party. Let's go join 'em.
SARA: It's all men.
LOUISE: Who told you about this place?
BOB: Kevin.
BOTH WOMEN: Kevin!
SARA: It's that beach.
BOB: What beach? What're you talking about?
SARA: The queer beach. Everybody knows Kevin's a queer.
ANDREW: Kevin's gay? I didn't know that.
LOUISE: Oh yuck! Let's get outta here. Before we catch it.
BOB: Catch what? What're you talkin' about? One of those fags come near us, I'll just bust him.
LOUISE: The gay plague.
ANDREW: The what?
LOUISE: Something only queers are getting. It's killing them left and right.
SARA: Oh yeah. I heard of it. It's contagious. My mother says it's God's punishment for their dirty sins.
BOB: Then get the hell outta here before we catch it. I'll kill that faggot Kevin. Forget this place.
ANDREW: (*To audience*) I didn't forget it. I kept sneaking peeks out the rear window at those men on the beach until the night swallowed them like morning swallows the stars. Needless to say, I didn't get laid that night. Everyone was so preoccupied with the gay plague that sex was the furthest thing from anyone's mind… even Bob's.

BOB: I'm never goin' back to that place.
SARA: I hope not, cause I'll never be there.
LOUISE: I'll never go anywhere near there.
ANDREW: Me neither. (*To audience*) But I knew that I would.
SARA: Where to now?
BOB: Let's go down to the Elbow Room.

(*ANDREW rises from his seat in the car, and speaks to the audience. SARA, BOB, and LOUISE exit.*)

ANDREW: (*To audience*) The next month before my sixteenth birthday, we didn't leave Glade. Bob was constantly giving me shit about not making with Louise, while he was banging his brains out with Sara.
BOB: (*Entering*) What do you mean you haven't done it yet? She told Sara she wanted to.
ANDREW: I don't know why. I've been tryin'. She just won't. (*BOB exits, and ANDREW turns to speak to the audience.*) I didn't have the nerve to tell him that it was me who didn't want to, not Louise. She would have. She loved me. She would have done anything for me, anything I asked. So Bob figured the only way I was ever gonna get laid was if he took me back to Fort Lauderdale and bought me a hooker. That would be my sixteenth birthday present from him. The plans were firmed up. To Fort Lauderdale we would go, and Bob would make sure I finally lost my virginity. On my sixteenth birthday, I got my license, and my parents lent me the car. I called Bob, but guess what? After all his big plans he was grounded. He had stayed out too late with Sara the night before, and now

he couldn't go out for a week. So now what was I to do? I suppose I could have called Louise. But I didn't want to. I kept thinking of that beach. The dancing fire, the many men around it, the happiness, the gay atmosphere... no pun intended. And, as you've probably figured out, that's where I went. Remember, I contracted AIDS on July 28, 1980—my sixteenth birthday. I'd love to be able to tell you that my first homosexual experience was a beautiful one. But I can't. It was horrible. When I got to the beach, it was raining... pouring. There was nobody there, no fire, no nothing. I decided it was probably a sign. I shouldn't be there. So I decided to just turn around and go home. (*TWO SAILORS appear.*) As I was driving away from the beach, I saw two sailors hitchhiking along the beach road. Probably from Port Everglades. Port Everglades is one of the deepest natural harbors in the South. A lot of naval vessels dock there. My father used to take me there on Sunday afternoons to look at the mighty ships, and I was always fascinated by the sailors. These guys ran aircraft carriers and submarines, they were protecting us, and now two of them were hitchhiking in the rain. There was no question in my mind that I should give them a ride.

(*TWO SAILORS run and get in the car.*)

SAILOR 1: Thanks for the lift, buddy.

ANDREW: No problem. Terrible night. You guys docked at Port Everglades?

SAILOR 2: Yeah. Just got in this morning. Been at sea for six months.

ANDREW: Wow! That must be fascinating.
SAILOR 1: Ah, it's okay. (*Insinuatingly*) But it gets awfully boring seeing the same ol' boys day after day.
ANDREW: Yeah, I bet.
SAILOR 1: So what are you doing out here on a rainy night.
ANDREW: Just cruisin'.
SAILOR 2: Bad night for cruisin'. You live around here?
ANDREW: I wish. I live in a small town about two hours from here.
SAILOR 2: Bummer. I grew up in a small town.
ANDREW: Yeah, it sucks.
SAILOR 1: Life sucks. Wanna get high?
ANDREW: No. I don't do drugs.
SAILOR 1: Mind if we do?
SAILOR 2: Why don't we go back to the beach, park the car there, and party?
ANDREW: Sure. If you guys want to.
SAILOR 1: You're in control, kid. (*The two SAILORS light up a joint.*) So, what're you doin' down here?
ANDREW: Nothin'.
SAILOR 1: I thought you said you were cruisin'. Lookin' for some action?
SAILOR 2: Well, you found it.

(*ANDREW steps out of the car, and addresses the audience. The SAILORS exit.*)

ANDREW: When I woke up, I was choking. I was lying facedown in a mud puddle on the beach. I'm lucky I didn't drown. My face and my body were covered in mud and blood and confusion. I ran to the ocean to clean myself. I don't know why, it was still raining, but there was something soothing about the ocean. I've always loved it. And the salt water probably helped me too. The one saving grace is that the jerks hadn't stolen my car. I drove home to Glade, shaking and sobbing all the way. I swore to myself then that I would bury these gay feelings, like a drunk swears he'll never take another drink, like a drug addict swears he'll go clean. I would lead a straight life, no matter what it cost. By the time I got home, I felt good. I felt strong… I didn't know then—but the book tells me now—that that night I became a carrier. I don't know which sailor I got it from, and it doesn't matter. I got it. (*BOB appears.*)

BOB: Sorry about your birthday, man. I think if you keep workin' on Louise, she'll probably go all the way.

ANDREW: You're right. I'm gonna go for it.

BOB: That-a-boy. It's an incredible feeling. You'll love it.

ANDREW: You only live once.

BOB: That's my man. (*BOB exits, as LOUISE enters, and ANDREW moves to her.*)

LOUISE: Where were you last night? I tried to call you.

ANDREW: I was at the park with some of the guys.

LOUISE: Who? Bob wasn't there. He's grounded.

ANDREW: Just some of the guys. Does it matter?

LOUISE: Well… Happy birthday.

ANDREW: Thanks. Where's my present. (*He takes LOUISE in his arms.*) Come on. If you loved me, you would.

LOUISE: You know I love you.

ANDREW: Then prove it.

LOUISE: What's gotten into you?

ANDREW: It's my sixteenth birthday. I'm a man now. (*LOUISE exits as ANDREW turns to the audience.*) I don't think I passed the virus to Louise that night. The experts say it takes three to four weeks to incubate in your blood system. But we continued to have sex—if you could call it that—throughout the summer. By the time school started in the fall, the virus had been passed to her. It wasn't knowingly, of course. She was the last person I wanted to hurt. But I did. An act of love turns ultimately into an atrocity.

(*BOB enters in a rage.*)

BOB: This sucks. Being a sophomore really sucks. We're at the top of the heap in junior high, and then we come to high school and end up at the bottom again. The juniors and seniors are treating me like crap.

ANDREW: It's not that bad.

BOB: It sucks. I'm telling you, it sucks.

(*SARA enters, elated.*)

SARA: Isn't this wonderful? Isn't high school wonderful?

BOB: It sucks. (*LOUISE enters.*)

LOUISE: I love it here. I never thought going to school could be so much fun. (*She kisses ANDREW.*)

Hi, honey. (*To SARA*) Don't you just love it here? (*To BOB*) What's wrong with you?
SARA: Bob's having a difficult time adjusting.
ANDREW: He thinks high school sucks!
BOB: I just don't like being on bottom.
LOUISE: I thought you liked it any way.
BOB: Maybe one day you'll find out.
LOUISE: (*Putting her arm around ANDREW*) I have my man. Thank you very much.
(*BOB, SARA, and LOUISE exit as ANDREW steps down and talks to the audience.*)
ANDREW: And she did have her man. The first few months of our sophomore year, we were inseparable. We spent every day together, and I realized how much I truly loved her… but not in a sexual way… more like a brother loves a sister. And by the time the presidential election finally ground to a merciful halt, we had stopped making love altogether. But that didn't seem to bother Louise. In a way, I think she was relieved. Now she didn't have to worry about getting pregnant. We shared many other things that year. The discovery of the Titanic. The assassination of John Lennon. And our consternation over the election of Ronald "Death Valley Days" Reagan as the fortieth President of the United States. Before I knew it, our sophomore year was over, summer was once again upon us, and Bob was back on his campaign to finally get me laid. The book tells me the next important date in my life was when I passed on the virus again. Well, it doesn't exactly say that, but

that's the way I feel now. What the book says, is that Bob succeeded in his quest. (*BOB appears.*)
BOB: July twenty-eighth, dude. Happy birthday. I didn't do it for you last year, but this year's different. We're gonna do it. You're finally gonna get some. You're gonna lose your virginity.
ANDREW: (*To audience*) Bob didn't know about Louise. I never told anyone. It's nobody's business. (*To BOB*) It's no big deal, man. I'm fine.
BOB: You'll be finer when you dine her.
ANDREW: (*To audience*) So we set out for Fort Lauderdale. What could I tell Bob?
(*Two HOOKERS appear.*)
BOB: Here we are, man. On the Strip, Fort Lauderdale. Look at all the babes. Just reach out and touch someone.
ANDREW: Thanks, Ma Bell.
BOB: Come on. Just wait till you experience it.
ANDREW: What if I told you I already experienced it? I don't need to, Bob.
BOB: Yeah, and fish don't need water to swim. You'll love it.
ANDREW: Let's just go home.
BOB: Look at that one. She looks exactly like Louise. You should take her. Come on, I'm paying for it.
ANDREW: (*To audience*) She did look like Louise. And, in a way, I missed being intimate with Louise. I also thought I had to prove myself to Bob. So I said: (*To BOB*) Yeah, you're right. Okay, let's go. (*They both approach ANGELA.*)
ANGELA: Hey guys, looking for a date?

BOB: He is. It's my main man's seventeenth birthday, and I'm payin'.
ANGELA: Last of the big spenders.
BOB: Make me proud, buddy. I'll wait for you on the beach by Las Olas Boulevard. (*BOB exits, and ANDREW and ANGELA move to the bedroom area.*)
ANDREW: (*To audience*) I must have been her worst trick ever. It was all over in about thirty seconds. I felt so stupid and embarrassed. I really didn't even want to do it. But peer pressure... what would I say to Bob if nothing happened? But Angela, that was her name, was a true lady —if that's possible for a hooker. She tried to make me feel better.
ANGELA: Don't worry. It happens to everybody their first time.
ANDREW: This isn't my first time, and I appear to be getting worse.
ANGELA: Don't worry about it. You're in a majority. Most of my clientele do the same thing.
ANDREW: Really?
ANGELA: You get used to it. Easy money. So... how long have you known?
ANDREW: Known what?
ANGELA: That you're gay.
ANDREW: I'm not gay!
ANGELA: There's nothing wrong with it. I'm a prostitute—I know I am, and I'm proud of it. You're gay, you should be too. The world is full of different types—that's what makes life interesting.
ANDREW: But I'm from a small town. If people find out I'm homosexual, I'll be run out on a rail for fear

that I'm carrying that… disease. What is it called? The gay plague.

ANGELA: That's only happening in San Francisco. No need to worry about it here in southern Florida.

ANDREW: I like you. You accept me for me. I could talk to you all night.

ANGELA: If you've got the money, honey, I've got the time. Otherwise, I've gotta get back to work, or my pimp will have my butt in a sling if I don't turn at least ten more tricks tonight. Go home, and quit lying to yourself, and to everybody else.

ANDREW: Thanks. (*ANGELA exits, as ANDREW turns to the audience.*) I liked her… And reading this book now, I feel terrible, knowing what I did to her, after what she had done for me. By the way, she didn't turn ten tricks after me that night—she did twelve. Does that add twelve more names to the roster of the infected? Probably not that night, if we believe what the experts say about the incubation period. But she did contract the disease from me. And within a month it had manifested itself in her body, and since that time who knows how many others she has passed it on to. Her pimp was one but, curiously, not through sex—he shared Angela's dirty needles and became one of the many junkies carrying the disease. Ironically, he died before he even knew he was infected… from an overdose of heroin. He shared Angela's needles. The book doesn't say what happened to Angela. I assume she's still out there turning tricks. Bob and I didn't talk much on the drive back to Glade.

Angela's advice reverberated in my head with each passing mile. And by the time I got to Glade, I knew what I had to do. I was going to come out and come clean once and for all. As you've guessed by now, I didn't heed Angela's advice. Glade was too narrow-minded, so to compensate for my cowardice, I went to the other extreme. Louise and I started to make love again, wherever we could, through mid-August. Mind you, it wasn't a lot. Maybe once a week. And then I just stopped calling her. I was still in the closet when school started that fall. (*LOUISE enters.*)

LOUISE: Hi, Andy…
ANDREW: Hi, Louise.
LOUISE: So, how was the rest of your summer?
ANDREW: Okay. How was yours?
LOUISE: Lonely.
ANDREW: Oh. Yeah. Mine too.
LOUISE: You could have called me.
ANDREW: Look, Louise, I'm really sorry about that.
LOUISE: That's okay. We don't have to make love to have a relationship.

(*BOB and SARA enter.*)

BOB: Well, if it isn't the two lovebirds!
ANDREW: Cool it, Bob.
SARA: Hey, Louise, aren't you the junior class president of the Red Cross blood drive?
LOUISE: That's right. And I expect to see all three of you in the gym seventh hour. (*As Dracula*) I vant your blood!
BOB: I bet that ain't all she wants.

LOUISE: How do you know I haven't gotten it already?

BOB: Andrew, you stud, you!

(*BOB, SARA, and LOUISE exit. ANDREW turns to the audience.*)

ANDREW: We all met in the gym seventh hour and did our good deed for the Red Cross. Each of us donating a pint of life-saving, healthy blood. That is, two pints of lifesaving, healthy blood. And two pints of poison—mine and Louise's. That was before blood was tested for the virus. Thank God they test it now. Who knows where our blood was destined to go. They told us we were doing great things for the entire world—that our blood could end up as far away as Africa, saving the life of a starving baby. Mine didn't make it that far. Matter of fact, mine didn't make it out of Glade. After the first week of school, there was a terrible automobile accident. Richie James was in critical condition after a head-on collision with a drunk driver on Alligator Alley. During the surgery, Richie went through ten units of blood. One of them was mine. Richie was the kid in our class that everybody called "the fag." He was skinny and smart and didn't stick up for himself, nonathletic, and more interested in poetry than punching. He didn't relate to the "guys" as well as everyone thought he should, so they all presumed he was a fag. I knew he wasn't. In '87, six years after the accident, when Richie was diagnosed as having AIDS, because of the blood transfusion, the suspicions of everyone in Glade were confirmed.

How simple-minded they were. Richie died shortly after being diagnosed. I saw him yesterday. He doesn't blame me. But he went through hell. He told me this story.

(*RICHIE appears in the clinic. FAY, a counselor, comes out of an office, and calls out a number.*)

FAY: 04736A.

RICHIE: Here.

FAY: Right this way. (*She leads RICHIE into an inner office, and they both sit.*) Now, 04736A, just a few questions before we do the test.

RICHIE: Why don't you call me by my name?

FAY: Everything here is strictly confidential. We don't even give test results over the phone. I don't want to know your name. Now. Are you homosexually active?

RICHIE: No.

FAY: Bisexually active?

RICHIE: No. Look, I came down here because my mom heard on the radio that anybody who had a blood transfusion between 1977 and 1983 should come be tested. I was in an accident in 1980, and was given a lot of blood. I resent the fact that you think I'm homosexual because I'm here.

FAY: Are you heterosexually active?

RICHIE: I just said that I wasn't homo- or bisexually active. So that must mean I'm not getting anything. Okay?

FAY: Do you use intravenous drugs?

RICHIE: No. I'm here because I had a blood transfusion.

FAY: (*Reciting from memory; coldly*) Thank you for coming in to be tested. We feel that education is the best way to inform society about AIDS. Already, AIDS is affecting people from all walks of life—no longer just the gay community. It is estimated that by the turn of the century, AIDS will reach epidemic proportions. You have done your part in fighting the battle against AIDS. Thank you very much.

RICHIE: When will I get my results?

FAY: In about thirty minutes. Please be seated in the waiting room. (*RICHIE exits. FAY speaks in a sotto voce*) Stupid faggot! (*FAY exits, and ANDREW steps forward.*)

ANDREW: (*To audience*) Humiliation. When will people learn? But back to 1981 and my junior year in high school. The class play that year was Kiss Me, Kate. I had never been in a play or done anything like that, but Bob had the idea that this would be a great way to meet chicks. Bob and Sara had broken up about halfway into the school year. Sara didn't want a relationship based only on sex. At least that's what she told Bob. The truth is she started going out with Joe Baker, the quarterback of the football team. But anyway... the three of us—Bob and Louise and I—auditioned for the play. I got cast in the chorus, but Bob and Louise got the leading roles. Actually, they were both quite good. Standing in the wings one afternoon during rehearsal was when I first noticed that they were falling in love. (*ANDREW steps back to watch as BOB and LOUISE enter, in rehearsal.*)

LOUISE: "Ha! Mov'd in good time. Let he that moved you come hither. Remove you hence; I knew you at the first, you were a movable."
BOB: "Why, what's a movable?"
LOUISE: "A joint stool."
BOB: "Thou hast hit. Come, sit on me." (*BOB slaps his knee.*)
LOUISE: "Asses are made to bear, and so are you."
BOB: "Women are made to bear, and so are you."
LOUISE: "No such jade as bear you, if me you mean." (*LOUISE bites BOB's hand. BOB starts laughing.*)
BOB: People don't talk like this. How are we supposed to say this and keep a straight face?
LOUISE: You're doing fine, Bob. Really. I'm really proud of how far you've come. You're really sweet.
BOB: You've always thought I was just a loudmouthed jerk.
LOUISE: But I'm seeing another side of you I really like.
BOB: Thanks. But people still don't talk like this.
LOUISE: Why don't you come over to my house tonight? I'll help you with your lines.
BOB: Sure. I'd like that. (*LOUISE and BOB exit. ANDREW turns to the audience.*)
ANDREW: Kiss Me, Kate was a smashing success. For me, the best part of the experience was that Bob, Louise, and I became inseparable. I guess art really does imitate life. It was no longer just Louise and I, or Bob and I; it was the three of us. The Three Musketeers. Bob even became a gentleman under Louise's tutelage. And I'm sure, if I hadn't been in the picture, Bob and Louise would have

started dating. But that didn't happen. All of us pretended that Louise was still my woman. And for all intents and purposes, she was. But I had a major conflict with that. I was still struggling with my sexual identity. And I knew the only way to come to terms with it was to face it head-on. I had to return to South Beach. (*He walks downstage and sits on the beach. Beat. TONY enters.*)

TONY: Hey, sailor. Got a light?

ANDREW: What? I'm not a sailor. What do you want?

TONY: I can see that. Unless you left your cute little bell bottoms back on the ship. Relax!

ANDREW: Sorry. It's just that I'm not too fond of sailors. I should be going. I shouldn't be here.

TONY: Bad experience with a sailor?

ANDREW: Two. How did you know?

TONY: That's why I'm here. You might say I'm the gay coast guard.

ANDREW: Does that make you better than the Navy?

TONY: Whoa, mate. I'm not in the military. I'm guarding our coast.

ANDREW: What?

TONY: Our beach. The police don't, so someone has to.

ANDREW: Guarding against what?

TONY: AIDS. Haven't you heard about AIDS? The gay plague.

ANDREW: Oh, that. But that's not here in southern Florida.

TONY: Do you want to take that risk?

ANDREW: So are we all going to die?

TONY: I hope not. There are things we can do. Condoms.
ANDREW: You mean, rubbers? Will that protect us?
TONY: Not absolutely. They're not 100 percent effective. The only absolute guaranteed safe sex is a lifelong monogamous relationship with a healthy partner. Or, of course, abstinence.
ANDREW: Oh. Great.
TONY: Relax. Come with me. I have some friends you should meet. (*TONY exits. ANDREW turns to the audience.*)
ANDREW: Tony—that was his name—and I were never lovers. But he did introduce me to a lot of interesting people and my first serious lover. It was a shame that I had to keep it a secret. But Smalltown, USA, was not ready for me to admit my homosexuality. They'd all heard of it—the Gay Plague—which I now knew was called AIDS—and they believed they could all get it from a faggot like me. That summer, in 1982, Bob, Louise, and I all got apprentice jobs at the Oslo Theatre in St. Petersburg. I wanted to tell them my secret, but I never did. So, on to our senior year. The three of us got the leads in our senior class play The Star-Spangled Girl, affirming in our minds that the theatre would be our future. And so it became. I, as a not-so-successful actor, waiting on more tables than appearing on stages. Bob, however, has built quite a name for himself as a playwright. But again, I'm getting ahead of myself. Graduation night, 1983, was a major stepping-stone into my future. (*LOUISE enters.*)

LOUISE: Hi, honey. Great party, huh? (*She kisses ANDREW.*) Do you believe we're finally finished?
ANDREW: Yeah. Great feeling.
LOUISE: Are you sure you don't want to go to college? Florida State's going to be awfully lonely without you.
ANDREW: Bob'll be there. He'll keep you company.
LOUISE: What's that supposed to mean?
ANDREW: Nothing.
LOUISE: Will you at least come and visit me? I'll have my own apartment.
ANDREW: Look, Louise. There's something I have to tell you.
(*BOB bursts in.*)
BOB: We did it! We did it! Doesn't it feel great? Almost as good as sex!
LOUISE: Is that all you ever think about?
BOB: (*After a beat as he thinks about it*) Yeah. (*To ANDREW*) So, Andy, we can't talk you into joining us at FSU? The theatre department could use a handsome leading man.
ANDREW: You know I'm moving to Fort Lauderdale. I'll try acting there for a while, see what happens. Maybe even move to New York.
BOB: Well, I'll leave you two alone. Mary Sue Hamilton's been making eyes at me all night. I think I'll go hunt her down.
ANDREW: Wait, Bob... Before you go, there's something I have to tell you both. I'm leaving tomorrow.
LOUISE: Tomorrow?
BOB: What?

ANDREW: Yeah, tomorrow. And Bob, I want you to take care of Louise.

BOB: Hey, she's your girl, buddy.

ANDREW: Who are we fooling? You two were meant for each other. And besides, I've been lying for too long.

LOUISE: What? Don't you love me?

ANDREW: Yes, I love you. I love both of you.

BOB: Hey, buddy, you're starting to sound like Richie. He never has been the same since that accident. Better watch it. People are going to start talking about you. (*He gives a limp wrist.*)

ANDREW: Richie's not that way.

BOB: How would you know? Don't tell me you're one.

ANDREW: I am.

BOB: Get outta here.

ANDREW: That's what I'm doing. That's why I have to leave. I'm tired of pretending.

BOB: You're not kidding, are you?

ANDREW: No.

BOB: How long have you known this?

ANDREW: All my life.

BOB: You jerk. Why didn't you tell me?

LOUISE: Or me?

ANDREW: I've wanted to so many times. I was afraid you would react… like you're reacting now.

BOB: You lying hypocrite. I stayed at your house. In gym class I showered with you.

ANDREW: And I never did anything.

LOUISE: But you did with me. I thought you said you loved me.

ANDREW: I do love you, Louise. That's why I'm telling you this. You think it's so easy?
BOB: You lied to us... your entire life. I never wanna see you again! Go to Fort Lauderdale! I hope you die of that queer disease!
ANDREW: AIDS. It's called AIDS. A-I-D-S. Acquired Immune Deficiency Syndrome.
BOB: Ass-Induced Death Syndrome.
(*ANDREW turns to the audience as BOB takes LOUISE in his arms, and they walk offstage.*)
ANDREW: I never saw either one of them again.
My mother wrote me that they were married after their junior year of college. The next day I moved to Fort Lauderdale to begin a new life. During the next few years, AIDS spread like wildfire, and even Angela's safe, southern Florida was invaded. As we watched our friends die, one by one, we realized how powerless we were against this killer. So the most important thing my friends and I learned was the practice of safer sex. One thing the homosexual community realized was that the saying "A tisket, a tasket, a condom or a casket" was more than just a saying on a bumper sticker. I'm sure if I looked in the book, it would tell me the most important date in my life was December 2, 1986. But I don't have to look in the book to remember that date. That's the day when I met my significant other—at least that's the way I thought of him—Sam. We had the perfect relationship for about a year. Then I got sick. At first it was no big deal. Mild fevers and colds that stayed a little too long. When I started

the night sweats, and we noticed the lesions, Sam insisted I go to a doctor.

(*SAM enters.*)

SAM: Enough is enough. Please go to a doctor.

ANDREW: No. It's just a rash. It'll go away.

SAM: You've had this rash for three months. You're going to a doctor if I have to drag you there.

ANDREW: I have it. I know I have it.

SAM: We'll cross that bridge when we get to it.

ANDREW: Would you leave me if I do?

SAM: Never. (*SAM exits, and ANDREW turns to the audience.*)

ANDREW: And he didn't. For the next two years, Sam was my friend, mother, lover, and, most of all, my nurse. I don't know how he survived. After the first year, it wasn't a pretty scene. It got pretty messy. Downright disgusting sometimes. There were times when I couldn't leave the bed for weeks. He changed my dirty diapers and soiled sheets sometimes three or four times a day. And he always kept his sense of humor. (*SAM enters.*)

SAM: You know I've always wanted kids. Changing diapers is just good practice for when we have some.

ANDREW: Right. When we have kids, you can change their diapers. (*SAM exits and ANDREW turns to the audience.*) That brings us to April 1, 1989. And as you all know, that's the day I died. The two months preceding my death aren't even worth discussing. Let's just say that my dying was the best thing for both Sam and me. Sam was just as wonderful after my death as he was for the three years we were together. The funeral was a tribute to my memory. Sam had orchestrated everything perfectly. I think of it as his last gift to me. Probably the best thing about it was that Sam invited Bob and Louise, and they came.

(*BOB, LOUISE, and SAM enter, and gather around a tombstone.*)

BOB: Sam, it was a beautiful ceremony. Thank you for inviting us.

SAM: Andrew wouldn't have had it any other way. I'm sure it would have meant a lot to him to have you here.

BOB: I didn't think Andrew liked us anymore.

SAM: Liked you? That's all he ever talked about. I couldn't shut him up. His best buddy, Bob, and his favorite lady, Louise.

LOUISE: And how are you?

SAM: What?

LOUISE: Are you okay?

SAM: Oh. You mean, do I have the virus? No. From the beginning of our relationship, we always practiced safe sex. It's just one of those precautions you learn to live with in the gay community.

BOB: It's not just the gay community anymore. Louise has tested positive and is beginning to show symptoms.

SAM: Because of Andrew?

LOUISE It had to be Andrew.

SAM: And you, Bob?

BOB: The three of us shared everything else. Why not this too?

ANDREW: (*To audience*) The three most important people in my life. Together. I loved those three more than anything I've loved in my life. And two of them were infected with the virus because of me. I can't reverse what has already happened or turn back time. Looking at them, standing over my grave, I became angry. I felt I had to do something. It's too late for Bob and Louise but not for others. I wanted to shout to the whole world that AIDS is out there; it's everywhere. In small towns, in big cities, and it's not just a gay plague. Anybody can get it. But what could I do? I was dead... Alone... Voiceless... with nothing but this book. And then it hit me. This book would make a wonderful play. I couldn't write it, but Bob could. All I had to do was get the information to him. (*BOB turns to the audience and crosses to ANDREW.*)

BOB: And he did. Thanks... (*Inserts name of the actor playing ANDREW, then introduces the rest of the cast to the audience, then speaks to the audience.*) The real Andrew was unavailable to play this part. He died of AIDS. And this was his story. The dreams started coming to me about a week after his funeral. I dismissed them as my mind still grieving over his loss. But when they persisted, I started writing them down, and I began to see a pattern developing. The images were so crystal-clear it was as though Andy were lying there next to me instead of Louise, whispering those messages in my ear. The hatred I had felt for Andrew on graduation night resurfaced. It was he who had infected Louise. And as my hatred increased and

Louise got sicker, the dreams intensified. Louise was the one who suggested I write this play based on the dreams... or thoughts... or whatever it was they were. She insisted it was Andy sending me these messages, and I was meant to do something positive with them. I'm glad she did that, and if one person is helped by it, it was worth my time. Louise is in the audience tonight, and I'd like her to join me on the stage. Louise, honey... (*The actress playing the REAL LOUISE comes from the audience and joins BOB on the stage.*) I almost lost her a short while ago. But thanks to AZT, Louise and I are getting a second chance at life.

REAL LOUISE: But we don't know for how long. Maybe long enough for a real cure to be found.

BOB: As you know, I, too, have tested positive. But my doctor tells us my chances of ever developing beyond carrier status are slim. Because of AIDS, we can never have a normal life. We've always wanted children.

REAL LOUISE: We were even trying when my symptoms started to appear. At first when I had the chills, nausea, and shortness of breath, I thought it was morning sickness. We were deliriously happy. But that was short-lived. Morning sickness can't compare to the agony I've experienced. We still talk about having children. But it wouldn't be fair to the baby, damned to a short, questionable existence. And it wouldn't be fair to Bob, having to care for an AIDS-infected infant once I was gone. The doctors have only given me three to five more years.

BOB: There are theories that if an AIDS baby can survive its first couple of years, it will live. And that baby would be a part of Louise.
REAL LOUISE: Everyone has to make choices when it comes to AIDS. But for us, the reality of AIDS makes our choices more difficult.
BOB: I wrote this play, with the help of my collaborator, Cris Tibbetts, to inform and educate the public. There's a lot we have to learn about AIDS, but we have to learn it, before it's too late.
REAL LOUISE: Pass the message along. Please.
BOB: One more thing. Thanks, Andrew. I don't hate you.

END

A Collection from a Career in Theatre

Go To...

a ten-minute play
by Bob May

© 1992/2008 by Bob May
All rights reserved

CAST OF CHARACTERS

SON
FATHER
WIFE
FRANK
COP/JUDGE—played by one actor

SYNOPSIS OF SCENES

Various scenes—all done with minimal sets—the action must flow from one scene to the next.

The premiere of *Go To...* was presented by the UNLV Theatre Department at the Grant Hall Little Theatre in Las Vegas, Nevada, in 1992.

(AT RISE: FATHER and SON are discovered standing in front of two big, brightly painted doors. The right door has a big number one painted on it. The left door has a big number two painted on it. The SON holds a suitcase.)

SON: Goodbye, Father. (*They embrace. SON moves to door number one. At the door he stops and turns to his FATHER.*) Do you think it's a good choice?
FATHER: It's a choice.
SON: But is it a good choice?
FATHER: It's your choice. At least you have one. When I was your age, I didn't have one. I was told what to do.
SON: Please tell me what to do.
FATHER: I can't. It's a new age you live in.
SON: Maybe I should choose this one? (*SON moves to door number two.*)
FATHER: I wish I had the answer.
SON: No, I think my original choice was correct. (*He moves back to door number one.*) Please try to explain my choice to her.
   (*SON opens door number one and enters. FATHER exits. The door shuts and immediately red LIGHTS start flashing, sirens SOUND. COP enters.*)
COP: You're under arrest.
SON: What did I do?
COP: You left your wife.
SON: But she was not being honest.
COP: Tell it to the judge.
   (*LIGHTS flash and SOUND is heard as COP drags SON to a table. The COP puts on a robe and becomes the JUDGE.*)
JUDGE: Guilty! You are sentenced to life in prison.
   (*JUDGE hits his gavel on the table. LIGHTS flash and SOUND is heard as JUDGE takes off robe to become COP, then drags SON to a prison cell. COP throws SON in the cell. FRANK catches SON. COP exits.*)
SON: Thanks.

FRANK: Frank. Just call me Frank.
SON: Thanks, Frank.
FRANK: What are ya in for?
SON: For making a choice.
FRANK: Me too. It was either him or me.
SON: Murder?
FRANK: Self-defense.
SON: Would you do it again? Now that you know the outcome? I wish I could choose again.
(*COP enters.*)
COP: You... son. You've been paroled! Make better choices in the future.
(*FRANK and COP exit. The two doors are discovered. LIGHTS flash and SOUND is heard as this shift takes place. FATHER enters and moves to SON.*)
FATHER: Did you learn anything, son?
SON: Hindsight is great.
FATHER: You mean you'd make a different choice if you could do it over?
SON: To avoid prison... yes. (*FATHER indicates door number two.*)
FATHER: Luckily, you have a choice. (*They embrace. SON walks to door number two. He stops and turns to FATHER.*)
SON: Do you think it's a good choice?
FATHER: It's a choice.
SON: But is it a good choice?
FATHER: It's your choice. At least you have one. When I was your age I didn't have one. I was told what to do.
SON: Please tell me what to do.
FATHER: I can't. It's a new age we live in.

SON: I hope things are different. (*SON opens door two and enters. FATHER exits. The door shuts. SOUND: Merry music. SON smiles. Then suddenly the LIGHTS begin to flash and SOUND is heard as a bed spins in with two people on it, laughing. The faces of the two in bed can't be seen.*) Nothing's changed, wife. You're still not being honest with me.
(*WIFE sits up. The man's face is still hidden.*)
WIFE: I thought you left.
SON: I chose to come back.
WIFE: You never could commit to a choice. (*The man sits up in the bed. It is FRANK.*)
SON: Frank? It was you? She was cheating with you?
(*FRANK gets out of bed with a gun in his hand and points it at SON.*)
FRANK: Self-defense!
SON: You mean… murder.
(*SON and FRANK fight. The gun goes off. FRANK falls to the floor. Immediately red LIGHTS flash and sirens SOUND. The bed spins off. FRANK and WIFE exit. COP enters.*)
COP: You're under arrest.
SON: It was self-defense.
COP: Tell it to the judge.
(*LIGHTS flash and SOUND is heard as COP drags SON to table. The COP puts on robe and becomes the JUDGE, who sits behind the table.*)
JUDGE: Guilty! You are sentenced to life in prison.
   (*JUDGE hits his gavel on the desk. LIGHTS flash and SOUND is heard as JUDGE takes off the robe and becomes COP. COP drags SON to a prison cell and throws him in. FRANK catches SON. COP exits.*)

FRANK: What are ya in for?
SON: For making a choice.
FRANK: Me too. Murder?
SON: Self-defense.
FRANK: Would you do it again?
(*The two men sit and stare at one another. Pause. The LIGHTS fade to black.*)

END

Paul Bunyan, Two Old Men, and a Wizard

Are There Really Any Kings?

a ten-minute play
by
Bob May

© 1992/2013 by Bob May
All rights reserved

CAST OF CHARACTERS

GARY, a father
BETH, his daughter at five years old.
ELIZABETH, his daughter at twenty years old.

SYNOPSIS OF SCENES

Scene One: Gary's house. 1985
Scene Two: Gary's house. Twenty years later. 2005

SCENE ONE

(AT RISE: BETH and GARY are discovered. They are playing cards.)

BETH: Do you have any… kings?

GARY: No. Go fish. (*BETH starts to fish for a card but stops and asks a question.*)
BETH: Daddy, are there really any kings? I mean, besides the kings on these cards?
GARY: England has had many kings. Some other countries are still ruled by kings too.
BETH: No, I mean fairy-tale kings. Are they real?
GARY: They are if you want them to be.
BETH: Kings are respected and loved.
GARY: Yes, they are. It's your turn to go fish and see if you can get one.
(*BETH fishes for a card.*)
BETH: I got one. I got a king. I win.
GARY: Do you have all four of them?
BETH: I got a king, Dad. I win.
GARY: But you must have all four of them. How many kings do you have?
BETH: Don't yell at me.
GARY: I'm not yelling. You know, you get that from your mother.
BETH: When are you taking me back to mom?
GARY: It's almost time. Now, do you have all four kings? Remember, the object is to get all four.
BETH: Why does Jack say you're an ass?
GARY: What? Who? Beth, you shouldn't talk that way.
BETH: That's what he says.
GARY: Who's Jack?
BETH: Mom's boyfriend.
GARY: Your mother has a boyfriend?
BETH: I only have three kings. I don't want to play anymore.

GARY: We don't have to play; it's almost time for, Hill Street Blues anyway. Do you want to watch it? I hear they're going to cancel it.
BETH: I don't know.
GARY: Come on let's watch it. Remember, it's our show. It began the year you were born.
BETH: I know, you watched it for the first time as you laid in the hospital bed with mommy…
GARY: That's right.
BETH: I can watch it at home.
GARY: You are home. This is your home too.
BETH: Daddy, don't fight with me.
GARY: I'm sorry. You're one of the lucky kids… you have two homes.
BETH: Why do you and mommy fight all the time?
GARY: So many questions.
BETH: Why can't you two be happy?
GARY: (*Playing the card game.*) Do you have any jacks?
BETH: I don't have any jacks. Go fish. (*GARY picks up a card.*) Did you get one?
GARY: No, I guess your mother has all the jacks.
BETH: Did you and Mom get divorced because of me?
GARY: What are you talking about? Of course not.
BETH: Rickie told me… it was my fault.
GARY: Your fault? What do you mean?
BETH: He says, when his mom and dad got divorced they said he should never have been born.
GARY: No. That's crazy. Who's Rickie?
BETH: A boy at my daycare.
GARY: Oh, so you have a boyfriend too?
BETH: Gross me out! I don't ever want a boyfriend.
GARY: Honey, I think you'll change your mind.

BETH: (*Back to the card game.*) Do you have any kings?
GARY: You already asked me that. Go fish.
BETH: I don't think there are any real kings.
(*The LIGHTS fade to black.*)

SCENE TWO

(*It is now twenty years later. AT RISE: GARY and ELIZABETH are discovered. ELIZABETH is BETH, who is now twenty-five years old.*)

ELIZABETH: Hi, Daddy. (*She kisses him.*)
GARY: Hey, honey, what's so important… that you had to interrupt a rerun of Hill Street Blues?
ELIZABETH: What do you like better… NYPD Blues or Hill Street?
GARY: You know my answer.
ELIZABETH: I know… Cop Rock. "They should have never canceled it!"
GARY: Well, they shouldn't have. What's wrong, honey?
ELIZABETH: Nothing's "wrong."
GARY: So why the unexpected visit?
ELIZABETH: Can't a daughter visit her father?
GARY: Of course, this is your house too. (*Beat.*)
ELIZABETH: Daddy, I'm getting married.
GARY: To Rickie. That's wonderful. So, why the long face?
ELIZABETH: We've both decided that we want you to give me away—
GARY: I'd be honored to—
ELIZABETH: —along with Jack.

GARY: What do you mean?
ELIZABETH: Do you think they will ever have reruns of Cop Rock?
GARY: Please, Beth, don't change the subject.
ELIZABETH: Daddy, you know I don't like being called Beth. I prefer Elizabeth.
GARY: I'd cross the street if I saw that ass coming toward me.
ELIZABETH: He's part of my life.
GARY: Then he can give you away.
ELIZABETH: I told Rickie you'd react this way.
GARY: How am I supposed to react? I'm your father.
ELIZABETH: But he is too!
GARY: That hurts.
ELIZABETH: I've known him more as a father figure than you.
GARY: We've had a great relationship. Haven't we?
ELIZABETH: Yes, it's just been different with him.
GARY: I'm your blood.
ELIZABETH: He did things just like a real father. Like when I broke my ankle. Or when I was sick.
GARY: You see what a good father I was? You never broke any bones or got sick on the weekends.
ELIZABETH: He taught me to drive a car
GARY: So the next time you get a speeding ticket, ask him to loan you the money to pay the fine.
ELIZABETH: Why do you hate him so much?
GARY: I don't hate him. I've always felt sorry for him. I feel sorry for him cause he married your mother.
ELIZABETH: (*A realization.*) You still love Mom, don't you?
GARY: Don't be insane.

ELIZABETH: I've suspected it for a long time, but never saw it until now.
GARY: I think we should watch the TV.
ELIZABETH: Do you love me?
GARY: What a dumb question.
ELIZABETH: Do you want me to be happy?
GARY: Was he a better father than me?
ELIZABETH: This isn't a competition.
GARY: Was he?
ELIZABETH: He was a different father.
GARY: I still don't like him.
ELIZABETH: Then don't kiss him after the ceremony. I need you, Daddy. You're the forth card in my suit. Mom, Jack, Rickie, and you.
GARY: Am I your fourth king?
ELIZABETH: No, I have a queen, a jack, and an ace. You are my only real king.
(*They embrace as the LIGHTS fade to black.*)

END

Paul Bunyan, Two Old Men, and a Wizard

9TH INNING WEDDING

a play
by
Bob May

© 1994/2017 by Bob May
All rights reserved

CAST OF CHARACTERS

JOAN, Terry's wife
SHELLY, Terry's sixteen-year-old daughter
TERRY, forty-five years old
LEALIA, Terry's mother
FRED, Terry's boss
FREDDY, Shelly's friend
BEN, Terry's father

SYNOPSIS OF SCENES

The Present.
Scene One: The living room of Terry's house
Scene Two: The same. An hour later

The premiere of *9th Inning Wedding* was presented at the University of Nevada, Las Vegas, Theatre on March 17, 1994, under the direction of Ann McDonough, with scenic design by Jeff Fiala and Rick Souza, costume design by Ellis Pryce-Jones, and lighting design by Joe Aldridge, under the stage management of Steve Emmerson, with the following cast:

Joan—Jackie Shick
Shelly—Corrine Grover
Terry—Herb Kayde
Lealia—Harriet Stich
Fred—Sandy Puryear
Freddy—Christopher Keefe
Ben—Paul Harris

In memory of my mentor... Jerry L. Crawford

SCENE ONE

(The scene is a living room. AT RISE: The room is empty. The phone is ringing. JOAN comes hurriedly through the front door. She is carrying a stack of books in one arm and a bag of groceries in the other. She scrambles to the phone. The books fall.)

JOAN: Oh... *(She yanks up the receiver)* Hello! *(Beat. She is clearly not happy that she has rushed to get the phone after finding out who it is. But at the same time, she can't show how she really feels.)* Oh... hi... Mama Lealia. *(Beat... she listens.)* No... you know he doesn't get home till about six on Friday nights. (*Beat... as she listens.*) Listen... this is not a good time... a bag full of groceries is about to slip from my arms... I'll see you later. (*Beat... as she listens.*) Of course you're still invited... you know that is a given. (*Beat... as she listens.*) You're doing what? (*Beat... as she listens.*) No... don't hang up. (*She hangs up the phone.*) She does that just to irritate me. (*She tries to pick up the books while still holding the grocery bag. Beat. SHELLY enters.*)

SHELLY: Hi, Mom. (*This scares JOAN. She drops the bag of groceries as she lets out a scream.*) What's up? (*As JOAN picks up the groceries, she responds with sarcasm.*)

JOAN: Just picking up a few groceries for tonight's dinner with your grandmother.

SHELLY: Mom, I met this man.

JOAN: That's nice.

SHELLY: He's in my math class. He looks just like Tom Cruise. (*Update or substitute another well-known name as desired.*)

JOAN: A new student?

SHELLY: Oh no. He just cut his hair. And he got a cool tattoo.

JOAN: I didn't know that Tom Cruise had a tattoo.

SHELLY: Does Tom Cruise have a tattoo?

JOAN: Will you help me with these groceries? (*They pick up the groceries.*)

SHELLY: I invited him over to dinner. And he said yes.

JOAN: Not tonight.

SHELLY: Mom, I really like this man. He asked me to marry him.
JOAN: First of all, he's not a man... he's a boy. If he's in your class... he's a junior... eleventh grade... and that's much too young to get married.
SHELLY: Oh no, he failed two years... he's two years older. I told him you made better fried chicken than the Colonel.
JOAN: You know your grandmother's coming over tonight.
SHELLY: I warned him. He's cool. I gotta call Pam. She'll flip. Thanks, Mom... I want you to be my maid of honor.
(*SHELLY runs off. JOAN drops the groceries in her hands because of what SHELLY just said.*)
JOAN: Does anyone remember what today is? (*JOAN begins to pick up the groceries once again. After a beat TERRY enters.*)
TERRY: Hi, love. (*JOAN lets out a scream and drops the groceries again.*) Gone shopping? (*He snuggles up behind JOAN.*) Do you know how much I want you?
JOAN: Today sure is full of surprises.
TERRY: Did I beat Shelly home? I sure hope so.
(*TERRY starts kissing JOAN's neck and hugging her.*)
JOAN: Your mother called.
TERRY: Let's do it right here on the floor... amid the vegetables. It'll be like being back home.
JOAN: She's coming over tonight.
TERRY: (*Still kissing her.*) Do you remember the first time we made love... in my father's cornfield?
JOAN: She's bringing a guest.

TERRY: It's a good thing... (*snuggling*) Iowa corn grows tall.
JOAN: Terry... stop! Have you heard anything I've said?
TERRY: My mother's bringing someone for dinner. Probably... Mrs. Strawderman.
JOAN: And Shelly invited someone too.
TERRY: The more the merrier. (*He snuggles up to her again.*) Have I told you lately... I love you?
JOAN: Terry... I have to start the chicken.
TERRY: I've been promoted.
JOAN: That's nice, dear.
TERRY: Joan, he finally did it. You're looking at a bank president.
JOAN: (*Pointedly*) Anything else exciting happen in your life today?
TERRY: Mr. Tightwad, finally did it. The old miser... Mr. Clark... finally gave up command.
JOAN: I'm proud of you.
TERRY: I invited him over for dinner tonight.
JOAN: You did what?
TERRY: I felt I owed it to him. He's so lonely.
JOAN: But your mother?
TERRY: She tolerated him last year... when they met.
JOAN: What about her friend?
TERRY: Shelly likes Mrs. Strawderman.
JOAN: I told you, Shelly's invited someone too.
TERRY: Who... Pam?
JOAN: No... her future husband.
TERRY: (*Joking*) What's his name?
JOAN: She didn't say. She only told me... he had a tattoo and looked like Tom Cruise.

TERRY: I didn't know Tom Cruise had a tattoo.
JOAN: (*Pouting*) Help me pick this mess up.
TERRY: What's wrong with you?
JOAN: Nothing… just help me.
(*TERRY and JOAN go to their knees and begin to pick up the groceries as the LIGHTS fade to black.*)

SCENE TWO

(*The scene is still the living room. An hour later. AT RISE: The room is empty. The phone rings. SHELLY comes running in.*)

SHELLY: I'll get it. (*She answers the phone.*) Hello. (*Beat… as she listens.*) No, he's not here yet. Boy, Pam… you're more nervous than I am. I'll call you as soon as he gets here. (*Beat… as she listens.*) I promise. (*The doorbell rings.*) Oh my gosh, Pam… he's here… what do I do? (*Beat… as she listens.*) If I answer it… he'll think I was waiting for him. (*The doorbell rings again.*)
JOAN: (*From offstage*) Answer the door, Shelly.
SHELLY (*Into the phone*) My mother wants me to answer the door. Gotta go.
(*The doorbell rings again.*)
JOAN: (*From offstage*) Shelly?
(*SHELLY hangs up the phone and then sits on the sofa. She picks up a magazine and begins to read it very nonchalantly. The doorbell rings again. SHELLY ignores it and continues to read. The doorbell stops ringing and a banging on the door begins. TERRY finally enters. He has changed clothes.*)
TERRY: Don't you hear that?

SHELLY: I'm sorry… what did you say?
(*TERRY shakes his head and exits to answer the door. SHELLY tries some different poses on the sofa. She finally settles on one in which she is seductively sprawled on the sofa. Meanwhile, the banging on the door has stopped. TERRY enters with LEALIA.*)
TERRY: I'm sorry, Mother, the doorbell must be broken.
(*TERRY and LEALIA see SHELLY posed on the sofa.*)
LEALIA: Is she sick?
(*SHELLY snaps to a sitting position. Then jumps up and kisses LEALIA.*)
SHELLY: Hi, Gramma.
TERRY: Where's Mrs. Strawderman?
LEALIA: What?
TERRY: Your dinner guest.
LEALIA: Went to buy a bottle of champagne. You can't celebrate without champagne.
TERRY: A bank president. Aren't you proud?
LEALIA: I love him.
TERRY: Thank you.
JOAN: (*Calling from offstage.*) Terry! (*As TERRY exits to the kitchen, the doorbell rings.*)
SHELLY: That's him.
LEALIA: I thought your father said the doorbell was broken?
SHELLY: I'm so nervous.
LEALIA: Relax. I know he likes you. He told me so.
SHELLY: You answer it. Please.
(*LEALIA exits. SHELLY does her different poses on the sofa once again. She finally settles into the same seductive pose. After a beat, LEALIA enters with FRED, an older*

gentleman, about the same age as LEALIA. They see SHELLY on the sofa.)
FRED: Is she all right?
   (SHELLY sees them and snaps up to a normal sitting position.)
SHELLY: Mr. Tightwad!!
LEALIA: *(Introducing)* Fred, you remember my granddaughter... Shelly?
SHELLY: Mr. Clark? What are you doing here?
TERRY: *(Enters)* Was that your boyfriend at the door? *(He sees FRED.)* Mr. Clark, I'm glad you could make it. You know my mother... and my daughter?
FRED: Please call me Fred.
TERRY: *(To LEALIA.)* Mrs. Strawderman's not back with the champagne?
FRED: Here's some champagne. *(He takes a bottle out of a sack.)*
TERRY: Thank you, Mr. Clark.
FRED: Fred... please.
TERRY: I couldn't.
FRED: Come on, Mr. President.
TERRY: Only if you call me... Terry? *(They smile at one another.)* Welcome to our home, Fred.
FRED: Terry... your mother and I would like to get married. *(The doorbell rings.)*
SHELLY: That's him... he's here... I know that's him!
TERRY: *(To FRED)* Excuse me... would you repeat that?
SHELLY: I can't answer the door.
FRED: Your mother and I would like to get married.
TERRY: My mother's already married.
SHELLY: Daddy, please answer it.

TERRY: (*Referring to the marriage proposal.*) The answer is no.
SHELLY: It's him, Daddy… please help me.
TERRY: Not now, Shelly.
(*The doorbell rings again. JOAN enters. She is not happy everyone has forgotten what day it is.*)
JOAN: Terry, answer the door.
TERRY: I told Shelly to answer it.
SHELLY: Gramma, please answer the door for me.
LEALIA: Fred, be a dear and answer the door.
FRED: Does this family have a phobia about answering doors?
(*FREDDY enters. He is eighteen years old. His hair is long. Although he is always called "Fred," for convenience sake, we'll refer to him as "Freddy" in the script.*)
FREDDY: Like… hello. The door was open… so I thought it was cool to let myself in. (*SHELLY screeches and runs to FREDDY. They embrace.*) Shelly, babe… I was worried I was at the wrong pad.
TERRY: Who's this?
JOAN: Tom Cruise.
TERRY: Tom Cruise doesn't have long hair.
JOAN: Or a tattoo.
FREDDY: Do you want to see my tattoo? It might still be bloody… I just got it yesterday. (*FREDDY starts to unbuckle his jeans. SHELLY stops him.*)
SHELLY: (*Softly to FREDDY.*) Not here.
TERRY: This is Tom Cruise?
FRED: (*To FREDDY.*) You look familiar… have we ever met?
FREDDY: I got lots of friends. What's the name?
FRED: Fred.

FREDDY: That's my name—don't wear it out. (*He laughs.*)
FRED: I know you.
JOAN: Shelly, I thought you said he got a haircut.
FREDDY: Bummer. You mean I wasted my dough?
SHELLY: Spit ends, Mom.
TERRY: I'd ask for my money back.
JOAN: Well, food's on in the dining room. (*FREDDY points to FRED.*)
FREDDY: Is this your father? Listen, dude, I'd like to marry your daughter.
FRED: (*Moves to TERRY.*) Terry, may I have your mother's hand in marriage?
FREDDY: (*To SHELLY.*) Far out! Your father wants to get married too?
SHELLY: (*Points to FRED.*) Not him. (*Points to TERRY.*) Him.
FRED: Well, Terry?
FREDDY: (*To TERRY.*) Dude, I'd like to marry your daughter.
TERRY: I told you... my mother's already married.
FREDDY: What?
LEALIA: Your father's been dead for five years.
FREDDY: (*To SHELLY.*) Your father's dead? I thought you said... (*Points to TERRY.*)... this was your father?
SHELLY: That's him. Ask him.
TERRY: (*To JOAN.*) Help me?
JOAN: (*Sarcastically.*) Happy Anniversary! (*JOAN moves away and sits. TERRY tries to move to JOAN, but the others surround him.*)
TERRY: I'm sorry, Joan. The promotion.

LEALIA: You know, son, I don't really need your blessing.

TERRY: (*To FRED.*) Is this why you promoted me?

FREDDY: Shelly told me you were at Woodstock?

FRED: We've been seeing one another since the last dinner we shared here.

SHELLY: Daddy, tell Fred about when Hendrix played.

TERRY: (*To LEALIA.*) How can you do this? He's dead.

FREDDY: And what a pity. One great guitar player. But he lives on in memory. (*FREDDY sings.*) 'Scuse me while I kiss the sky. (*FREDDY mimes playing the air guitar, as he screeches the guitar sounds.*)

TERRY: You've been dating my boss?

FREDDY: Dude, I think your daughter's "boss."

FRED: I love her.

TERRY: (*To SHELLY.*) You're too young to get married. (*To LEALIA.*) And you're too old to get married. (*TO JOAN.*) Help me.

JOAN: And you're too stupid to be married.

TERRY: I'm sorry I forgot. (*All start bombarding TERRY with demands. It builds to a peak. TERRY can't take anymore. He shouts.*) This was supposed to be a celebration of my promotion. What happened? (*All freeze except TERRY.*) Dad? Dad… please help me.

(*LIGHTS flicker. We hear a chorus of "Take Me Out to the Ballgame" as BEN enters. He wears a New York Yankees uniform.*)

BEN: Son… life is about choices. Football… baseball… it's up to you. Baseball is the older of the sports.

TERRY: Oh Dad, help me, Dad.

(*BEN claps his hands. The others come to life, but they can't see BEN.*)

JOAN: Soup's on in the dining room. (*All exit except BEN and TERRY.*)

BEN: Personally, I don't like football. You don't need a mind to play football. Baseball's a mind game. But it's your choice.

TERRY: I sure have missed you, Dad.

BEN: But I never could tell you anything.

TERRY: I know you preferred baseball.

BEN: The generation gap will always exist.

TERRY: Shelly wants to marry a hippie.

BEN: I hated the sixties. And your involvement.

TERRY: I hope I wasn't like this guy.

BEN: What was the girl's name you wanted to marry after that silly concert you went to in upstate New York?

TERRY: Clare. Boy, I sure thought I loved her.

BEN: Did you marry her?

TERRY: Mother wants to marry my boss.

BEN: Why did you marry Joan?

TERRY: Didn't you hear what I said?

BEN: I heard you.

TERRY: Doesn't it bother you that your wife wants to marry another man?

BEN: I'd be more worried about your daughter.

TERRY: I can't believe you're so unconcerned.

BEN: Again, I ask you… why did you marry Joan?

TERRY: Forget about Joan and me. I blew that. What about Mom?

BEN: Is she happy?

TERRY: What?

BEN: Your mother. Is she happy?

TERRY: No, she's crazy. Dad, I don't think you understand me... your wife wants to marry another man.

BEN: How long were your mother and I married?

TERRY: Forty-six years.

BEN: Only forty-one.

TERRY: I'm forty-five years old. I was born one year after you were married. Forty-six years.

BEN: I've been dead for five years.

TERRY: What does that have to do with it? You're still married to her.

BEN: I am that. And I still love her.

TERRY: Then do something.

BEN: But she's a widow.

TERRY: What do you mean?

BEN: Do you know why your mother and I stayed married for forty-one years?

TERRY: It sounds like you were into the swinging singles scene.

BEN: We cared about each other's happiness.

TERRY: How can she do this?

BEN: Would it help you to know that we made a pact... that if either one of us died... it would be all right for the other to marry?

TERRY: No!

BEN: Good... we never made any such agreement.

TERRY: So, you're jealous?

BEN: You bet I am. Whoever she's marrying... you say your boss? Well, he better darn sure treat her with the respect and love that she... the best woman in the world... deserves.

TERRY: I'll stop it from happening. (*Beat*)
BEN: I always wanted you to be a baseball player.
TERRY: Do we have to bring that up again… now?
BEN: I supported you as a quarterback.
TERRY: And I was good.
BEN: You would have been a better pitcher.
TERRY: Get off my back. This is not about throwing a baseball versus a football. It's about Mom.
BEN: Your mother was the one who got me off your back.
TERRY: I love her, Dad.
BEN: Then let her be happy.
TERRY: Do I let Shelly do the same thing?
BEN: I never was very good with kid problems. Ask your mother.
TERRY: I don't know what to do.
BEN: I'd start with giving this to your wife. (*BEN hands TERRY a box of candy and a card.*) For forty-six years, I never once forgot our anniversary.
TERRY: I feel bad enough… without that.
BEN: Take it.
TERRY: Wait a minute. Remember, you've only been married forty-one years. So, forget the last five.
BEN: Your mother and I communicate every December second.
TERRY: Proof positive that she still loves you.
BEN: There's no doubt in my mind that she does.
TERRY: How can she marry another man if she loves you?
BEN: Take these. (*He holds up the candy and card.*)
TERRY: I think it's too late for Joan and me.
BEN: Just pretend you're back in the cornfield.

TERRY: What are you talking about?
BEN: Iowa corn might be tall, but it's not soundproof.
TERRY: You knew?
BEN: Your mother told me.
   (*TERRY flinches with embarrassment. Both men begin to laugh. The laughter grows until they embrace one another.*)
TERRY: I must confess... the older I get, the more I prefer baseball over football.
BEN: Did I tell you... I'm traveling with the Yankees.
TERRY: Can you do that?
BEN: You get the team of your choice.
TERRY: But you hated Steinbrenner. He's such a fool.
BEN: The year of your choice too. I'm with the '61 Yanks. I think Maris is going to break the Babe's home-run record.
TERRY: You know he does.
BEN: It's hard not telling everyone.
TERRY: I'm a bit old for a stepfather.
BEN: The bottom line is... is your mother happy?
TERRY: She seems to be.
BEN: Then give those things to your wife... and let mine be happy.
(*LIGHTS flicker. BEN is gone. JOAN, SHELLY, LEALIA, FRED, and FREDDY enter. They have just finished dinner.*)
FREDDY: That chicken was better than the Colonel's. (*As he passes TERRY, he flashes a "peace sign."*) Hey, dude.
LEALIA: Well, Terry? You said you'd give us your answer after dinner.
TERRY: You're right. Joan, happy anniversary. (*He gives Joan the candy and card.*)

JOAN: I thought you forgot. (*They kiss.*)
LEALIA: (*To TERRY.*) You know, we don't need your blessing.
TERRY: How can I say "yes" to you and, well, what about Shelly?
(*Just as Ben said, LEALIA takes control of the situation.*)
LEALIA: (*To FREDDY.*) So, Fred, you want to marry my granddaughter?
FREDDY: (*To FRED.*) You old letch, so do I.
LEALIA: What grade are you in?
FREDDY: It's not my fault that I failed two times. I need to be free… freedom. The teachers have never liked me.
LEALIA: Why do you want to marry my granddaughter?
FREDDY: Hey listen, granny… she came on to me.
SHELLY: I did not.
TERRY: Hey, dude, watch your tone with my mother.
LEALIA: Does she make you happy?
FREDDY: Shelly, you said your parents were cool.
LEALIA: I'm cool. Don't you think I'm cool, Fred?
FRED: Ice! That's how cold I think you are.
LEALIA: Cool, Fred, not frigid. (*To FREDDY.*) So, Mr. Love and Peace… does she make you happy?
SHELLY: Gramma, what are you doing?
LEALIA: It's a simple question. (*To FREDDY.*) Does she make you happy?
FREDDY: Listen, if I flunk again… my probation officer says I'll do some hard time for the bank job I did.
FRED: I knew I recognized him. He robbed my bank.

LEALIA: Bottom line, kid… the bases are loaded… bottom of the ninth… the score is tied… a base hit could win the game… give us your best pitch.
FREDDY: What is she talking about?
SHELLY: Do you want to marry me?
FREDDY: She said that?
SHELLY: Indirectly.
FREDDY: I'm sorry, Shelly. You're so smart… I thought you could help me graduate. (*He kisses SHELLY.*) See ya around. (*FREDDY exits.*)
SHELLY: I feel like a fool. (*She starts to exit.*)
LEALIA: Don't leave, Shelly.
SHELLY: I thought I loved him. I thought he loved me.
LEALIA: First love… you'll never forget it.
SHELLY: I don't think I want to ever love again.
LEALIA: I thought the same thing after my first love… and then I knew I never would after being married to Ben. But, to quote your grandfather… "life is like baseball… a curveball is just part of the game."
SHELLY: Grandpa's baseball metaphors never made sense to me.
LEALIA: (*To TERRY.*) So son, what's your answer?
TERRY: Father says, he loves you.
LEALIA: I know.
TERRY: Do you really?
LEALIA: He thinks Maris will break the Babe's home run record.
(*Beat… TERRY and LEALIA share a moment.*)

TERRY: Mr. Clark, I'd be honored to give you my mother's hand in marriage.

(*The LIGHTS fade to black.*)

END

Paul Bunyan, Two Old Men, and a Wizard

The Clown, the Penguin, and the Princess

---

a fantasy adventure
by
Bob May

© 1993/2016 by Bob May
All rights reserved

CAST OF CHARACTERS

BARB, Alan's mother
ALAN, ten-year-old boy
TED, Alan's father
JACK, Alcohol personified
TEDDY, Alan's father as a ten-year-old
CLOWN, Teddy's toy
PENNY, Teddy's toy stuffed penguin

The roles of Alan and Teddy should be played by young-looking adult actors. They could even be done by women, playing young boys. Ted is an alcoholic, but he should never play drunk.

SYNOPSIS OF SCENES

ACT ONE
Scene One: Alan's bedroom. An early summer's eve.
Scene Two: Alan's bedroom. Not long after.
ACT TWO
Scene One: Alan's bedroom. Not long after.

The premiere of *The Clown, the Penguin, and the Princess* was presented by the UNLV Theatre Department, Las Vegas, Nevada, in the Black Box Theatre on June 10, 1993, under the direction of Davey Marlin-Jones.

ACT ONE SCENE ONE

(AT RISE: BARB and ALAN are discovered in his bedroom. There is a toy box up center, a bed stage left, and a desk stage right. They are playing a game. There is a door to the hallway and a door to the bathroom. BARB stands down center on a large cube painted to look like an oversized numbered or lettered building block. She has chains around her wrists. ALAN fights off an invisible Dark Lord with a wooden sword. After he defeats the Dark Lord he touches the chains around BARB's wrists with the tip of his sword. The chains fall from her wrists.)

BARB: Thank you, Sir Knight. You have saved me from the evil clutches of the Dark Lord.
ALAN: Tis nothing, oh beautiful princess. It's all in a day's work.
BARB: How shall I ever thank you?

ALAN: By placing your fair hand in mine and saying those words that will make me the happiest knight in all the kingdom.
BARB: And what words are those, Sir Knight?
ALAN: That you will be my princess for life and become my ever-loving wife.
BARB: Happily, I accept the role of your princess wife for life.
ALAN: Let us seal our love with a... (*ALAN pauses.*)... with a handshake.
BARB: No, Alan, it was a kiss.
(*ALAN stops playing the game and is now talking as himself.*)
ALAN: Mom!
BARB: (*Still lost in the game.*) A tender kiss... to seal our love.
ALAN: Mom? Mom! Are you all right?
BARB: (*As herself.*) What dear? I'm sorry.
ALAN: You know I don't like the kissing part.
BARB: Oh, but that's how it happened.
ALAN: I just like playing the part when the knight rescues the princess.
BARB: But I do enjoy the proposal and the marriage. It was a dream come true.
ALAN: Did this really happen to you?
BARB: It seems like a million years ago, but yes, it happened.
ALAN: You know, the kids at school say our family is crazy.
BARB: It's all true, Alan. Every word of the story we play is true.
ALAN: It's really hard to think of dad as a prince.

BARB: He was much younger, and it was before he met—
(*From offstage TED calls.*)
TED: I'm home, Barb.
BARB: (*Calling to TED.*) Up here, dear. In Alan's room.
ALAN: I don't like it when Dad comes home.
TED: And I'm hungry.
BARB: (*Still calling to TED.*) I'll be right down, dear. I'll fix you something to eat.
ALAN: And I hate his friend, Jack.
BARB: He's your father. You must love him.
ALAN: My friends say he's a drunk...
BARB: No, he's a good man.
ALAN: ...an alcoholic.

(*TED bursts into the room, accompanied by JACK. JACK is alcohol personified. JACK is dressed in a white suit and he follows TED everywhere. He is always just over TED's shoulder so he can speak into his ear.*)

TED: What's going on up here?
BARB: Nothing. You're home early. How did the job search go?
TED: No one is hiring.
BARB: How many places did you go to?
JACK: Tell her to, "shut up and sit down."
TED: Shut up and sit down.
ALAN: Stop yelling at mom.
JACK: The kid too.
TED: You heard him, Alan. Sit down.
BARB: Come downstairs, dear, you need to eat. Some food will make you feel better. I can make you anything you want.
JACK: You don't need anything to eat.

TED: But Jack, I think I do.
JACK: Teddy boy, have I ever let you down?
BARB: Yes, Ted, a person has to eat.
TED: I am hungry.
JACK: (*To TED.*) Have you forgotten why you came up here?
TED: (*Confused.*) Yes. Yes, I have.
JACK: I told you… if she…
TED: I know… if she really loved me, she would be waiting downstairs for me to get home and welcome me back with a kiss. And she'd have a warm meal on the table, inviting me to sit down and eat.
BARB: If I knew when you'd be home… I'd do all that for you. (*She kisses TED on the check.*) Ted, I do love you.
JACK: Ah, words, just words with no meaning. She doesn't love you.
BARB: Come on, Ted, let's go downstairs. I'll fix your favorite meal.
TED: You see, Jack… she does love me.
BARB: I do, Sir Knight… I do.
TED: (*Something clicks in TED's mind.*) Knight. And you are… my princess. (*They embrace. JACK talks in TED's ear.*)
JACK: She's with the kid an awful lot. They spend a lot of time together.
(*TED pulls away from BARB.*)
TED: Jack is right. Why are the two of you always together?
JACK: I wonder what they were doing up here together?

TED: What were you doing up here?
BARB: Come on, dear, let's go downstairs and eat.
JACK: I'm sure they were plotting against you.
(*TED gets in BARB's face.*)
TED: Were you? Is that what you were doing? (*ALAN tries to distract TED.*)
ALAN: I was playing you… when you rescued Mom from the Dark Lord.
(*TED pulls away from BARB.*)
TED: (*Softening a bit.*) What did you say?
JACK: Nonsense… utter nonsense.
BARB: Ted, there's no reason to do this. Come on, let's go eat.
TED: (*Very touched.*) Barb, my dear, do you still play those games?
JACK: She's filling the boy's head full of fantasies.
ALAN: I don't think you were ever brave enough to save Mom from anything.
TED: I did. I once saved a princess… a princess Barb… your mother.
ALAN: In your drunken dreams.
BARB: Please, stop this. Let's go eat.
JACK: Are you going to take that from a kid? He called you a liar.
TED: (*To ALAN.*) Who's not brave enough to save her?
BARB: It doesn't matter, Ted. Please, let's just go downstairs.
ALAN: You're not brave enough. You're a coward. You always let Jack do your talking.
JACK: Will you listen to that mouth!

TED: Watch your mouth... boy. (*TED slaps ALAN. ALAN starts crying. BARB comforts ALAN.*)
BARB: Oh my God. Please, Ted... stop. No violence. You promised you'd stop. We weren't doing anything. We were playing. I was happy. He's just a boy. Please, let's just go eat.
JACK: Don't eat any food from her. I'm sure she's probably poisoned it.
TED: I wouldn't eat anything you prepared for me. You want to kill me.
BARB: No! This is not you talking. It's Jack.
JACK: Come on, Ted, let's go.
TED: I knew I shouldn't have come home.
BARB: No, Ted. Don't go. Please don't go.
JACK: They just don't understand what you're going through.
TED: You know, all I want is a little love and respect. Why can't I get it?
JACK: Why, Ted? Because they don't really love you.
BARB: We do, Ted, we do. Stop listening to Jack.
ALAN: I don't! I hate you.
BARB: No! He doesn't mean that.
JACK: You heard the kid! Come on, let's go. Let me show you a good time. I can give you the love and respect you seek.
ALAN: Why don't you just leave? Get out of here.
BARB: Alan, don't say that.
JACK: Come with me, Teddy. Have I ever let you down? I'm your blanket for life! I give you comfort.
BARB: Teddy, you have to stop this madness.
TED: My name is Ted... not Teddy. I'm an adult now.

JACK: Sorry, Ted. Come on. Relax! We're a team. Comfort!

BARB: Teddy… remember what your mother use to say?

TED: You're right, Jack… there's no comfort here. Let's go. (*TED and JACK start to exit.*)

BARB: (*Shouting at TED.*) She would say, "Look to the woods!"

(*This statement means something to TED. He stops.*)

TED: What?

BARB: The woods! Do you see all the oak in our family?

TED: Mama?

BARB: Fight, honey. Fight for love. Believe.

JACK: Oh, give me a break. What a dreamer. She lives in a fantasy world.

TED: The woods? Go to the oak trees!

BARB: Yes.

JACK: No, wood rots. (*JACK pulls TED offstage.*)

ALAN: Are you?

BARB: Am I what?

ALAN: What Jack said.

BARB: A dreamer?

ALAN: Are you?

BARB: Yes, I will always be one.

ALAN: You're both crazy.

BARB: Both?

ALAN: You and dad. The kids at school are right. You're both just crazy.

(*BARB begins to play the game. She stands on the block.*)

BARB: Thank you, Sir Knight—

ALAN: I'm too old to be playing your dumb games.

BARB: I play… am I too old? You have to save me from—
ALAN: What's wrong with daddy?
BARB: —from the evil clutches of the—
ALAN: Yes, I know. The Dark Lord. (*He shouts.*) Truth! I want the truth.
(*BARB sits on the block.*)
BARB: He's sick.
ALAN: You mean crazy?
BARB: No. It's a disease.
ALAN: It's Jack, isn't it? I don't like Jack.
BARB: Yes, Jack is his sickness, his Dark Lord.
ALAN: Is Dad an alcoholic?
BARB: Yes, he has to get rid of Jack. And we have to help. We have to save him from Jack! Make him see the woods.
ALAN: Jack scares me.
BARB: And he should. Jack has changed your father. Turned him into something he is not.
ALAN: I hate Dad.
(*BARB starts the game again. She stands on the block.*)
BARB: Once upon a time…
ALAN: You were never a princess.
BARB: There was a young boy.
ALAN: And Dad was never a knight. (*BARB steps off the block and moves to ALAN.*)
BARB: You can help your father by believing the story.
ALAN: No.
BARB: The young boy had a vivid imagination.
ALAN: I don't want to hear it.

BARB: Believe in the story. It can teach us how to defeat Jack. It's true.... if you believe.
ALAN: I don't want to believe anymore.
BARB: The boy had two friends.
ALAN: Toys don't come to life.
BARB: One was a clown doll. His grandmother had given it to him for his fifth birthday.
ALAN: I talked to my teacher about Daddy.
BARB: The other was a stuffed animal...
ALAN: I'm sorry. She asked me about Dad.
BARB: ...and of all things.... a penguin. A stuffed toy penguin. She, too, had been passed on to Teddy... by his grandmother.
ALAN: She said she was going to call you.
BARB: The boy had a father who drank too much. Just like you.
ALAN: Did she call you?
BARB: The clown and the penguin were the boy's only friends.
ALAN: I told her about this story.
BARB: The boy believed in those friends so much...
ALAN: My teacher says it can't happen.
BARB: ...that they became real.
ALAN: No, mother, it can't happen.
BARB: You have to believe. The boy believed. Have you stopped believing?
ALAN: I'm too old.
BARB: Too old for what? To stop caring? Your father needs us.
ALAN: Yes, he does. I'm sorry. (*ALAN embraces his mother.*) What can I do?
BARB: Believe in the story.

ALAN: I do want to.
BARB: Tell it to me.
ALAN: This boy...
BARB: What was his name?
ALAN: Teddy.
BARB: That's right, Teddy... your father.

(*TEDDY, as a ten-year-old, enters. He is talking to the CLOWN, who is in the hallway. TEDDY is dressed like a wizard.*)

TEDDY: Are you ready yet?
CLOWN: (*From off.*) I don't think I really want to do this.
BARB: And who is he talking to?
ALAN: His friend, the clown, who is standing in the hall just outside the bedroom.
TEDDY: (*To BARB.*) Oh, no. Are you back again?
BARB: Yes, I want to play with you and the clown.
TEDDY: No, I don't want to play with you.
BARB: But Teddy... I am your princess.
TEDDY: You're my sister's friend, Barbie. Go back to her room.
ALAN: (*To BARB.*) Come on, Mom, let's go. I believe the story.
TEDDY: Go play with my sister.
CLOWN: (*From off.*) All right, I'm ready.
TEDDY: Please, I must ask you to leave.
ALAN: Mom, we have to go.
BARB: Why?
ALAN: So the clown can enter.
BARB: And then Teddy can rescue me?
ALAN: Yes!

TEDDY: Rescue you? I don't think so. Why would I want to rescue my sister's friend?
BARB: Because I'm your princess.
ALAN: Mom, I'm hungry. We can finish telling the story downstairs. Come on.
BARB: Okay, let's go eat. (*ALAN and BARB exit.*)
TEDDY: (*To the CLOWN.*) Are you ready?
CLOWN: (*From off.*) No.
TEDDY: You just said you were.
CLOWN: I've changed my mind.
TEDDY: Oh, come on out. (*The CLOWN enters. He is dressed as a knight.*)
CLOWN: I feel silly.
TEDDY: You look great.
CLOWN: I'm a clown... not a knight.
TEDDY: Come on, you promised me that you'd play the knight.
CLOWN: I'm sorry. I just can't do it.
TEDDY: Sure you can. And even Penny thinks you can.
CLOWN: What does a penguin know?
 (*PENNY, the penguin, enters from the bathroom. She is dress as a princess.*)
PENNY: I know a lot. I know you wear silly looking clothes and too much makeup.
CLOWN: Well, you're too proper. Always in a tux. And you need to relax.
PENNY: That's it. I'm not playing anymore. I'd rather be sleeping. This princess doesn't want to be rescued by a fool.
TEDDY: Please, Penny, do it for me.
CLOWN: And this knight doesn't want to rescue you.

TEDDY: Come on, you two, this is my game. And I want to play it. I'm the wizard and I command you to play.
PENNY: I'll play with you. But not with him.
CLOWN: And I don't want to play with you.
TEDDY: No! All right. I'll be the knight. I'll rescue her. You be the wizard.
PENNY: If you make him the wizard… I'm for sure not playing.
CLOWN: I've always wanted to be the wizard.
TEDDY: Good, then you be the wizard and I'll be the knight. (*TEDDY and the CLOWN start switching costumes.*)
PENNY: No, I'm telling you… if you do that, you'll have to find another princess to rescue… cause I'm leaving. I'd much rather be sleeping. (*PENNY starts to exit.*)
TEDDY: Penny!
PENNY: A clown as a wizard is the most ridiculous thing I've ever heard of. I'm going back into the bathroom. It's the only place I can get away from the two of you and get some privacy. (*PENNY exits into the bathroom.*)
CLOWN: She's such a stuffed shirt.
TEDDY: No, she's trying real hard not to be.
CLOWN: I'm sorry, now we can't play.
TEDDY: We don't need her. We can play something different. I know, make me invisible.
CLOWN: What? I can't do that.
TEDDY: Sure you can. You're a wizard.
CLOWN: I'm just a pretend wizard.

TEDDY: How many times have I told you... you have to believe! If you believe... anything can come true.
CLOWN: All right, I believe.
TEDDY: Great, then make me invisible.
CLOWN: I, the great wizard... What's my name?
TEDDY: Merlin.
CLOWN: Too famous.
TEDDY: Marvin.
CLOWN: Not his brother.
TEDDY: I didn't know he had a brother.
CLOWN: Just call me, Mr. Wizard.
TEDDY: No first name?
CLOWN: No, I like it... Mr. Wizard!
TEDDY: I do too. Now, do you believe?
CLOWN: Yes, I believe... I mean, Mr. Wizard believes.
TEDDY: Great, then make me invisible.
CLOWN: All right, here it goes. (*Beat.*) How do I do it?
TEDDY: I don't know... you're the wizard.
CLOWN: Okay. Do this: wave a hand... whistle with your eyes closed... jump up and down three times... and...
TEDDY: Yeah?
CLOWN: Do all that and you'll be invisible.
TEDDY: That's all?
CLOWN: Try it.
   (*TEDDY waves a hand, whistles with his eyes shut, and jumps up and down three times.*)
TEDDY: Well?
CLOWN: I can still see you.
TEDDY: Sure you can... cause you're the wizard.

CLOWN: Then you must be invisible.
TEDDY: Let's ask Penny.
CLOWN: Do we have to? (*TEDDY walks to the bathroom door.*)
TEDDY: Penny!
PENNY: (*From in the bathroom.*) Leave me alone. I'm trying to sleep.
TEDDY: Can you see me?
PENNY: No.
CLOWN: You see… it worked.
TEDDY: Of course you can't see me with the door closed. Please come out here and tell me if you can see me.
PENNY: Didn't you hear me? I want to go to sleep.
TEDDY: If you come out here… I don't think you'll be able to see me.
PENNY: If I open the door… I'll see you.
TEDDY: I don't think so. The clown made me—
CLOWN: Remember, I'm a wizard.
TEDDY: The wizard made me invisible.
PENNY: If that fool made you invisible, I'm sure I can see you. (*She opens the bathroom door.*) There you are. You are dressed as a knight. There he is. He is dressed like a foolish clown wizard. Neither one of you is invisible. Now, I would love to go to sleep. May I?
TEDDY: Are you sure you can see me?
PENNY: I'm positive. Good night. (*PENNY exits into the bathroom, shutting the door.*)
CLOWN: I'm sorry. I'm not a wizard. I'm a good clown. Let me make you laugh. I'll be a jester.
(*The CLOWN does some pratfalls.*)

TEDDY: It didn't work because you didn't believe.
CLOWN: It didn't work because I'm not a real wizard. I'm just a clown.
TEDDY: Are you real?
CLOWN: I am to you.
TEDDY: You're real because I believe. (*Shouts.*) NOW, MAKE ME INVISIBLE.
CLOWN: (*Shouts and gestures with his hands like a magician.*) OKAY… YOU ARE INVISIBLE! (*A magical SOUND effect is heard, and a flash pot goes off as TEDDY disappears.*) Teddy? Teddy! Where are you?

(*In the following, TEDDY's lines are voice only. Ideally from a microphone backstage coming through a speaker on stage.*)

TEDDY: Relax. I'm right here.
CLOWN: Where? I don't see you.
TEDDY: I'm right beside you.
CLOWN: I can't see you.
TEDDY: That's because it worked. I'm invisible.
CLOWN: I don't believe it.
TEDDY: Believe this! (*The CLOWN reacts as if he were kicked in the behind.*)
CLOWN: Who did that?
TEDDY: (*Giggling.*) Me! I'm telling you… it worked. I'm really invisible.
CLOWN: Wow, I did it.
TEDDY: Yes, you did it because you believed. You can do anything… if you believe in yourself.
CLOWN: I believe I'm more than a silly clown. I believe I'm a wizard.

TEDDY: Yes, you are. You are Mr. Wizard. Now, make me reappear; make me visible again.
CLOWN: How do I do that? I've never made anyone visible.
TEDDY: Do the opposite of what you did to make me invisible.
CLOWN: All I did was yell… "You are invisible."
TEDDY: Try it again.
CLOWN: (*He shouts.*) YOU ARE INVISIBLE. (*Nothing happens.*)
TEDDY: No, I'm already invisible. This time say "make yourself visible" and really believe.
CLOWN: All right. Here it goes. Teddy… MAKE YOURSELF VISIBLE. (*The clown gestures and a magical SOUND effect is heard, along with another flash pot, and TEDDY appears.*)
TEDDY: Can you see me?
CLOWN: Yes, you're right there. (*The CLOWN and TEDDY jump and scream with joy. PENNY enters.*)
PENNY: Would the two of you please keep it down out here? Some of us are trying to sleep.
CLOWN: Penny, I made Teddy invisible.
PENNY: It didn't work again. I can still see him.
TEDDY: Penny, he really did it.
PENNY: All right, I'll play your game. I don't see you. Now, I'd love it if I couldn't hear you either. Goodbye. (*PENNY exits into the bathroom.*)
CLOWN: She's so uptight.
TEDDY: Make me tall!
CLOWN: What?
TEDDY: Forget her. Make me tall!

CLOWN: Okay, you are tall. (*The CLOWN gestures. A magical SOUND effect is heard, as TEDDY becomes ten feet tall. LIGHTS can create shadows to create this illusion.*)

TEDDY: Wow, look at me... I'm a giant!

CLOWN: Hail to Teddy! The tallest knight in the kingdom.

TEDDY: Yes, I am. Now make me tiny. Teeny tiny!

CLOWN: Shrink! From tall to small. From giant to mouse! (*The CLOWN gestures. A SOUND effect of a slide whistle is heard as TEDDY becomes as tiny as a mouse. A hand puppet can be used here.*)

TEDDY: I'm so small. This is scary.

CLOWN: Normal! Return to normal size. (*The CLOWN gestures. A SOUND effect of slide whistle in reverse is heard as TEDDY grows to normal size. CLOWN and TEDDY giggle with glee.*)

TEDDY: Now what, oh great and powerful wizard... now what?

CLOWN: Fat! You are fat. Fat as an elephant! (*The CLOWN gestures. The SOUND of stretching rubber is heard as TEDDY becomes as fat as an elephant. This can be achieved by TEDDY squatting, pulling his clothes out, holding his arms like they were the expanse of his fat body and puffing out his cheeks.*)

TEDDY: (*Laughing and having fun.*) Oh... too much! Make me skinny! Please, Mr. Wizard.

CLOWN: You are thin as a rail. (*The CLOWN gestures. The SOUND of wind escaping from a balloon is heard as TEDDY becomes as thin as a pole. This can be accomplished by having TEDDY stand tall, suck in his cheeks, and put his arms to the side of his body like at *attention.*) That's no good! I can't see you. Normal… return to normal size! (*The CLOWN gestures. A popping SOUND effect is heard as TEDDY grows to his normal size.*)

TEDDY: I want to fly. Make us both fly like birds.

CLOWN: We can't fly. Only birds can fly.

TEDDY: Peter Pan did.

CLOWN: Then so can we. (*Shouting.*) FLY! WE BOTH CAN FLY!

(*The CLOWN gestures. A magical SOUND effect is heard. TEDDY takes off first and then the CLOWN. They both fly around the room. This is wonderful if the actors can actually be flown, but if that is not possible, this can be simply done by having the actors stand on a desk, chair, or bed, and as they fly, hold their arms out, illuminate them with a colored LIGHT, play some flying music, and have the actors believe they are flying. Do this each time they fly and the audience will accept the convention of flying.*)

TEDDY: Weee! We're flying.

CLOWN: Yes, we are. I did it.

TEDDY: I'm as free as a bird.

CLOWN: I'm the greatest wizard in the world.

TEDDY: We can do anything.

CLOWN: Yes, we can… anything. (*PENNY enters.*)

PENNY: All right, I've had enough. Do I have to get angry at… (*PENNY sees the TEDDY and the CLOWN flying about the bedroom. She screams.*) Ahhh!

CLOWN: Mellow out, you miserable penguin and join us.

PENNY: You're flying.

TEDDY: Yes, we are. We're flying, just like Peter Pan. Come on up.

PENNY: Penguins can't fly.
TEDDY: Mr. Wizard... make her a believer.
CLOWN: Penny... you can fly! (*The CLOWN gestures. A magical SOUND effect is heard. PENNY takes off and joins the others in flight around the room.*)
PENNY: AHHH!!!
TEDDY: The world's first flying penguin.
PENNY: NOOOOOOOO!!!
CLOWN: Come on, Penny, let your collar down and enjoy.
PENNY: PLEEESSSSE!!
TEDDY: He's right, Penny, you need to relax.
PENNY: Let me down and I will. I'll relax better when I'm standing on the bedroom floor.
TEDDY: All right. Mr. Wizard, let her down.
CLOWN: Do I have to?
PENNY: YEEESSS!!
TEDDY: It's time we all touched down.
CLOWN: Flying stop. To land we go. (*The CLOWN makes a gesture. A magical SOUND effect is heard. All three stop flying and stand on the floor. They jump off whatever they were standing on, LIGHT special out on them, and flying music stops.*)
PENNY: Please tell me I'm dreaming. I'm asleep in the bathroom and this is all just a bad dream.
CLOWN: Nope. You're wide-awake and I made you fly.
PENNY: You? No way! You're a clown that can't even make people laugh.
CLOWN: (*To TEDDY.*) Tell her who I am now.

TEDDY: He's a powerful wizard now and he just made us fly. Please, Penny, won't you play with us now? Be the princess and let us rescue you.
PENNY: No, I will not play with a clown who thinks he's a wizard.
TEDDY: You were just a flying penguin.
PENNY: I refuse to believe it. It was nothing but a dream. Good night. (*PENNY exits into the bathroom.*)
CLOWN: What a bore. Where did she come from?
TEDDY: My grandmother gave her to me. She used to belong to my father.
CLOWN: That explains it. If she belonged to your father, she's probably drunk too.
TEDDY: Hey, you promised not to talk about that.
CLOWN: I'm sorry, Teddy, but you have to talk about it.
TEDDY: No! I just want to be a knight and rescue a princess.
CLOWN: Have you seen your father lately? Is Jack still with him?
TEDDY: I'll make Penny play with us. (*Yelling to the bathroom door.*) Penny, come out.
CLOWN: No, she's too stubborn. Forget her.
TEDDY: You know, my daddy used to play the wizard with me.
CLOWN: Hey, I'll gladly give up the costume if you want him to be the wizard.
TEDDY: No, Jack won't let him play anymore.
CLOWN: (*Getting an idea.*) Barbie!
TEDDY: Mama lied to me! She told me that the foundation of the family unit is the strongest bond there is. Solid as the oak trees that fill our backyard.

She always told me I could find strength in those trees. She would go there and find comfort when things got too bad for her. But our family is not as solid as oak! I don't want to play anymore.

CLOWN: Barbie can be your princess.

TEDDY: I tried some whiskey! I liked this girl at school... Cathy. I had a ring for her. She laughed at me, so I drank some of Dad's Jack Daniel's. It was awful.

CLOWN: You did what?

TEDDY: Don't worry; I'll never drink again.

CLOWN: You better not. If you turn into your father, I'll not be your friend.

TEDDY: I do love you.

CLOWN: Don't make me cry. It's bad for the image... if people see a clown crying.

(*TEDDY laughs. He snaps out of his funk and gets back to playing the game.*)

TEDDY: But you're not a clown... you're a wizard.

CLOWN: Yes, I am, and a powerful one at that.

TEDDY: Oh powerful Mr. Wizard, this knight needs a princess to save.

CLOWN: Barbie! I'm telling you, she can be our princess.

TEDDY: Not my sister's friend.

CLOWN: Penny won't do it, so who else?

TEDDY: Okay, Barbie can do it. I'll go get her.

CLOWN: No... I'll make her appear here! In your bedroom.

TEDDY: All right, now you're truly thinking like a real wizard.

CLOWN: Barbie... come. Appear here... in Teddy's room... before us!
(*The CLOWN makes a gesture. A magical SOUND effect is heard. BARB appears before TEDDY and the CLOWN. BARB acts like a young girl.*) Hey, I'm getting good at this!
BARB: What? Where am I? Who? Don't hurt me.
CLOWN: Don't be afraid... it's only us.
BARB: How did I get here?
TEDDY: The wizard did it.
BARB: The Wizard of Oz?
TEDDY: Nope, better than that!
CLOWN: I, Mr. Wizard, did it.
BARB: You?
CLOWN: Yes, me.
BARB: What do you want?
TEDDY: We want you to play with us.
BARB: Play what?
CLOWN: Will you be our princess and let us rescue you?
BARB: What do I have to do?
CLOWN: Go sit over there, and we'll save you in a second.
BARB: Over here?
CLOWN: That's fine.
TEDDY: Now what?
CLOWN: I don't know.
TEDDY: We don't have anything or anyone to save her from.
CLOWN: Yes, that is a problem.
BARB: Please save me!

TEDDY: I know! A dragon! Let me save her from a dragon.
CLOWN: Great idea. Knights always save princesses from dragons. (*The CLOWN moves the block center stage and then leads BARB to it. BARB stands on the block. CLOWN talks to TEDDY.*) Are you ready? (*TEDDY holds a wooden sword up.*)
TEDDY: Yes.
CLOWN: Sir Knight… you asked for a dragon… a dragon you will get! (*The CLOWN waves his hands, a magical SOUND effect is heard, and a dragon appears. The dragon, like the kind that is in a Chinese New Year's parade, can be played by the actors playing TED, PENNY, and ALAN.*)
BARB: Help! Save me from the dragon!
    (*TEDDY has a choreographed fight with the dragon and defeats it.*)
CLOWN: Congratulations, oh strong and wondrous knight… you defeated the dragon.
BARB: My hero!
TEDDY: It was too easy. You helped me. You helped me win!
CLOWN: No, I didn't. I only made the dragon appear. I swear I didn't do anything else.
TEDDY: Then let me save her from something else.
CLOWN: Okay, gimme a sec… let me think.
BARB: The dragon! I liked that. Save me from the dragon again!
TEDDY: No, I've done that. It's not a challenge anymore!
    (*SOUND: A loud thunderclap is heard. The LIGHTS flash. JACK appears before the others.*)

JACK: How about me? Am I a worthy opponent? (*JACK grabs BARB.*)
CLOWN: Look out; it's the Dark Lord!
JACK: Teddy, owning your father has become so boring lately. It's time I move on a generation. Did you like the whiskey, Teddy?
CLOWN: I command that you go away.
JACK: Ha! It's going to take more than a clown-wizard to make me go away. I control this family.
BARB: Help me, Teddy!
JACK: Your father is mine… and now it looks like your princess is too.
CLOWN: I have more power than you.
JACK: I'm talking to Teddy… not you! (*JACK gestures toward the CLOWN. A magical SOUND effect is heard. The CLOWN falls down as if dead.*) I want you now, Teddy. Come play my game. (*JACK laughs as he and BARB disappear. TEDDY runs to the CLOWN.*)
TEDDY: Mr. Clown, Mr. Clown? (*He shakes the CLOWN.*) Wake up! You can't be dead. Please wake up! I don't want to play anymore. This is not real. Please! (*TEDDY starts crying. After a few beats the CLOWN stirs and wakes up.*)
CLOWN: What happened?
TEDDY: You're alive?
CLOWN: Is Jack still here?
TEDDY: I thought you were dead.
CLOWN: Where did he go?
TEDDY: Are you hurt?
CLOWN: Did he take Barbie?
TEDDY: Yes, he took her. And he says, now he wants me.

CLOWN: I knew it was only a matter of time before he came for you. We have to talk about him now.
TEDDY: You're breaking your promise… you said you wouldn't talk about him.
CLOWN: You have to face the facts. Alcohol is serious business. The games have become very real now.
TEDDY: But I'm only a boy.
CLOWN: You made me a wizard. It's time I made you a man. (*Pause.*)
TEDDY: I'm scared.
CLOWN: So am I.
TEDDY: Okay, what do we do?
CLOWN: We have to defeat Jack. Stop him from entering your life.
TEDDY: What about Barbie?
CLOWN: To find Barbie we have to find Jack.
TEDDY: That's easy. You know he's always with my dad. Find my dad and you'll find Jack. I bet they're in the study. Let's go.
CLOWN: No. We need to get Jack on our turf. He has to come back to us.
TEDDY: He won't do that.
CLOWN: I think he will because of his ego!
TEDDY: Right! I'll go down and invite him up.
CLOWN: In a minute. First we must orchestrate our plan of attack. Come on.
(*TEDDY and the CLOWN exit into the bathroom. As they enter we hear PENNY.*)
PENNY: You two are my worst nightmare!
(*The LIGHTS fade to black. In the black ALAN and BARB talk.*)

BARB: And what happened next?
ALAN: Teddy went down to the study and invited Jack up to his bedroom, promising him he'd like to hear what Jack had to offer that was so great.

ACT ONE

SCENE TWO

(*The action is continuous. JACK is heard talking in the dark.*)
JACK: Hey, what's going on? You invite me up to your bedroom and greet me with darkness. (*The LIGHTS snap on like someone turned on a light switch. JACK is discovered in the middle of the bedroom... alone.*) Thank you. Now I can see. And I see that I'm alone.
TEDDY: (*Voice only.*) Where's Barbie?
JACK: Oh! I guess you don't want to hear about the benefits I can offer you.
TEDDY: (*Voice only.*) No, we want Barbie back.
JACK: Are you hiding? I can find you. This room isn't that big. Under the bed? (*JACK bends over and looks under the bed.*)
CLOWN: (*Voice only.*) Now! Kick him now!
(*JACK reacts as if he were kicked in the bottom. JACK falls down. TEDDY and the CLOWN laugh. JACK stands up.*)
JACK: Are you in the bathroom? (*JACK walks toward the bathroom.*)
TEDDY: (*Voice only.*) Don't trip, Jack.
(*JACK trips and falls. TEDDY and the CLOWN laugh again.*)

CLOWN: (*Voice only.*) Did you have a nice trip, Jack?
JACK: Where are you?
TEDDY: (*Voice only.*) We want the girl.
JACK: Sorry, she's mine.
TEDDY: (*Voice only.*) Mr. Wizard, what do we do to those who don't do what we ask them to do?
CLOWN: (*Voice only.*) We make them fat.

(*The SOUND of stretching rubber is heard as JACK becomes as fat as an elephant. This can be achieved by JACK squatting, pulling his clothes out, holding his arms like they were the expanse of his fat body and puffing out his cheeks.*)

JACK: Leave me like this and I'll sit on Barbie.
TEDDY: (*Voice only.*) Oh no, make him thin.
CLOWN: (*Voice only.*) Jack, you're no longer fat. You're thin... thin as a pole.

(*The SOUND of wind escaping from a balloon is heard as JACK becomes as thin as a pole. This can be accomplished by having JACK stand tall, suck in his cheeks, and put his arms to the side of his body, like at attention.*)

JACK: I can stop this with double vision!
CLOWN: (*Voice only.*) NO!
TEDDY: (*Voice only.*) What's wrong?
CLOWN: (*Voice only.*) He knows what we're doing.
JACK: And I can see you with double vision. (*JACK gestures. A magical SOUND effect is heard. JACK returns to his normal shape. TEDDY and the CLOWN pop into view before JACK.*) Not bad! The old invisible trick. I'm impressed. You had me fooled, Mr. Clown.
CLOWN: I'm a wizard now... and we demand that you release the princess.
TEDDY: Yes, we demand the release of Barbie.

JACK: Teddy, my boy, she and your father are both happy. And they want you to join them.
CLOWN: If you don't release your prisoners and leave this boy alone, you'll be sorry.
JACK: Nice try, Mr. Clown… Wiz! I admire your faithfulness, but it's going to take more than a powerless threat for me to let them go.
CLOWN: FLY! Fly like a bird! I command that you fly!

(*The CLOWN gestures, a magical SOUND effect is heard. JACK takes off. He flies like a crazy bird throughout the bedroom.*)

TEDDY: Very good, Mr. Wizard.
CLOWN: Now where is the princess? Release her at once.
JACK: Is this flying supposed to make me release her?
CLOWN: I can make it rougher!
JACK: I've had bumpier rides in Teddy's father's Chevy after a Saturday night binge at the bar.
CLOWN: You leave me no alternative. (*He waves his hands as he speaks.*) Make Jack's flight as bad as —
JACK: All right! Don't do it. If you want the girl that bad… here she is. (*JACK gestures. A magical SOUND effect is heard. BARB joins JACK flying about the room. JACK laughs triumphantly.*)
BARB: Help! Help me, Teddy! Please!
JACK: You forgot one thing, Mr. Clown, I love to fly. The higher I am, the better I feel!
BARB: Stop this. I'm getting sick.
JACK: Uh oh, I don't think our princess likes it as much as your father and I do.
BARB: Please, do something.

TEDDY: Mr. Wizard, you better bring them down.
CLOWN: To the ground... both of you come. Stop flying. Stop at once. (*The CLOWN gestures. A magical SOUND effect is heard. JACK and BARB land. JACK grabs BARB.*)
JACK: Now, where were we? I believe in the middle of a princess rescue?
(*TEDDY steps forward... proud and tall*)
TEDDY: That is correct.
JACK: I'm not going to just hand her over to you. I want a little action in my life. Your father's become such a bore.
TEDDY: Leave my father out of this.
JACK: He's always out of it. It's you I really want... Teddy.
CLOWN: Be careful, Teddy.
(*TEDDY pulls his wooden sword out.*)
TEDDY: I challenge you to a fight.
JACK: Oh, give me a break. I haven't used a weapon like that for thousands of years. Your great, great, great... I can't remember how far back... it was one of your grandfathers of year's past. He tried to fight me off with a crude sword like that.
TEDDY: (*To the CLOWN.*) Do something.
CLOWN: I'm sorry, Teddy, I'm afraid he's won.
(*Suddenly PENNY bursts out of the bathroom.*)
PENNY: He hasn't won anything.
JACK: Who are you?
PENNY: Someone who is not afraid of you.
TEDDY: Be careful, Penny!
JACK: Oh, it's Penny, the stuffed shirt!
PENNY: I am not a stuffed shirt.

JACK: You know, Penny, Teddy and the Clown don't like you. Why don't you join me? I could use someone with your talents.
TEDDY: Don't listen to him Penny, we like you.
JACK: We could rule this house together.
PENNY: Can I boss the Clown around?
JACK: If that's what you want, you got it.
PENNY: Let's shake on it.
JACK: You got it, partner.
(*PENNY and JACK shake. As they do, PENNY flips JACK over with a karate move and then pins him to the floor.*)
PENNY: Okay, Wizard, do your thing. Get some rope so we can tie this evil creature up.
   (*The CLOWN claps his hands. A magical SOUND effect is heard as a rope flies to him from offstage. The CLOWN and TEDDY tie JACK up.*)
JACK: Oh, Penny, I'm so disappointed. We could have been so powerful as a team.
PENNY: Hail to Teddy for saving the princess.
BARB: Thank you.
CLOWN: Hail, Sir Knight.
TEDDY: I couldn't have done it without the two of you. My friends.
JACK: You think these ropes are going to stop me?
CLOWN: I banish you from this kingdom.
JACK: I've been around a long time.
PENNY: Make him disappear, Mr. Wizard!
CLOWN: Disappear! Be gone! We don't want you here. Get out of this house.
JACK: Beware, Ted, you're the next chapter in this family's biography. You'll find me.

CLOWN: Away! Disappear! (*The CLOWN gestures, a magical SOUND effect is heard, and JACK disappears, TEDDY, the CLOWN, PENNY, and BARB begin to celebrate.*)

PENNY: Since the knight saved the princess from the Dark Lord…

CLOWN: He's the bravest knight in all the kingdom.

PENNY: …he must take the princess's hand in marriage.

TEDDY: What? Do I?

CLOWN: That is usually what is done after a knight saves a princess.

TEDDY: Okay.

(*The CLOWN leads BARB to the block at center stage. She stands on it. The words of the game are said.*)

BARB: Thank you, Sir Knight. You have saved me from the evil clutches of the Dark Lord.

TEDDY: Tis nothing, oh beautiful princess. All in a day's work.

BARB: How shall I ever thank you?

TEDDY: By placing your fair hand in mine, and saying those words that will make me the happiest knight in the kingdom.

BARB: And what words are those, Sir Knight?

TEDDY: That you will be my princess for life and become my ever-loving wife.

BARB: Happily I accept the role of your princess wife for life.

TEDDY: Let us seal our love with…

BARB: A tender kiss. (*TEDDY and BARB kiss.*)

CLOWN: By the power vested in me as Mr. Wizard… I now pronounce you… husband and wife. Knight and Princess! (*ALAN bursts into the scene.*)
ALAN: Father didn't save you, Mom.
BARB: I love you, Teddy…
ALAN: It was the penguin who saved you.
BARB: …and I always will.
ALAN: Mom, you are crazy.
BARB: No, Alan, you have to believe. What have you learned from the story?
ALAN: That the clown and the penguin don't exist. They are not real.
BARB: Don't say that.
ALAN: Well, I do say it. They are not real and I don't believe this story.
   (*A sucking SOUND is heard and TEDDY, the CLOWN, and PENNY disappear.*)
BARB: Don't go. Come back.
ALAN: Stop living in a fantasy. Jack got to Dad… just like he said he would. Dad is nothing but an alcoholic… and I hate him.
BARB: No, your father saved me. He's a good man.
ALAN: Why do you put up with Dad? Jack owns Dad. Jack has won.
(*With a flash and a magical SOUND effect JACK appears.*)
JACK: Hello, Alan. You don't know how long I have waited for you to say that. Let me show you a good time.
ALAN: Go away. Just get out of our life. I'll never surrender to you.
JACK: (*Laughing.*) Oh, I do love a challenge.

ALAN: I'll not fight you. Take my father and leave us in peace.
JACK: That's not very loving.
ALAN: What do you know about love? (*JACK grabs BARB.*)
JACK: I know you love her.
ALAN: Let her go. Don't hurt my mother.
JACK: I've been in your family far too long. You can't get rid of me so easily. You're stuck with me. I have no place else to go.
ALAN: What do you want?
JACK: As I've said for generations... I want you! The next in line. I need you. You can make me continue to live.
BARB: Help me, Alan.
ALAN: I can kick you, Jack.
JACK: Oh, kid, I love your spunk!
(*With a magical SOUND effect, JACK and BARB disappear. JACK laughs as they disappear. The laugh lingers on even after JACK is gone. ALAN stands there for a beat and then says...*)
ALAN: This means war!
(*The LIGHTS fade to black.*)
END ACT ONE

ACT TWO

(*The scene is still ALAN's bedroom. Only now there is a bunker built of various things that were in the bedroom; chair, deck, toy box, etc. AT RISE: "Also Sprach Zarathustra" by R. Strauss blasts over the sound system. ALAN rises from the behind the bunker to the music. He is dressed as a makeshift futuristic knight.)*

ALAN: The calm before the storm.
(*SOUND: Several explosions go off at the base of the bunker as if someone were firing a cannon at ALAN and the bunker. BARB appears in a LIGHT special. Her arms are bound at the wrists with rope.*)
BARB: Help me, Alan. Please come and rescue me.
(*ALAN sees his mother. He talks to himself.*)
ALAN: Be firm. Don't go to him. Fight him on your own turf. (*SOUND: Some more explosions.*)
BARB: Save me.
ALAN: Tell Jack to come to me.
BARB: He won't.
ALAN: If he wants me bad enough… he'll come.
BARB: He's hurting me.
ALAN: I'm sorry, Mama. Have faith. I will rescue you.
BARB: You're not man enough to rescue me. You don't love me.
ALAN: Jack is making you say those things. (*BARB screams out in pain. ALAN yells to JACK.*) Jack, stop hurting my mother. If you want me… come and get me. Can't you talk to me yourself? Afraid to face me? Jack the user. Jack the abuser. Jack doesn't exist without someone else.
(*With a flash of LIGHTS and a magical SOUND effect, BARB disappears and JACK appears in the bedroom.*)
JACK: I just love your spunk, kid.
ALAN: Leave my parents alone.
JACK: (*JACK holds out a whiskey bottle.*) Drink this and I will.

ALAN: I've updated my sword. (*ALAN leaps over the bunker, light saber in hand.*)
JACK: I see that you have. (*JACK produces his own light saber.*) And so have I.
(*A choreographed fight ensues. It looks like ALAN is going to win, but JACK finally wins. JACK holds his light saber above ALAN, who is trapped beneath JACK on the floor.*)
ALAN: Go ahead, kill me!
JACK: Now why would I want to do that?
ALAN: Then set my parents free.
JACK: I told you I will… if I can have you.
ALAN: All right, how do I know I can trust you?
(*JACK moves away from ALAN. ALAN scrambles to his feet.*)
JACK: Read the label on the bottle… satisfaction guaranteed. (*JACK throws ALAN his saber.*)
ALAN: Now my parents.
JACK: I'll start with your father. You want him? You can have him! (*JACK gestures, a magical SOUND effect is heard, and TED stumbles into the bedroom.*)
ALAN: Dad, are you okay?
TED: Yes, I'm sorry. I should have fought off Jack before it got to this. I love you, son. (*They embrace.*)
JACK: Oh, how cute! Alcoholic father and son in a loving embrace.
ALAN: Let's fight for Mom together!
TED: Yes, we must be strong.
JACK: Alan, you lied to me.
ALAN: You have a way of making people do that.
JACK: You're not in my control yet, but your father is. Be careful, Ted… I'll leave you!

ALAN: Don't listen to him, Dad, believe in the woods. The foundation of family.
JACK: Believe in this, Ted. (*JACK, like a magician, produces a drink. A magical SOUND effect accompanies this.*) Drink up, Teddy. (*TED takes the drink.*)
ALAN: No, Dad, don't do it. (*TED drinks the drink and passes out.*)
JACK: Now, what was it you were saying to me about trust?
ALAN: Where are you keeping my mother?
JACK: (*Laughing.*) Why don't you ask your father?
ALAN: Okay, if you want me, let me see my mother. Then I'm yours.
JACK: I don't think I can trust you anymore.
ALAN: There doesn't seem to be any other options for me.
JACK: Ask and you shall receive! (*JACK claps his hands, a magical SOUND effect is heard, and BARB bursts into the bedroom. ALAN starts to move to BARB.*)
ALAN: Mom! (*JACK steps between BARB and ALAN.*)
JACK: No, keep your distance from each other. Come to me, Alan.
BARB: Has he hurt you, Alan?
ALAN: Mother... I know you believe in the woods?
JACK: No! (*He moves to BARB.*) I trusted you, Alan.
ALAN: You know people can't be trusted when it comes to alcohol. My mom's not as weak as my dad. See the woods, Mom!
BARB: I see... (*JACK cuts her sentence off by covering her mouth with his hand.*)
JACK: She sees nothing.
ALAN: She saw it, Jack.

JACK: You're good, Alan… real good! Just drink this and end all this back and forth on who is stronger.

ALAN: Never.

JACK: Oh, this is going to be fun! (*JACK laughs. He and BARB disappear in a cloud of smoke, accompanied by a magical SOUND effect. ALAN moves to TED.*)

ALAN: Dad? Wake up, Dad! Please. Wake up! (*TED stirs and wakes up.*)

TED: Where is he?

ALAN: Are you all right?

TED: I can kick him.

ALAN: You've been saying that for years, but you're always a little too late.

TED: Are you okay?

ALAN: What do you care?

TED: I do care, a lot. (*Pause.*) I suppose it's too late to say I'm sorry. I haven't been much of a father the past few years.

ALAN: That's an understatement. I hardly know you.

TED: We had a good time when you were younger.

ALAN: Sorry, I don't remember.

TED: You know, this is not easy for me.

ALAN: Why should I make it easy for you?

TED: I guess I deserve that. (*Pause.*)

ALAN: Why did you let Jack into your life? You had him defeated.

TED: I guess because I thought I could never live up to the knight your mother made me.

ALAN: Mama never made any demands. She loves you.

TED: I'm just a big disappointment in her eyes.

ALAN: You stopped believing.

TED: Does she?
ALAN: What?
TED: Love me? Does she really still love me?
ALAN: With all her heart.
TED: Then I must save her. (*TED starts to run off. As he does he yells...*) Barbie, I'm coming. (*TED runs a bit and all of the sudden he stops dead in his tracks. He mimes as if he were caught in a glass prison. After a beat JACK enters.*)
JACK: How heroic! (*He mockingly applauds for TED.*)
TED: Let me out of here.
JACK: Ted, how long have we known each other?
TED: Too long!
JACK: You're right. (*JACK jumps up on the desk behind TED, raises his hands, and starts waving them around as though he were controlling a puppet. And he is! He makes TED go through some crazy gyrations.*) Alan, why do you hang around with these drunk puppets? You and I could make such a good team. You're so strong, but with me, I can make you feel stronger. (*JACK gestures like he drops TED. A magical SOUND effect is heard. TED falls to the floor.*) Come here, Alan, I have a secret I know you will grow to love.
ALAN: If you have something to say to me... say it out loud. The only thing I want from you is my mother.
JACK: Come and find her. (*JACK disappears laughing. ALAN moves to TED. TED is very weak.*)
TED: We need help.
ALAN: The police?
TED: No, the clown and the penguin!

ALAN: Who?
TED: My clown and Penny, the penguin!
ALAN: Your toys?
TED: Yes, get them.
ALAN: Where are they?
TED: In my past.
ALAN: Does Granny Mae have them?
TED: Go back to my past and find them.
ALAN: What? Your past? How?
TED: Believe! You must believe! (*TED passes out. ALAN begins to pace back and forth in the bedroom.*)
ALAN: How do I go back in time? How? (*He stops pacing, he clenches his fists, and he shuts his eyes.*) Believe! A time jump! I must make a time jump. Twenty years. I need to go back in time twenty years. (*The LIGHTS flicker. A strobe LIGHT flashes. ALAN spins around the room flailing his arms. Wild music plays. TED must exit in this transition. The bunker furniture must be moved back to their original positions in the transition. Then just as suddenly as this madness began... it stops abruptly. ALAN falls to the floor. He is still in the same room. He gets up and moves about the room cautiously.*) Hello?
(*ALAN moves around the room looking at things. TEDDY runs into the room being chased by the CLOWN. They laugh as they move around and over the bed. The CLOWN finally tags TEDDY.*)
CLOWN: You're it!
TEDDY: Not for long. (*TEDDY jumps for the CLOWN. They giggle as they play. They finally see ALAN.*)
Hello.
ALAN: Hi.

TEDDY: Do I know you?
ALAN: Ah… in the future, you will.
TEDDY: Are you one of my sister's friends?
CLOWN: Her friends like Teddy's room better than her room.
TEDDY: I don't think I know you, but you do look familiar.
ALAN: I don't know how to say this.
CLOWN: The truth is always the best way. It's one of the rules of the bedroom. Honesty! No lying.
ALAN: Okay!
TEDDY: I feel like I know you.
ALAN: You do.
TEDDY: Who are you?
ALAN: I'm your son.
TEDDY: (*To the CLOWN.*) What did he say?
CLOWN: He said he's your son.
TEDDY: But I'm not old enough to have a son.
CLOWN: (*To ALAN.*) Remember, there's no lying in this room.
ALAN: I'm not lying. I'm his son.
CLOWN: You mean you want to play his son. We love to play games.
ALAN: No, I'm his son. I'm his son in the future.
TEDDY: We especially enjoy playing futuristic games.
ALAN: This isn't a game. You marry Barbie and the two of you produce me.
TEDDY: Yes, I married Barbie, right after I saved her from the Dark Lord.
CLOWN: Where is Barbie? We haven't seen her in weeks.

ALAN: She kept believing... and somehow... I don't know... when you grew up... you married her. And I am your son!
CLOWN: Wow! What a fantastic imagination.
ALAN: Jack!
TEDDY: What did you say?
ALAN: Jack has captured Barbie and...
TEDDY: I don't know any Jack.
ALAN: ... and in the future Jack controls you... just as he controls your father now, my Grandfather... Papa Foss.
TEDDY: (*To the CLOWN.*) Is this some trick of yours to get me to talk about Jack?
CLOWN: No. I've never seen this boy before. But you do have to stop denying Jack.
ALAN: I need your help to once again save Barbie from the Dark Lord.
TEDDY: Go away.
ALAN: Where's Penny?
TEDDY: How do you know about her?
ALAN: My mother... Barbie... told me about her. She's told me the whole story, and I've played you a million times... "Tis nothing, oh beautiful princess. All in a day's work."
CLOWN: (*As the princess, standing on the block.*) How shall I ever thank you enough?
ALAN: By placing your fair hand in mine, and saying those words that will make me the happiest knight in the kingdom.
TEDDY: And what words are those, Sir Knight?
ALAN: That you will be my princess for life and become my ever-loving wife.

(*TEDDY and the CLOWN look at one another, astonished. The CLOWN steps off the block.*)
CLOWN: He knows it. Word for word. (*TEDDY looks at ALAN.*)
ALAN: You must believe me.
TEDDY: Do I have any other children?
ALAN: No, but I wish I had a brother.
TEDDY: Let me get used to you first. What's your name?
ALAN: Alan. I really need your help.
TEDDY: How did you get here?
ALAN: Time jumping.
TEDDY: Time what?
ALAN: I made it up. But I believed and it worked. You must help me. Come with me into the future and help me destroy Jack and save my mom and you from him.
CLOWN: Jack controls Teddy in the future?
ALAN: I'm very sad to say… but yes, he does.
TEDDY: Never. I've seen what Jack has done to my father…
CLOWN: Alan, I'll go with you and help you.
TEDDY: …and I won't let him do the same to me. I hate Jack.
CLOWN: Sir Knight… you can save the princess once again.
ALAN: And a son. You can save me. Jack wants me now.
TEDDY: Okay. I don't believe you, but I'll play along.
ALAN: Where's Penny?
CLOWN: We don't need her.
ALAN: My father… you… Ted… says that we do.

CLOWN: She's sleeping. That's all she ever does.
ALAN: (*Shouting.*) Penny. Penny the penguin! Wake up. You are needed. Wake up!
(*PENNY enters from the bathroom.*)
PENNY: Again you wake me up. You two are always waking me up.
ALAN: Form a circle and take each other's hands.
(*ALAN grabs PENNY's hand. The four of them join hands and form a circle. ALAN shuts his eyes, and chants.*) Time jump! Let us time jump! The four of us must jump twenty years. Time jump! Take us forward! Take us to the future!
(*The LIGHTS flicker. A strobe LIGHT flashes. All four spin about the bedroom flailing their arms. Wild music plays. Then it is all over as quickly as it started. All four fall to the floor. TED has come in during the transition and falls to the floor in the same spot he was before ALAN went back in time. The furniture must be moved back to the bunker too.*)
PENNY: This has to be a bad nightmare.
ALAN: I think we made it back.
CLOWN: In our case, I think you mean… we made it forward.
TEDDY: We didn't go anywhere. We're still in my bedroom.
ALAN: Yes, but now it's my bedroom.
PENNY: Would someone please explain what's going on?
ALAN: Papa Foss left you the house when he died. I… we live here now. Your bedroom is now mine.
TEDDY: It looks the same.
ALAN: Mother insisted it should never be changed.

TEDDY: What do you think, Mr. Clown?

CLOWN: We all just experienced something. What? I don't know. I do know I'm in the same room. It all looks familiar… except for that. (*The CLOWN points to TED. PENNY sees the passed out body of TED and screams.*)

TEDDY: Who's that?

ALAN: It's you. (*Pause.*)

TEDDY: That's not me.

ALAN: Yes, it is, under the influence of Jack.

TEDDY: No more about Jack. (*To the CLOWN.*) Tell him to get out of my bedroom.

ALAN: Believe. Mother taught that to me. She told me you taught her how to believe.

TEDDY: Penny, will you escort Mr. Imagination back to my sister's room.

(*PENNY has been rifling through TED's pockets. She has his wallet and is looking at his driver's license.*)

PENNY: This guy has the same name as you.

TEDDY: So?

PENNY: What's the date of your birthday?

TEDDY: You know when my birthday is.

PENNY: This guy has the same birthday.

TEDDY: So does Columbus. October twelfth. That doesn't make him me.

PENNY: But not the same year.

CLOWN: Teddy, I think we did it.

TEDDY: Did what?

CLOWN: (*To ALAN.*) What did you call it?

ALAN: Time jumping.

PENNY: We did what?

TEDDY: I like to play games. But that is not me.

PENNY: This is all very weird.
ALAN: Mr. Wizard... (*Referring to TED.*) Wake him up!
CLOWN: I'm not a wizard.
ALAN: You were once upon a time. Tall... short... fat... thin... you made them all fly! Mr. Wizard, wake him up!
CLOWN: I don't think I can.
PENNY: He was never a wizard.
(*The CLOWN gets mad at what PENNY said and shouts to TED.*)
CLOWN: Wake up! Whoever you are... wake up!
(*The CLOWN gestures. A magical SOUND effect is heard. TED stirs and wakes up.*)
TED: I'll kick you, Jack. Leave my son and wife alone. (*He sees the others.*) Where's Jack?
ALAN: (*To the others.*) Welcome to the future.
CLOWN: Oh my gosh, I guess I am still a wizard.
TED: What do you what? Who are you?
CLOWN: Teddy, don't you recognize us?
TED: Are you friends of Alan's?
ALAN: Dad... I got them. Just like you said to do.
TEDDY: I refuse to believe this. That is not me.
PENNY: Who is that?
TED: Penny?
CLOWN: Teddy.
TED: My clown! (*TED and the CLOWN embrace.*)
PENNY: That's Teddy? It can't be.
TED: Thanks for coming, Penny. (*TED embraces PENNY.*)
PENNY: Oh, yeah, well, I didn't really have much of a choice.

TED: You're the same ole penguin.
TEDDY: This can't be happening.
ALAN: Dad... I'd like you to meet—
TED: I know myself.
TEDDY: You don't know anything.
TED: Your favorite color is orange.
TEDDY: The clown knows that.
TED: Our favorite number is—
TEDDY: Seven. I've told Penny that millions of times.
TED: How old are you?
TEDDY: You're supposed to be me... you tell me how old I am.
TED: Ten.
TEDDY: Wrong. I'm ten and a half!
TED: You have a crush on Cathy.
TEDDY: I do not.
TED: The cute little girl with red hair in your class.
TEDDY: I don't like her.
TED: You... we tried to give her a ring. (*Pause.*)
TEDDY: She wouldn't take it.
TED: That night we drank Jack Daniel's whiskey. I was so sad.
TEDDY: Drinking whiskey always seemed to help my dad.
ALAN: Jack helps no one... but himself!
TED: I'm sorry I haven't done much with our life.
TEDDY: We're both to blame.

(*TED and TEDDY embrace. Pause. Explosions rivet the bedroom. The five dive for cover behind the bunker. JACK appears in a LIGHT special. He is lounging in a lawn chair, sipping a drink through a straw from a coconut. He wears sunglasses. The five talk straight out. They can't see JACK.*

He is in another part of the house. They can only hear his voice.)
JACK: Very touching, reunions always bring tears to my eyes. (*He sips from his drink.*) Hi, Penny, and the worthless clown that thought he could be a wizard.
CLOWN: Once a wizard... always one.
JACK: Hi, Teddy, do you like what you've become?
TEDDY: We beat you once... we can do it again.
JACK: That was over twenty years ago. Who'd of thought to bring these fools back into the battle? Applause to you, Alan.
ALAN: Actually, my father thought of it.
JACK: Ted? Then let me give you a hand. (*He begins to clap his hands.*) And I thought you were brain dead. (*TED leaps over the bunker.*)
TED: Come to us. Face us. You have always hidden behind this door... or that. If you are so strong come face us now. I don't think you have the guts.
JACK: Guts? Did you say guts?
TED: You heard me. You don't have any.
JACK: But Ted... I do! I have yours. Just watch! (*JACK takes a big drink from his coconut drink. TED reacts as if he just swallowed poison, passes out, and falls to the floor.*) Oh, what a bore you have become, Ted. (*TEDDY jumps over the bunker.*)
TEDDY: He's right. You're afraid to show yourself.
JACK: At least you're not contradicting yourself. Get it. (*He laughs at his own joke.*)
TEDDY: How can we fight you if you avoid us? (*Several explosions go off. TEDDY stands firm.*)
JACK: I'm not avoiding you. Look around there are signs of me everywhere.

(*ALAN jumps over the bunker and stands next to TEDDY.*)
ALAN: My turf, Jack! You think you're so brave!
JACK: I just love that spunk, kid.
ALAN: You're a coward.
  (*SOUND: There is a gigantic explosion and smoke fills the bedroom. ALAN and TEDDY fall to the floor, and JACK appears.*)
JACK: Here I am! (*The CLOWN hurdles the bunker.*)
CLOWN: You are fat, Jack. (*The CLOWN gestures. A magical SOUND is heard. Nothing happens to JACK.*) Thin! You are thin! (*The CLOWN gestures again. Another magical SOUND is heard. Nothing happens. JACK laughs.*) FLY! (*The CLOWN makes another gesture and another magical SOUND is heard. Nothing happens.*)
JACK: I think you should be the one that flies, Mr. Clown. (*JACK waves his hands. A magical SOUND is heard The CLOWN begins to fly. PENNY jumps over the bunker.*)
PENNY: I beat you once, you evil creature, and I can do it again.
  (*PENNY attacks JACK. She is no challenge for JACK. He flips her with the same karate move she used on him before and pins her to the ground.*)
JACK: (*To ALAN.*) Is this the best you have to offer? Prehistoric! I've dealt with all this before and I've adjusted. I'm like a cockroach... I'll be around forever. (*JACK gets off of PENNY.*) I expected more from you, Alan.
ALAN: I want my mother.
TEDDY: And I want my princess.

JACK: Teddy, you don't know what you want. Look at yourself. (*JACK points to the passed out TED.*) Oh, but you do like to fly. (*JACK waves his hands, a magical SOUND is heard, and TED is airborne.*)
TEDDY: You've gained lots of power over the years, Jack.
JACK: It's easy when you don't have any resistance. (*PENNY has had enough. She once again attacks JACK.*)
PENNY: Leave my boy alone.
JACK: Oh, please. (*JACK waves his hands, a magical SOUND is heard, and PENNY joins the others flying.*)
PENNY: NOOOOOO!
JACK: I owe everything to you, Teddy.
TEDDY: You do seem to control me now, so what do you want?
ALAN: Me! I told you he wants me!
TEDDY: Well, he can't have you.
JACK: You both seem to have forgotten Barbie? (*JACK claps his hands, a magical SOUND is heard, and BARB bursts onto the scene.*)
BARB: Teddy... don't let him get Alan.
JACK: Oh save it, you romantic. (*JACK waves his arms, a magical SOUND is heard, and BARB joins the others in flight.*) I usually hate puns... but this one I can't resist. Alan, your whole life hangs before you.
(*JACK laughs. ALAN clinches his fists, shuts his eyes, and shouts...*)
ALAN: WOOD!! I see the woods! You must see it, too! All of you! See the woods!
(*The CLOWN, PENNY, TED, and BARB drop to the ground.*)

JACK: They see nothing. In fact, you don't see them at all. (*JACK claps his hands, a magical SOUND effect is heard, and the CLOWN, PENNY, TED, and BARB disappear. JACK is left alone with ALAN and TEDDY.*) You're good, Alan, you're very strong. But I'm stronger.

ALAN: They all saw the woods, Jack.

JACK: Maybe they did.

ALAN: Teddy and I are standing side by side to let you know…

TEDDY: …you are not wanted in this family anymore.

JACK: Nobody ever really wants me. But they can't seem to get rid of me. And now I not only control you, Teddy, and your princess… the clown and the penguin seem to be mine also. I believe I'm winning. It's only a matter of time, Alan, and you'll be mine too.

ALAN: Teddy… don't believe.

TEDDY: We must believe.

ALAN: Don't believe in Jack.

TEDDY: What?

ALAN: If you don't believe in him… he won't exist.

TEDDY: But we have to believe.

JACK: Yes, you do, or you don't feel good. And I'm all about feeling good.

ALAN: Don't you understand? That is our problem.

JACK: The kid is crazy.

ALAN: Believe in not believing.

(*It finally dawns on TEDDY what ALAN is doing. He begins to play the game. He moves the block to down center and stands on it as he plays BARB's part.*)

TEDDY: Thank you, Sir Knight. You have saved me from the evil clutches of the Dark Lord.
ALAN: Tis nothing, oh beautiful princess. It's all in a day's work.
JACK: That's not the princess. You can't save her by doing this.
ALAN: Continue, Teddy.
TEDDY: And what words are those, Sir Knight?
ALAN: That you will be my princess for life, and become my ever-loving wife.
JACK: Stop! Stop this nonsense.
TEDDY: Happily, I accept the role of your princess wife for life.
ALAN: Let us seal our love with—
JACK: With a bottle of booze. Jack, old number seven.
ALAN: With true love, Jack. We both love Barb.
(*An explosion is heard and BARB bursts into the bedroom.*)
BARB: Yes, love. Love without Jack.
TEDDY: A love without you, Jack. We don't need you.
JACK: You two fools haven't won anything.
ALAN: We saved the princess again.
JACK: Bravo, you saved her, but you forgot about Teddy. Let me show you what I mean. (*JACK waves his hands. A magical SOUND is heard. TEDDY goes into a trance.*) Teddy, after Cathy refused the ring, you never stopped sneaking sips from your dad's whiskey. Isn't that right? (*JACK waves his hands toward TEDDY. A magical SOUND is heard. TEDDY moves into JACK's arms.*)
TEDDY: Yes, you're right. Oh, Alan, he feels so nice.

ALAN: DAD!
TEDDY: Jack, you do make me feel so good.
JACK: Yes, Teddy, ole buddy. Thank you. I know you enjoy me and I have to admit I've enjoyed you too. Tell Alan how good it is.
TEDDY: Welcome him into your life, son.
ALAN: Dad, don't forget the clown, the penguin, and the princess!
BARB: Teddy, you don't need him!
(*JACK waves his hands, a magical SOUND effect is heard, and BARB goes into a trance.*)
JACK: Woman, I've owned you for years. You just didn't know it!
BARB: Yes, Jack, I've been an enabler for you.
ALAN: Mother! (*BARB has walked to JACK. He puts his arms around her.*)
JACK: Checkmate, Alan.
ALAN: All right, you win. Please don't hurt them.
JACK: I've told you all along, come to me, and I won't do a thing to them.
ALAN: What do I do?
JACK: No tricks this time?
ALAN: You have my word.
JACK: Just relax and enjoy.

(*JACK, TEDDY, and BARB open their arms to ALAN welcoming him to join them. ALAN walks to them. They embrace as one. TED bursts into the room and sees the situation. He has a plan.*)

TED: Jack! Don't leave me!
JACK: Alan has found me at last, Ted. I don't need you anymore.

ALAN: I finally understand, Dad, why Jack makes you feel so good.

TED: I'm glad, son, Jack is a good spirit.

JACK: You are too kind, Ted.

TED: But why take Teddy? You don't need him. He's past history. I'm the one you need now. Take me. You already own me. Let Teddy go! Take me, Jack.

JACK: If I did that, I'd have the whole family.

TED: Yes, you'd finally have us all. We'd all be one. And all be yours.

JACK: If you try to trick me, Alan and your wife will suffer.

TED: How long have I been telling you I wish my family understood you?

JACK: Cheers to you, Ted. (*Very cautiously JACK exchanges TEDDY for TED.*)

TEDDY: You can't leave me alone. Let me come with you.

TED: (*Pointedly.*) Teddy, go back to the past and play your games.

TEDDY: What? I can't play games after all this.

JACK: Time to leave. I've waited a long time to control this whole family. I'm so happy that Alan is finally with us. Let's take a vacation.

TEDDY: Please, take me with you.

JACK: Stop your sniveling. Go play your silly games with your clown and penguin.

ALAN: Jack, can you make me fly?

JACK: Oh yes, higher than the silly clown ever made your father fly.

TED: And it feels so much better too.

BARB: Ted, I love you. It's good to finally be a family. No more fighting.

TED: I'm so happy we all finally understand one another.

JACK: See ya, Teddy. (*JACK claps his hands, a magical SOUND effect is heard JACK, BARB, TED, and ALAN disappear.*)

TEDDY: No, don't leave me here alone, Jack, take me. (*TEDDY runs to the bed, falls on it, and begins to cry. After a beat the CLOWN and PENNY enter.*)

CLOWN: I never want to hear you say that again.

PENNY: For the first time in my life, I agree with the fool.

TEDDY: Penny! Mr. Clown! (*TEDDY runs to them. All embrace.*)

CLOWN: Where's Jack?

PENNY: Yes, where is the villain? I was so worried about you.

CLOWN: He's very powerful now. He had us trapped in limbo. I'm not sure how we escaped.

TEDDY: Jack has won. He has them. He has them all. The whole family. And they don't even care. Ted even told me to go back and play games. Then Jack vanished. All of them did.

PENNY: He got what he wanted. Alan! He controls Alan now. That's why the clown and I were freed.

TEDDY: We have to save them.

PENNY: Yes, come on. (*TEDDY and PENNY start for the bedroom door.*)

CLOWN: No. Ted was right. We have to go back to the past. We have to save them in the past. We have to stop Jack before he controls you… not after.

PENNY: I never thought I'd hear myself say this, but the clown is making sense.

CLOWN: If we stop him in the past… this moment won't exist.

PENNY: But how do we get back?

CLOWN: What did Alan do? The time warp.

TEDDY: No, that wasn't it.

PENNY: Time trip?

CLOWN: Something like that. Hop? Skip?

TEDDY: Jump.

CLOWN: Time jumping.

TEDDY: Yes, that's it. Come on, make a circle and hold hands. (*The three form a circle, hold hands, and shut their eyes.*) Take us back, Mr. Wizard.

CLOWN: Here we go. Time jump. We must time jump. (*Nothing happens.*)

PENNY: Why do I waste my time with a clown that thinks he's a wizard?

TEDDY: That's it. I know what went wrong. Time. We didn't set a time. If we're going to time jump… we have to say where we want to go.

CLOWN: I knew that.

TEDDY: Please, Mr. Wizard, send us back to our time.

CLOWN: Yes, my knight. (*He shuts his eyes and clenches his fists.*) Time jump. We have to time jump. Time jump… backward… we need to go back in time. Twenty years… we need to go back to our real time. Let us… time jump.

(*The LIGHTS flicker. SOUND: Wild music plays. A strobe light flashes. All three flail about the room. The furniture must be moved back to its original positions. Then as suddenly as it all began, it stops. All three fall to the floor.*)
TEDDY: Is everyone all right?
CLOWN: Did we make it?
PENNY: You know, I'm aging twice as fast as I want to because I hang out with the two of you.
TEDDY: We made it, Mr. Wizard.
CLOWN: Where are the costumes?
PENNY: In the bathroom. I'll get them. (*She exits into the bathroom.*)
CLOWN: Teddy, you need to put on the knight's costume. And give me the Wizard's.
(*PENNY opens the door.*)
PENNY: Here they are. (*PENNY throws out the costumes, and the CLOWN and TEDDY dress.*) I'll be in here if you need me. (*She shuts the bathroom door.*)
TEDDY: What do we do now?
CLOWN: We need Barbie.
TEDDY: Jack has her.
CLOWN: He has the Barbie in the future. We need the Barbie in the past. (*He shuts his eyes and chants.*) Barbie. Come to Teddy's room. Come now. We need you. I, Mr. Wizard… command you to come.
(*LIGHTS flash and a magical SOUND effect is heard. BARB appears in the bedroom.*)
BARB: Do you boys play twenty-four hours a day?
CLOWN: We're not playing tonight.
BARB: The tone in your voice scares me.
TEDDY: We need your help.
CLOWN: We have to rescue you again.

BARB: From the dragon?
CLOWN: No, from Jack.
BARB: No, not Jack.
CLOWN: We have to rescue you once again from him. And when we do... this time we'll destroy him.
TEDDY: Before anything bad can happen in the future.
BARB: You two are as crazy as the kids at school say... (*She gestures to TEDDY.*)... your father is.
TEDDY: We have to do this... or I end up just like my dad.
CLOWN: Please, Barbie, we need you.
BARB: Get on your knees and beg me.
CLOWN: What?
BARB: I'll help you if you get on your knees and beg me.
TEDDY: Beg you?
BARB: Are you deaf? I want you on your knees.
TEDDY: Why are you doing this?
CLOWN: (*To TEDDY.*) We need her. Do as she says.
(*The CLOWN goes to his knees. BARB starts to laugh.*)
TEDDY: Forget it. I don't want to rescue her.
BARB: (*Still laughing.*) To your knees, boy.
CLOWN: Come on, Teddy, you must do as she says. Get down.

(*TEDDY goes to his knees. BARB's laughter increases and soon JACK's laugh is heard. And in a flash BARB is gone and JACK stands where she was. He continues to laugh.*)
JACK: On your knees before me? I didn't think you liked me. (*The CLOWN and TEDDY scramble to their

feet and move as far away from JACK as possible.) Thank you. Now I know your plans.

TEDDY: You tricked us.

JACK: Of course, I did. Teddy, my boy, you can't change what the future has in store for you.

CLOWN: Yes, you can, Teddy.

JACK: Why do you continue to fight me? You and your family are very happy in the future. Would you like to see them?

TEDDY: Yes, bring them here.

JACK: What?

TEDDY: If you're so powerful bring them here. Time jump them back to us.

JACK: Fine. Time jump. Time jump twenty years to the past. Happy Ted, Barb, and Alan. Come to us. *(JACK claps his hands. A magical SOUND is heard. TED, BARB, and ALAN appear in the bedroom. They are posed in a family portrait, smiling.)* As you can see, I haven't hurt anyone. Be happy, Teddy. Most people don't know what their future has in store for them. See you later, Teddy. *(PENNY enters.)*

PENNY: The woods. See the woods. Everyone must see the woods.

CLOWN: Yes, believe in the foundation of family.

TEDDY: See it.

JACK: I'm sick of all this "woods" nonsense. Wood rots over many years and burns very easily, especially oak. *(ALAN is the first to break the family pose.)*

ALAN: I see it. Mom, Dad, you must see the woods too. Fight to see it.

(*TED and BARB break the pose. All then scatter and surround JACK.*)
PENNY: Believe in the woods. The woods are strong.
BARB: Yes, a strong foundation.
JACK: Your foundation fell apart generations ago.
PENNY: Believe in the family.
JACK: You asked for it. (*JACK waves his hands. SOUND: Thunder is heard. LIGHTS turn dark and ominous.*)
TED: I remember. Mama said it… "foundation… family… strong." Woods! And ours can be as solid as oak. She wasn't lying.
JACK: I'm finished playing your childish games.
CLOWN: You screwed up, Jack.
JACK: I know what happens in the future, and you can't change it.
CLOWN: You can when you're given another chance.
JACK: And who gave you that?
PENNY: You did.
JACK: I didn't give you anything.
TEDDY: Yes, you did, when you brought them back to us in the past.
ALAN: Goodbye, Jack, you're not wanted here anymore.
CLOWN: Teddy, you must deny Jack.
JACK: Denying me is only a temporary fix. It won't make me go away.
CLOWN: But with love and support…
PENNY: …from his friends…
BARB: …and his family…
TED: …we can stop you.
JACK: You've never seen me at full strength. I'm tired of this babble. (*JACK gestures. A rumbling SOUND*

fills the room. JACK starts a soft growl and it grows in volume as he too grows in size.) No one can stop me.

CLOWN: We must band together… become one. *(All huddle together.)*

JACK: I am too powerful. *(JACK gestures toward the group, an explosion SOUND is heard, sending the group stumbling in different directions.)*

CLOWN: We have to get back together.

JACK: Never. I'm too good at breaking up the family unit. *(JACK gestures. The SOUND of a strong wind blowing is heard. All try to walk to one another, but this isn't easy. SOUND: Thunderclaps serve as exclamation points after everything that JACK says.)* It's too late, Ted, you can't deny me.

TEDDY: It might be too late for Ted to do it… but I can. I deny you, Jack.

JACK: And I'll soon have you too, Alan.

ALAN: No, you won't. I deny you too. *(JACK laughs at them.)*

CLOWN: Come on, we all must unite.

PENNY: Unite, and become one.

(The group continues to struggle as they move to one another.)

JACK: You'll never defeat me. *(JACK laughs hysterically. The wind SOUND continues. The group finally gets together.)*

CLOWN: Teddy, you must deny him.

TED: He's already done that. It didn't work.

CLOWN: But not united with all of us.

PENNY: Speak English, you silly clown.

CLOWN: He must say it when the group is united. Together with the strength of our united love and support we can be more powerful than Jack.
BARB: But he's so big.
CLOWN: We can be bigger. We must become one.
(*The group starts forming a pyramid—like cheerleaders, with TEDDY on the top.*)
TEDDY: Go away, Jack. You're not wanted here.
JACK: I've owned this family far too long.
TEDDY: Not anymore, your dominance over this family will stop with me.
JACK: You make me laugh. (*JACK's laughter fills the room. TEDDY is finally on the top of the pyramid, and shouts over JACK's laughter.*)
TEDDY: I DENY YOU, JACK! (*JACK stumbles. The wind SOUND stops.*)
ALL: WE ALL DENY YOU, JACK!
(*JACK explodes. SOUND and LIGHTS illustrate this. JACK disappears. The group breaks up the pyramid. There is a long pause before anyone speaks.*)
BARB: Is he really gone?
CLOWN: Ask Ted.
TED: I think so.
CLOWN: How do you feel?
TED: Free. Empty. Good.
TEDDY: That means he's gone.
ALAN: Teddy, you saved us all.
TED: Thank you. (*BARB begins the words of the game. She stands on the block.*)
BARB: Thank you, Sir Knight. You have saved me from the evil clutches of the Dark Lord.

TEDDY: Tis nothing, oh beautiful princess. All in a day's work.
BARB: How shall I ever thank you?
TEDDY: By placing your hand in mine, and saying those words that will make me the happiest knight in the kingdom.
BARB: And what words are those, Sir Knight? (*TED takes over for TEDDY.*)
TED: That you will be my princess for life and become my ever-loving wife.
BARB: Happily I accept the role of your princess wife for life. (*Pause.*)
TED: I'm sorry for all the years of pain.
BARB: A kiss... a tender kiss... to seal our love.
TED: I do love you, my princess.
BARB: And I you, my knight. (*BARB and TED kiss.*)
ALAN: Excuse me; can this wait until we get home?
BARB: He doesn't like the kissing part.
ALAN: We do have to get back.
TED: Yes, back to be a family. (*BARB and TED welcome ALAN into their arms.*)
TEDDY: Watch out for Jack. He'll be waiting to get you.
TED: It will be tougher for you.
CLOWN: We'll watch over Teddy.
TED: And I have my solid oak family to watch me.
PENNY: And Papa Foss used to talk about a support group...
CLOWN: That's right... Triple A.
PENNY: No, you clown, it was AA.
TED: I'll look into it. Well, I guess this is goodbye. (*All embrace, saying, "goodbye."*) Take us home, Alan.

ALAN: Mr. Wizard, will you do the honor?
CLOWN: I'd be very honored.
PENNY: Do I have to live with this ego now? (*All form a circle and hold hands.*)
CLOWN: Time jump, my friends... my family. They must time jump. Send them into the future. Twenty years. Time jump... now.
(*The LIGHTS begin to flicker. SOUND: Wild music plays. TED, BARB, and ALAN spin around, arms flailing, then all three disappear. All SOUND and LIGHTS stop.*)
TEDDY: Well done, Mr. Wizard.
CLOWN: Thank you, Sir Knight.
PENNY: Oh, please.
CLOWN: What shall we play now?
PENNY: I'm going to bed. (*PENNY walks toward the bathroom.*)
TEDDY: Let's invent video games.
CLOWN: Video what?
PENNY: Good night. (*She exits into the bathroom.*)
TEDDY: Games that can be played on the TV. I found this in Alan's room.
(*The CLOWN holds up a videodisk. PENNY opens bathroom door and looks to the CLOWN and TEDDY. In a LIGHT special, ALAN, TED, and BARB are posed looking at the CLOWN and TEDDY. All freeze as LIGHTS slowly fade to black and happy music fills the theatre.*)

END

A Collection from a Career in Theatre

For the Love of a Woman

a noir play

by

Bob May

© 1994/2018 by Bob May
All rights reserved

CAST OF CHARACTERS

DICK
RICK
LOUIE
WOODY
BROWN
LAUREN
GRANT
OLD MAN JORDAN

SYNOPSIS OF SCENES

TIME: 1940s
PLACE: Various locations in and around Los Angeles, the City of Angels

Although there are several locations, the script is written so that the action is continuous. There are speeches written to cover the scene shifts. Dim the lights to focus on the character delivering the scene covering speech and shift the scene as the character speaks. There should never be a complete blackout. The sets are very simple, all in front of the same backdrop.

The premiere of *For the Love of a Woman* was presented by the University of Nevada, Las Vegas, at the Paul Harris Theatre, in 1993.

(As the house LIGHTS fade and we sit in black, music fills the theatre. It is ominously played with a full orchestra sound. Back lighting soon reveals two figures. We can't identify them. They stand on opposite sides of the stage. They have guns pointed at one another. They both move, in a half circle. One figure upstage, the other down. Guns pointed at each other the entire time. Once this move is completed, they speak.)

DICK: Why do you haunt me?
RICK: You haunt yourself.
DICK: Leave me alone.
RICK: This hellhole ain't big enough for both of us.
DICK: You need to die!
RICK: If that's what you want. Make your move.

(The LIGHTS blackout. In the dark, we hear two gunshots. Beat. The LIGHTS rise. DICK stumbles into his office. He stops in the doorway to light a cigarette. We see that he holds

a bloodstained hanky to his stomach. He makes his way to his desk at SL. As he picks up a phone and dials, he begins to speak.)

DICK: He got me, Lieutenant Brown. I knew he would. You never believed me… about him. But he was real. As real as the sorry sun that will set over our graves. I told you he'd get me, ole buddy! And he did! (*He listens on the phone for a beat and then hangs up.*) Where are the police when you need them? (*He flinches in pain and coughs. Blood trickles from his mouth. He laughs. He opens a drawer and pulls out a Dictaphone. He inserts a cylinder and then begins speaking into the microphone.*) What a fitting way to go. Honest cop… turned murderer. I think I'm guilty! I don't know! Was it him or me? He played such an important part. (*He laughs and then flinches in pain.*) You gotta get him. Revenge my death. (*Beat.*) And you gotta believe this recording… no matter how farfetched it sounds. (*He coughs.*) I hate Dick. I mean Rick. I hate Rick. He didn't deserve to breathe the good air God gave us here in LA. (*He laughs and flinches in pain.*) But then he wanted me to be yesterday's laundry too. (*Sarcastically.*) Can you believe that anyone could hate me… Dick Powell? (*The LIGHTS fade to a spot on DICK. He stands up and moves downstage. He talks to the audience. He no longer reacts to the fact that he's been shot. As he moves stage right, WOODY enters and sits at the same desk.*) I don't know where to start. I guess when I met her. I don't know who's more evil? Him or her? You remember her. The

Antenucci dame! The day I brought Lucky Louie into the station house.

(*The LIGHTS fade up to revel WOODY at the desk. He smokes a cigar. DICK enters dragging, a handcuffed, LOUIE with him. They move to Sergeant WOODY's desk.*)

WOODY: (*Sarcastically.*) Well, look who we got here.

DICK: Is Brown in?

WOODY: Hotshot cop turned private.

DICK: Is the Lieutenant here?

WOODY: Too good for us Powell? Mr. Private Dick Powell! Y'know the boys and me ain't sorry you left.

DICK: Save it for your mother. Get Brown for me.

LOUIE: You gotta help me… this guy's a maniac.

WOODY: Brown's busy. Some high society dame and her husband. Whadda ya got here?

DICK: Lucky Louie Fremont. Jumped bail… connected to Old Man Jordan's crime family.

LOUIE: I ain't go nuttin' to do with that wop… but I'll take the wrap to get away from this chump.

WOODY: Reduced to being a bounty hunter.

DICK: Ole Woody… the police sergeant in the City of Angels who thinks he's God. I'll tell you what, let's pretend this wanted felon is a fallen angel… maybe even Lucifer. And I'm turning the Prince of Darkness over to you… your highness… the proper law enforcement agency. I trust he'll receive the proper care and rehabilitation. (*Beat.*) And I'd like a receipt. (*DICK lights a cigarette.*)

WOODY: You know, Powell, that's one of your big problems. You don't know how to communicate.

DICK: Oh, I communicate... it's just that some people are too ignorant to comprehend.

WOODY: Take your felon to another precinct. All my cells are full.

LOUIE: Hey, Sarge, your beef with this maniac ain't my problem. I never thought I'd be begging to get into the joint... but don't make me go anywhere else with him.

(*Lt. BROWN, LAUREN, and GRANT enter from BROWN's office. LAUREN is a very sensuous woman of the '40s, in her twenties. GRANT is a man in his sixties.*)

BROWN: I promise you, Mr. and Mrs. Antenucci we'll do everything we can.

GRANT: Thank you, Lieutenant Brown. Come, dear. (*GRANT and LAUREN start to exit. LAUREN sees LOUIE and attacks him.*)

LAUREN: You! It was you! I know you stole him! You took my baby! (*It takes DICK, BROWN, and WOODY to pull her off LOUIE. There are ad-libs as this happens.*) Arrest that man. I know he's responsible.

DICK: If you'll look, lady, the man is sporting some very unflattering bracelets.

(*There is a moment between DICK and LAUREN that always happens in those '40's films. She makes a very long, silent cross to DICK. All the men watch her.*)

LAUREN: I don't think I've had the pleasure... Mr. Bright Eyes.

GRANT: (*He's jealous. She does this all the time.*) It's time we left Lauren.

LOUIE: Mr. Antenucci... you gotta help me.

GRANT: Excuse me... do I know you? (*Beat. LOUIE knows he better shut up.*)

LOUIE: Ah... no sir... it's just... I thought a man of your influence could do something to get me away from this insane man.
DICK: Stop bothering the rich lady and her father.
GRANT: Husband, sir. I am her husband!
BROWN: I'll call you as soon as we get any leads.
LAUREN: (*Referring to LOUIE.*) He knows something.
GRANT: (*Pointedly.*) Please, my dear. We've filed a complaint. It's time to go.
LAUREN: Goodbye, Mister Bright Eyes.
DICK: Bye. (*To BROWN.*) So, Brown, take this goon off my hands.
BROWN: Lucky Louie Fremont! (*To LOUIE.*) I guess your luck ran out, Louie. (*To DICK.*) I know one bail bondsman that's gonna love you, Dick. (*To WOODY*) Woody, take him downstairs and put him in a holding cell. (*WOODY drags LOUIE off, past LAUREN and GRANT.*) So, how are ya, buddy?
DICK: Rick's back. And he wants to kill me.
BROWN: I thought we got rid of that guy?
LAUREN: I want that insubordinate cop's name.
WOODY: He's no cop... he's a private dick. Powell's his Christian name, but that's the only thing godly about him. He's bad news. Yeah, his rep is gettin' the job done, but he's fightin' with a big demon in that overintelligent psyche of his. Stay away from him, Mrs. Antenucci.
GRANT: Thank you for the advice, Sergeant Woody. I trust you heard it, my dear?
(*DICK sits on the desk. The LIGHTS fade to a spot on him. All others exit. He talks to the audience/Dictaphone.*)

DICK: When I left the station house, I tied one on with the reward money so good that the Boy Scouts are considering adding to their list of famous knots. I floated home, to the office. Yeah, I'm living in the office. My ego might be big, but the paychecks aren't. It was either a bed or an office. Why can't one be both? (*Knocking is heard on a door.*) I dreamed the pounding was the devil's way of welcoming me to the hell I belonged in. But when I woke up… I knew it was him! It was Rick! I was confused why he was knocking. He usually just bursts into my life. Now that I reflect on it… my dream was more accurate… it was the devil. (*The LIGHTS fade up as DICK moves to the door. He opens it and LAUREN enters.*)

LAUREN: Does it always take you so long to answer your door?

DICK: What time is it?

LAUREN: Now, I'm not so sure that I want your services.

DICK: Isn't today Saturday? (*He looks at his watch.*) It's seven o'clock in the morning. What are you crazy?

LAUREN: I need your help.

DICK: I don't work on Saturday. Come back tomorrow.

LAUREN: You don't work on Saturday… but you work on Sunday? You know that's a sin. God says we should rest on the sabbath.

DICK: And that's what I'm trying to do. Goodbye.

LAUREN: But it's not Sunday.

DICK: I'm Jewish.

LAUREN: You don't remember me?

DICK: I remember you. You're the bundle of trouble I met down at headquarters yesterday.
LAUREN: Please help me.
DICK: I'm closed for the weekend.
LAUREN: I'll triple whatever your fee is.
DICK: I get twenty-five bucks a day plus expenses.
LAUREN: I'll give you a hundred.
DICK: I need a cup a coffee. (*DICK prepares coffee as they talk.*) So, how'd ya know I'd be here?
LAUREN: Your home number listed in telephone directory has been disconnected.
DICK: Those living arrangements didn't suit me. I'm looking for something more classy… to reflect my personality.
LAUREN: I hear there's a vacancy back on the police force?
DICK: Do you want a cup?
LAUREN: Do you have cream?
DICK: Don't use it.
LAUREN: I didn't think so.
DICK: Is that a "no?"
LAUREN: Yes!
DICK: So, what do you want?
LAUREN: Direct. I like that in a man. Right to the point.
DICK: I just want to start earning my hundred dollars a day.
LAUREN: Oh, am I on the time clock already?
DICK: That's right, doll… from the moment I let you through that front door.

LAUREN: If I'm going to pay you a hundred dollars a day... I'd appreciate it if you didn't call me doll... or babe... or lady. The name is Lauren.
DICK: I don't call any dame by her name.
LAUREN: And I don't like dame either.
DICK: Feisty! I like that in a broad.
LAUREN: Boy, you're a walking thesaurus of names that won't get you into bed with a woman.
DICK: You know, I don't have to work for you.
LAUREN: Then don't. (*LAUREN starts to exit.*)
DICK: Don't go... the coffee's ready.
LAUREN: I told you, I don't drink it without cream.
DICK: How can I help you... Lauren? (*LAUREN stops.*)
LAUREN: Do you have sugar?
DICK: How many lumps? (*DICK talks to the audience.*) Beside "him"... Rick... she was the first person to challenge me... hell, excite me since I was a kid. With every word she uttered, I fell helplessly into her bottomless pit of love. (*DICK turns back to LAUREN.*)
LAUREN: I liked your coffee. I hope you're just as good?
DICK: You lost your dog? And you want me to find him? I'm sorry I let you in. I'm a professional. Not a dogcatcher.
LAUREN: I'll give you two hundred dollars a day.
DICK: You must really love that dog?
LAUREN: Chanel is very precious to me.
DICK: Why don't you talk straight to me?
LAUREN: What do you mean? I am.
DICK: No dog is worth two hundred dollars a day.
LAUREN: I can see you're not an animal lover.

DICK: And I can see you're trying use that figure of yours to persuade me to help you.
LAUREN: I think I've come to the wrong man.
DICK: Why did you come to me at all?
LAUREN: In a backhanded compliment sort of way, Sergeant Woody said you get the job done.
DICK: And I'm still asking myself why you went to the police? If I lost a dog… I'd go to the dog pound. Or did you think your rich husband's opium money could buy the police… just as you thought it could buy me?
LAUREN: The accusations about my husband's involvement with opium are completely unfounded.
DICK: Tell it to the judge when they throw the book at him. (*Beat.*)
LAUREN: The dog was wearing a collar.
DICK: Dogs are required by state law to wear tags. A collar is a convenient way to display them.
LAUREN: This collar was special. It was a birthday present from the president of Columbia.
DICK: Studio heads have always irritated me. No mind fools, in positions of power.
LAUREN: I beg your pardon?
DICK: What is your dog… the next Lassie?
LAUREN: Chanel is a Yorkshire terrier. A tiny baby that could fit in the palm of your hand. And the president I am referring to is the leader of a country in South America. You've probably heard of neither.
DICK: Tell me about this collar.
LAUREN: Diamonds.

DICK: How many?

LAUREN: Let's just say it's worth more than you'll earn in your lifetime.

DICK: When I was a kid, a leather collar worked just fine on my dog.

LAUREN: Chanel didn't wear it all the time. But the night she was abducted, she had it on. We had some people over.

DICK: And Lucky Louie just happened to be one of them.

LAUREN: No, he was over earlier in the— I'm sorry who did you say?

DICK: You heard me.

LAUREN: I don't know a... Lucky Louie.

DICK: You knew him yesterday... when you left your fingernail calling card on his face.

LAUREN: I thought he was someone else.

DICK: Who?

LAUREN: I don't know!

DICK: Your story's so full of holes... the truth drowns with every word you utter. I'm sorry, I refuse to swim in the deceptive river you want me to dive into.

LAUREN: Sergeant Woody also said you were insane. I'm beginning to believe that part of his Powell biography and I should have heeded his words of staying away from you.

DICK: Let me put it another way. If you want me to find your dog, don't lie to me. If you don't lie to me... I'll find your dog. You continue to lie to me... your dog is dead. And your husband will never get his diamond collar back.

LAUREN: Lucky Louie works for the Jordan family.
DICK: So, tell me something I don't know.
LAUREN: My husband has had some business dealings with the Jordan's.
DICK: I've read this newspaper before.
LAUREN: The Jordan family was at the party. Old Man Jordan and Grant had a misunderstanding.
DICK: Grant?
LAUREN: My husband.
DICK: What were they fighting about?
LAUREN: My husband is an insanely jealous man.
DICK: I can see why.
LAUREN: He's also very violent. If he knew I was here… you'd be dead.
DICK: So why do you continue to play in his backyard?
LAUREN: (*Seductively*) It's the best offer I've had.
DICK: You don't want me. I'm only makin' a hundred bucks a day.
LAUREN: I thought I raised it to two hundred.
DICK: I think you did. (*DICK sweeps LAUREN into his arms and they kiss passionately throughout the following.*)
LAUREN: I knew you were the man to find my dog… my baby Chanel. Grant is so cold. All he cared about was the collar. I love that dog more than all the diamonds in the world.
(*DICK stops the kissing abruptly.*)
DICK: What a minute, sister! Diamonds can buy you hundreds of dogs.
LAUREN: Whoever has the collar can have it. I just want my Chanel.

DICK: That dog is yesterday's news by now. Whoever lifted that canine wasn't from the humane society. They were rock collectors.
LAUREN: Don't say that. I have this. (*LAUREN hands DICK a letter. He reads it.*)
DICK: Why didn't you show me this earlier?
LAUREN: (*Seductively.*) I wanted to make sure I'd found the right man.
DICK: Who were the other guests at the party? Other than the Jordan family.
LAUREN: It had to be them.
DICK: Old Man Jordan doesn't need another diamond necklace.
LAUREN: He did it to get even with Grant.
DICK: He doesn't work that way.
LAUREN: Do you really think she's dead?
DICK: Not from the sounds of this letter.
LAUREN: Oh, thank God.
DICK: God has nothing to do with it!
LAUREN: But you think she's safe?
DICK: The letter says... "If you ever want to see your dog alive..." So she's not dead yet.
LAUREN: What do they want?
DICK: That's a good question. They got the jewels.
LAUREN: There's no finish to their sentence. Just... "if you ever want to see your dog alive..."
DICK: They're greedy. Probably want some of that Antenucci opium cash.
LAUREN: Please get my precious Chanel back.
DICK: Give me names. Who was at the party?
LAUREN: I'm scared. (*DICK takes LAUREN into his arms.*)

DICK: I'll not let anyone hurt you. And that's a promise you can deposit in the bank.

LAUREN: Start with that Lieutenant, back at headquarters.

(The LIGHTS fade to a spot on DICK. He talks to the audience as though into the Dictaphone. As he speaks, BROWN enters and sits at the desk. The same desk is used for all the scenes.)

DICK: Sure, I quit the force... with only two honest cops... I didn't stand a chance of advancement. You'd been stuck at Lieutenant for how long? And nobody liked me. It was him. They didn't like Rick! But you've heard all this before. And I'm not talking to you. You can't hear this. You're not there when I need you. Somebody hear these words. I'm sure there's an honest cop somewhere out there. *(The LIGHTS fade up.)*

BROWN: Hey, Buddy... you're up pretty early. *(DICK moves to the desk.)*

DICK: I hate it... but one has to earn a living.

BROWN: Why don't you come back? I need good cops like you.

DICK: How's Sharron?

BROWN: I'm sorry I brought it up again. But I can really use you back here on the force. Besides... you're my friend. I miss stopping at O'Shea's after our shift.

DICK: Sharron always hated that. She thought I was a bad influence on you. I was corrupting you. A husband should go home to his wife after work.

BROWN: Being a cop is a tough life. She understood my stops at O'Shea's with you.

DICK: She never liked me. Just as the other guys at the precinct didn't.
BROWN: They like you. It's Rick they didn't like.
DICK: Don't patronize me! Somehow he became real! And he's back... and this time with a vengeance.
BROWN: This always happens when you're bored. You've told me this yourself. You push yourself too hard. Come back to the department. I'll keep you busy. With all the crime this city produces... you won't have time to fight with demons inside yourself.
DICK: He's back... and he's real.
BROWN: He seems real to you. You've even admitted to me you created him. Listen, why don't you come with Sharron and me to our next church social?
DICK: You still don't believe me.
BROWN: There are a lot of single women who attend. Maybe we can hook you up with one.
DICK: I hear you attend Antenucci parties!
BROWN: What? What are you talking about? Who told you that?
DICK: I thought you were an honest cop. Not many of us left.
BROWN: The Captain asked me to cover for him. He had to attend his Granddaughter's christening.
DICK: Did you see the collar?
BROWN: I'm sorry if I offended you about coming to the church social.
DICK: Don't play dumb. I'm talking about the diamond collar Chanel was wearing.
BROWN: I really don't know what you're talking about.

DICK: Is that why the Antenuccis were here yesterday? They got you in their pockets. You can service them directly? You're their private cop?
BROWN: I didn't even meet them at the party. I met them for the first time here at the station house yesterday.
DICK: First, you play the dunce... and now you take on the role of the dissembler.
BROWN: Did they hire you to find that dumb dog?
DICK: So, you do know about the dog?
BROWN: Of course I do. That's why they were here yesterday. They wanted to fill out a missing person's report for the dog. I suggested the dog pound.
DICK: You seemed awfully friendly.
BROWN: That's my job... to serve the people. Are you working for them?
DICK: So tell me... who else was at this party?
BROWN: Stay away from Lauren... that dame's crazy.
DICK: How long you been on a first-name basis with the Antenucci dame?
BROWN: You sound jealous. (*Beat as DICK digests what BROWN just said.*)
DICK: I want to talk to Lucky Louie.
BROWN: Lucky Louie got bailed out this morning.
DICK: I guess Lucky Louie really is lucky. Why would any bail bondsman post bail for someone who just jumped bail? It had to be an inside job. You better dust your furniture. There's someone dirty in your house.
BROWN: That's why I'm a cop... I want to change the system.

(*The LIGHTS fade on that scene to a spot on DICK. He talks to the audience, the Dictaphone.*)

DICK: I could see it in your eyes as I left your office. The same thing all the other boys on the force thought… "He's crazy! Dick Powell's insane!" And at the moment, I'll agree with you. This is all so insane! (*He moves to the desk.*) Talking into a Dictaphone to catch a murderer… my murderer. Who you don't even think exists. I need some help and I need it now. (*He turns the Dictaphone off and picks up the phone. He doesn't get a dial tone, so he taps the button on the phone.*) Hello? Hello? (*He blows into the receiver.*) Rick is doing this. (*Beat. He turns on the Dictaphone.*) My phone's dead, so this recording is all that I have. (*As DICK talks, we see him stand up, and pull out his gun.*) When I returned to my office that morning… I knew someone was in it. And I knew it was… Rick. (*A toilet flushes. DICK aims his gun toward the bathroom.*)

DICK: Damn you, Rick! Leave me alone! I should kill you right now!

(*LOUIE enters, zipping up his fly. He sees the gun pointed at him and reacts.*)

LOUIE: Don't shoot, crazy man… please don't shoot me. It's only me… Lucky Louie.

DICK: Your luck almost ended.

LOUIE: Never… why do you think I got my name. (*He does a shuffle-step as he moves to pour himself a drink.*)

DICK: How'd you get in here?

LOUIE: You should really invest in a new lock. Not that there's anything in this dump anyone would want to steal.

DICK: The door swings both ways. I didn't invite you in, but I am asking you out.
LOUIE: Now, don't do nothin' crazy. I want to hire your services.
DICK: Yesterday you couldn't sever the cord that held us together fast enough.
LOUIE: A lot can happen in twenty-four hours.
DICK: Why would a two-bit crook like you want my services?
LOUIE: I don't know nobody that could protect me better than you.
DICK: Why would you need protecting? It looks to me like you already have a guardian angel… that posts bail.
LOUIE: That angel's really a devil.
DICK: I'm sorry to hear that.
LOUIE: Does that mean you won't help me?
DICK: Do you know what happened to the Antenucci dog?
LOUIE: I don't know Grant Antenucci.
DICK: Mrs. Antenucci seemed to know you yesterday at the police station. Your face still carries her mark.
LOUIE: That woman's crazier than you are.
DICK: So, you do know them?
LOUIE: I didn't take that ugly mutt.
DICK: A diamond collar is a big temptation.
LOUIE: What are you talking… diamond collar? It ain't no diamonds that make the collar worth so much. If I'da taken it, I'd haveta hit the road. My boss don't cotton to thieves.
DICK: What's your boss got to do with it?

LOUIE: Why do you even care about that tiny excuse for a dog?
DICK: I'm an animal lover.
(*LOUIE starts to panic.*)
LOUIE: You're working for her. Oh no! I thought I could trust you. She got to you too.
DICK: Relax. I might be odd… but I think I'm honest.
LOUIE: Relax? Who do you think sprung me? She wants to kill me. I saw her and Old Man Jordan. (*LOUIE starts to exit. DICK stops him physically.*) That woman is the devil. She possesses all the men she touches.
DICK: Are you saying she and Jordan were having an affair?
LOUIE: I've said too much. Let me out of here. That dame is evil.
DICK: Don't say anything bad about my Lauren.
LOUIE: You're working for her… you can't protect me from her. Let me go.
(*There is a struggle. LOUIE escapes. He runs to exit. But RICK enters, gun drawn. He aims it right into the face of LOUIE. As he speaks, he backs LOUIE back into the office.*)
RICK: (*To DICK.*) Dick, you really embarrass me. How can I teach you anything? I thought you were more intelligent than this. (*DICK turns his back on the situation.*)
DICK: (*Shouting.*) Leave me alone!
LOUIE: I swear. Tell Lauren, I won't say nothing to Grant about Old Man Jordan.
RICK: Are you ready to die?
DICK: Yes.

LOUIE: No!! (*RICK fires his gun. LOUIE falls. DICK turns to face RICK.*)
DICK: What do you want, Rick?
RICK: After all this time… and you're just now asking that question?
DICK: You just murdered a man.
RICK: So put me behind bars… honest cop! (*DICK pulls his gun.*)
DICK: Drop your weapon.
RICK: What, are we gonna have a shootout, right here in your office?
DICK: Drop the gun!
RICK: I'll do better than that. (*RICK raises his gun. It looks like there's going to be a shootout. Beat.*) I'll give it to you. (*RICK tosses the gun to DICK. DICK catches the gun. RICK starts to leave.*) Wake up, Dick… don't be so stupid.
DICK: I'm not stupid.
RICK: That's not what our father says.
DICK: I said don't move.
RICK: No dame is worth it.
DICK: I swear I'll shoot you.
(*During the following, RICK moves to DICK. He pushes the gun DICK has pointed at him to the ground.*)
RICK: You ain't got the guts. That's the difference between you and me. If I had a gun aimed at you… I'd pull the trigger. (*RICK starts to leave.*)
DICK: Why did you come back?
RICK: You invited me. Hasn't it always been that way? Life was boring until you invented me.
DICK: I've changed my mind.
RICK: For the love of a woman?

(*DICK raises the gun and aims it at RICK. There is a moment. Will he shot? After a beat, DICK lowers the gun.*)

DICK: Please, just leave me alone.

RICK: If this were a final exam… you just failed…

(*RICK exits, with a laugh. The LIGHTS shift to a spot on DICK. He talks to the audience/Dictaphone.*)

DICK: When I was a boy… my father used to make me read the newspaper cover to cover and then quiz me on it. I just wanted to play baseball. But he said baseball players didn't have any brains.

(*The LIGHTS crossfade to revel BROWN standing over the dead body of LOUIE. BROWN lights a cigarette.*)

BROWN: What happened?

DICK: He wanted to hire my services.

BROWN: Do you always shoot your clients?

DICK: It was Rick. When are you going to believe me, that he's real? I hope this proves it. Here's the murder weapon. Dust it for prints and then we can catch this maniac. (*DICK gives the gun to BROWN. BROWN refers to LOUIE.*)

BROWN: He didn't say anything about the Antenucci dog, did he? (*Beat.*)

DICK: Have you suddenly taken an interest in saving dogs?

BROWN: Just doing my job. You were right. Rumor has it; the dog collar is what we're really looking for.

DICK: Are you telling me or asking me?

BROWN: The dog was a mule.

DICK: From what I understand, Chanel's a Yorkshire terrier.

BROWN: A drug mule. The collar was loaded with opium.
DICK: What stool pigeon you been chatting with?
BROWN: A good cop never reveals his sources.
DICK: I thought you were my friend.
BROWN: Don't leave town. (*BROWN exits as the LIGHTS shift to a spot on DICK. He talks to the audience/Dictaphone.*)
DICK: I always respected the relationship you had with Sharron. I also got a kick out of the way that Sharron insisted on spelling her name with two Rs. You let me down, buddy. (*DICK moves to the whiskey. As he does so, the LIGHTS fade up. A knock at the door is heard. We are in DICK's office.*) Go away.
LAUREN: Darling, it's me.
DICK: It's open. (*LAUREN runs in. DICK meets her. They kiss passionately.*)
LAUREN: Are you all right? I came as soon as I could. I think Grant suspects something.
DICK: Time creeps like a snail when we're apart. (*They kiss again.*)
LAUREN: Did he say anything about Chanel before he died?
DICK: He said a lot. His mouth ran like a well-plumbed faucet.
LAUREN: Is she safe?
DICK: How well do you know Old Man Jordan?
LAUREN: I'm sure the Old Man has her.
DICK: Why? Cause you were sleeping with him? And that's what Grant and the Old Man were fighting about the night of the party!

LAUREN: That's absurd. Have you ever seen the Old Man?
DICK: Has anyone ever seen him?
LAUREN: I have, and he doesn't hold a prayer to your precious looks. (*They kiss.*)
DICK: I want you. More than life.
LAUREN: You have me.
DICK: All to my own. Do me the honor of sharing my life with me?
LAUREN: But I'm already married.
DICK: Get a divorce.
LAUREN: Grant would never allow that. Death is the only way I'll ever be free of him.
DICK: Yours or his?
LAUREN: His.
DICK: What are you suggesting? (*LAUREN kisses DICK.*)
LAUREN: Keep those lips warm. (*She starts to exit.*)
DICK: Where are you going?
LAUREN: Trust me.

(*The LIGHTS shift to a spot on DICK. He talks to the audience/ Dictaphone. During this monologue, RICK enters and sits on the desk.*)

DICK: My father instructed me on how to make love to a woman in a way that she'll adore you forever. Now, that seems ironic... seeing as my father was divorced three times.

(*The LIGHTS shift. LAUREN enters. DICK and LAUREN kiss passionately. And continues to do so throughout the following.*)

LAUREN: I love you, darling. And I want to be free. I want a white picket fence in front of a farmhouse in Iowa.
(*As DICK speaks his lines, RICK mouths the words, as he sits on the desk.*)
DICK: Let's run away. We can change our names. Start all over again. Begin new lives.
LAUREN: It sounds so easy. But Grant would find us. He's a powerful man. He must die.
DICK: So, he is tied to the Jordan family?
LAUREN: No more questions. Just hold me. (*They kiss.*)
RICK: But Dick I thought you wanted me? (*LAUREN screams.*)
DICK: The police are looking for you.
RICK: You're not falling for the song this canary's singing, are you? I thought you were more intelligent than that. (*DICK pulls out his gun.*)
DICK: Dial the police, Lauren. We just caught ourselves a murderer. (*LAUREN moves to the phone.*) They say a criminal always returns to the scene of their crime.
RICK: But I didn't do anything… I'm innocent.
DICK: Just like all the other crooks in the big house.
RICK: I came back to warn you about the broad that's gonna be your downfall.
DICK: I want you to leave me alone.
RICK: I suppose you don't want to hear it. I'll come back when you're alone. (*RICK starts to exit.*)
DICK: I'll shoot.
RICK: You didn't last time… you won't this time.
DICK: I swear I will.

RICK: The things one will do to impress the opposite sex. (*RICK starts to exit. DICK shoots him. RICK falls to the floor. LAUREN screams and drops the phone receiver.*)

LAUREN: You killed him. Oh my God… you killed him. You killed him.

DICK: No one believed me about him. They said that he didn't exist. Well, now he doesn't.

LAUREN: You just murdered a man.

DICK: He's not a man.

LAUREN: Sure… not anymore!

DICK: Believe me… no one will miss him.

LAUREN: I've been involved with other men since I married Grant. And I think he suspects it. But I've never… Oh my God, what are we going to do?

DICK: We'll take him up to Topanga Canyon and bury him.

LAUREN: I'll not be a partner to murder.

DICK: I'm sorry, darling… you're already involved. Just help me get him into the car. I swear I'll protect you. (*A knock is heard at the door. DICK speaks in a whisper.*) Grant?

LAUREN: No one knows about you and me.

DICK: Hide. In the bathroom.

LAUREN: What about him?

DICK: Help me. (*LAUREN and DICK drag RICK to the bathroom. RICK's hat is left behind. Another knock is heard. DICK calls from off.*) Coming. (*A toilet flush is heard. DICK enters and answers the door.*) Well, look who's here. Come on in.

(*BROWN enters. He smells the air. He can smell LAUREN's perfume.*)

BROWN: Am I interrupting anything? (*DICK moves to pick up RICK's hat.*)
DICK: Only the flow of some whiskey down my throat.
BROWN: Shoot me some. (*DICK moves to the whiskey. He puts the hat on the bar.*)
DICK: I thought Sharron forced you to jump on the wagon?
BROWN: I think we need to talk about Rick.
DICK: Did you catch him?
BROWN: Where's that drink?
DICK: This sounds serious.
BROWN: You know I'll stand behind you all the way.
DICK: Don't feed me ice cream and cake. Just cut to the quick!
BROWN: You're under arrest for the murder of Lucky Louie Fremont.
DICK: I swear to you I didn't shoot him. Rick did it. Didn't you check the prints on the gun?
BROWN: They came up... Richard Powell.
DICK: Dick... Rick... Richard! We got the same name. He's haunted me since childhood!
BROWN: They were your prints.
DICK: Sure my prints were on the gun. He threw the gun to me. I held it.
BROWN: There were no other prints. Just yours.
DICK: He must have wiped them off before he tossed the gun to me. No, he was wearing gloves. I'm telling you... we're dealing with a very intelligent criminal.
BROWN: Rick doesn't exist. (*DICK looks to the bathroom.*)

DICK: But he does.
BROWN: I think you better come downtown with me.
DICK: I wouldn't do a thing like this. Come on, Buddy. You know I wouldn't. You just asked me to come back to the force. I'm honest.
BROWN: Don't say anything more. I'll have to use it against you in court.
DICK: Save it... friend.
(*BROWN puts handcuffs on DICK and leads him out. Beat. LAUREN enters. She crosses to the whiskey. She pours a drink and then speaks.*)
LAUREN: Were you wearing a bulletproof vest?
(*RICK enters and moves to her.*)
RICK: Nope... he just missed me.
LAUREN: And you say he invited you here? What kind of game are we playing? (*LAUREN hands RICK the drink.*)
RICK: (*Suggestively.*) Would you like to join?
LAUREN: You could be his twin!
RICK: Do you want me to be?
LAUREN: Leave Dick alone!
RICK: Is that a request or a demand?
LAUREN: Take it any way you want.
RICK: Gutsy dame! I can see why Dick is attracted to you.
LAUREN: Please just leave us alone. I really can't explain it. But I need him. I'll pay you ten thousand dollars to forget you ever knew him.
RICK: And they say you can't buy love.
LAUREN: Do we have a deal? (*RICK downs the drink.*)

RICK: I want cash. Small bills. And no funny business… like marked money. (*RICK hands LAUREN the empty glass. She hands him his hat. He moves to the door.*) I'll be in touch.
(*LAUREN and RICK share a moment before he exits. The LIGHTS cross to a spot on DICK, who enters. He speaks to the audience/Dictaphone.*)

DICK: When I was a kid I had an English setter… Black lab mix. His name was Buddy. I loved that dog. So did my dad. But his wife… my stepmother… hated any kind of animal. She ran over the dog with the car. She said it was an accident. I know she was guilty. (*Beat.*) I'm amazed at how easily felons are released on bail at your jail.
(*The LIGHTS revel LAUREN and DICK. WOODY is at the desk. He is giving DICK his belongings.*)

LAUREN: Are you all right, my darling? (*LAUREN tries to embrace DICK.*)

DICK: Careful. Not in here.

LAUREN: I don't care who sees us.

WOODY One wallet. Two hundred dollars cash. What bank did you rob? One ring of keys. Your piece. (*He gives DICK his gun.*) Sign here.

DICK: Where's my belt?

WOODY Damn, I told them to leave it with you. I was hoping you'd hang yourself. (*WOODY exits.*)

DICK: How'd you get me free? (*LAUREN tries to hold and kiss DICK.*)

LAUREN: It doesn't matter. We're together again. That's all that I want.

DICK: What about your dog?

LAUREN: She doesn't matter, as long as you're safe.

DICK: Do you really mean that?
LAUREN: Forever.
DICK: Then we'll spend it together with Chanel!
(*DICK embraces LAUREN.*)
LAUREN: I knew you were the right man.
DICK: Give me a couple of hours to take care of Rick and then meet me at my office.
LAUREN: He's taken care of.
DICK: What?
LAUREN: I took him to Topanga Canyon... just like you suggested.
DICK: I love you. (*DICK and LAUREN kiss.*)
LAUREN: But what about Grant?
DICK: Meet me at my office in half hour. You've already made a big mistake by coming here and being seen with me.
LAUREN: I was so worried about you.
DICK: My office. We'll discuss Grant's future there.
LAUREN: Let me stay with you.
DICK: Go, before Woody comes back. (*DICK leads LAUREN to the door and she exits. WOODY enters.*)
WOODY: Where's your broad? How does a louse like you get such a classy number?
DICK: Communication Woody. I know how to talk to them. (*WOODY throws the belt at DICK.*)
WOODY: Here's your belt. But I don't think you're gonna need it to hang yourself.
(*The LIGHTS fade to a spot on DICK. He speaks to the audience/Dictaphone.*)
DICK: My father hung himself. Oh, not literally. He got married a fourth time, to an absolute terror. She made his life a living purgatory, for the two

short years they were married, before he died. I once asked him, "Why don't you divorce her? You've done it three times before?" He replied, "'It's time I faced the music!'" I know that fourth wife killed him. (*The LIGHTS crossfade to revel LAUREN in the office. She runs to DICK.*)

LAUREN: I thought you'd never get here.

DICK: Woody didn't make my exit an experience I'm going to write about in my memoirs.

LAUREN: This came to the house this morning by special delivery. (*LAUREN hands DICK a note. He reads it.*)

DICK: Why didn't you tell me about this at the police station?

LAUREN: You were in such a hurry to get rid of me. I didn't have a chance.

DICK: I'm sorry, my love.

LAUREN: I used it to persuade Grant into buying the judge. That's how we got you bond.

DICK: What do you mean?

LAUREN: I told Grant you were under my employ. Of course, he went off the deep end with jealousy. But I calmed him down when I told him you'd go with him. To protect him.

DICK: Why would anyone who has a diamond collar worth ten times a million dollars, be willing to give it back for that amount?

LAUREN: Who's going to give them that kind of money for a collar that every crook in America knows belongs to Grant? Besides, Grant is sentimental. He wants that stupid collar.

DICK: I guess the thief doesn't know the collar is loaded with opium.
LAUREN: Who told you that?
DICK: So it's true?
LAUREN: Now you know why Grant wants the collar back.
DICK: Doesn't Grant have other henchman to protect him?
LAUREN: His low-life flunkies aren't willing to shoot him… once the deal is done. Do you want to take advantage of this gift handed to us or not? It'll look like a drug deal gone bad. I'll be the grieving widow for a couple of months and then we'll leave this godforsaken city. We can have that white picket fence in Iowa.
DICK: Chanel is still alive?
LAUREN: Yes, and so happy to see me. She was delivered with the letter.

(*DICK and LAUREN kiss. Beat. The LIGHTS fade to a spot on DICK. He talks to the audience/Dictaphone. As he talks, LAUREN exits and GRANT enters.*)

DICK: I never knew what unconditional love was… until I met Lauren. It's amazing the things you'll do. An intelligent person is reduced to a moron. Objective thinking is a thing of the past.

(*The LIGHTS crossfade to a dark alley. DICK and GRANT are discovered.*)

GRANT: So, Mr. Private Eye… you're here to protect me from Old Man Jordan?
DICK: Old Man Jordan?
GRANT: I see Lauren neglected to tell you that detail.

DICK: Mrs. Antenucci is paying me very handsomely to protect you, sir… and I do thank you.
GRANT: And I appreciate the fact that a gentleman like you knows where the money's coming from.
DICK: Oh, sir… I've never forgotten that. (*Beat.*)
GRANT: So, Mr. Dick… how well do you know my wife?
DICK: What is that supposed to mean?
GRANT: You know perfectly well what it means.
DICK: Look… I said I come here to protect you. The deal doesn't include talking to you. I think we've flapped our jaws too much already.
GRANT: Well, then just listen! I don't like men sleeping with my wife. I can't stop her from doing it, so I let her do it. Then I just eliminate the ones that have known her.

(*DICK pulls his gun out.*)

DICK: I was going to do this after you got the dog collar back, but I'll just dispose of you and receive the collar on your behalf.
GRANT: Dog collar?
DICK: The diamond collar filled with opium that Jordan is giving back to you tonight.
GRANT: Whoever took the dog, kept the collar, which was filled with opium, but the diamonds were nothing but rhinestones. And, yes, I am meeting Jordan tonight. He is a man of honor and to show his faith in our partnership and to illustrate he didn't steal the collar, he is going to give me another opium shipment on the house.
DICK: You're lying to save your neck.
GRANT: Too bad you'll never find out.

DICK: You seem to forget I have the gun pointed at you.
(*WOODY enters with his gun drawn.*)
WOODY: I think you should lower that firearm.
DICK: Sergeant Woody, you're a disgrace to the department.
WOODY: A rat smells his own hole first.
GRANT: So, Mr. Dick, tonight I get two birds with one stone. You and Old Man Jordan.
DICK: Lucky Louie was telling the truth! Lauren does like 'em old. I'm surprised she even stopped on her journey through the land of dinosaurs to even grace me with a hello.
GRANT: And thanks to you... I didn't have to silence Lucky Louie's big mouth.
DICK: Thank Rick... not me.
GRANT: Do you have any last words?
DICK: Yeah, boy, what a chump I've been!
GRANT: Don't be too hard on yourself.
DICK: So, why involve Lt. Brown?
GRANT: As you know, Lauren also likes men with a badge. (*Beat.*)
DICK: He wouldn't do that to Sharron!
GRANT: You made a much better pawn than he. He'll get his soon. It'll look like you were trying to be the hero and bust Old Man Jordan for the dognapping. Now, give the good Sergeant your gun. (*DICK tosses the gun to WOODY.*)
DICK: This will never work.
GRANT: He doesn't seem to want to play the game, so shoot him now, Sergeant Woody.
(*WOODY takes aim. DICK holds up his hands.*)

DICK: So, you're the bad seed within the department.
WOODY: I've always hated your intellect. (*LAUREN enters.*)
LAUREN: No, Grant. Don't do it.
GRANT: Hold on, Sergeant! (*To LAUREN.*) Hello, my dear. I was wondering if you'd make it. I know how you like to watch the disposal of your lovers.
LAUREN: How many times do I have to tell you, darling… I've done nothing wrong, and you are the only man I love? (*From offstage we hear OLD MAN JORDAN call.*)
JORDAN: Hello?
LAUREN: It's Jordan. He's coming, Grant.
GRANT: You know what to do, Woody. Shoot each one with a different gun.
(*WOODY exits.*)
DICK: (*To LAUREN.*) You're going to let this happen? I know what we shared was real. And so do you.
LAUREN: (*To DICK in a soft voice.*) Relax.
(*OLD MAN JORDAN enters. He's a very young, good-looking stud.*)
JORDAN: Grant. (*He gestures to DICK.*) What is this? (*He moves to LAUREN. She offers her hand. He takes it and then kisses her on the cheek.*) Lauren. You're as beautiful as ever.
LAUREN: Thank you, Jordan.
DICK: This is Old Man Jordan?
JORDAN: I'm disappointed, Grant… after all these years of meeting me alone… tonight you have to bring a guest.

GRANT: I thought you'd like to meet Mr. Powell... seeing as you're both adulterers and you're both going to meet your creator together.
LAUREN: Grant, stop all this talk of death. I'm sure we can work this all out. (*To JORDAN.*) Do you have the opium?
JORDAN: Next to my heart, and you know both belong to you.
GRANT: You're a fool, Jordan.
JORDAN: Is that any way to talk to your friend and number one business partner?
GRANT: Now, Woody! Shoot! (*A shot rings out. All look confused.*)
JORDAN: For some reason I thought I too should bring protection tonight. (*Calls out.*) Come on in. (*BROWN enters.*) Did you get him?
BROWN: They're gonna need a new sergeant over at the station house.
JORDAN: So, do we do it here? Shoot all three of them. It'll look like jealous husband gone crazy over catching his cheating wife with lover. Then he turns the gun on himself.
BROWN: This is as good a place as any.
JORDAN: You'll be rewarded handsomely, Lieutenant.
(*BROWN raises his gun. DICK starts to move out of the picture.*)
DICK: Are there any honest cops anymore?
BROWN: (*To DICK.*) I'm sorry, buddy, but being honest just never paid the bills.
(*RICK enters gun drawn.*)
RICK: But yes it does, Lieutenant!

BROWN: Who the hell are you?
DICK: That's him, Brown… that's Rick. I told you he was real.
RICK: What better introduction could I have?
BROWN: I suggest you drop that gun.
RICK: Should I? Oh, I do love a challenge.
(*Blackout. We hear four shots. A spot illuminates DICK, as he speaks to the audience/Dictaphone.*)
DICK: Do you gamble? For as long as we've known one another… that's one thing I don't know about you. There were six people standing in that alley when four shots rang out. There were two guns. Was it equally divided? Two shots per gun… or was it three to one. Or did one gun shoot all four shots? As you'll never know… it was three direct hits from Rick and you did manage to get off one round before you fell. I don't know if I could have shot her. (*The LIGHTS crossfade to the alley. DICK and RICK are discovered.*) Why did you spare me?
RICK: Someone has to take the blame.
DICK: I killed you once. You're supposed to be dead.
RICK: Childhood buddies wearing plaid can't be killed in front of girls.
DICK: I want this to end.
RICK: What do you suggest?
DICK: A final shootout. Gimme a gun. (*RICK tosses him a gun.*)
RICK: Now what?
DICK: Put your gun on the ground in front of you. I'll do the same. (*DICK and RICK very cautiously put their guns on the ground in front of themselves.*) Make your move. (*RICK goes for his gun. So does*

DICK. *Blackout. We hear two gunshots. The LIGHTS come up to reveal DICK at his desk. He is hurting, once again, like at the beginning of the play. He holds the microphone.*) So, why am I talking to you, Lieutenant Brown? You'll never answer your phone again. Or even hear this recording. I'm hoping, maybe, there's an honest cop somewhere in the system that can put this crazy story straight?
(*RICK walks into the office. He is bleeding from the stomach.*)
RICK: Hey, Dickie boy.
DICK: Die... you devil... die!
RICK: I can't. Imaginary friends never die. And you did ask me to do this.
DICK: But Father is dead now.
RICK: He was such an evil man.
DICK: Please, leave me in peace.
RICK: I have to destroy that cylinder. (*RICK grabs the cylinder. He pulls the roll from the Dictaphone and steps on it.*)
DICK: No, don't do that.
RICK: Here. (*RICK holds out an envelope.*)
DICK: What's that?
RICK: Your suicide note. (*RICK throws the note on the desk. LAUREN enters. She too is bleeding from the gut.*)
LAUREN: Haven't you done it yet? Hurry!
RICK: Did you get the opium Jordan had?
LAUREN: Both shipments. (*LAUREN throws a rhinestone dog collar, center stage.*) Come on, we both need to get to a doctor.
DICK: (*To LAUREN.*) Why Rick?
LAUREN: He's the real man.

(*RICK puts his gun to the back of DICK's head. The LIGHTS cross to a special on the dog collar. We hear a gunshot. Beat. Blackout.*)

END

A Collection from a Career in Theatre

TABLE STAKES

a comic fable in two acts

by
Bob May

© 1994 by Bob May
All rights reserved

CAST OF CHARACTERS

PAULA
MARK
HOWARD HUGHES
CHARLES "POP" SQUIRES
HELEN STEWART
BENJAMIN "BUGSY" SIEGEL

SYNOPSIS OF SCENES

TIME: Tonight
PLACE: Paula's apartment, Las Vegas, Nevada

The premiere of *Table Stakes* was presented by the University of Nevada, Las Vegas, at the Paul Harris Theatre on August 4, 1993, under the direction of Davey Marlin-Jones, with set design by Yale Yeandel, costume design by Gail Lehtinen, lighting design by

Joe Aldridge and Yale Yeandel, and sound design by Keith Corning with the following cast:

Paula—Maggie Winn-Jones
Mark—Charles Paddock
Howard Hughes—Michael Serna
Charles "Pop" Squires—Dax Pagan
Helen Stewart—Christie Parker
Benjamin "Bugsy" Siegel—Gregory Gaskill

(AT RISE: PAULA, a forty-year-old writer, and her boyfriend, MARK, enter her apartment. She is a very hyper person, always on the run. Some of the scenes should be played as if she were running a race. PAULA sits at her desk and prepares to start writing.)

PAULA: Thanks, honey. I had a wonderful… ah, well, I had a wonderful time.
MARK: Can you believe those morons?
PAULA: Don't worry. I wasn't hungry anyway. Thanks a bunch.
MARK: I should write the manager. No, he was one of the morons. The owner.
PAULA: Call me tomorrow. Thanks again. Love you. *(PAULA kisses MARK. MARK smiles lovingly at her.)* I gotta get to writing—
MARK: Who owns it?
PAULA: Forget it.
MARK: I shouldn't have let you talk me into going there.
PAULA: Mark… please.
MARK: I knew I wouldn't like it.

PAULA: It was a Mexican restaurant—
MARK: Are we gonna get married or what?
PAULA: —and I'm sorry they didn't serve steaks. I really wanted to go there. After all, it's my birthday.
MARK: Now I'm starving. Let's go somewhere else.
PAULA: It's okay. Go without me.
MARK: Have you slept with the waiter?
PAULA: What?
MARK: The waiter at the restaurant. He was overly friendly to you.
PAULA: He was uncomfortable with the way you— (*She breaks off.*) Mark, I really have to write tonight.
MARK: The guys at Yucca Mountain warned me about you. Why does it have to be tonight? It's not like Las Vegas will disappear if you don't write.
PAULA: Deadlines.
MARK: I am not.
PAULA: Obviously, you've never had one.
MARK: I'm sorry I'm not the liberal artist.
PAULA: Oh stop. I'm a playwright. Tomorrow is it. I've run out of time.
MARK: Hypermaniac.
PAULA: Please go home.
MARK: Is the president of the chamber a man?
PAULA: You're the only man in my life.
MARK: You spend more time with your plays than you do with me.
PAULA: You know, Mark, I don't really think I want this relationship.
MARK: And that's not fair to us.
PAULA: Mark, I really have to work.
MARK: I thought you wanted to get married?

PAULA: Thanks for the birthday, honey.
MARK: What's the president's name?
PAULA: Would you hand me that file folder, please? (*MARK gets the file folder.*)
MARK: Are you trying to get rid of me? (*He throws the folder to the floor.*) I don't need this crap.
PAULA: You can come back later. Just give me a couple of hours.
MARK: So you can meet your waiter friend?
PAULA: Okay, you can stay.
MARK: I'm outta here.
PAULA: Please don't go.
MARK: Paula, the educated woman. You think you're so smart… just cause you're older than me.
PAULA: So what? Is this "goodbye?" What? What are you doing?
MARK: I'm going out to get me the biggest, fattest, juiciest steak in the world. I live in Las Vegas. I can do that all night long. And very cheaply.
PAULA: I'm sorry. You can say. I'll cook you something. I'll call the chamber president in the morning.
MARK: Tell him I said hello.
PAULA: She's a woman.
MARK: Probably a lesbian.
PAULA: Don't do this.
MARK: You did it to yourself.
PAULA: Mark, don't do… call me… please.
MARK: I'll get you for this. (*MARK exits.*)
PAULA: (*Attitude shift.*) Domineering ass. (*She looks at a photo of MARK.*) Where am I without him? (*She

plays a hand-held tape recorder. We hear PAULA's voice.)

TAPE: Las Vegas .. Spanish for The Meadows. A half billion years ago or so, Nevada was underwater. During the Paleozoic era... *(PAULA talks to the tape.)*

PAULA: What era?

TAPE: ...which took 340 million years...

PAULA: A long time.

TAPE: ...the ocean floor raised and the sea drained leaving towering mesas and alluvial plains... *(She turns off the tape.)*

PAULA: What the hell does alluvial mean? *(The phone rings. She answers it.)* Hello.

(HUGES appears in a LIGHT special. He is on the phone.)

HUGHES: Hughes here.

PAULA: Who?

HUGHES: Howard, you idiot. Now listen up. I can't believe it. Moe Dalitz wants me out of his Desert Inn. Who the hell does he think he is? I don't care who he is. I'm comfortable. I don't want to move. Buy the goddamn thing.

PAULA: Mark, is that you?

HUGHES: I don't care what it costs. Buy it. I have a major plan for Las Vegas. Phone Jean for me. She's back in Ohio. *(HUGHES slams the phone down. The LIGHT special goes out.)*

PAULA: Hello? Dammit, Mark, leave me alone. *(New thought.)* So, how much of this history do I use? Maybe I could have a dinosaur do the prologue? *(She goes back to her notes, reading them in a deep voice as a dinosaur.)* Two billion years ago the first of four great ice ages began. The basin was drowned...

(*She is now a drowning dinosaur.*) drained... then, ground down by glaciers. (*She sits up.*) Jurassic Vegas. (*An aside.*) Damn, there's a lot of water in the Vegas past. Maybe that's a theme, Paula. Water does seem to be a dominant theme with the hotels on the Strip now. The desert was once flooded and now they seem to be trying to do it again. Nah, people won't want to be reminded that Las Vegas is supposed to run out of water soon. (*New thought.*) Water. I am definitely using— Squires.

(*PAULA starts flipping through her notes. SQUIRES appears in a LIGHT special. He is talking to an unseen Herbert Hoover.*)

SQUIRES: Charles Squires at your service.

(*PAULA finds the name SQUIRES in her notes. She does not see SQUIRES.*)

PAULA: Because of you, Mr. Squires, Vegas will once again be swimming in an ocean of water.

SQUIRES: It's nice to meet you, Mr. Hoover. Please call me, Pop. My friends call me Pop. And this is Vicki, my fiancée.

PAULA: I know the campaigning will pay off. You bet your sweet butt it will.

SQUIRES: Thank you. Enjoy your visit, Mr. Secretary.

(*The LIGHT special goes out on SQUIRES.*)

PAULA: No problem, Pop. That's good, Pop. Who the hell is Pop? Probably some chauvinist like Mark. I can't believe he doubts my fidelity. I should probably just call him and tell him to forget it. (*She picks up the phone. Pause. Then puts the phone back down.*) Read on, McDuff. (*She picks up her*

notes.) And how does Las Vegas look today? Bad. Dominated by men. Men... one man... a man named, Mark. Yes, damn it... call him. He probably won't be home. He went to get a steak.
(*PAULA dials the phone. We hear it ring. STEWART answers the phone in a LIGHT special.*)
STEWART: Hello.
PAULA: Who's this?
STEWART: Helen.
PAULA: Who? Where the hell is Mark?
STEWART: And may I ask who I'm talking to?
PAULA: What are you doing... why are you answering his... where is that two-timing hypocrite?
STEWART: Those rumors about my conduct during Archibald's absences are nothing but that... rumors.
PAULA: Let me talk to Mark.
STEWART: And I will not be intimidated off my land.
PAULA: Do I have the right number? Is this—
STEWART: If I am patient, I know the railroad will come to Las Vegas.
PAULA: Tell Mark that this is Paula.
STEWART: Grace was right. Thank you, my friend.
PAULA: Tell Mark, I will get him for this. (*She hangs up the phone. The LIGHT goes out on STEWART.*) He wants to play games? That's fine. I can play too.
(*She takes the phone off the hook and turns on the tape.*)
TAPE: The first Spanish explorers stumbled upon this life-saving...
(*PAULA once again makes comments to the tape.*)

PAULA: Oh please.
TAPE: ...and named it... (*PAULA turns off the tape.*)
PAULA: That snake. And he has the nerve to ask me if I have another man in my life. (*She turns the tape on again.*)
TAPE: ...people inhabited the valley as early as 11,000 BC.
PAULA: Stupid jerks.
TAPE: By the year 1000, Pueblo Grande had become Nevada's first ghost town. (*PAULA turns off the tape.*)
PAULA: Who the hell is Helen? And why was she at his house? The hell with this, let's fast forward to the good stuff. (*The sound of the tape on fast forward is heard.*) The "hot" stuff. The Warren Beatty years. (*The phone rings. She looks at it. This is weird because the receiver is off the hook. She finally picks up the receiver.*) Dammit, Mark, what do you want?
(*SIEGEL appears in LIGHT special. He is on the phone.*)
SIEGEL: Virginia, my love, thank you. The only thing that could improve this moment is... if we could be together.
PAULA: How did you make this phone ring?
SIEGEL: What a vision. It's a grand vision.
PAULA: Who the hell is Helen?
SIEGEL: What? Who?
PAULA: Helen. She answered your phone earlier.
SIEGEL: No one... I called you. The idea... the vision... a casino in the middle of the desert. Brilliant. It's a credit to your intelligence. I'm going to start the ball rolling tonight.

PAULA: Is there another woman? Is that why you're doubting me?
SIEGEL: I love mountains. I love valleys. But my favorite thing is the Virginia Hill that comes between them.
PAULA: Helen? Virginia? You have two other women?
(*HUGHES appears in a LIGHT special.*)
HUGHES: I wish you were with me, Jean, and not back in boring Ohio. I'm about to embark on the most exciting thing I think...
PAULA: Jean?
HUGHES: ...I've ever done.
SIEGEL: Vice and glamour. It's a grand vision. And mix women with gambling.
HUGHES: I'm going to buy Vegas and clean it up. Change the image.
SIEGEL: It's brilliant.
PAULA: Dammit, Mark, how do you expect me to write?
HUGHES: I'm going to start tonight. I am buying the Desert Inn.
SIEGEL: I'm going to bring flamingos to the desert.
PAULA: Very funny, Mark. Or should I call you Howard Bugsy Hughes Siegel?
SIEGEL and HUGHES: I love you...
SIEGEL: ...Virginia.
HUGHES: ...Jean.
PAULA: Fine. I never want to speak to you again... for the rest of my life. (*She slams the phone down.*)
HUGHES: Hello... Jean? I hate that. (*He redials the phone.*)

SIEGEL: Damn phone company. What a monopoly.
(*He redials the phone.*)
(*The LIGHTS go out on SIEGEL and HUGHES. PAULA goes berserk and starts ripping up her notes. She throws them in the air. She stomps on the pages. As she does this, the four characters spin offstage... as if thrown.*)
PAULA: I hate you. You son of a bitch. I have to get out of this damn town... this relationship. I want out. Three women. I want out. I don't care if this play ever gets written. This town shouldn't be here. I want out. (*PAULA's tantrum stops. She surveys the damage.*) Oops! Damn! Now look what you've done. (*She picks up her notes and tries to piece them back together in the correct order. As she does this, her apartment begins to take on the shape of a departure terminal. Or depending on the character, a stage depot, a train station, or an airport. A sign that reads TICKETS drops in above where PAULA sits. Throughout the shift, PAULA reads different sections of her notes.*) Rafael Rivera, the first non-Indian... (*A new page.*) built a giant volcano that erupts every half hour in front of his mega-hotel and casino... the Mirage. (*An aside.*) That's not right. (*Back to notes.*) Brigham Young had a plan to... (*An aside.*) No, I don't want to use him as a character. (*She throws the slip of paper in the trash. The goes back to her notes.*) Around 1858, the Comstock Lode was discovered and O. D. Gass was among those gold miners that poured into this... (*An aside.*) stupid desert. (*Back to her notes.*) Vegas is now a family town... (*An aside.*) What a joke. (*Back to her notes.*) With the new Luxor and MGM Grand Theme Park, Vegas tries in vain to

change its image from sin city… to Disneyland.
(*And aside.*) Sounds like the story of my life. (*Joking*)
Ah, now I know why they hired me to write this
damn play. (*She shuffles a few pages.*) Here we are.
This is important to know in the Helen Stewart
story. (*Reads from a new page.*) Gass built a ranch
house in the Valley. The Gass family irrigated 640
acres, raise produce, grain, fruit, and cattle. By the
mid-1870s, Gass had bought up or taken most of
the homesteaded land in the valley and owned the
rights to most of the water.

(*The scene shift is completed by now. HUGHES, SQUIRES, STEWART, and SIEGEL are discovered as the LIGHTS fade up. HUGHES and SIEGEL are on the phone. STEWARD steps up to the ticket window and talks to PAULA. SQUIRES is in line behind STEWARD. All their attitudes have shifted from positive to negative.*)

HUGHES: (*On the phone.*) Hello, Jean. I hate that. (*He redials the phone.*)

SIEGEL: Damn phone company. What a monopoly. (*He redials the phone.*)

STEWART: (*To PAULA.*) Is there a stage out of here soon?

PAULA: (*Still reading her notes.*) The Gass ranch was taken over by Archibald Stewart in 1881.

STEWART: Excuse me, when does the next stage leave Las Vegas?

PAULA: (*Still in her own world.*) After he was murdered in 1884, his wife, Helen…

STEWART: Excuse me…

SQUIRES: Is the train back east on time?

STEWART: ...are you deaf? (*PAULA becomes aware of the people.*)
PAULA: Oh my God.
HUGHES: (*On the phone.*) Jean, honey, you hung up on me.
SIEGEL: (*On the phone.*) Virginia Hill, please, room 321.
HUGHES: Jean, please don't do what you're thinking of doing.
PAULA: Who are you? All of you? How did you get in here?
STEWART: (*To SQUIRES.*) Excuse me, did you say train?
SQUIRES: Yes, the sooner it gets here the better.
SIEGEL: Hi, Virginia, doll.
PAULA: Please don't hurt me.
HUGHES: Jean, I swear, I've been faithful.
STEWART: The train will pass Vegas by.
SIEGEL: (*He discovers he is talking to his wife and not his girlfriend, Virginia.*) Esta, honey, my lovely wife. What are you doing at Virginia's... I mean, what are you doing in LA?
SQUIRES: The train? I can't have missed it.
PAULA: Get out... or I'll call the police.
HUGHES: Hepburn and Marlowe are history. I promise.
STEWART: (*To PAULA.*) Are you finally awake?
SIEGEL: Oh baby, I need to be with you. Things are falling apart.
HUGHES: Las Vegas is a pit of corruption. There's nothing here for me. Not if you go through with it. Such a foul act.

PAULA: Do I know you?
SQUIRES: When is the next scheduled train out of here?
SIEGEL: You can't possibly mean that.
STEWART: I think your only way out will be a stagecoach. But you can join me. I can't get out of this godforsaken desert fast enough.
SIEGEL: Just calm down. I'll catch the next flight out of here.
HUGHES: You can't stop me from coming. I'll buy the goddamn state of Ohio. (*He hangs up the phone and moves to the ticket window.*)
PAULA: Mark put you up to this.
SIEGEL: I love you, Esta. Let's talk this out.
HUGHES: (*To PAULA.*) When is the next flight to Columbus?
SIEGEL: I'm coming home. What? Don't be silly. Meyer won't hurt me. (*He hangs up the phone and moves to the ticket window.*)
PAULA: Is this Candid Camera?
SIEGEL: (*To PAULA.*) Book me on the next flight to LA.
HUGHES: Excuse me, sir, I was here before you.
SIEGEL: Buzz off.
STEWART: Ah, gentlemen, I was here before both of you.
PAULA: All of you, get the hell out of here. This is my apartment.
SQUIRES: The lady was at the head of the line.
(*The four start squabbling over who was the first in line.*)
PAULA: Okay, if you won't leave, I will. Matter of fact, you can tell Mark I'm taking the next plane

out of this town. (*She gets a suitcase and starts to pack.*)

SIEGEL: Where the hell is she going?

HUGHES: What kind of terminal is this?

PAULA: This would have never happened back in Iowa. (*The phone rings. She yells at the phone.*) Leave me alone, Mark.

HUGHES: Is she the only one working? (*The phone continues to ring.*)

SIEGEL: (*To PAULA.*) Hello, your telephone is ringing.

PAULA: Tell the unfaithful bastard to go to hell. (*All look at her like she's crazy. Finally she can't take it any longer and she answers the phone.*) Leave me alone. I am going back to Iowa. (*She slams the phone down and moves to the suitcase.*) I don't need this. Just get out of here. (*She moves to the door. A note is slipped under the door. PAULA is startled by its sudden appearance, but she picks it up and reads it.*) You ripped up history. It's up to you to fix it. (*She wads up the note and then shouts.*) You're crazy, Mark. You're the one who's history. (*The phone rings. PAULA is frightened by the ring. She lets out a scream, then shouts at the phone.*) I've had enough, Mark. (*Referring to the four characters staring at her.*) And you've gone too far with these jokers. Please stop.

(*SQUIRES, STEWART, SIEGEL, and HUGHES all freeze on the word "stop." PAULA runs out the door. She is gone for a few beats, then returns. She is in shock. The phone is still ringing.*)

PAULA: It's gone. There is nothing there. My apartment is standing in the middle of the desert. Las Vegas is gone. (*SQUIRES, STEWART, HUGHES, and SIEGEL all come to life on the words "Las Vegas" and start ad-libbing, demanding a ticket out of Vegas on their mode of travel. The ad-libbing builds. PAULA can take no more. She screams...)* STOP!! (*SQUIRES, STEWART, HUGHES, and SIEGEL freeze. The phone is still ringing. PAULA answers it.*) What have you done, Mark? (*MARK, on a phone, appears in a LIGHT special. He is trapped in his apartment and not happy.*)

MARK: Goddamn you, Paula, who are these morons?

PAULA: Mark, I don't find this game very funny.

MARK: Are they from the Mexican restaurant? They got me locked in my apartment and won't let me out... "until you fix it."

PAULA: What have you done to the city?

MARK: Will you listen to me. Who are these guys?

PAULA: That's what I'd like to know.

MARK: Paula, I don't think you understand... I got four morons keeping me prisoner in my own apartment. They say they won't let me go until you write your play.

PAULA: Have you looked outside?

MARK: Didn't you hear me? I'm a prisoner.

PAULA: Look out a window.

MARK: Paula, this is not the time to—

PAULA: Just do it, dammit.

(*MARK sets the phone down and moves to look out a window. He looks and then moves back to the phone stunned.*)

MARK: What have you done?

PAULA: How did you do this?

MARK: I can't see your apartment building.

PAULA: I can't see anything. Do you have frozen people in your apartment?

MARK: Frozen what?
PAULA: Mark, I think I need your help. Please come over here.
MARK: Paula, just do what they're asking. Fix it.
(*The sound of the phone line being disconnected is heard.*)
PAULA: Hello? Hello, Mark?
MARK: Paula? Hello? Are you there?

(*The LIGHT goes out on MARK. PAULA surveys the scene.*)

PAULA: Who are you people? Answer me. (*She jabs at them.*) What the hell? This isn't Candid Camera… it's The Twilight Zone. What does he mean, "fix it"? Who are you people? (*She looks in SIEGEL's breast pocket and gets his wallet. She looks at his license and reads his name.*) Benjamin Siegel. (*She does the same for HUGHES.*) Howard Robard Hughes. (*She does the same for SQUIRES.*) Charles Squires. (*She looks at STEWART.*) You have to be Helen Stewart. In my living room. Only in Las Vegas. (*SIEGEL, HUGHES, STEWART, and SQUIRES once again become alive and begin demanding tickets.*) Why do all of you want out of town? Enough. Stop! (*SIEGEL, HUGHES, STEWART, and SQUIRES freeze once again.*) I hate Las Vegas. (*SIEGEL, HUGHES, STEWART, and SQUIRES once again come alive and start demanding tickets.*) No. I can't take anymore. This has to… stop! (*SIEGEL, HUGHES, STEWART, and SQUIRES freeze once again. Something dawns on PAULA.*) Las Vegas. (*SIEGEL, HUGHES, STEWART, and SQUIRES once again come alive and start demanding tickets.*) Stop. (*SIEGEL, HUGHES, STEWART, and SQUIRES freeze once *again.*) Twilight Zone. (*There is a comical sequence where PAULA says, "Las Vegas" and "Stop" at various speeds. She also discovers that she can control them with a wink, a nod of the head, a cough, a point, anything that the actress can come up with. Thus eliminating all the times PAULA says, "Las Vegas" and "stop." Each time the four demand tickets or freeze... depending on the appropriate phrase or gesture. PAULA ends this comical sequence with a...*) Stop! (*The four freeze.*) I've been drugged. Something from Yucca Mountain. It came in through the air conditioning. (*She screams.*) Why don't you get out of here? (*She thinks.*) I wonder? (*She touches SQUIRES and says...*) Las Vegas. (*SQUIRES comes to life.*)

SQUIRES: The next train... a ticket, please. I'd like to get out of here as soon as possible.

PAULA: Stop. (*SQUIRES freezes. PAULA touches STEWART and says...*) Las Vegas. (*STEWART comes to life.*)

STEWART: You can't stop me, Grace. I am taking the next stage out.

PAULA: I'm not Grace.

STEWART: I thought you were my friend.

PAULA: Stop. (*STEWART freezes.*) Good. I can control them. Why does Charles Squires... (*She checks her notes. She scrambles through the pages of her notes. She finally finds what she is looking for.*)... who campaigned tirelessly for the building of Hoover Dam. The Publisher of the Las Vegas— (*SIEGEL, HUGHES, STEWART, and SQUIRES come to life... etc.*) Stop. (*The four freeze.*) The publisher of the... blah, blah "Age." And a gung ho supporter of Las... of

this hole. (*An aside.*) So what is his problem? Why does he want to get out? (*She touches SQUIRES and says...*) Las Vegas.
SQUIRES: I'm sorry, miss. I've just gone through something very... (*He breaks off.*) After she left me... life became a joke.
PAULA: Stop. (*SQUIRES freezes. PAULA touches HUGHES and says...*) Las Vegas.
(*HUGHES comes to life. He sees PAULA and thinks she is Jean.*)
HUGHES: Jean, thank god you've come back. Did you do it?
PAULA: Who?
HUGHES: I'm sorry, madam, I thought you were someone else.
PAULA: Jean who?
HUGHES: I need to get to Ohio State University. When is the next flight to Columbus?
PAULA: (*Making a joke.*) Will that be cash or charge?
HUGHES: I don't find this situation comical at all.
PAULA: (*An aside.*) Me either.
HUGHES: May I see your superior. I will have your job.
PAULA: Oh... stop. (*HUGHES freezes. PAULA reads her notes.*) Howard Robard Hughes... like this city and Bugsy Siegel... Hughes was born in 1905. (*An aside.*) Mmmm, that is interesting. (*Back to her notes.*) At age twenty-one, inherited multimillion-dollar Hughes Tool Company. Made a beeline for Hollywood. There he launched a crazy career... film producer, airplane designer, pioneer pilot, airline mogul, and sex investor. (*An aside.*) What is

a sex investor? (*Back to her notes.*) He'd sold TWA for half a billion bucks, cash, giving him a larger bankroll than anyone else in the world, and he felt like spending some. And he does in Sin City. (*An aside.*) So, why does he want to leave? (*She looks at the four frozen folks. She singles out SIEGEL.*) Okay, Bugsy, why do you want to leave? (*She touches SIEGEL and says...*) Las Vegas. (*SIEGEL comes to life.*)

SIEGEL: If I don't get some assistance soon I'm not going to be a very pleasant person.

PAULA: I'm sorry to have kept you waiting, sir. Say, aren't you Bugsy Siegel?

SIEGEL: I allow people to call me that only once. I prefer... Benjamin or Ben Siegel.

PAULA: (*Referring to his looks.*) Warren Beatty didn't do you justice.

SIEGEL: When is the next flight to LA? I've got to get out of this hell hole.

PAULA: But I thought Las Vegas— (*HUGHES, SQUIRES, and STEWART, and along with SIEGEL, all demand tickets.*) Oh dammit... I can't say that. Stop. (*The four freeze.*) I thought... (*As she says...*) Las Vegas... (*She touches SIEGEL. He comes to life.*)... was a getaway for you and Virginia?

SIEGEL: Do you know Ginger?

PAULA: I know you call her Flamingo. And you're going to name a casino and hotel after her.

SIEGEL: Are you a fortune teller?

PAULA: It's all here in my notes. Somewhere.

SIEGEL: What the hell is this? Are you with the crime commission?

PAULA: Don't be silly. I'm a writer.

SIEGEL Just get off my back. I've not done anything... and believe me, the sooner I can get out of this town, the better. And I'm never coming back.

PAULA: Stop. (*SIEGEL freezes. She looks at STEWART.*) So, am I right about you? You have to be... (*She looks at her notes and reads...*) Helen Stewart, ten years married with four kids, and three months pregnant with the fifth, buried her husband and ran the ranch. She reigned as the first lady of Las... (*She catches herself almost says "Vegas."*)... the first lady of "stink city" till her death in 1926. (*An aside.*) And I bet she too wants to get out of... (*She touches STEWART and says...*) Las Vegas. (*STEWART comes to life.*)

STEWART: I'm sorry, Grace, there's nothing you can say that will keep me here.

PAULA: (*Playing as though she were Grace.*) You can't let Archibald's death be forgotten.

STEWART: What? Death? Who died?

PAULA: Your husband.

STEWART: If you're trying to be funny... you're not succeeding. You know Mark jilted me.

PAULA: Who? Did you say, Mark?

STEWART: I've always known he's loved you. Well, you can have him. I'm leaving town.

PAULA: Hold on. I don't think I want the two-timer either.

STEWART: He told me, he didn't want me anymore. He wanted you.

PAULA: Are we talking about the same person?

STEWART: I'm on the next stage out.

PAULA: Stop. (*STEWART freezes.*) They all want out... and they haven't done what it is they're noted for doing to help Las Vegas. That's what Mark means by... "fix it." This should be a breeze. Let's write some history. (*She pages through her notes and finally finds and reads.*) It all begins when, a young Archibald Stewart, eighteen, came from Scotland to the California gold fields. (*An aside.*) This better work. (*Back to the notes.*) By the time he turned thirty he owned a big freighting company. He relocated to Pioche, Nevada, during the silver-mining heyday. His ore hauling expanded into lumber milling and then he got into cattle ranching. At forty-five, in 1874, the mines began to decline... (*She touches SIEGEL and says...*)... but Stewart remained prosperous in... La Vegas.
(*SIEGEL comes to life, but he is now Archibald Stewart. He is waiting for someone to show up. He is impatient because the person is late.*)
SIEGEL/ARCHIBALD: (*To PAULA.*) Excuse me, do you have the time?
PAULA: I don't believe it.
SIEGEL/ARCHIBALD: The time, please.
PAULA: Archibald?
SIEGEL/ARCHIBALD: Do I know you?
PAULA: Twenty past three.
SIEGEL/ARCHIBALD: Dammit, he's late. (*PAULA half reads her notes and touches SQUIRES and says...*) Enter O. D. Gass, always out of money, but the owner of 400 head of cattle and an 800-acre... Las Vegas... ranch. (*SQUIRES comes to life, but he is now O. D. Gass.*)

SQUIRES/GASS: Archibald, I'm sorry I'm late.
SIEGEL/ARCHIBALD: Mr. Gass, I don't appreciate being kept waiting.
PAULA: This is great.
SQUIRES/GASS: A friend of mine needed some help.
PAULA: You're on, Helen. Make your entrance... your mark... (*An aside.*) No pun intended. (*She touches STEWART and says...*)... your mark on the history of Las Vegas.
STEWART: O. D., I really don't—
SQUIRES/GASS: Arch, I'd like for you to meet—
STEWART: No, O. D., it's too soon after Mark.
SQUIRES/GASS: (*An aside to STEWART.*) Are you going to help me or not? I need that loan.
SIEGEL/ARCHIBALD: Mr. Gass, I'm a busy man.
STEWART: All right, go ahead.
SQUIRES/GASS: Archibald, I'd like for you to meet...
PAULA: Stop. (*STEWART, SQUIRES, and SIEGEL freeze. PAULA touches SIEGEL and says...*) Your future wife. You got that? (*She removes her hand from SIEGEL.*) I hope so. Okay, let's continue with the making of... Las Vegas.

(*The three come to life as the characters PAULA has made them. But HUGHES also comes to life. He is himself.*)
SQUIRES/GASS: I'd like for you to meet...
SIEGEL/ARCHIBALD: My future wife.
SQUIRES/GASS: ...Helen... a...
HUGHES: What airline is this?
SQUIRES/GASS: (*To STEWART.*) What's your last name?
SIEGEL/ARCHIBALD: Will you marry me?

HUGHES: Damnit, I need to get to Ohio.
STEWART: I just met you.
PAULA: (*Referring to HUGHES.*) How the heck did you get here?
(*The next lines should overlap and build to mayhem.*)
SQUIRES/GASS: What about my loan?
SIEGEL/ARCHIBALD: Please marry me.
HUGHES: I'm getting angry.
STEWART: I want to leave. (*To SQUIRES.*) Will you get me out of here?
SIEGEL/ARCHIBALD: My future wife.
HUGHES: And you don't want to see me angry.
SQUIRES/GASS: (*To STEWARD.*) Please pacify him.
(*The four ad-lib and this builds until finally, PAULA yells...*)
PAULA: STOP! (*The four freeze. PAULA catches her breath. She touches STEWART.*) So, what is happening in your... Las Vegas? (*STEWART comes to life.*)
STEWART: He asked me to marry him.
PAULA: Not yet... Stop. (*STEWART freezes. She touches SIEGEL and SQUIRES and says...*) Gass was desperate. Stewart had insight. And together that gave birth to... Las Vegas.
(*SIEGEL and SQUIRES come to life. SIEGEL is Archibald and SQUIRES is Gass, once again.*)
SQUIRES/GASS: I need five thousand dollars or I'll lose my ranch.
SIEGEL/ARCHIBALD: Where's Helen?
SQUIRES/GASS: You're my last resort. Believe me, if I had another way, I would take it.

SIEGEL/ARCHIBALD: Thirty percent interest rate. Due in one year.
SQUIRES/GASS: Agreed. (*The two men shake hands.*)
PAULA: Stop. (*SIEGEL and SQUIRES freeze.*) Okay, now let's get you married. (*She touches STEWART and says...*) Forget Mark and see the future of... Las Vegas. (*STEWART comes to life.*)
STEWART: (*Saying "yes" at her marriage ceremony.*) I do.
PAULA: (*As she touches SIEGEL.*) Archie baby, meet your new wife and the first lady of... Las Vegas. (*SIEGEL comes to life.*)
SIEGEL/ARCHIBALD: Yes, I love you. And no, I don't believe the rumors.
SQUIRES/GASS: You stole my ranch!
SIEGEL/ARCHIBALD: Your year is up. The loan... plus interest... is due.
SQUIRES/GASS: An extension! Please!
PAULA: Give him nine months!
SQUIRES/GASS: Helen, please talk to him. Help me!
STEWART: He's my husband!
SIEGEL/ARCHIBALD: Times up!
SQUIRES/GASS: What?
PAULA: Your nine months are up!
SQUIRES/GASS: This isn't fair!
SIEGEL/ARCHIBALD: It's called foreclosure!
PAULA: STOP! (*SQUIRES, STEWART, and SIEGEL freeze.*) All right, Howard, we need you now. (*She refers to her notes.*) Enter Schuyler Henry, a ranch hand on the only other ranch in the area. (*She touches HUGHES and says*) Howard, be our Henry...

our history... your history! (*She pauses and says*) Las Vegas!
(*HUGHES comes to life. He is Schuyler Henry.*)
HUGHES/HENRY: (*To PAULA.*) Stewart cheated Gass out of his ranch.
PAULA: He gave him an extension. Gass couldn't pay!
HUGHES/HENRY: And his wife's not much better.
PAULA: Helen Stewart is a strong decent woman.
HUGHES/HENRY: He's old enough to be her father. And she's too much for that old man to handle. (*He talks to the frozen STEWART.*) I bet you're quite the playful kitten when daddy's out of town on business.
PAULA: Helen happens to be a friend of mine and I'd appreciate it if you'd not start such vicious rumors about her.
HUGHES/HENRY: A friend? I've never seen you around Las Vegas!
(*Because HUGHES said, "Las Vegas," all come to life. All are themselves and they all once again begin demanding a ticket.*)
PAULA: Oh my God... it happens if anyone says it. (*Pause.*) Stop! (*All four freeze.*) This will have to be carefully orchestrated! (*She reads her notes.*) Stewart, 48, (*She touches SIEGEL.*) warns Henry, 33, (*She touches HUGHES.*) to stop suggestively looking at his wife Helen, 29. (*She touches STEWART.*) Come on, gang... we need the railroad to come to... Las Vegas.
(*SIEGEL as Archibald, HUGHES as Henry, and STEWART as herself come to life.*)
SIEGEL/ARCHIBALD: I'll not stand for it any longer.

HUGHES/HENRY: I don't know what you're talking about.
PAULA: (*She yells out.*) By the way… you're all in a saloon.
(*Honky-tonk piano music begins to play.*)
HUGHES/HENRY: Hey, Pop, give me a whiskey.
(*SQUIRES comes to life and becomes a bartender. He pours a shot of whiskey.*)
PAULA: All right!
SIEGEL/ARCHIBALD: I'm warning you, Schuyler Henry… stop dragging my wife's name through the mud. And cease the suggestive sexual looks you give her each time you see her.
STEWART: Archibald… please! Let's just go home.
SIEGEL/ARCHIBALD: Do it again and it'll be the last act you ever do!
HUGHES/HENRY: You're crazy, old man. Leave me alone.
(*HUGHES moves to a different area.*)
PAULA: Fast forward to the business trip! (*All move quickly to new positions.*)
SIEGEL/ARCHIBALD: I won't be gone long.
STEWART: Why don't you sell the house in Pioche?
SIEGEL/ARCHIBALD: The lumber mill is so near.
STEWART: I don't like that house.
SIEGEL/ARCHIBALD: What's really bothering you?
STEWART: You're away from me more than you're home.
SIEGEL/ARCHIBALD: Talk to me, Helen!
STEWART: It's nothing! I'm fine!
SIEGEL/ARCHIBALD: Is it Schuyler Henry?
STEWART: It's really nothing.

SIEGEL/ARCHIBALD: For ten years now... each time you've told me "it's nothing," I know it's something!
STEWART: Will you be gone long?
PAULA: Oh for Christ's sake, tell him!
STEWART: I'm pregnant!
SIEGEL/ARCHIBALD: Honey, that's wonderful.
(*They embrace.*)
SQUIRES/BARTENDER: If nobody else wants a drink... I'm gonna close this place.
PAULA: I forgot about him.
SIEGEL/ARCHIBALD: A drink to celebrate?
STEWART: When are you leaving?
SIEGEL/ARCHIBALD: In the morning.
STEWART: Let's just go home and spend the night together.
(*SIEGEL and STEWART move to go. PAULA snaps her fingers and SIEGEL and STEWART freeze.*)
SQUIRES/BARTENDER: (*To PAULA.*) How about you pretty lady? Another drink?
PAULA: I beg your pardon?
SQUIRES/BARTENDER: Are you alone?
PAULA: I still haven't figured out how you came to life.
SQUIRES/BARTENDER: I'm hungry. When I close this place, I was going to grab me something to eat. Would you like to join me?
PAULA: I am famished!
HUGHES/HENRY: Hey, Pop... another whiskey!
SQUIRES/BARTENDER: A steak dinner.
PAULA: Is that all you men eat?

SQUIRES/BARTENDER: We can eat something else. How about Mexican?
PAULA: (*With a smile.*) No steaks are fine!
SQUIRES/BARTENDER: A candlelit table... with wine and steaks.
PAULA: Table steaks!
SQUIRES/BARTENDER: What did you say?
HUGHES/HENRY: I asked for another whiskey.
SQUIRES/BARTENDER: Please join me.
PAULA: I have to get the railroad here first.
SQUIRES/BARTENDER: What?
HUGHES/HENRY: Whiskey.
PAULA: Let me check on something. (*PAULA walks toward SIEGEL and STEWART.*)
HUGHES/HENRY: Goddammit, I want a drink.
SQUIRES/BARTENDER: We're closed, Schuyler!
PAULA: (*Over her shoulder to HUGHES.*) Cut it out, Howard.
HUGHES/HENRY: The name's Henry.
PAULA: You're playing the part great... but... STOP! (*HUGHES freezes.*)
SQUIRES/BARTENDER: I'm impressed! I've been trying to shut that fool up for years. How about that dinner?
PAULA: Stop! (*SQUIRES freezes. PAULA stares at SQUIRES.*) You're hot, Pop... you're hot! But I have to make sure! (*PAULA walks over to SIEGEL and STEWART.*) We're going to close. Another drink?
SIEGEL/ARCHIBALD: (*To STEWART.*) Honey?
STEWART: Do you?
PAULA: (*To herself.*) What am I doing? Get them out of the bar!

SIEGEL/ARCHIBALD: Do you want to go?
PAULA: Yes.
STEWART: If you want to!
PAULA: Home! You're at home. You've just made mad passionate love!
SIEGEL/ARCHIBALD: I don't think I could be a happier man. Another baby. I'll hurry home.
(*They kiss. PAULA touches them and says...*)
PAULA: Stop! (*SIEGEL and STEWART freeze.*) We're okay there. At least for now! (*She looks at SQUIRES.*) Did you say dinner? But first I better bone up on my Hoover Dam history. (*She plays her cassette tape. As she listens to the tape she acts out, ala Kabuki, what she hears.*)
TAPE: The 1,400-mile Colorado River has been digging canyons and valleys for nearly ten million years. But in 1905—
PAULA: (*Talks to tape.*) Boy, that was a busy year.
TAPE: —a wet winter and abnormally severe spring rains combined to wreak havoc. For nearly two years, engineers and farmers fought the water back into place. But the message was clear. The Colorado must be tamed.
PAULA: Dream ballet.
TAPE: Over the next fifteen years the U.S. Bureau of Reclamation narrowed the list of possible dam sites from seventy to two— Boulder and Black canyons in southern Nevada. It took another three years to negotiate an equitable water distribution among the affected states and Mexico.
PAULA: That could be very dramatic.

TAPE Another six years for Congress to pass the Boulder Canyon Project Act.

PAULA: (*Turns off the tape.*) Okay… that puts us at about… Time: 1928. Place: A small cafe. (*She puts her hand on SQUIRES.*) At rise, Paula and Charles "Pop" Squires are discovered sitting at a table in the small café, which is located on the outskirts of… Las Vegas. (*SQUIRES comes to life.*)

SQUIRES: I'm honored that you decided to join me for dinner.

PAULA: It sure took the Bureau of Reclamation long enough to narrow the list of possible dam sites. What was it? From seventy to two!

SQUIRES: How did we get here? I don't remember leaving the train depot.

PAULA: So, do you think Congress will choose Boulder Canyon?

SQUIRES: Have you seen a waitress?

PAULA: Why are you ignoring this DAM issue? (*She laughs at her pun.*)

SQUIRES: I think maybe this wasn't such a good idea. Maybe we should go back to the depot. I need to get out of this town.

PAULA: Why are you giving up? It's because of you that Boulder Canyon is still in the running.

SQUIRES: I thought I knew everyone involved with the project.

PAULA: I just recently got involved.

SQUIRES: It doesn't matter. I'm through with that folderol.

PAULA: You can't quit now. Siegel is betting on you and Hughes is banking on you.

SQUIRES: I haven't had the pleasure. Have you seen any waitresses?
PAULA: If we get the dam here, I'm sure you'll meet Bugsy. I'm not sure about Howard. When did you die?
SQUIRES: What are you rambling about?
PAULA: One more letter. Write one more letter to the Secretary of Commerce... ah... oh, damn, you know... what's his name? (*She looks in her notes.*)
SQUIRES: Herbert Hoover.
PAULA: Yeah, that's him! The President they named the dam after! Even though it's named for him because he was Secretary of Commerce not because he was President. Roosevelt was President when the Dam was completed. He dedicated it!
SQUIRES: And what crystal ball have you looked into?
PAULA: Now that you've mentioned it... I haven't seen a waitress! I'll go get one. (*PAULA gets up.*)
SQUIRES: Where are you going?
PAULA: Ah... ah! Oh just... Stop! (*SQUIRES freezes. PAULA runs to HUGHES, touches him and says-*) We need a waitress... a waiter! Come take our order. Las Vegas!

(*HUGHES come to life. He is a waiter, complete with French accent.*)

HUGHES/WAITER: May I take your order, Madame?
PAULA: Over there. (*PAULA runs to the table and sits. HUGHES walks to the table.*)
HUGHES/WAITER: May I take your order?
PAULA: (*To SQUIRES.*) What would you like?

(*HUGHES and PAULA look at SQUIRES. He doesn't move. He is still frozen.*)

HUGHES/WAITER: Is he all right?

(*PAULA realizes what is wrong. She laughs as she reaches across the table and touches SQUIRES.*)

PAULA: Oh stop it... please! He's rehearsing. He's an actor. He's in a play and he has to play dead. Very good, dear. It looks good. Come and see it. It opens tonight in... Las Vegas. (*SQUIRES comes to life.*) Look... I found a waiter.

HUGHES/WAITER: (*To SQUIRES.*) You were very good, sir. You had me convinced you were dead. What's the name of the play?

SQUIRES: (*To PAULA.*) Do you have any idea what this man is talking about?

PAULA: (*To HUGHES.*) It's called Table Stakes.

SQUIRES: A steak sounds good to me.

HUGHES/WAITER: And how would you like that cooked?

SQUIRES: Medium rare.

HUGHES/WAITER: And you, Madame?

PAULA: The same.

SQUIRES: Can you put a rush on that? I've got a train to catch!

HUGHES/WAITER: I thought your show opened tonight?

PAULA: (*To HUGHES.*) Thank you... that will be all! (*HUGHES moves to another area of the stage and walks in circles.*) There, now that we've ordered, I can't convince you to continue your campaigning for the dam? (*As HUGHES walks in circles, he mumbles to himself.*)

HUGHES/WAITER: (*Mumbling.*) Where do I go? Where? I don't know where to go!
(*PAULA sees HUGHES.*)
PAULA: Oh my God! (*To SQUIRES.*) Don't move. (*PAULA gets up.*)
SQUIRES: Let's just go back to the terminal.
PAULA: No... not yet!
SQUIRES: I'm going without you. (*SQUIRES stands. PAULA touches him and says...*)
PAULA: Stop! (*SQUIRES freezes. PAULA rushes to HUGHES.*) What's wrong?
HUGHES/WAITER: I can't find the steaks. I don't know where to go. Where are the steaks?
PAULA: We changed our minds.
HUGHES/WAITER: I'm sorry. This is my first day on the job.
PAULA: You were magnifique!
HUGHES/WAITER: Merci! By the way... your friend... he's a terrible actor. I know a little about acting. Have you ever heard of Jean Peters? You remind me of her!
PAULA: Stop! (*HUGHES freezes.*) Womanizer! (*She runs back to SQUIRES. She touches him and says...*) Dinner's over! The steaks were wonderful. You're stuffed! You couldn't eat another bite. You'll continue your battle to get the dam built at Boulder Canyon! Without the dam... Las Vegas— (*SQUIRES comes to life.*) —doesn't grow!
SQUIRES: I'm stuffed.
PAULA: You shouldn't have eaten half of mine too.
SQUIRES: Did I?
PAULA: You pig.

SQUIRES: I couldn't eat another bite.
  (*PAULA smiles. SQUIRES is saying everything she wants him to say.*)
PAULA: I'll be damned!
SQUIRES: Don't start in about that Goddamn dam!
PAULA: Why? What happened?
SQUIRES: I'm going back to the terminal. (*SQUIRES stands.*)
PAULA: Please! Sit down.
SQUIRES: Thank you for joining me for dinner.
PAULA: I'm sorry. Don't leave. (*SQUIRES walks out a door.*) Come back. (*PAULA walks through the door. SQUIRES and PAULA are now in 1928 Las Vegas. PAULA notices the change.*) No one is ever going to believe this! This must be what things look like in 1928. (*She yells to SQUIRES, who is still walking away.*) Please! Don't leave me… especially now!
SQUIRES: Go away!
PAULA: Where the hell are we? Where are you going?
SQUIRES: I don't know about you, but I'm going to get drunk! (*SQUIRES walks to HUGHES and speaks to him.*) Hi… give me a whiskey! (*HUGHES comes to life. He's a bartender.*)
HUGHES/BARTENDER: Charles… welcome home! Where have you been? What's it been… a year or more?
SQUIRES: Whiskey… please!
HUGHES/BARTENDER: Where's Vicki? Is the wedding still on?
SQUIRES: You've always talked too much!

HUGHES/BARTENDER: And what will the lady have?

PAULA: Truth?

HUGHES/BARTENDER: I don't know how to make that.

PAULA: You don't make it... you tell it!

SQUIRES: My whiskey, please!

PAULA: Are you running because your wedding is off?

SQUIRES: Go back to your ticket counter.

PAULA: Oh... stop! (*HUGHES freezes, but SQUIRES does not.*)

SQUIRES: I think you should... stop. I thought I liked you. I thought you could help me forget her. I guess I was wrong!

PAULA: Stop!

SQUIRES: Where is my whiskey?

PAULA: Stop! Stop!! STOP! (*SQUIRES finally freezes.*) I wonder why it took so long to work? (*She looks around. Then talks to SQUIRES.*) So, this is 1928? What happened that made you want to leave... Las Vegas!

(*The four come to life. HUGHES as the bartender, STEWART as Vicki, SIEGEL as Hoover, SQUIRES as himself, and PAULA as herself.*)

SQUIRES: I'd like to propose a toast! Set 'em up bartender. (*HUGHES/BARTENDER pours out five drinks.*)

SQUIRES: (*cont'd*) To our great country's finest Secretary of Commerce...

STEWART/VICKI: Herbert Clark Hoover!

SQUIRES: Thank you... Vicki, my love! (*SQUIRES tries to kiss STEWART/VICKI. She turns her head.*) To Mr. Hoover... may he choose Boulder Canyon as the site for the dam. (*All drink.*)
SIEGEL/HOOVER: Thank you, Mr. Squires... but you know the Congress will make that decision.
SQUIRES: Based on your recommendation, Mr. Hoover!
PAULA: The dam is the key to Las— (*She catches herself.*) —to this area's resurrection.
SIEGEL/HOOVER: Yes... Well, thank you for your hospitality during my stay. I'm off to inspect the other site. (*To STEWART.*) Coming, my dear?
SQUIRES: Vicki?
STEWART/VICKI: I'm sorry, dear.
   (*SIEGEL/HOOVER and STEWART/VICKI move to another area of the stage. PAULA snaps her fingers and they freeze.*)
SQUIRES: And I haven't seen her since!
PAULA: Is she still with him?
SQUIRES: She's his little Washington secret.
PAULA: You fought so long and hard. Don't make them rewrite the history books. Besides, I'd like to make you my leading man!
SQUIRES: Pardon?
PAULA: In my play.
SQUIRES: Who are you? All I know about you is you sell railway tickets and predict the future quite a bit.
PAULA: I write plays.
SQUIRES: Do I know any of them?

PAULA: I'm writing one now on the history of... Las Vegas.

(*Because PAULA has said, "Las Vegas," all switch characters. SIEGEL is Archibald, HUGHES is Henry, SQUIRES is Gass, and STEWART is herself.*)

SIEGEL/ARCHIBALD: (*To STEWART.*) Is what I hear true?

STEWART: Welcome home, Archibald. How's the house in Pioche?

SIEGEL/ARCHIBALD: I told him I'd kill him!

PAULA: Oh no... what's happening?

SQUIRES/GASS: Schuyler Henry propositioned Helen Stewart.

PAULA: (*To herself.*) How did we get here?

STEWART: Forget it... he was drunk!

SIEGEL/ARCHIBALD: He's a dead man. (*He gets a gun.*)

STEWART: Please, Archie, it was nothing.

SIEGEL/ARCHIBALD: (*Calling him out.*) Schuyler Henry. (*STEWART runs to PAULA.*)

STEWART: Can't you stop this?

SIEGEL/ARCHIBALD: Schuyler Henry... if you don't come out... I'm coming in.

PAULA: Believe me... it has to happen.

SIEGEL/ARCHIBALD: I'll count to three.

HUGHES/HENRY: Do you want another drink?

SIEGEL/ARCHIBALD: One!

STEWART: Nothing justifies violence.

SIEGEL/ARCHIBALD: Two!

SQUIRES/GASS: I think he's serious.

HUGHES/HENRY: Where's the bartender when you need one?

SIEGEL/ARCHIBALD: Three!
(*SIEGEL/ARCHIBALD walks toward HUGHES/HENRY. STEWART stops SIEGEL/ARCHIBALD's advance.*)
STEWART: Archibald—
HUGHES/HENRY: Hey, Stewart… four comes after three… if you're wondering!
SIEGEL/ARCHIBALD: Please apologize to my wife.
HUGHES/HENRY: I didn't know that tramp was married!
(*SIEGEL/ARCHIBALD pulls his gun. So does HUGHES/HENRY. Both guns fire. STEWART screams. PAULA yells…*)
PAULA: Stop! (*All four freeze. PAULA measures the distance the bullets have traveled. She ponders…*) Helen's right. Nothing justifies violence. (*She looks at the four characters and knows that she can't change fate.*) Oh… just do it! LAS VEGAS! (*All four come to life.*)
SIEGEL/ARCHIBALD: I just shot you.
HUGHES/HENRY: You missed.
SIEGEL/ARCHIBALD: So did you.
HUGHES/HENRY: Not this time.
(*HUGHES/HENRY shots SIEGEL/ARCHIBALD. STEWART runs to SIEGEL/ARCHIBALD.*)
STEWART: He's dead.
PAULA: I'm sorry!
HUGHES/HENRY: Hey, Mr. Gass, maybe you can get your ranch back now!
STEWART: The stupid fool.
PAULA: I'm sure you're proud! He died sticking up for your honor!
STEWART: I've got to get out of here.

PAULA: Now you can revenge his death by... doing what?
STEWART: When can the next stage get me out of here?
SQUIRES/GASS: Helen Stewart, your husband stole my ranch from me. I want it back.
PAULA: Uh oh! I'm losing control.
STEWART: Take your ranch! I don't want it anymore.
PAULA: No! You can't do that!
HUGHES/HENRY: Helen Stewart, you— (*HUGHES/HENRY makes sarcastic kissing sounds.*)
STEWART: Leave me alone. All of you! I just want to get out of this town.
HUGHES/HENRY: —you harlot!
PAULA: Helen... your foresight...
SQUIRES/GASS: Take your children and get out of here.
HUGHES/HENRY: You're not wanted.
STEWART: Daddy! I want my daddy!
PAULA: Stop! For crying out loud... stop! Just stop! (*All four freeze. PAULA speaks to STEWART.*) Helen, what are you doing? Your husband is dead. You're supposed to be strong now. (*She looks through her notes.*) You can't wimp out. We're all counting on you. I thought you were the first lady of Las Vegas—
(*Because PAULA said LV all four come to life. HUGHES as himself, STEWART as Moe Dalitz, and SQUIRES as MARK, a HUGHES flunky. SIEGEL remains himself... lost.*)
HUGHES: Mark!
PAULA: Where? Is Mark here?

SQUIRES/MARK: Yes, Mr. Hughes?
HUGHES: He said what?
PAULA: Where are we?
STEWART/DALITZ: I said, I want you and your Goddamn entourage out of my hotel!
HUGHES: He said that... did he?
SQUIRES/MARK: Yes.
PAULA: I can't let Helen leave Las Vegas.
   (*All switch characters. STEWART is herself, SQUIRES is Gass, and HUGHES is Schuyler Henry. SIEGEL falls dead to the floor as Archibald Stewart.*)
SQUIRES/GASS: Helen Stewart, I want my ranch back.
STEWART: You can have it.
PAULA: Helen, you don't want to do that!
STEWART: Just give me enough money to get me and my children back east.
HUGHES/HENRY: The sooner you get out... the sooner we can clean up Las Vegas.
   (*ALL switch characters. STEWART is Moe Dalitz, HUGHES is himself, and SQUIRES is Hughes' flunky. SIEGEL stands as himself.*)
SQUIRES/MARK: What's your response, Mr. Hughes?
STEWART/DALITZ: Tell him he doesn't have enough money to buy my hotel.
PAULA: Stop. (*ALL freeze. PAULA looks at them.*) Where are we? (*To HUGHES.*) I know you're Hughes and... (*To SQUIRES.*)... you're Mark! Some sort of flunky to Hughes. (*To STEWART.*) But who are you? (*PAULA snaps her fingers. STEWART comes to life as Moe Dalitz.*)

STEWART/DALITZ: The nerve of that asshole, Hughes! And his wife is a thief.
PAULA: Excuse me.
STEWART/DALITZ: I'll run him out of Las Vegas.
(*ALL switch characters. SIEGEL is himself, STEWART is Esta, and SQUIRES is Meyer Lansky.*)
SIEGEL: I swear to you, Esta... my affair with Virginia is over.
STEWART/ESTA: That's not what Meyer tells me.
SQUIRES/LANSKY: I hear she wants you to build a casino in the desert.
SIEGEL: Dumb! I'll never do it. A casino in Las Vegas.
(*ALL switch characters. SQUIRES is himself, STEWART is Vicki, HUGHES is the bartender, and SIEGEL is Hoover.*)
SQUIRES: The hell with you, Vicki... and the entire Boulder Dam project.
PAULA: Everyone stop! (*ALL freeze.*) I'm the controlling playwright here. We'll do things my way. (*To STEWART.*) Now, who the hell were you back in the Hughes scene? (*She touches STEWART. STEWART comes to life as Moe Dalitz.*)
STEWART/DALITZ: Who the hell are you?
PAULA: I asked you first.
STEWART/DALITZ: Are you one of my girls? Why aren't you working?
PAULA: Is this twenty questions?
STEWART/DALITZ: Oh Christ, another one of Hughes's flunkies! Tell the rich weirdo he's worn out his welcome at my DI.
PAULA: Thank you... stop! (*STEWART freezes.*) The DI— The Desert Inn. (*She skims her notes.*) Opened 1950... initial investment $1.5 million... three years

later... Moe Dalitz... invested $3 million... (*She looks at STEWART.*) So, you're Moe Dalitz... owner of the DI. We must be back in 1967... March... when Hughes was about to buy the DI. But now he's refusing to do so. (*HUGHES comes to life.*)

HUGHES: I'm sorry Mr. Dalitz.

(*PAULA continues to talk and is unaware the characters are coming to life.*)

PAULA: And Bugsy hasn't built his Flamingo. (*SIEGEL comes to life.*)

SIEGEL: Don't call me that again.

HUGHES: We'll move from your hotel.

PAULA: Boulder Dam's not a sure thing. (*SQUIRES comes to life.*)

SIEGEL: Stop pressuring me...

SQUIRES: What a waste of one's life.

PAULA: Helen's not cooperating. (*STEWART comes to life.*)

STEWART: Mr. Gass you can have your ranch back.

PAULA: Maybe I have to do this in chronological order?

(*The phone rings. ALL turn on PAULA as though she were the character they were talking to. She now becomes aware of them.*)

STEWART: Gass, you can have the farm.

SIEGEL: Virginia, a casino in the desert is the dumbest thing I've ever heard of.

PAULA: Helen, you can't give up the... No, Bugsy... a casino in the desert will make you a—

HUGHES: Tell Mr. Dalitz politely to... (*He's thinking for the correct word.*)

PAULA: Well, it won't make you a millionaire...

SQUIRES: (*Referring to the phone.*) You better answer that Vicki.
HUGHES: ...to politely...
PAULA: ...but it will make the mob a ton of money.
STEWART: Why do I want to be a rancher?
SQUIRES: It's probably your boyfriend... Mr. Hoover.
HUGHES: Tell him my answer is...
STEWART: Answer me.
SQUIRES: (*Referring to the phone.*) Answer it!
SIEGEL: I have no answer.
HUGHES: ...my answer is... (*ALL turn to HUGHES.*) Please answer that damn phone.
SQUIRES: No dam!
PAULA: (*Answers the phone.*) This better be good!
(*MARK appears in a LIGHT special, on the phone.*)
MARK: What is taking so long?
PAULA: Mark!
HUGHES: We've been here long enough.
PAULA: (*To HUGHES.*) It's not been that long.
MARK: An hour?
PAULA: Not you, Mark. I was talking to—
HUGHES: We're moving to Ohio.
MARK: Haven't you got rid of them yet?
PAULA: (*To HUGHES.*) Not yet... don't move yet!
MARK: What?
STEWART: I'm moving east.
MARK: Do you love me?
PAULA: (*To STEWART.*) No!
(*MARK hears the "no." Remember he's on the phone.*)
MARK: You don't love me?
SQUIRES: Without love... I don't care where I go.
PAULA: You can't leave me.

MARK: I don't want to leave you... I want to get to you.
HUGHES: We're moving everything to Columbus.
PAULA: Mark... I need some help... please try to get over here.
SIEGEL: Esta, I'm moving back to NYC.
PAULA: They're all leaving me.
MARK: I'm sorry I was an ass on your birthday.
PAULA: What did you say? (*ALL bombard her with demands. This all peaks... and she shouts—*) Intermission!!
END ACT ONE

ACT TWO

(*AT RISE: All are in the same positions they were in for the end of Act One.*)

PAULA: Now where were we? Las Vegas! (*All come to life and once again bombard her with demands.*) Stop! (*All freeze.*) We need to rewind just a bit more. (*All move backward.*) Let's try here! (*All stop.*)
MARK: I'm sorry I was an ass on your birthday.
PAULA: (*To the others.*) There did you hear that?
MARK: I promise you... when this is over... I'll take you out to where ever you want to go.
PAULA: Thank you, Mark, that's the kind of support and strength I need. (*PAULA hangs up the phone. The LIGHT goes out on MARK. She looks at her players and says...*) Now that's love. And with that I can do anything. Now, listen up and listen good. I'm the boss here. What I say goes. We have some history

to fix… and you have to help me fix it. Give up those thoughts of leaving. (*She touches STEWART.*) Now, tell me about yourself Moe Dalitz.
(*STEWART comes to life as Moe Dalitz.*)
STEWART/DALITZ: I move to town from Cleveland to run the DI.
PAULA: Big time bootlegger—
STEWART/DALITZ: That's me!
PAULA: Ran a string of illegal casinos in the Midwest.
STEWART/DALITZ: Good training for the DI.
PAULA: In 1967… sold the whole schmear to Howard Hughes for $13.2 million.
(*HUGHES comes to life.*)
HUGHES: I wouldn't give you a plug nickel for this dump.
STEWART/DALITZ: I wouldn't take all of your Mormon money for my hotel.
PAULA: It's your destiny, Howard.
HUGHES: Just get me to Columbus.
PAULA: I guess I do have to do this in chronological order.
HUGHES: I don't care how you do it… just get me there.
PAULA: Stop. (*STEWART and HUGHES freeze.*) Back to July… 1884. The death of Archibald Stewart. (*She touches SIEGEL.*) You're dead, Archie! (*She touches HUGHES.*) You're proud Schuyler Henry. (*She touches STEWART.*) You're strong Helen. (*She takes a deep breath and says…*) Las Vegas!
(*The three comes to life as the people PAULA made them. They move to the same positions they were in the previous*

scene when Archie was shot and he fell. STEWART runs to his side.)
STEWART: He's dead!
PAULA: I'm sorry.
STEWART: I want to get out of here! I hate this town!
PAULA: No… you're supposed to be strong. STOP! (*All freeze. PAULA pages through her notes. She reads various sections.*) Helen married her longtime foreman. (*An aside.*) No! (*Back to noes.*) She befriended the Paiutes… buried her husband and ran the ranch. Time off only to give birth to son—Archibald Junior. Her parents moved to town. She and her father speculated in real estate. (*An aside.*) That's it! (*She touches SQUIRES.*) Pop… be a father! Helen's father. (*She touches STEWART and says…*) Las Vegas.
(*SQUIRES comes to life as STEWART's daddy. STEWART comes to life as herself.*)
STEWART: Daddy! (*STEWART runs to SQUIRES/DADDY and embraces him.*)
SQUIRES/DADDY: My baby!
STEWART: Oh, Daddy… thank you for coming.
SQUIRES/DADDY: Have you buried him yet?
STEWART: Yesterday!
SQUIRES/DADDY: I got here as soon as I could.
STEWART: Just help me pack and get the kids and me out of this awful town.
PAULA: No!
SQUIRES/DADDY: Is this a friend of yours?
STEWART: More like a nuisance.

PAULA: Hi... I'm Paula! Speculation is the name of the game!
SQUIRES/DADDY: How do you do—
PAULA: Speculation... as in real estate.
SQUIRES/DADDY: —I'm Helen's father.
PAULA: The railroad... Salt Lake to LA... is coming through.
STEWART: She's crazy, daddy.
PAULA: Are you hungry?
SQUIRES/DADDY: I'm famished.
STEWART: Daddy!
PAULA: Steaks?
SQUIRES/DADDY: Medium rare!
STEWART: I'm going home to pack!
PAULA: Oh, chill, Helen... stop! (*STEWART freezes. She speaks to SQUIRES.*) I know a very cozy place. (*She points to the table they sat at before when they ate dinner earlier.*) Right over there. You go ahead. I'll join you in a sec... I've got to powder my nose. (*SQUIRES/DADDY sits at the table. PAULA moves to HUGHES.*) I need your help again, Howie! Put on your waiter face... (*She touches HUGHES.*) Las Vegas. (*HUGHES comes to life as the Waiter.*)
HUGHES/WAITER: Where are the steaks? I don't know where they are!
PAULA: Excuse me, sir. Could you take our order?
HUGHES/WAITER: Pardon m'oui... do you know where the steaks are?
PAULA: We haven't ordered them yet.
HUGHES/WAITER: This is all so strange to me. (*They are at the table. He recognizes SQUIRES.*) Oh

hello... it's the actor! How did your opening night go?

SQUIRES/DADDY: I beg your pardon?

PAULA: Two steaks... medium rare! Isn't that what we want?

HUGHES/WAITER: Would you care for anything to drink?

PAULA: Just the water rights please.

HUGHES/WAITER: That will be... two steaks... medium rare and the water rights.

PAULA: Yes... thank you! That'll be all. (*HUGHES/WAITER moves to another area of the stage and begins to walk in circles.*) Did you know that Archibald owns the rights to most of the water in this valley? And now that he's dead... your daughter owns them!

SQUIRES/DADDY: I should be with my daughter. (*SQUIRES/DADDY starts to leave.*)

PAULA: If you and your daughter were to buy some certain parcels of land... that I'd be happy to point out to you... you'd both become very rich people. (*SQUIRES starts to leave.*) Trust me! Please don't let your daughter leave this town.

SQUIRES/DADDY: She hates... Las Vegas.

(*Because he said LV... STEWART and SIEGEL come to life. SIEGEL is himself. STEWART is Esta, his wife. SQUIRES becomes Meyer Lansky and HUGHES becomes Clark Gable.*)

SQUIRES/LANSKY: Over here, Benny!

PAULA: Here we go again!

(*SIEGEL takes STEWART/ESTA by the arm and they walk to the table. HUGHES/GABLE moves to the table also.*)

SIEGEL: Meyer... you know my wife, Esta.
SQUIRES/LANSKY: A pleasure.
STEWART/ESTA: It's all mine... Mr. Lansky.
SQUIRES/LANSKY: And I'm sure you recognize Clark Gable?
SIEGEL: I'm a big fan.
PAULA: (*To herself.*) This is great.
HUGHES/GABLE: I'm intrigued! Meyer's told me so much about you, Bugsy.
(*SIEGEL catches his breath. STEWART/ESTA holds him back.*)
SIEGEL: That's not my name.
(*HUGHES/GABLE looks at SQUIRES/LANSKY.*)
SQUIRES/LANSKY: Benny... call him Benny!
(*SIEGEL looks at PAULA.*)
SIEGEL: I don't think I've had the pleasure.
SQUIRES/LANSKY: How rude of me. Please let me introduce Miss Virginia Hill.
PAULA: Oh God... now I'm an actor.
SQUIRES/LANSKY: Yes... she thinks she's an actress.
SIEGEL: I'm sure she's wonderful.
STEWART/ESTA: Benjamin, don't you have business to take care of?
SIEGEL: What was that? Did you say something? Dammit, Esta... don't do that! You know I don't like that!
SQUIRES/LANSKY: Benny... Benny... How's it going in... oh crap... what's the name of that hole in the desert? How's our interests going there?
SIEGEL: Please forgive me, Miss Hill.
SQUIRES/LANSKY: Vegas—
PAULA: No! Don't say it!

SQUIRES/LANSKY: Las Vegas.
(*All shift characters again. SQUIRES becomes STEWART's father, HUGHES becomes the waiter again, SIEGEL becomes William Clark, and STEWART is herself. We are back at the dinner with PAULA and STEWART's father. HUGHES is walking in circles once again.*)
SIEGEL/CLARK: (*To HUGHES.*) I'm looking for a Helen Stewart!
HUGHES/WAITER: I can't find the steaks.
SQUIRES/DADDY: (*To PAULA.*) Why are you doing this for me? For my daughter... for us?
PAULA: You remind me of a friend.
SIEGEL/CLARK: Excuse me... do you know a Helen Stewart?
SQUIRES/DADDY: That's my daughter's name.
SIEGEL/CLARK: Clark's the name. William Clark.
PAULA: (*To SQUIRES.*) Don't trust him!
HUGHES/WAITER: (*To SIEGEL.*) Will you be eating, sir? (*STEWART enters the scene.*)
STEWART: I've packed what I want. The children are waiting, Daddy.
SIEGEL/CLARK: Miss Stewart? What luck to find you. My railroad is prepared to pay you a handsome sum for your property near... ah...
PAULA: (*Checking her notes.*) Ah...
HUGHES/WAITER: (*To STEWART.*) I suppose you want to eat also?
PAULA: ...Jean!
SIEGEL/CLARK: That's correct. Jean, Nevada.
SQUIRES/DADDY: I'm sorry Mr. Clark... my daughter's husband has just died.
PAULA: (*To SIEGEL.*) How much?

SIEGEL/CLARK: Are you a relative?
STEWART: My husband didn't own any land out there.
SQUIRES/DADDY: Please leave us alone.
PAULA: Will you shut up.
STEWART: You're insane.
SIEGEL/CLARK: I'm sorry if I've bothered you.
PAULA: No, don't leave.
STEWART: Daddy… please.
HUGHES/WAITER: I promise I'll find them.
PAULA: STOP! (*ALL four freeze. She checks her notes.*) Helen and her father speculated in real estate along the imagined right-of-way of the rumored Salt Lake-Los Angeles railroad. Finally, in 1902, at forty-seven, she had amassed 1,800 acres to sell to William Clark for fifty-five thousand. (*She looks at the four.*) Got the picture? Las Vegas!
(*All four come to life as the same characters they were in the previous scene.*)
SIEGEL/CLARK: We are prepared to offer you thirty thousand for your land.
PAULA: Ask for more.
STEWART: Take it, Daddy… let's go!
SQUIRES/DADDY: Are you sure you want to sell?
PAULA: (*To SIEGEL.*) Seventy-five thousand!
SIEGEL/CLARK: Do you represent them?
PAULA: Yes.
STEWART: No.
PAULA: Shut up.
STEWART: I told you she was crazy.
PAULA: Helen… stop! (*STEWART freezes.*)
SQUIRES/DADDY: What have you done to her?

PAULA: You too! (*SQUIRES freezes.*)
HUGHES/WAITER: He's an actor. He's rehearsing being dead!
PAULA: Stop! (*HUGHES freezes.*)
SIEGEL/CLARK: I think you're all insane. The desert heat has fried your minds.
PAULA: Seventy-five thousand.
SIEGEL/CLARK: Thirty is all we can give!
PAULA: Eighty!
SIEGEL/CLARK: We'll run the railroad elsewhere.
PAULA: Go ahead.
SIEGEL/CLARK: Thirty-five thousand!
PAULA: We own the water rights.
SIEGEL/CLARK: Forty thousand!
PAULA: Mrs. Stewart's husband was just killed.
SIEGEL/CLARK: Forty-five!
PAULA: A widow with four kids and one in the oven.
SIEGEL/CLARK: Cut to the core… top dollar… fifty-five thousand!
PAULA: Seventy… and not a penny less!
SIEGEL/CLARK: All right!
PAULA: Step one complete in the making of… Las Vegas!

(*STEWART comes to life as herself, SQUIRES as her daddy, and HUGHES as the waiter.*)

HUGHES/WAITER: I apologize! It's never taken this long before! Perhaps you would like to try the chicken!
SQUIRES/DADDY: I think we have a deal… Mr. Clark!

(*SQUIRES/DADDY offers SIEGEL/CLARK his hand.*)

PAULA: You're gonna love it, Helen!

SIEGEL/CLARK: Fifty-five thousand... correct?
(*SIEGEL/CLARK shakes SQUIRES/DADDY's hand.*)
SQUIRES/DADDY: Yes.
PAULA: No!
SIEGEL/CLARK: It's been a pleasure doing business with you.
STEWART: Can we go, Daddy?
PAULA: Stop! (*All four freeze.*) Siegel... It doesn't matter who you play... you're still a manipulating son of a bitch! At least the railroad is here. (*To SQUIRES.*) Let's get Pop here to deal with Hoover and the dam and then... (*To SIEGEL.*) I can face you, Siegel. (*She looks at her notes and reads.*) Wide-open gambling was legalized in 1931. Divorce residency requirement reduced to a scandalous six weeks. Combined with unimpeded bootlegging, quasi-legal prostitution, prizefights, and no-wait marriages, Nevada became the only state in the union to spurn the moral backlash that followed the Roaring Twenties. Vice-starved visitors and hopeful dam workers flooded southern Nevada, thereby converting— (*She touches SQUIRES.*) Las Vegas— (*SQUIRES comes to life as himself.*) from a dusty railroad stopover into a spot on the gloomy horizon of the Great Depression— first step on the yellow brick road to becoming the ultimate Oz.
SQUIRES: That's beautiful. I do believe you are a writer.
PAULA: Thank you.
SQUIRES: A dreamer... but a poet!
PAULA: Actually I didn't write that.
SQUIRES: It sounds like you.

PAULA: It's my notes. From a book by— (*She checks her notes.*) Deke Castleman.
SQUIRES: So, what else does your book predict?
PAULA: Nothing... if the dam isn't build! (*She snaps her fingers... SQUIRES freezes. She continues to read her notes.*) The closest civilization... to the dam site... was at the sleepy railroad town of Las— (*She looks at SQUIRES and says...*) Forget Vicki. You'll find someone else. Get on with your life. (*She touches SQUIRES affectionately and say...*) Vegas. (*SQUIRES comes to life.*) Write another letter to Hoover. Get the dam here.
SQUIRES: I did that already. A site was chosen.
PAULA: They passed us by?
SQUIRES: (*He smiles.*) No, they're bringing in power from San Bernardino. Tracks are being laid... equipment will be shipped in!
PAULA: Step two... complete! (*PAULA starts to move on to face SIEGEL. SQUIRES wants to talk more. His love for her is increasing.*)
SQUIRES: What else do you know?
(*PAULA delivers this as a love poem. She's falling for SQUIRES too.*)
PAULA: The dam, when completed, will be sixty stories tall, six hundred feet thick at the base, and nearly a quarter mile long at the crest— the sum total of over three million cubic yards of concrete.
SQUIRES: You're sure?
PAULA: All because of you, Pop.
SQUIRES: What do you want from me?
PAULA: I think I might need your help.
SQUIRES: Anything.

PAULA: Do you know Benjamin Siegel?
SQUIRES: Slimy hood that appeared in town in the late thirties!
PAULA: We have to convince him to build a casino—
SQUIRES: The Flamingo.
PAULA: Of course you'd know.
SQUIRES: This town would be better off if that mobster would've never shown up!
PAULA: This town wouldn't be what it became without him!
SQUIRES: What did it become?
PAULA: We haven't got time.
SQUIRES: What do I do?
PAULA: May I ask you something?
SQUIRES: Anything.
PAULA: Do you still want to leave?
SQUIRES: Will you come with me?
PAULA: I think I'd like that... but I don't think that's possible!
SQUIRES: Siegel has to build his casino first?
PAULA: Charles, I... (*Pause.*)
SQUIRES: Me too.
PAULA: I know... thank you!
SQUIRES: What do you want me to do?
PAULA: Stop! (*SQUIRES freezes.*) I like you! Just trust me! (*She reads her notes.*) Benjamin Siegel, born Brooklyn, New York. By the time he was eighteen, he'd committed every heinous crime in the book: assault, burglary, bookmaking, bootlegging, extortion, hijacking, murder, mayhem, narcotics, numbers, rape, white slavery. (*An aside.*) I won't hold that against you! (*Back to her notes.*) Virginia

Hill, would-be actress, was his mistress with whom he had a love affair from hell with. She was known as "Mistress of the Mob." (*An aside.*) A match made only real in Hollywood. (*She talks to SIEGEL.*) So, why do you want to leave this fair city… the city of your dreams… your— (*She touches SIEGEL.*) Las Vegas!

(*SIEGEL comes to life.*)

SIEGEL: If I can't get a plane out of here… I know there's a train out.

PAULA: Thanks to Helen Stewart.

SIEGEL: Is this a history class or a ticket terminal?

PAULA: Why do you want to leave?

SIEGEL: The hell with this… I'll just steal a car.

PAULA: This isn't working.

SIEGEL: You're damn right it isn't. Get me the hell out of this place.

PAULA: I guess we have to go back to the beginning.

SIEGEL: Back what? Where?

PAULA: The night you met me.

SIEGEL: I've never seen you before.

PAULA: You were just about to ask me out.

SIEGEL: Dream on, doll. You're not my type.

PAULA: Stop! (*SIEGEL freezes.*) I didn't think you had enough class to have a type. (*She checks her notes.*) Back to Hollywood, the night you met Virginia… that's me… minus, of course, your wife, your boss, and Gable. (*She touches SIEGEL.*) Go for it you stud of… Las Vegas! (*SIEGEL comes to life.*)

SIEGEL: We're alone?

PAULA: I fixed it that way.

SIEGEL: Where are the others? Esta?

PAULA: Does it matter?
SIEGEL: I know another place... quiet and cozy!
PAULA: Are you insinuating that I leave this place with you?
SIEGEL: What?
PAULA: Are you asking me out?
SIEGEL: Well, I...
PAULA: Can't you say it?
SIEGEL: I can say it!
PAULA: Then say it!
SIEGEL: Yes.
PAULA: Yes, what?
SIEGEL: Yes... I'm asking you out.
PAULA: But I'm not your type.
SIEGEL: Who said that?
PAULA: You did.
SIEGEL: I would never have said that about you!
PAULA: Why?
SIEGEL: I don't believe this.
PAULA: Tell me why... Bugsy!
SIEGEL: Don't call me that.
PAULA: I don't go anywhere... until I hear why!
SIEGEL: Feisty! I like that.
PAULA: Dream on. (*PAULA starts to exit.*)
SIEGEL: I think you're beautiful. (*PAULA stops.*)
PAULA: What?
SIEGEL: You heard me.
PAULA: Say it louder.
SIEGEL: I don't do this for any woman.
PAULA: You'll do it for me! (*SIEGEL goes to his knees and repeats what he said louder.*)
SIEGEL: I think you're beautiful.

PAULA: Thank you. Now, show me this quiet, cozy place you know.
SIEGEL: My suite at the Hollywood Hotel. (*SIEGEL begins kissing her neck.*)
PAULA: Ah… won't your wife be there?
SIEGEL: I think I sent her back to New York. If I haven't… I will. (*PAULA is having a difficult time fending off SIEGEL.*)
PAULA: I'd rather you took me to Vegas.
SIEGEL: That hole! Why?
PAULA: I really believe your future is there.
SIEGEL: The only future I have is with you in room 321.
PAULA: I can't sleep with you there. It has to be in Vegas.
SIEGEL: Stop teasing.
PAULA: I'm serious.
SIEGEL: You're driving me crazy, Virginia. I need you. I want you.
PAULA: No!
SIEGEL: I must have you! Now!
PAULA: Stop! (*SIEGEL freezes.*) When are you men going to learn that when a woman says "No," she means it! (*An aside.*) Oh God, Paula… I can't believe you just said that. No one will ever believe this. (*SQUIRES comes to life.*)
SQUIRES: I will.
PAULA: What?
SQUIRES: I'll believe you.
PAULA: Only cause you— Wait a minute! How'd you do that?
SQUIRES: Get on with it!

PAULA: How'd you come to life?
SQUIRES: Did I? (*SQUIRES freezes.*)
PAULA: So you suggest I "get on with things?" (*SQUIRES moves slightly.*) Can you hear me? (*SQUIRES doesn't move.*) Okay, Bugsy! We're here. I loved the long, boring drive across the desert. We're in... (*She touches SIEGEL.*) Las Vegas! (*SIEGEL comes to life.*)
SIEGEL: We're here, Virginia. We made it.
PAULA: Have you ever thought about building a casino?
SIEGEL: We made it. I must have you.
PAULA: Gambling is legal in Nevada!
SIEGEL: Right now. I can't wait any longer. (*SIEGEL embraces PAULA. She fends him off.*)
PAULA: What are you doing?
SIEGEL: We're here. I must have you. You promised.
PAULA: Oh my God!
SIEGEL: I love it when you scream.
PAULA: Stop! (*SIEGEL freezes.*) I wish it were always that easy. (*She talks to SIEGEL.*) We've already made love. You were terrible. No, I better not do that to his ego. You were... (*An aside.*) No, I can't say it. Say it, Paula... say it! (*Back to SIEGEL.*) You weren't terrible... you were... terrific! (*She touches SIEGEL.*) Las... (*An aside.*) And I was the best you've ever had! (*She smiles.*) Las Vegas! (*SIEGEL comes to life.*)
SIEGEL: Holy Mother Mary... Saints be praised!
PAULA: I thought you were Jewish?
SIEGEL: I think I just saw the light!
PAULA: Do you love me?
SIEGEL: Let me show you again... just how much!

PAULA: That's all right! I believe you.
SIEGEL: Come on… one more time.
PAULA: Would you do anything for me?
SIEGEL: Name it!
PAULA: Build me a monument. Show me how much you love me. Make the Phoenix rise once again out of the desert sand.
SIEGEL: Build a monument here… in this dump!
PAULA: Where then? New York? So your wife can see it! Hollywood? So Lansky will know our business! This is our town, baby. Our special place. Our hideaway.
SIEGEL: I'd kill for you.
PAULA: No… you don't have to do that.
SIEGEL: Who do you want dead?
PAULA: I want a casino. And we mix sex with gambling. Provide easy sex to seduce, service, and satisfy the suckers.
SIEGEL: I need you, Virginia.
PAULA: At the Flamingo a lucky man could spend every night with a different lady.
SIEGEL: I'll do anything for you.
PAULA: Divorce Esta! Build me my monument!
SIEGEL: It should have separate modular wings, accessible without ever having to pass through a lobby or a main entrance.
PAULA: Now you're turning me on… you big, hot lady's man!
SIEGEL: And dress it up with lots of girls.
PAULA: Everywhere.
SIEGEL: Young and pretty!
PAULA: Suggestively attired.

SIEGEL: Everywhere! Coat-check girls.
PAULA: Hatcheck girls.
SIEGEL: Cigarette girls.
PAULA: Shills! Escorts! Loungers! Showgirls!
SIEGEL: And lots of barely clad cocktail waitresses.
PAULA: Gambling and sex—
SIEGEL: An accessory to the world's most sophisticated, most flattering larceny.
PAULA: Do it for me!
SIEGEL: God, you excite me. Make love to me!
PAULA: My monument!
SIEGEL: It's a nice dream, Flamingo… but how do we afford it?
PAULA: Ask Meyer. Call Mr. Lansky.
SIEGEL: Touch me.
PAULA: Just a second.
SIEGEL: Feel how hard I am for you.
PAULA: Pick up a phone.
SIEGEL: I love you, Virginia.
PAULA: Stop! (*SIEGEL freezes. PAULA touches SQUIRES.*) Don't let me down, Pop! Please become Meyer Lansky. The mob will give Bugsy the bankroll to build his beginning in… (*She touches SIEGEL and SQUIRES.*) Las Vegas!

(*SQUIRES comes to life. He answers a phone that is ringing. He is Meyer Lansky.*)
SQUIRES/LANSKY: Hello.

(*SIEGEL comes to life and talks on a phone to SQUIRES/LANSKY.*)
SIEGEL: Did I wake you, Meyer?
SQUIRES/LANSKY: Who the fuck is this?
SIEGEL: I'm gonna make you a bundle of money!

SQUIRES/LANSKY: Siegel, are you still screwing that slut?
SIEGEL: How would you like to invest in a casino?
SQUIRES/LANSKY: She's not that good.
PAULA: You don't have to play the part that well.
SIEGEL: A first-class casino for the highest-class clientele.
SQUIRES/LANSKY: That woman's made you lose your mind completely.
PAULA: Just give him what he wants.
SQUIRES/LANSKY: How much do you need?
SIEGEL: Only three million.
PAULA: He'll need six!
SQUIRES/LANSKY: This better work, Benny!
SIEGEL: Thank you, sir.

(*They both hang up their phones. SIEGEL turns to PAULA. SQUIRES freezes.*)

PAULA: Well, what did he say?
SIEGEL: Get me the number of the Del Webb Company. Honey, I'm about to put your name in lights. Give me a hug! (*SIEGEL advances on PAULA.*)
PAULA: Stop! (*SIEGEL freezes.*) Goodbye! (*She reads her notes.*) Construction began in January. The Flamingo opened its doors the day after Christmas, 1946. (*She looks at HUGHES.*) So, now we move on to your wacky-world! (*The phone rings. PAULA looks at it.*) Screw you, Mark… I'm doing just fine. (*PAULA checks her notes. The phone continues to ring. She answers it.*) What do you want? (*She realizes it's not Mark.*) I'm sorry… what did you say? (*STEWART comes to life. She is on the phone. She is Esta Siegel.*)

STEWART/ESTA: May I speak with Benjamin?
PAULA: What do you want?
STEWART/ESTA: Is this Virginia?
PAULA: You've got the wrong number!
STEWART/ESTA: I've known about you two for years.
PAULA: Lady, I don't know what you're talking about. But I got a bigger problem than you right now to—
STEWART/ESTA: Put Benjamin on the phone!
PAULA: Oh my God... is this Esta?
STEWART/ESTA: May I speak to my husband?
PAULA: Does he let you call him Bugsy?
STEWART/ESTA: Please! Haven't you caused enough pain?
PAULA: I'm not who you think I am.
STEWART/ESTA: Spare me! Please put my husband on the phone!
PAULA: I truly am sorry... (*Pause... no response from STEWART/ESTA.*) I'll get him. (*She talks to SIEGEL.*) You've been caught, big boy! (*An aside.*) No, I shouldn't say that! Don't want to feed his ego! (*Again to SIEGEL.*) You've been caught with your pants down in... (*She touches SIEGEL.*) Las Vegas! (*SIEGEL comes to life.*)
SIEGEL: Virginia, my Flamingo... I think it's time for you to take another trip to Switzerland.
PAULA: Telephone, Bugsy!
SIEGEL: If anyone knew I let you call me that... Oh, never mind, my love... Forget it!
PAULA: (*She shakes the phone in her hand.*) This is for you.

SIEGEL: If it's Lansky, tell him I'm not here.
PAULA: It's Esta.
SIEGEL: Who?
PAULA: Your wife.
SIEGEL: What does she want?
PAULA: Don't ask me... (*She gives the phone to SIEGEL.*) ask her!
SIEGEL: Hello, Esta, honey!
STEWART/ESTA: Benjamin...
SIEGEL: Yes, my love.
STEWART/ESTA: I'm tired of it all.
PAULA: All right, Esta!
SIEGEL: I'll come to New York soon.
STEWART/ESTA: I'm not in New York. I'm in LA.
SIEGEL: That's better.
STEWART/ESTA: I want a divorce!
PAULA: Right on, sister!
SIEGEL: Esta, don't do anything on the spur of the moment.
STEWART/ESTA: Goodbye! (*STEWART/ESTA hangs up the phone and freezes.*)
SIEGEL: Esta? Hello? (*SIEGEL slams the phone down.*) Goddamn phone company! They have a monopoly! (*He moves to PAULA.*) Can I get a ticket out of the hole!
PAULA: What?
SIEGEL: A ticket... I need a ticket! I really have to get out of here!
PAULA: Oh no!
SIEGEL: Get me out of Las Vegas!
PAULA: Don't say that!

(*Because SIEGEL said LV... all come to life. HUGHES as himself, STEWART as Moe Dalitz, SQUIRES as Mark, HUGHES'S flunky.*)
SQUIRES/MARK: Are you the manager?
PAULA: Where are we, Pop?
STEWART/DALITZ: I'm Moe Dalitz.
PAULA: I know that name!
SQUIRES/MARK: I asked to see the manager.
HUGHES: Let's go to the Flamingo!
STEWART/DALITZ: I'm the owner.
PAULA: All right... of the DI... 1966-67! (*HUGHES mistakes PAULA as Jean Peters.*)
HUGHES: (*To SQUIRES.*) What is she doing her?
SQUIRES/MARK: I'm sorry, Mr. Hughes.
HUGHES: Jean.
SQUIRES/MARK: That's not Miss Peters.
HUGHES: Looks like her. Give her a thousand dollars and tell her to come up to our floor.
PAULA: Stop! (*All four freeze. PAULA reads from her notes.*) Jean Peters. Would be actress... under contract to Fox! Born in Ohio. Beauty queen at Ohio State but still just a small-town farm girl. Married Hughes... (*An aside.*) Why the hell would he marry her... when he could have had anyone? Hepburn... Harlowe! (*She talks to HUGHES.*) You were about to embark on the most robust buying spree in Nevada history. What made you change your mind? Well, let's find out together! You think I look like Jean... I'm kinda enjoying this acting... I'm your wife Jean Peters and you are yourself. The year is March 1967. We're in your newly decorated penthouse at the Desert Inn in... (*To the others.*)

You three can sit this one out. (*STEWART, SIEGEL, and SQUIRES move and sit. PAULA touches HUGHES.*) Las Vegas! (*HUGHES comes to life. He is setting up a table for a poker game.*)

HUGHES: I don't want to hear another word about such a foul act.

PAULA: (*To herself.*) Oh boy... right in the middle of... what's he talking about?

HUGHES: Go get dressed... you know I have the game tonight.

(*PAULA attempts to figure out what HUGHES is talking about.*)

PAULA: Why is it a... foul act?

HUGHES: I've told you a thousand times my feelings on the subject.

PAULA: I forgot.

HUGHES: Are you going to change? I hope you're not going to wear that.

PAULA: I don't think it's a foul act!

HUGHES: That's obvious!

PAULA: What is?

HUGHES: That you feel that way.

PAULA: How do I feel... dammit?

HUGHES: I don't want to discuss this anymore.

PAULA: Well, I do! (*HUGHES continues to set the table. He does not respond.*) Do your other woman think it's a foul act?

(*HUGHES gives her a look, but decides to ignore her comment.*)

HUGHES: I don't think you want our guests to see you dressed like that.

PAULA: How can a man who has invested as much money in sex as you have find anything foul?
HUGHES: You've changed so much, Jean.
PAULA: Well, I'm doing the best I can.
HUGHES: Do you know why I married you? Of course you do... I've told you so many times.
PAULA: Tell me again. You know how much I love to hear it!
HUGHES: You were so real. So true... honest! You radiated the purity and innocence of the Midwest. You didn't belong in Hollywood. I hated your involvement in that sick business. (*He kisses her.*) Please don't do this! Don't even think of doing it! You know how much I want an heir!
PAULA: Abortion!
HUGHES: Such a foul act.
PAULA: You think she's... I'm... going to have abortion?
HUGHES: Don't make fun of me.
PAULA: You're supposed to be buying the DI. It's a woman's right.
HUGHES: My father always made fun of me. Always made demands on me. Yes, he gave me the money... but I think I've proved myself.
PAULA: Yes, you've proved yourself. (*She kisses him on the cheek.*) Now, have you ever thought about owning half the casinos on the Strip? Changing the image of... Las Vegas?
(*STEWART, SIEGEL, and SQUIRES stand. PAULA yells at them.*) Not yet! Sit down! Stop!
(*The three sit again and freeze.*) There's too much sex in... this town!

HUGHES: Do you really think I've proved myself?
PAULA: Buy Las... (*She catches herself.*) Buy the Meadows. Turn it into... the Midwest. I love Ohio.
HUGHES: Promise me you won't do it.
PAULA: Turn this city around.
HUGHES: Will you promise me?
PAULA: What? Promise you what?
HUGHES: Please have the child.
PAULA: You really want a baby?
HUGHES: I hope it's a girl.
PAULA: Do you promise me?
HUGHES: Anything for an heir.
PAULA: Start with buying the Desert Inn.
HUGHES: I'm not interested in Hotels.
PAULA: Promise me.
HUGHES: Do you?
PAULA: My word of honor as a writer!
HUGHES: I love spring. I love this town in the spring. I love you. I love... Las Vegas!

(*The three come to life. STEWART as Moe Dalitz, SQUIRES is Mark, and SIEGEL is just a big spender/gambler. A knock is heard.*)

SQUIRES/MARK: The guests have arrived. Should I let them in?
PAULA: The door's wide open... let 'em in!
HUGHES: Thank you, Mark. (*To PAULA.*) I'll cut the game short.
PAULA: Thanks, dear!
STEWART/DALITZ: Hughes, I like what you've done to these penthouses.
HUGHES: Thank you, Moe. I like the way I'm treated here at the Inn.

STEWART/DALITZ: Let me introduce you to Mr. Seagul. A Scottish gentleman from New York who spends a lot of time here with us!
HUGHES: Related to Bugsy?
SIEGEL/SEAGUL: (*Laughing.*) Please... no... don't call me that! Not in this town. Please! (*He spells his name.*) S-E-A-G-U-L. Like the bird.
HUGHES: You both know Mark... And this is my wife... Jean.
PAULA: I'm sorry I didn't change.
STEWART/DALITZ: Ready to lose some cash HH?
HUGHES: Moe, you know I love stealing your mob money. (*The phone rings.*)
PAULA: If it's Mark... tell him to get over her! (*She smiles at SQUIRES/MARK.*) Just kidding... Mark! (*SQUIRES answers the phone.*)
SQUIRES/MARK: Hello. (*He listens for a bit and then the phone up.*) Meyer Lansky sends his regrets. He's in Havana... something to do with the Flamingo!
STEWART/DALITZ: We can't play without a fifth!
SIEGEL/SEAGUL: You promised me a game, Moe!
HUGHES: We can play with four.
SIEGEL/SEAGUL: Mr. Hughes, we're not playing Old Maid!
HUGHES: I'm sorry, Moe... maybe we shouldn't play tonight.
SIEGEL/SEAGUL: Maybe I should take my action to the Flamingo?
STEWART/DALITZ: Mr. Seagul, you don't want anything to do with that place.
SQUIRES/MARK: Perhaps Miss Peters could join us?
HUGHES: Not my wife!

PAULA: I don't know how to play poker.
SIEGEL/SEAGUL: Then by all means… please join us.
PAULA: Well, I can play a little… Mark has been trying to teach me.
(HUGHES looks to SQUIRES/MARK.)
SQUIRES/MARK: I don't know what she's talking about, sir.
PAULA: Oops… not this Mark! It was another Mark. Besides, I wouldn't know what to do.
SQUIRES/MARK: I'll help you. (SQUIRES/MARK smiles at PAULA. HUGHES looks at them.) If that's all right with you Mr. Hughes?
STEWART/DALITZ: We do need a fifth, Hughes!
HUGHES: (To PAULA.) Do you really want to?
PAULA: I'll probably lose all your money.
HUGHES: I think that would be hard to do, dear. (They all sit at the table. HUGHES passes the cards to SIEGEL/SEAGUL.) The deal is to our guest!
SIEGEL/SEAGUL: Table stakes?
PAULA: I'll take mine medium rare! (They all look at PAULA.)
STEWART/DALITZ: Unlimited! The game of your choice.
SIEGEL/SEAGUL: Five-card stud!
PAULA: Oh… it sounds sexy! (They all look at PAULA. SIEGEL/SEAGUL deals the cards. They all look at their cards.) What do I do now?
HUGHES: Shut up!
SQUIRES/MARK: You'll get three more cards.
(PAULA shows SQUIRES/MARK her cards.)
PAULA: Is this any good?

SIEGEL/SEAGUL: I think maybe the Flamingo has my name on it.

STEWART/DALITZ: Jean dear, the proper etiquette in poker is to keep your cards to yourself.

PAULA: Sorry. I'm sorry. If Mark were here, he could play with you. He knows poker.

SQUIRES/MARK: But I am here.

PAULA: I mean my boyfriend.

HUGHES: Excuse me?

PAULA; I mean my friend... ah... Helen... ah... her father! He's a gambler!

HUGHES: Jean?

PAULA: He invested in water and the railroad. And it paid off.

SIEGEL/SEAGUL: Are we going to play poker... or talk about old friends?

PAULA: Right on! (*The doorbell rings.*)

HUGHES: What was that?

STEWART/DALITZ: These Penthouses don't have doorbells. This evening is getting very bizarre. (*The doorbell rings again.*)

HUGHES: Mark, go see who it is.

(*SQUIRES/MARK moves to the door. At the same time MARK enters.*)

MARK: Paula, are you all right?

HUGHES: Who the hell is that?

PAULA: Mark?

SQUIRES/MARK: Yes!

MARK: What is going on?

HUGHES: Mark, get rid of him.

MARK: Paula, I don't know how I got here.

SQUIRES/MARK: Excuse me, sir...

MARK: Paula, is this some kind of theatre trick?
HUGHES: Who the hell is Paula?
SQUIRES/MARK: Excuse me… you'll have to leave…
MARK: Are you all right dear?
SQUIRES/MARK: … Mr. Hughes's penthouse.
  (*MARK is holding PAULA.*)
HUGHES: Jean! What is the meaning of this?
STEWART/DALITZ: How did you get up here? I'll have security's ass for this.
MARK: (*To PAULA.*) I love you.
HUGHES: Do you know this man?
SIEGEL/SEAGUL: Are we going to play poker or matchmaker?
MARK: Tell these jerks to get out of here.
HUGHES: Mark, get rid of him. (*SQUIRES/MARK moves toward MARK.*)
SQUIRES/MARK: I'm afraid I'm going to have to ask you to leave.
MARK: You've done your duty… now back off.
SQUIRES/MARK: You leave me no alternative.
  (*SQUIRES/MARK grabs MARK. A fight ensues. SQUIRES/MARK gets the upper hand. It looks like he is going to hurt MARK.*)
PAULA: Pop, don't hurt him. (*SQUIRES/MARK hesitates when he hears "POP." He releases MARK. PAULA runs to MARK.*) Are you hurt?
HUGHES: (*To SQUIRES/MARK.*) What are you doing? Get him out of here.
SQUIRES/MARK: I'm sorry, sir… I think I love her.
HUGHES: You love my wife?
SQUIRES/MARK: Yes.
MARK: You're married?

PAULA: It's not what you think.
SQUIRES/MARK: I've loved you for years.
HUGHES: You're fired.
SIEGEL/SEAGUL: I've had enough of this.
PAULA: Oh the hell with this. So have I! (*They all look at her.*) With all the games I'm playing now... why am I playing this silly one?
HUGHES: Jean, please!
PAULA: Shut up, Howard! (*HUGHES freezes.*)
SIEGEL/SEAGUL: I'm going to the Flamingo.
PAULA: You shut up too, Bugsy! (*SIEGEL freezes.*)
STEWART/DALITZ: I'm sorry, Mr. Seagul. Have you ever met Judy Garland?
PAULA: And you too, Moe! (*STEWART freezes.*)
MARK: Paula, be careful! These people are weird.
PAULA: They're only who I want them to be.
MARK: What about your future husband?
SQUIRES/MARK: How about that steak?
(*MARK points to SQUIRES. PAULA looks at him and snaps her fingers. SQUIRES freezes.*)
MARK: How did you do that?
PAULA: All good playwrights are in control of their characters.
MARK: I don't think I like this theatre shit.
PAULA: Mark, you should shut up too. (*MARK freezes. But he can still talk.*)
MARK: What have you done?
PAULA: I'm not sure why it didn't work all the way—
MARK: You're a witch!
PAULA: If you don't shut that big mouth of yours... I'll tape it shut.

MARK: Paula, you're talking to your Mark. I know you. You're not strong enough to do something like that.
(PAULA *doesn't say a thing. She moves to her desk. She gets a roll of duct tape from a drawer and moves to* MARK. *He protests as she tapes his mouth shut. She then talks to the frozen four.*)
PAULA: I'm not stupid. And Howard… from what I read in my notes neither was Jean. No, that was Virginia! I think! (*She reads her notes.*) Yes. She had an IQ of a hundred and sixty. It doesn't matter… the point is… Jean… Virginia… me… we're all… we're woman. Intelligent… strong… and capable of taking control. (*A new thought.*) Scene: Hughes's DI penthouse. Poker night. I just beat all you high-rolling men at your game. I'm a rich woman now. How rich? (*Beat.*) A hundred and fifty million. That's what I got from you when I divorced you. (*To all of them.*) Twist the screw! (*To* SIEGEL.) You… you, pompous jerk. You lost a mill! No… two! (*To* STEWART.) Only cause you're a woman playing a fool… Moe, you only lost a half a mill. And Howie gets to live here rent free in the DI for as long as he likes! I hope he buys the damn place. But I've learned I can't push the future. (*To* SQUIRES.) Pop, I'll let you off the hook! (*To all of them.*) You've all done what you had to do. The railroad. The Dam. And the Flamingo. Maybe we don't need you Howard? Are we back to normal? Here in… Las Vegas! (*The five come to life.*)
MARK: (*As he rips the tape off his mouth.*) You're crazy, Paula.

SIEGEL/SEAGUL: She must have cheated. I owe her two million dollars!! I demand satisfaction, Dalitz!
STEWART/DALITZ: Where did she go, Hughes?
HUGHES: Oh my God... my heir. She left to do it!
Mark, catch her! She can't leave... Las Vegas.

(*They all switch characters to people they have played before. SQUIRES pulls out a gun and fingers it. The action should start to get frantic.*)

SQUIRES/LANSKY: Where's Benny, Esta?
STEWART/ESTA: Can I see him first, Mr. Lansky?
SQUIRES/LANSKY: I'll give you a day.
STEWART/ESTA: God bless you.
MARK: Have they gone crazy?
SIEGEL: Esta, please! No divorce!
STEWART/ESTA: Is Virginia with you?
HUGHES/WAITER: May I take your order?
SIEGEL: I'll get rid of her.
HUGHES/WAITER: I'm sorry we're out of steaks.

(*SIEGEL pulls out a gun.*)

SIEGEL: Take a hike, pal!
HUGHES/WAITER: I'll get that right away, sir!
PAULA: I've lost control.
SIEGEL: I love you, Esta.
MARK: We better leave.
STEWART/ESTA: I've always hated... Las Vegas!

(*They all switch characters. HUGHES pulls out a gun as Schuyler Henry.*)

HUGHES/HENRY: Hey, Stewart, four comes after three... if you're wondering?
SIEGEL/STEWART: Please apologize to my wife.
MARK: What's going on?

HUGHES/HENRY: I didn't know that tramp was married.
PAULA: History!
STEWART: Archibal, let's just leave... Las Vegas! (*They all switch.*)
SIEGEL/SEAGUL: Mr. Hughes, your wife is a low life scum.
SQUIRES/LANSKY: (*Fingering his gun.*) Your day is up, Esta!
HUGHES: Mark, please find her! Stop her!
STEWART/DALITZ: Hughes, I want you and your goddamn entourage out of my hotel!
HUGHES: Shut up, Dalitz! I don't like you. I don't like the way you run your hotel. I don't like the image of this city. This is a bad city.
STEWART/DALITZ: Has God spoken?
HUGHES: I'm going to buy your damn hotel!
PAULA: He did it! I guess you can't change history! All four of them have done it!
MARK: What are you screaming about?
HUGHES: I'll buy all of it—
PAULA: Howard Hughes just fulfilled his destiny.
HUGHES: —I'll soon own... Las Vegas! (*They all switch.*)
SQUIRES: (*Fingering the gun.*) He's President Hoover now?
PAULA: No, Pop! Don't do it!
MARK: Is that really Howard Hughes?
HUGHES/WAITER: There should be plenty of steaks in... Las Vegas! (*They all switch.*)
SIEGEL: Esta, this is a bad time. The Flamingo's not doing too good!

STEWART/ESTA: I'm sorry to hear that, Benjamin. (*She walks away.*) He's all yours, Mr. Lansky.
SIEGEL: Meyer, give it another month! I know it'll work. The Flamingo is going to be a gold mine.
MARK: And that's Bugsy?
SQUIRES/LANSKY: The boys and me… we took a vote in Havana!
SIEGEL: How are the boys?
MARK: Is this when the mob kills Bugsy?
PAULA: Stay out of it, Mark.
SQUIRES/LANSKY: They said to say goodbye…
 (*SQUIRES/LANSKY aims gun at SIEGEL.*)
MARK: Don't shoot him.
SQUIRES/LANSKY: What the…
MARK: Give it another month.
PAULA: Don't interfere.
MARK: What would this town be like… if Bugsy lived?
(*SIEGEL grabs PAULA and shields himself with her.*)
SIEGEL: Shoot me… you'll kill her.
MARK: Leave my Paula alone.
PAULA: Back off, Mark… be cool.
SQUIRES/LANSKY: I'm sorry, Virginia… you got so involved.
HUGHES: Don't hurt my, Jean… and my heir.
MARK: I'll save you from this pit… I'll save you from… Las Vegas! (*They all switch.*)
HUGHES/HENRY: I shot you… Archibald Stewart.
SIEGEL/STEWART: You missed!
HUGHES/HENRY: Not this time!
 (*HUGHES/HENRY shoots SIEGEL/HENRY. SIEGEL reacts as though he were shot, but he recovers.*)

SIEGEL: (*To SQUIRES/LANSKY.*) I've done nothing wrong.
SQUIRES/LANSKY: The Havana vote dictates my action.
(*SQUIRES/LANKSY shoots SIEGEL. SIEGEL reacts as though he was shot, but he recovers. He clings to PAULA.*)
SIEGEL: I am Las Vegas.
(*Total mayhem erupts. All four people repeat various lines from previous scenes. SIEGEL gets shot over and over. The following lines are said at the same time. There are three sections. Each section is punctuated by a gunshot from SQUIRES shooting SIEGEL.*)
HUGHES: Helen Stewart... you harlot!
STEWART: He's dead... the stupid fool!
SIEGEL: I love you, Virginia. I'll do anything for you!
SQUIRES: It doesn't matter. I'm through with that folderol! This isn't fair.
(*SQUIRES shoots SIEGEL. SIEGEL falls down, but gets up. The next set of lines are also said at the same time.*)
HUGHES: He's an actor... he's rehearsing being dead.
STEWART: Hughes, I want you and your goddamn entourage out of my hotel.
SIEGEL: Please apologize to my wife.
SQUIRES: I hear she wants you to build a casino in the desert? Meyer Lansky sends his regrets. He's in Havana... something to do with the Flamingo.
(*SQUIRES shoots SIEGEL. SIEGEL falls down, but gets up. The next set of lines are also said at the same time.*)
HUGHES: Looks like her, give her a thousand dollars and tell her to come up to my floor.
STEWART: I'm sorry, dear. I'm pregnant!

SIEGEL: I'll not stand for it any longer.
SQUIRES: I'm impressed. I've been trying to shut that fool up for years.

(*SQUIRES shoots SIEGEL. SIEGEL falls once again. It should look like PAULA is going to get hurt. MARK grabs SIEGEL's gun and points it at SQUIRES.*)

MARK: Stop!

(*ALL four freeze. The above lines are only suggestions. The actors may find they need to cut some or add some. The important action is the gunshots.*)

PAULA: Thank you, my love... thank you.
MARK: What the hell do we do with them?
PAULA: We end the play.
MARK: Will you marry me?

(*PAULA takes the gun from MARK. She speaks into the handle of it... as though it were a microphone.*)

PAULA: Welcome travelers to McCarron International Airport. One of the most technologically advanced airports in the world!
MARK: Will you answer me?
PAULA: We hope for whatever reasons—
MARK: You're ignoring me again.
PAULA: Just give me a second to finish. We hope for whatever reasons you've come to... Las Vegas— (*The four come to life.*) all your dreams will come true. Enjoy your stay! (*The four look around as if lost.*) What are you waiting for... go!
STEWART: The epilogue!
MARK: Can't you get rid of them?
SQUIRES: We take after our creator!
MARK: What are they talking about?
PAULA: I have to put them to rest.

MARK: Paula, I'm really hungry.

PAULA: It'll just take a second.

HUGHES: (*To MARK.*) Obviously, you don't know the first thing about women or love.

MARK: Blow it out your duff!

HUGHES: Mankind is not worth communicating with!

(*Throughout the following, PAULA checks her notes periodically.*)

PAULA: (*To HUGHES.*) Those were the last words you will utter in public. You'll become a hermit in your Desert Inn penthouse! But you will change the face of Vegas. You're about to become the proud owner of the Sands, Castaways, the Landmark, and the Silver Slipper — the deal on the Stardust falls through... so don't waste your time. In all... get ready to drop $300 million! (*HUGHES slips offstage.*)

MARK: Did you see his fingernails?

PAULA: (*To STEWART.*) You will reign as first lady of Las Vegas till you die in...

STEWART: Please.

PAULA: Oh sure! On the bright side... You'll marry again. And you won't have to change your name. It's another Stewart. His name is...

STEWART: Don't tell me!

PAULA: Do you know that in the future... they'll be able to tell you the sex of your baby before it's born?

STEWART: Did you really know, Mark... or have you always been a matchmaker?

PAULA: Oh, I know him!

MARK: She's gonna marry me.

STEWART: You've got good intentions! Trust them... and yourself! (*STEWART exits.*)
PAULA: (*To SIEGEL.*) I'm sorry... I can't change history!
SIEGEL: They haven't got me yet.
PAULA: You made this city what it is!
SIEGEL: Do you like what it's become?
PAULA: I don't know. Let's just say that I don't feel the same as I did an hour or so ago.
SIEGEL: Stop by the Flamingo! (*SIEGEL exits.*)
PAULA: (*To SQUIRES.*) I'm sorry about Vicki.
SQUIRES: It wasn't meant to be!
PAULA: Then why does one stay... work so hard?
SQUIRES: I've eaten twice in the past hour and I'm still famished. How would you like to have dinner with me?
PAULA: Steaks?
SQUIRES: Medium rare!
MARK: What's going on? (*Pause.*)
PAULA: I can't!
SQUIRES: Well, I've got to go get a dam built!
PAULA: I have to write a play.
SQUIRES: And obviously I'm supposed to do it without a woman in my life.
PAULA: God knows I can't write when I have a man in mine.
MARK: What does that mean?
SQUIRES: So, I should vote for Hoover? I was going to support Al Smith!
MARK: Paula?
SQUIRES: Is that your real name?
MARK: And soon to share my last name too.

SQUIRES: Goodbye, Paula.
MARK: Get rid of him, Paula.
PAULA: Charles "Pop" Squires will always be remembered as a founding father of… Las Vegas.
SQUIRES: Goodbye! Good luck with the writing! (*SQUIRES exits.*)
PAULA: Bye. He became the successful editor and publisher of the Las Vegas Age. He got married in—
MARK: You liked him didn't you?
PAULA: Don't start in.
MARK: You artists are too bizarre for me.
PAULA: Mark, I'm starved!
MARK: You mean I can finally get my steak?
PAULA: You said I could choose!
MARK: I suppose you'll want some "wop" food… or "chink" vegetables?
PAULA: Stop! (*There is a pause as they stare at each other.*)
MARK: What did you say?
PAULA: Do you know who Helen Stewart is?
MARK: Are you all right?
PAULA: Helen Stewart! Who is she?
MARK: I don't know! You just said goodbye to her.
PAULA: Is that all you know?
MARK: They named a school after her!
PAULA: You don't know! Who was Charles Squires?
MARK: I know you were sleeping with him. I saw it in the way you said goodbye to him.
PAULA: He was a— is… a gentleman. Do you know what that is?
MARK: What are you talking about?

PAULA: Good answer, Mark. Good answer.
MARK: I've put up with enough of your crap today.
PAULA: Get out, Mark.
MARK: Enough is enough.
PAULA: Goodbye.
MARK: You don't mean that.
PAULA: Don't slam the door when you leave.
MARK: You'll be sorry.
PAULA: Tell the guys at Yucca Mountain... they were right. I am a woman. Educated. And proud of it.
MARK: Don't come crawling back to me... cause I won't take you back.
PAULA: Please leave, Mark.
MARK: I'm hungry... dammit. (*PAULA moves to her computer and begins to type.*)
PAULA: Table Stakes. A play by Paula Squires. At rise—
MARK: That's not your last name.
PAULA: At rise... Paula, a writer, is discovered in her apartment at her computer.
MARK: What are you doing?
PAULA: Her husband, Charles Squires, enters after a long day's work at Hoover Dam. (*SQUIRES enters.*)
SQUIRES: Hi, my Polly Pop!
MARK: What's going— what's he doing back here?
PAULA: He embraces her as he tells her... I love you! (*They embrace.*)
MARK: Your husband?
SQUIRES: How's the writing going?
PAULA: You didn't say, you "loved me!"
MARK: I love you.
SQUIRES: I love you.

PAULA: The writing's going great. I started a new play tonight.
MARK: I hate this writing world of yours.
SQUIRES: I'm behind you all the way. I'm sure it will be a hit.
MARK: Get rid of him.
PAULA: No! (*PAULA goes to her computer and types.*) The nuclear storage site at Yucca Mountain was shut down… thus putting Mark out of a job… and he moved away.

(*A sucking/vacuum sound is heard. It sucks MARK out the door.*)

SQUIRES: Nuclear?
PAULA: It's a power thing.
CHARLES: Have you thought at all about our two worlds coexisting?
(*PAULA hits the keys on her computer.*)
PAULA: Please, save file. (*PAULA moves to SQUIRES. They kiss.*)
SQUIRES: One more thing. Are we a hit?
PAULA: I think we might just run for centuries.

(*They start to exit. HUGHES, STEWART, and SIEGEL enter and are illuminated by specials. PAULA turns to them and waves. They smile and wave back. PAULA and SQUIRES exit. The LIGHTS fade to the specials on the three. Beat. The LIGHTS fade to black.*)

END

A Collection from a Career in Theatre

HINDSIGHT

a play by Bob May

© 1998/2018 by Bob May

All rights reserved

CAST OF CHARACTERS

KEVIN
CASSIE
JESSICA
GRETEL
KATE

SYNOPSIS OF SCENES

There are multiple locations in the script, with most of the action revolving around a prom and a class reunion, which can share set decorations. Other locales can be suggested. The show is written so that the action is continuous. Use lighting to suggest different locations. There should never be a complete blackout.

The premiere of *Hindsight* was presented by the Clay County High School Theatre Department in Rector, Arkansas, under the direction of Gail Burns.

(AT RISE: The scene is a high school prom. CASSIE and KEVIN are discovered. KEVIN is on his knees in front of CASSIE.)

KEVIN: Well, will you?

CASSIE: I wonder where Jessica is? It's not like her to be late.

KEVIN: Will you forget about your sister? Cassie, I'm on my knees. It's prom night... our senior year. Our high school days are almost over. Will you please answer me?

CASSIE: You better get up off your knees. That tux is rented. If you get it dirty... you're gonna end up paying two times what it usually costs.

KEVIN: Why are you avoiding the most important question I have ever asked?

CASSIE: I ain't!

KEVIN: You mean... "You're not?" How many times have I told you... to get ahead in the world you have to talk properly.

CASSIE: Thank you, Kevin. The number of times you have blessed me with that valuable information has to be equal to the number of incomplete passes you've thrown as this loser school's lousy quarterback!

KEVIN: Well, excuse me, Miss I'm-gonna-be-a-Broadway-star, who forgot the lyrics to "People," during the senior class musical Funny Girl cause she was trying so hard to be Barbara Streisand.

CASSIE: I'll make it on Broadway long before you make it in the NFL!

KEVIN: Come on, let's stop this. What are you really going to do? You know this town doesn't have many jobs for single women in the arts. Will you please answer the question? I'm back on my knees.

CASSIE: You've not asked me anything except… "Well, will you?"
KEVIN: Well, will you?
CASSIE: Will I what?
KEVIN: Look. I have bad knees from playing football.
CASSIE: Why can't you say it?
KEVIN: I only want the best for the two of us.
CASSIE: You mean the three of us.
KEVIN: I wasn't going to bring that up. But now that you have, I thought you told me you took care of that problem.
CASSIE: All right, I've heard enough. We've played enough touch football. I think it's time to put on the pads and play some tackle. Why are you asking me to marry you… at least I think that's what you're doing. Are you?
KEVIN: Why do you always have to make things so dramatic?
CASSIE: You know what I think? I think you just don't want me to go away to college.
KEVIN: All right, so you're right! It's not the first time. You always know what I'm thinking. But come on! What you're thinking of doing is stupid. It's just plain dumb. How are you going to pay for college?
CASSIE: I ain't going… excuse me… I'm "not" going off to college. I'm moving to New York City. The Big Apple! The next time you see this face it's going to reflect Broadway and the Great White Way!
KEVIN: Dream on.

CASSIE: This relationship is so negative. Can't you see that? We hold on to each other only cause we live and are stuck in this small town. You have dreams that I know I'm holding you back from fulfilling… go for them. I got dreams too. I can't just sit here as a wife and mother and never see if I'm going be a star.

KEVIN: You'll be my wife long before stardom ever comes.

CASSIE: Maybe one day I will. But right now I don't appreciate being told what I'm going to do like I'm one of your wide receivers going long.

KEVIN: You don't know anything about football.

CASSIE: I know I've just tackled you in your own end zone and got a safety. Now you have to kick off to me. But I'm going to ignore your kick off. I guess this is goodbye.

KEVIN: Please don't leave me.

(*Smoke or a strobe light is used to help with the transition. CASSIE is discovered with JESSICA. The time is now five years later. The scene is an all-class reunion.*)

JESSICA: Oh, Cassie, I'm so happy that you made it.

CASSIE: (*Still caught up in the previous scene.*) Why can't you just let me do this? Fine! Why don't you just get a gun and shoot us both? I doubt your aim is any better with a gun than it was with a football.

JESSICA: Hello… Cassie, are you there?

CASSIE: I'm sorry, what? Jessica! Just lost in an old memory, my dear sister.

JESSICA: Half sister!

CASSIE: Dear half sister.

JESSICA: I only have half your bad faults. I mean... I wouldn't want people to talk.
CASSIE: Oh, thanks! It's so good to see you! (*They embrace.*)
JESSICA: Are you sure you're all right? You were really out of it a minute ago.
CASSIE: Don't worry about me. I'm fine. It's just really weird being back here.
JESSICA: You've been in New York City too long. Five years. The pace is too fast there. You'll live years longer if you move back here to the South.
CASSIE: Thank you, Mother. Oh, how many times have I heard that? I didn't know they were cloning humans yet?
JESSICA: I don't exactly enjoy playing the role of the daughter-left-home to deal with our mother. I'm not the actress.
CASSIE: Wait a minute. I didn't ask you to stay here and be the family martyr.
JESSICA: Someone had to do it.
CASSIE: I knew I shouldn't have come back here.
JESSICA: I'm sorry. (*She says a catchphrase from their youth.*) Yip... yip!
CASSIE: (*Answering with the correct loving response.*) Yoy... yoy! (*They embrace.*) I'm sorry too.
JESSICA: Welcome to the all-class reunion.
CASSIE: Nothing has changed. It looks just like it did on prom night five years ago.
JESSICA: Didn't you know that prom and reunion decorations haven't changed in the past two hundred years?
CASSIE: So, how is Mom?

JESSICA: Looking more like Nanny every day that passes.
CASSIE: Oh, please, God, don't do that to all the women in this family.
JESSICA: What an awful thing to say.
CASSIE: Is it the mother's genes that are dominant with fat cells or the father's?
JESSICA: I think it's the mother's, so we're both destined to be Porky Pigs!
CASSIE: Not as long as I keep doing my Road Runner imitation at the gym each morning.
JESSICA: You are looking trim and fit.
CASSIE: Oh, my gosh, is that him?
JESSICA: Excuse me?
CASSIE: Is that Kevin?
JESSICA: You can't be serious. Are you suffering from jet lag or what? You really want to talk to that zero?
CASSIE: I gotta talk to him. Excuse me… it's proper to say "have" to talk to him.
JESSICA: What do mean, "you have to talk to him?" What really happened at your disastrous senior prom night?
CASSIE: Maybe I've been lying to myself all these years. Maybe it wasn't him as much as it was me.
   (*KEVIN enters from the opposite side of the stage and gets down on one knee. CASSIE moves to him. We are once again back at the prom five years earlier.*)
KEVIN: Well, will you?
CASSIE: You want to marry me? I can't believe this. Are you sure you really want to do this?
KEVIN: I can't think of a more romantic night… the senior prom… to propose to you.

CASSIE: This is too good to be true. I've lain awake in bed at night dreaming of this moment.

KEVIN: Come with me. I want us to get away from this place. I think I have a good shot at getting a football scholarship at the university. They're courting and sparking me more than I did you last Valentine's Day. Remember that? We had Cupid blushing behind his arrow quill.

CASSIE: Stop it... you're embarrassing me.

KEVIN: We can both go together and escape from this podunk place. We'd be living in a university town. Things are a lot more liberal there than they are here.

CASSIE: But can we afford it?

KEVIN: I told you... they're giving me a scholarship. And I've applied for some government grants.

CASSIE: Does that really mean we can get out of here?

KEVIN: You have the summer to pack your bags. Come fall, this husband and wife team will have a new address.

CASSIE: This isn't a prom night joke... is it?

KEVIN: Cassie, will you marry me and accompany me to the university?

CASSIE: Do you remember the night when I first let you?

KEVIN: Sex has nothing to do with this.

CASSIE: That night I gave my heart to you.

KEVIN: It didn't come easy for me either.

CASSIE: I was a virgin.

KEVIN: So was I.

CASSIE: Well, there's something I gotta tell you.

KEVIN: Tonight you can tell me anything you "gotta!"
CASSIE: I'm pregnant.
KEVIN: What?
CASSIE: You heard me.
KEVIN: But you told me you were safe.
CASSIE: I ain't too happy about this either.
KEVIN: You mean… "you're not" too happy about this.
CASSIE: Stop telling me how to talk.
KEVIN: (*Gently, as to say, "We can deal with this."*) How you talk is not the problem now.
CASSIE: (*Totally misunderstanding him.*) Go ahead and go off to the university… I'm moving to New York City. I guess we're changing the play at the line of scrimmage. It's third down and one to go… I mean two to go. Me and our baby! You always loved football more than me anyway. (*CASSIE runs from the scene.*)
KEVIN: We can talk about this. Timeout.

(*Back at the reunion. CASSIE is in a daze because of the dream.*)

JESSICA: Timeout! Please, calm down.
CASSIE: You know what I love about the theatre? There are no timeouts in the theatre… only in sports. We do things on the spot in the theatre. It's like we're walking a tightrope. If you fall… there is no second chance.
JESSICA: Is that what really happened between you and Kevin?
CASSIE: Details… you say potato… I say potato!
JESSICA: But I drove you to the family planning clinic. Didn't you take care of it?

CASSIE: I'm sorry, what? I'm feeling a little faint. I think I'm going to have a miscarriage.
JESSICA: Very funny! You do know, that's what mama told everyone in town happened.
CASSIE: Mama just never wanted to be a grandmother.
JESSICA: Well, is she? The rumors about you and Kevin are still the talk of the Mid-town Cafe. You know, there's even a special reunion thing planned tonight, spoofing the two of you and your mysterious child.
CASSIE: You gotta be kidding.
JESSICA: Give me the dirt. Do I have a five-year-old niece or nephew I've never met? I have an inquiring mind and have always wanted to be "a source" for the Enquirer.
CASSIE: This reunion spoof is probably all your idea. You are not my sister. I don't have any sisters.
JESSICA: You got more sisters than the colonel has chicken.
CASSIE: I sure feel alone right now.
JESSICA: Maybe you shouldn't have come back.
CASSIE: Yip... Yip?
JESSICA: Yoy... Yoy!
CASSIE: Kevin is supposed to be here... and I have something I've waited five years to tell him.
JESSICA: You are one sick sister. I'm not so sure I'm even going to claim that I'm related to you. After five years and all the grief you've gone through with him. Remember, I was on the other end of the telephone every time he would hurt you.
CASSIE: I didn't come back here to fight with you.

JESSICA: Why did you come back?
CASSIE: Well, besides the fact that you begged me to come... Do you want the truth?
JESSICA: No, I want to live in a fantasy world where we both win the Publishers Clearing House and move to southern Florida... where we'll meet the two half brothers that won the Ed McMahon and Dick Clark contest. The four of us will fall in love and get married. Then we'll all live happily ever after sharing all our millions. Just four lucky kids from small-town USA.
CASSIE: Kevin also begged me to be here. He wants to ask me something.
JESSICA: Oh, isn't that cute! You have something to tell him and he has something to ask you! Do you tell him your thing before he asks you his?
(GRETA *enters and runs up to* CASSIE *and hugs her.*)
GRETA: CASSIE! You made it. I love you. And I've missed you. This all class-reunion is now complete. Hi, Jessica!
JESSICA: (*To herself.*) Phony!
GRETA: (*To* CASSIE.) How do you like the Big Apple? I just love it that you are a mega-star! I always knew that you would be.
CASSIE: (*To* JESSICA.) Who is this?
JESSICA: Don't you remember, Greta, your stepsister? My daddy's daughter from his first marriage.
GRETA: You don't remember me? I know I was only thirteen when you left town to become a star. I sure remember you in the high school class plays. I saw you in Funny Girl. My daddy took me. I remember telling him... that I wanted to be just

like you. I felt so sorry for you when you forgot the lyrics to "People." (*CASSIE gives JESSICA a look.*)

CASSIE: This is Greta? She's developed so.

GRETA: And please don't think of me as... One Flew Over the Cuckoo's Nest! I got it together and I know if you and me team up we can be a hit like Two For the Seesaw. The high school did Funny Girl my senior year and I was lucky enough to play your part... I mean Barbara's part... I mean I played the character. I know that acting is about playing characters. I've studied Stanislavski. Will you please help me become a Broadway star... just like you?

CASSIE: I'm not a Broad—

GRETA: Can I just tell you, when I played Fanny I didn't forget the lyrics to "People." Oh, I'm sorry. I'm not saying I'm better than you. I could never be that. I just graduated from the high school, otherwise, I wouldn't be able to come to this here reunion unless I had a date with a graduate or something. I'm so glad I could come. Meeting you is actually like meeting Barbara Streisand. Daddy still tells me I'm a lot like she is... you are. Even though we're not any blood... or nothing like that. I feel really close to you. I wanna be an actress. Just like you.

(*CASSIE gives JESSICA another look.*)

JESSICA: She never stops talking. Thank goodness she always lived with her mama.

GRETA: You and Babs were my idols. I mean... you still are. Both of you. When I was in middle school and you won the high school talent

contest, I would spend hours imitating you. I was so disappointed when you moved to New York. Especially when my daddy married your momma. I wanted you to be my acting teacher. I'm a singer now. Do you want to hear me sing?
(*GRETA begins to sing "People."*)
CASSIE: I'm going back to New York!
(*Flashback time. CASSIE moves to the opposite side of the stage and meets KEVIN who enters. The scene is now New York City.*)
KEVIN: Well, will you?
CASSIE: What are you doing in New York? You have really come at a bad time.
KEVIN: I've always wanted to take a bite out of the Big Apple. I just didn't know I'd be fortunate enough to have my baby-cake here as I was munching.
CASSIE: You're just making fun of me… cause I've not made it as an actress yet and it's been three months. I gotta go. I have an audition that I'm going to be late to.
KEVIN: Contrary to popular belief… I am not making fun of you. I am here to ask you to please come home.
CASSIE: What makes you think I would believe the words of a future used car salesman?
KEVIN: Cause he flew all this way to see you and ask you… "will you?"… once again. And by the way… it's been four months… that you've not made it as an actress. Summer's over. And I'm not going to be a used car salesman. I've been accepted at the university.

CASSIE: (*Happy.*) Did you really? I'm so proud of you. I knew you could do it.

KEVIN: Why don't you come with me? I've brought you an application and a class schedule.

CASSIE: You always were so thoughtful.

KEVIN: I had a good teacher.

CASSIE: Don't embarrass me. You love to do that.

KEVIN: Come here. (*They embrace.*)

CASSIE: I've really missed you.

KEVIN: The university will probably accept you as a late student if you are married to one of their star football players.

CASSIE: Do you think so? I could major in theatre.

KEVIN: You know, maybe you should reconsider that.

CASSIE: You're probably right. Maybe a double major in theatre and radio-television-film. That would probably help me more.

KEVIN: Will either of those degrees really help us in the future? Maybe home economics or something like that would be better. Look at all this time you have wasted in New York chasing this acting dream.

CASSIE: You haven't changed a bit.

KEVIN: What do you mean?

CASSIE: You are still trying to control my life.

KEVIN: I'm just trying to be sensible and logical.

CASSIE: Thank you, Mr. Spock... I am not a puppet that you can play with. I have a mind.

KEVIN: Oh yeah, you don't seem to be using it right now.

CASSIE: You know, I didn't ask you to come here.

KEVIN: I'm sorry, from your letters you sounded pretty lonely.
CASSIE: I only wrote you cause you sounded so bored back home. I got a great life here in the big city.
KEVIN: Being a maid during the day for some sleazy motel in Manhattan and waiting tables at night at a Chili's sure sounds like a great life.
CASSIE: Ask anyone here in the "City"… and they'll tell you… all the talented actors in New York are waiting tables.
KEVIN: So, tell me… Miss Broadway Star… if you were almost six months pregnant when you left home, and you've been here four… that equals ten! And even this dumb football player knows that babies are born in nine months. I want to see our kid.
CASSIE: I told you I'm gonna be late for an audition. You can stay here if you want to. I share a toilet with three other people on this floor and the door don't lock.
KEVIN: It "doesn't" lock.
CASSIE: That's what I said. Oh, and by the way, one of the people I share it with is gay!
KEVIN: This decadent life you are living can't be healthy. Your sister wants you to come home too.
CASSIE: I "don't" got no sisters.
KEVIN: You mean you don't "have any" sisters.
CASSIE: Maybe you should major in English at the university. Goodbye! (*CASSIE exits. She walks from one side of stage to the other.*)

GRETA: What do you mean you don't got any sisters? You got me, and Jessica. And with you, we got... The Three Sisters. Just like Chekhov.

CASSIE: I always hated Star Trek. I refuse to act in television.

GRETA: How do you keep such a clear complexion? I swear, I'll win the battles over blemishes! I mean, how can an actress like you or me ever have pimples and expect to make it. Barbara's never had zits.

JESSICA: Kirk to Enterprise. Two to beam aboard!

CASSIE: You planned this. Didn't you?

GRETA: Does she know?

CASSIE: Be quiet! (*KATE enters.*)

KATE: Cassie! What are you doing here? Daddy bet me ten-to-one you'd never come back here for this all-class reunion. He's going to owe me big time when I get home.

CASSIE: (*To JESSICA.*) This has your name written all over it. This little family reunion at the all high school reunion is all your doing.

JESSICA: She's not my sister. Why would I ask her to come?

KATE: What a welcome. Don't I get a hug?

GRETA: So, that's the other half sister?

JESSICA: Greta... please don't give it away.

CASSIE: Don't be silly, Kate... (*CASSIE and KATE embrace.*) I'm just wondering what you are doing? Las Vegas is a long way from here.

GRETA: Wow, four sisters! This blows the whole Chekhov theory. And we're no longer The Three Musketeers either. It's a nightmare... Chekhov is rolling over in his Russian grave. Oh, no, John Guare wrote a play, Four Baboons Adoring the Sun. I sure hope that title is not a reflection of the four of us!

JESSICA: Greta, please shut up... this is not an audition.

GRETA: I'm not so sure. What your mama says about their daddy would make a great monologue.

KATE: Do I know this obnoxious little girl?

JESSICA: This is Greta, our stepsister.

KATE: You need say no more. Oh my, I'm not sure I can do this. I really think it's all the stress of being a doctor's wife. He gets so many calls late at night. It's awful. Sometimes I can't sleep cause I'm waiting for the calls to come.

GRETA: What did she mean by that?

JESSICA: Relax, Greta.

GRETA: Maybe she needs to get an answering machine. And caller ID is great too. She could screen the calls then.

KATE: Excuse me, young lady. I did not come all this way to be badgered by some snot-nosed stepsister who isn't even related to me.

GRETA: You know, in the musical Nine, the leading lady has to ignore hateful comments from an overbearing press just to endure. I guess I'll just have to do that with you.

JESSICA: Please, let's not get into anything ugly. That's not why we're here.

CASSIE: Why are we here? I know why I'm here. Jessica, what have you done?

JESSICA: Don't be silly. We're here to enjoy the reunion. I haven't done anything.
GRETA: Yes, she did.
JESSICA: Greta, please!
GRETA: No. I don't like the way I'm being treating by any of you. I can't help it that I am the youngest. She got all your sister's here tonight to make fun of you.
CASSIE: You did what?
GRETA: She wrote a skit… just like on Saturday Night Live. It makes fun of you and Kevin and your mysterious baby. Do you really have a baby?
CASSIE: (*To JESSICA.*) How could you? So, I'm tonight's entertainment.
JESSICA: I thought it would be fun for you to have all your sisters here to support you when Kevin doesn't show up.
CASSIE: He'll be here.
GRETA: I tried to talk her into doing a musical revue so I could sing "People," but she wouldn't listen to me. I reminded her how successful musicals like Seven Brides for Seven Brothers are. Musicals always fill the house and make the audience smile.
CASSIE: What is it with you and show titles with numbers? You're driving me crazy. Ever since you got here I feel like you've been quoting from a book of Tony award winners.
GRETA: I'm so happy that you picked up on that. I knew we were real sisters at heart. I am gonna put together a book. An acting book. The tentative title is… Play Titles… One Through Ten… To Help You Get the Part. You know like, One Flew Over

the Cuckoo's Nest and Two for the See Saw. I still don't got a title for number five or eight. Can you help me?

KATE: (*As though saying, "shut up!"*) How about… Eight is Enough!

GRETA: Wow, that's great! I never thought about TV shows.

JESSICA: All right, fine. Now that the cat is out of the bag. We still need to rehearse this little spoof. You are more than welcome to watch what we do and make any changes that you want to.

KATE: Before we do that I really have to talk to Cassie in private.

GRETA: Oh my gosh, Cassie, you could direct the skit. What an honor that would be.

CASSIE: I didn't come to this reunion to deal with family.

(*KEVIN enters.*)

KEVIN: Why did you come here? This is family weekend and we're not family.

(*CASSIE moves to the other side of the stage and the new scene, which is the campus of the university.*)

CASSIE: Do you know how hard it was for me to get here?

KEVIN: I don't have a lot of time. Coach wants us all to be at football practice early this afternoon.

CASSIE: (*Not angry.*) Oh, thanks a lot for such a romantic welcome.

KEVIN: I didn't ask you to come.

CASSIE: That doesn't matter. Aren't you going to ask me… the question? Please ask me. I really need you to ask me.

KEVIN: Ask you what?
CASSIE: You know. Those three simple words.
KEVIN: Why should I? You haven't written to me. Or returned my calls since I visited you in New York.
CASSIE: Come on… you're my foundation. The anchor to my ship.
KEVIN: What are you doing here?
CASSIE: I really need to tell you something. It's time I told you!
KEVIN: As far as I'm concerned it is over between us
CASSIE: Someone has to hear what I've done, what has happened.
KEVIN: Besides, I've found a new life here.
CASSIE: I really like the campus.
KEVIN: What do you know about the campus?
CASSIE: A lot. I've been here almost a week wandering around… afraid to knock on your door… wondering if you still loved me?
KEVIN: You've been doing what?
CASSIE: You don't have to lie to me about going to practice early. I'm sorry you didn't make the football team as a free agent.
KEVIN: It's called a "walk on" in college sports… and I ain't worried about it. I didn't really want to play football anymore. It's time I grew up.
CASSIE: You mean… "you're not"… worried.
KEVIN: Don't make fun of me. I've lost my mind going away to college. I can't function without you.
CASSIE: I'm sorry. I'll never make fun of you again.
KEVIN: Oh, Cassie, I miss home and you. Thank you for coming. I wish you'd leave New York and keep me company here.

CASSIE: I do feel comfortable here.
KEVIN: What did you want to tell me?
CASSIE: That I've missed your embrace.
KEVIN: Thanks... me too. But what was it when you first got here that was so important?
(*She looks at him and decides not to tell him the real reason she came.*)
CASSIE: We were wondering if you'd visited the theatre on campus yet?
KEVIN: Here is this mysterious "we" again. Who are you talking about? Your sister told me she took you to the clinic.
CASSIE: Aren't you going to ask me? I came all this way.
KEVIN: All right. Fine! (*He gets on his knees.*) Will you?
CASSIE: You don't really mean it! You're too upset about not making the football team.
KEVIN: You and I were two big fish in a small pond back home, but now that we're away from the security of small town... we're just two minnows lost in the big sea. You shouldn't have come.
CASSIE: That's very obvious. I'll never come back again.
(*From the opposite side of the stage JESSICA enters.*)
JESSICA: Don't say that. We need you here. (*CASSIE moves into the new scene.*)
CASSIE: Why, so you can make fun of me?
GRETA: No, you are the only other person in this town... shoot this county... that knows that Pirandello wrote a play Six Character's in Search of an Author. Most people have heard of Ten Little

Indians, but you are the only one that would know my number six title. Besides, we can't do this spoof without the star.

KATIE: I have no idea what she just said, and I hate to say this, but I think I agree with her.

CASSIE: Why should I let you make fun of me?

JESSICA: Because we are your sisters and who better than blood? Would you rather have the rest of the town do it? We all love you.

CASSIE: Kevin will be here.

JESSICA: But we three are here now.

GRETA: Chekhov is blessing us now! Three Sisters who care about the fourth!

CASSIE: Let me see this script.

GRETA: You can have my copy.

JESSICA: Does that mean you'll help?

KATE: Before we do that… I really have to talk to Cassie in private.

JESSICA: You're not gonna wig out on us, are you?

KATE: It's a father thing I have to share with her.

CASSIE: Don't tell me he's sick!

KATE: He's fine. Jessica can we have a moment?

JESSICA: And what are we supposed to do?

CASSIE: Go look for Kevin.

JESSICA: You know, you are so crazy, sister… I should call you, "crazy sister!"

CASSIE: As crazy as I am… please give me a moment with my other crazy sister.

JESSICA: We really have to rehearse this skit. I will not be made a fool in front of this town.

CASSIE: Oh, but, it's all right for me to be made the fool?

KATE: Just give us a few minutes. (*JESSICA and GRETA exit.*)
CASSIE: What's wrong? You're acting like a caged animal. Is it really that tough for you to leave the big city and come back to this small town life? I miss my life back in New York too.
KATE: I can't do this skit Jessica has planned.
CASSIE: Don't worry about me. Go ahead and do it.
KATE: No, you don't understand. It's not the skit.
CASSIE: What's wrong? (*KATE can't tell the truth, so she says the next line.*)
KATE: Fred and I are having problems.
CASSIE: I'm sorry to hear that. What does that have to do with the skit?
KATE: Actually, we're not really. He was very supportive of me coming back to this reunion. Well, he is a little mad at me.
CASSIE: For coming back without him?
KATE: No, he won an award for some 911 saving thing he did.
CASSIE: That's wonderful.
KATE: He wanted me to read his acceptance speech the night of the award ceremony cause he was on duty at the emergency room. He thought it would be hypocritical if he was accepting the award when he was supposed to be working.
CASSIE: That sounds admirable. I'd like to meet him one day. How did it go?
KATE: Why do you hate me?
CASSIE: Don't be ridiculous. I don't hate you.
KATE: Ever since Daddy and I moved to Las Vegas you have hated me.

CASSIE: I missed having you just a block away. I could always go over to your house when I was having a problem at home with my mom or Jessica. Why didn't he take me?
KATE: Cause you lived with your mother. At least you had a mom. Remember, mine deserted me.
CASSIE: I missed him so much... and you too... when you left.
KATE: Me too. Why do you think I called you all the time?
CASSIE: Thank you. I really did, and still do appreciate the love and support you give me every time you call.
KATE: You have always returned it twofold.
CASSIE: Stop... I'm getting teary-eyed! I'm happy for you. It sounds like you have a wonderful marriage. I wonder if it will ever come to me? A doctor. You're set for life. I'm so jealous. Now, do you want to stop all this avoiding? Kate, what are you trying to tell me?
KATE: What do you mean?
CASSIE: I'm an actress. It's part of my training to observe people and study their behavior. You've been beating around the bush more than a man does when it comes to matrimony.
KATE: Jessica sent me the script to the spoof several months ago.
CASSIE: What... you don't like it?
KATE: No, it's not that... it's just... I think it's great.
CASSIE: So, what the problem?
KATE: (*Blurts it out.*) I can't read.
CASSIE: You gotta be kidding me!

(*KEVIN enters on the opposite side of the stage. KATE freezes.*)

KEVIN: I know it's been a while. (*CASSIE moves to the flashback. The scene is New York City.*)

CASSIE: You got to be kidding me. You want me to do what?

KEVIN: Now that you're a Broadway star, I wouldn't blame you if—

CASSIE: I've only acted off Broadway. I haven't conquered Broadway yet!

KEVIN: You're a star in my eyes no matter where you act and I wouldn't blame you if you said no.

CASSIE: Maybe I will. Just give me a second. This has really caught me off my guard. How long has it been?

KEVIN: Well, here I am in the Big Apple on my junior year spring break… you made the visit to the campus not long after I was accepted… you were always better at math than me.

CASSIE: "Than I!"

KEVIN: I did the "me" thing because of the alliteration with "math." I thought it would appeal to your artistic side. I really need your help.

CASSIE: (*Laughing.*) And what did you say your major is?

KEVIN: Pre-Law.

CASSIE: So, the future used car salesman is now a future lawyer running for president of the student body. And you want me to help you act out your speeches. Are you a republican or a democrat?

KEVIN: Political parties don't really play a part in university elections.

CASSIE: And playing up to the director at the auditions didn't help me get the parts in the Off-Broadway plays I've been in.
KEVIN: I'm really proud of you. I knew you would make it in the Big Apple.
CASSIE: Three Off-Broadway plays in three years is not making it.
KEVIN: Has it really been three years since I've been to New York?
CASSIE: It seems three times as long when the heart has been aching. Three seems to be our magic number!
KEVIN: You're just saying that cause you're in a slow period with your career.
CASSIE: Ask me those three words now and I swear I'll give up the theatre and live wherever you want to. And I'll be more devoted to you than the Golden Retriever you had as a child ever was.
KEVIN: A pre-law-major friend of mine at the university knows a friend of a producer in Branson. He thinks he can get you into a show there.
CASSIE: What is this the barter system? I don't want your pity.
KEVIN: I wasn't offering that out of pity.
CASSIE: Look, I'm on the verge of making it here… not off Broadway… but on Broadway. I've struggled and fought… and made some tough sacrifices since I got here. And I think it's all finally gonna pay off. Real soon.
KEVIN: I'm going to get married next month.
CASSIE: What?

KEVIN: She's a legal assistant at the law firm I'm interning with.
CASSIE: What about our child?
(JESSICA and GRETA enter. KATE unfreezes. KEVIN exits.)
JESSICA: Enough about this child of yours. I took you to the clinic.
GRETA: Your mama swears you had a miscarriage.
KATE: I always believed it was adopted.
CASSIE: My baby is alive and well and back in New York with a friend. Jessica, look at the time. Don't you have to perform your little spoof soon?
JESSICA: She's right, sisters. Let's at least read through it once before we have to perform it before an audience.
KATE: I'm not feeling too well.
GRETA: Too bad your doctor-husband ain't here. He could give you something for whatever's ailing you.
JESSICA: Kate, don't do this to me now. You promised. Did everyone remember to bring their scripts?
GRETA: Here's mine, but I don't need it. I memorized my part the day after I got it.
KATE: I have mine, but I forgot my glasses back in Vegas. I can't do it.
GRETA: What else did you leave in Vegas?
CASSIE: Greta, give me your script. I'll read her lines and then she can learn them.
JESSICA: Whatever! Now, I know why I never got involved in the theatre.
CASSIE: Thank you, mother, can we move on?

JESSICA: Okay, so, I'm the narrator. Greta plays Kevin and Kate plays you... Cassie. I begin with... "There was a girl born unto—

CASSIE: Wait a minute! What is this a Passion Play? "Born unto?" You make me sound like some biblical character.

JESSICA: Please keep your comments to yourself until we are finished.

CASSIE: I'm sorry.

JESSICA: There was a girl born unto this town. Her name was Cassie. She had two half sisters. One begot of her mom and the other from her dad. I'm from her mother.

CASSIE: And I'm from her father.

JESSICA: No, that's what Kate says!

CASSIE: I know. I'm feeding her the line. Remember she forgot her glasses.

JESSICA: So, say it, Kate.

KATE: And I'm from her father.

GRETA: I don't think she said it with the right inflection!

JESSICA: Greta, please!

GRETA: Look if I'm gonna act in this skit, I want it to be good. There could be an agent in the audience.

CASSIE: Relax, Greta. The skit will be great. Continue, Jessica.

JESSICA: I don't have to keep the part about the sisters in. I mean, after all the skit is really about you and Kevin.

CASSIE: Leave it in. I like the fact that you are including my family.

JESSICA: No, I'll just make it simple and say... Cassie hated all this confusion with all these sisters. Enter Kevin into her life.

GRETA: Hi, Cassie! I'm playing Kevin. Can we stop for a sec? Let me tell you, Cassie, it is an honor to play Kevin. But please... tell me... what was he really like? I need to know to fully understand my character.

JESSICA: Greta, just say your line.

GRETA: (*As KEVIN. She gets to her knees in front of KATE.*) Cassie, I have loved you since I first seen you in second grade. Will you marry me?

CASSIE: Excuse me, I have to stop again. Actually, he didn't ask me that until third grade. He hated me in second grade. And he would never say, "since I first seen you!"

JESSICA: These early facts are not important. Kate say your line.

KATE: I can't read.

GRETA: What was that?

KATE: Nothing. Remember, I forgot my glasses.

CASSIE: You say, "we're too young to get married. If you still feel this way when we are old enough... Ask me at our senior prom and I'll give you my answer then."

KATE: I can't remember all that. Say it again.

JESSICA: Never mind! That's all right. Let's fast forward to the senior prom. Greta, your line.

GRETA: So, we're at the senior prom? And he's loved you all these many years... through elementary school... through middle school... and finally the big night he's been waiting for... the high school senior prom… is finally here. Wow, I can just imagine the pressure he is under.

JESSICA: Greta, just say what's in the script. Three simple words.

GRETA: (*As KEVIN. She once again gets on her knees in front of KATE.*) Well, will you?

(*The sound of a telephone is heard. CASSIE walks into a LIGHT special and answers the phone. JESSICA, KATE, and GRETA freeze.*)

CASSIE: (*Lost in the past.*) Hello?

(*KEVIN appears in a LIGHT special on the phone.*)

KEVIN: Well, will you?

CASSIE: Oh, Kevin, I was so scared when the stage manager told me I had a call. I couldn't imagine who it was. I am so nervous. How did you find this backstage number?

KEVIN: Relax, you'll be great. I am so jealous of you. You're dream come true.

CASSIE: It's not that big a part.

KEVIN: But you're about to open in a show on Broadway. I'm very proud of you.

CASSIE: I'm so scared. Will I be good? This is so much more nerve-racking than opening in any other show I've ever been in.

KEVIN: Well, you've hit the big time and you must pay big-time dues. You'll knock 'em dead.

CASSIE: I wish you could be here.

KEVIN: The theatre gods and the university board are fighting more than Democrats and Republicans do when they try to agree on funding for the arts. I'm sorry my graduation and your opening fall on the same night.

CASSIE: You mean a top-flight lawyer like you're going to be couldn't get them to change the graduation date?
KEVIN: Believe me, honey, I don't think even a fast-talking used car salesman could do that.
CASSIE: There are some complimentary tickets in your name at the box office any time you want to see the show. I hope you come soon.
(*GRETA, JESSICA, and KATE break their freeze.*)
GRETA: Wait a minute! I thought he got married?
JESSICA: Greta, can't you just read the lines as written?
GRETA: You obviously don't understand the craft of acting. How am I supposed to honestly say "Well, will you?" when I know my character is already married.
CASSIE: (*Still on the phone.*) And bring the wife too. But she has to pay for her ticket.
(*GRETA, JESSICA, and KATE freeze.*)
KEVIN: What? Haven't you heard? You mean the small-town rumor mill hasn't reached New York yet? I'm not married anymore. It didn't work out. If you want me to go into details… I will… but I hope it's enough to say that you were the problem in my marriage.
CASSIE: I can't believe you even did it.
KEVIN: We all make stupid mistakes. So, are you going to go to the five-year class reunion?
CASSIE: What for? So they can make fun of us.
KEVIN: If those people back home are so bored that they have nothing better to do than make fun of

the ones that have ventured out into the world...
let them.
CASSIE: Are you going to go?
KEVIN: I've been thinking about it.
CASSIE: Why?
KEVIN: At first I wanted to go back just to show off my degree, but I really think it's cause I miss home.
CASSIE: You gotta be kidding me.
KEVIN: I'd really like it if you'd meet me back home for the reunion.
CASSIE: Kevin, you know I'm in a show.
KEVIN: Football teams have a second string. I'm sure you have one.
CASSIE: They're called understudies!
KEVIN: If you ask your understudy to take over for you... I'll ask my fellow-flunkies at the law firm to cover me. Besides, I have something I need to ask you.
CASSIE: I don't know what to say.
(*The LIGHT special goes out on KEVIN and he exits. GRETA, JESSICA, and KATE unfreeze.*)
GRETA: All right I'll say it! (*As KEVIN.*) Besides, I have something I need to ask you. Well, will you?
JESSICA: Kate, it's your line. You have to respond.
KATE: I don't know what to say. Cassie, help! (*CASSIE joins the scene.*)
CASSIE: What?
KATE: Help me! I don't know what to say.
CASSIE: And that's just what I said to Kevin. "I don't know what to say!" Very good, Jessica. Have you ever thought about a playwriting career?
GRETA: This is a cover-up! Kate can't read.

KATE: What? You're crazy! I can too! I told you I forgot my glasses.
GRETA: I've been observing you. People who wear glasses, and don't have them, usually squint when they try to read. When it comes to a line of yours, you don't even look at the script.
KATE: Don't be ridiculous. I am an honor student graduate of this high school. Otherwise, I couldn't be at this reunion.
GRETA: Did you read the play when Jessica mailed it to you?
KATE: Why are you doing this to me?
GRETA: What is the climax? Does Kevin show up and ask Cassie to marry him?
JESSICA: No time to answer! I'm getting our cue. We're on… it's time to perform!
GRETA: I'll get to the bottom of this.
JESSICA: Stop it, Greta. Stop making a fuss! We are being stared at. I hope everyone is ready! (*JESSICA addresses the audience as though they were the reunion guests.*) Hi, everyone. Welcome to the all class high school reunion. For those of you who don't know me, my name is Jessica. I'm in charge of the entertainment for tonight. I sure hope everyone is having a great time. I know I am.
   (*A phone rings. CASSIE moves away from group and answers a cell phone. JESSICA, KATE, and GRETA freeze as CASSIE and KEVIN talk.*)
CASSIE: How did the graduation go?
(*KEVIN appears in a LIGHT special on a cell phone.*)
KEVIN: Cassie, is that you?

CASSIE: I'm sure it was great. I was just calling to see. I know it's late. Real late! Probably too late! I'm sorry.
KEVIN: That's all right. I tried to call you after the graduation. Where have you been?
CASSIE: At a stupid cast party at Sartre's.
KEVIN: Wow, I bet that was a dream come true. The big question is how did your opening night on Broadway go?
CASSIE: I'm so embarrassed. I forgot the lyrics to the second verse of my song.
KEVIN: Relax. I'm sure that no one noticed.
CASSIE: The critic for the Village Voice did. I overheard him at the cast party tell the director... that if they replaced me the show might have a life.
KEVIN: What do critic's know?
CASSIE: Obviously a lot! The director gave me my walking papers as I was leaving the party.
KEVIN: Can I do anything for you?
CASSIE: Come to New York and comfort me.
KEVIN: (*Comforting.*) I wish Scottie could beam me to you right now.
CASSIE: As much as I hate Star Trek... I wish that's how my night could end.
KEVIN: Please meet me at the reunion.
CASSIE: Why? We've done nothing but fight with each other this entire relationship.
KEVIN: I prefer to think of it as two stubborn people chasing their dreams.
   (*KEVIN exits as the present takes control. KATE, GRETA, and JESSICA unfreeze.*)

JESSICA: And as entertainment director for tonight and being tired of all the jokes I've suffered over the years… since my sister, Cassie, left town… I thought we'd finally tell the truth about what really happened on prom night all those years ago. Greta, ask the question this entire city wants to hear the answer to.

GRETA: Now?

JESSICA: Now!

GRETA: Hi, everyone. My name is Greta, remember… I'm playing Kevin. And if there are any agents in the audience… my home phone number is—

JESSICA: Greta!

GRETA: (*As KEVIN asking KATE.*) Well, will you?

KATE: Is this where I'm supposed to say, "Are you only asking me to marry you because I'm pregnant?"

JESSICA: You're holding the script in your hands.

CASSIE: Yes, Kate, say that line now.

KATE: Are you only asking me to marry you because I'm pregnant?

GRETA: (*As KEVIN.*) You told me you took care of that problem.

(*KATE stops acting.*)

KATE: Cassie, you could never really do that… could you?

JESSICA: That's not in the script. Can't you just read… sorry… you forgot your glasses. Can't you remember the correct lines?

KATE: I've had enough. Do you want to know the truth about me?

CASSIE: Kate, you don't have to do this.
KATE: No, I can't read! Oh, I sorta can. And I've been embarrassed about this all my life. Going to a restaurant with a date and playing the dumb woman who coyly asks the man to order for me. Hiding this from my husband has not been fun or easy.
GRETA: I knew it all the time! How in the world did you ever graduate?
KATE: It was easy. By using my femininity and playing the game I could get anything by saying what men in this male-dominated world wanted to hear me say. Not anymore. I'm at this reunion to say I'm going back to school, and with the help of my sister, Cassie, I'm going to make a mark in this world without the help of a man. Well, perhaps a little help from my doctor-husband.
CASSIE: Kate, you don't even have to ask. You have my support.
GRETA: I'm sorry... this is too much... I can't act under these conditions.
(*JESSICA addresses the audience.*)
JESSICA: I'm sorry, ladies and gentleman. Tonight I planned to make fun of my sister, but I've changed my mind! I think we should honor her. We've all made fun of her over the years... and thought she'd never be a Broadway star. But she is one. She is currently starring in a show on Broadway and even took time off from that show to be here with us tonight.
CASSIE: Thank you, Jessica, but you know not what you speak of!

JESSICA: And I propose that instead of this silly skit... I think the Broadway-star-come-home should sing and really entertain us.
GRETA: Bravo! I second that! I think she should sing "People."
CASSIE: Don't do this! I appreciate your love, but this is silly.
KATE: Please, sing! Get me off the hook.
(*KEVIN enters singing "People."*)
KEVIN: PEOPLE!
PEOPLE, WHO NEED PEOPLE!
ARE THE LUCKIEST PEOPLE
IN THE WORLD!
CASSIE: Have you ever thought about performing? I never knew that you had such a beautiful singing voice.
KEVIN: Our future will have no more secrets.
CASSIE: I don't know what to say. It's so good to see you. Oh, that sounds so stupid.
KEVIN: I'm sorry about the Village Voice critic.
CASSIE: Maybe it was a sign.
GRETA: So, this is Kevin,... not bad... and he actually showed up.
JESSICA: Ladies and gentleman, let the real entertainment begin!
(*JESSICA, GRETA, and KATE scurry away from KEVIN and CASSIE and form a picture as they eagerly listen.*)
KEVIN: I wasn't accepted at law school.
CASSIE: You must be disappointed.
KEVIN: No, I've had five years to think... and in that time I've learned lots of lessons. And the biggest one is... I now know I honestly mean the three

words I am about to say. (*He goes to his knees.*) Well, will you?

KATE: Wait a minute! Cut! Don't answer that until he tells you why he didn't go to law school. This audience wants to know.

GRETA: Go, Kate, you tell 'em. Twelve Angry Men is a play title... and I don't really need it for my book, but I feel more angry than twice all those guys did combined. What is he doing? You think all these people came to this reunion to hear you say, yes, after that lame proposal? What a boring climax to a five-year ordeal! Good plays don't end that way. There are too many questions unanswered!

JESSICA: Greta, I know I've asked you to be quiet more than one time tonight... and now, I'm sorry. Right now, I can't shout loud enough for Cassie to wake up!

CASSIE: They're right! Kevin, I want to know why you weren't accepted to law school?

KEVIN: Very simple. I didn't apply.

CASSIE: Are you crazy?

KEVIN: The news will break soon. I've accepted a position as head football coach at the high school here.

CASSIE: Wait a minute! Head football coach? Used car salesman to lawyer back to jock!

KEVIN: Isn't hindsight great?

CASSIE: Meaning what? Why do you want to marry me?

KEVIN: What we had five years ago was wonderful. We had dreams. We split to follow them. We sure did waste a lot of time finding out what we had was what we want.

CASSIE: Our baby is a boy. I gave birth to him not long after I got to New York. I was at an audition for a bus and truck tour of Funny Girl. Imagine this… a nine-month pregnant me… singing for the role of Fanny… you know Bab's part! What a picture! I was right in the middle of "People" when I went into labor. And… get this… it happened in the same spot in the lyrics that I forgot back in high school. That song is my curse! The theatre paid for the ambulance to the hospital, but they didn't give me the part.

KEVIN: I can't wait to meet him.

CASSIE: Making it in New York is really tough. It demands all your energy. Being a single mom made it even tougher. I wasn't making hardly any money. I didn't know what to do with myself. For him. Adoption was my life line! Our son now lives a very comfortable life in Connecticut with a doctor and his wife… who couldn't have children.

KEVIN: Oh, Cassie, I'm so sorry. I remember when you tried to tell me.

CASSIE: It was a horrible experience to face alone. (*They embrace.*) Thank you for never giving up on me.

GRETA: Come on, already! Ask her! Before I cry!

CASSIE: Oh, by the way, Greta… Peter Schaefer wrote a play titled Five Finger Exercise. I hope that helps you with your book.

GRETA: Thanks, sis. You're even better than Barbara in my eyes.

CASSIE: And, Kate... glasses can help you see words... but it takes courage to read them.
KATE: I can't do wrong with your blood in my veins.
JESSICA: Yip... yip?
CASSIE: Yoy... yoy! (*They embrace.*)
JESSICA: Ladies and gentleman... please, let me proudly be the first to welcome the strays back home, and ask Kevin to put an end to this five-year ordeal. (*KEVIN goes to his knees.*)
KEVIN: Well, will you?
CASSIE: Oh my, this is so un-theatrical! I'm sorry Greta. But yes... I will marry you!

(*THEY kiss and embrace as we hear Barbara Streisand singing "People." The mood is festive as the LIGHTS fade to black.*)

END

Paul Bunyan, Two Old Men, and a Wizard

Sleeping Beauty

a play

by Bob May

© 2017 by Bob May
All rights reserved

CAST OF CHARACTERS

LORDS AND LADIES OF THE COURT
THE STEWARD
KING
QUEEN
CANDIDE (*Can-deed*)
MIETTES (*My-tis*)
LILAC
CARABOSSE (*Cara-bossy*)
GUARDS
AURORA at EIGHT
PHILAMUND at TEN
AURORA at THIRTEEN
PHILAMUND at FIFTEEN
AURORA at SIXTEEN
PHILAMUND at EIGHTEEN
ELDEEN
JIMI
JANIS

SYNOPSIS OF SCENES

Scene One: The Great Hall in the castle of the King and Queen
Scene Two: The Secret Spot, immediately following.
Scene Three: The Great Hall, two days later.
Scene Four: The Great Hall. When?
Scene Five: The Great Hall, immediately following.
Scene Six: The Great Hall, immediately following.

The premiere of Sleeping Beauty was presented by Children's Theatre to Go, Inc. at Reynolds Performance Hall in Conway, Arkansas, on August 1, 2008, under the direction of Bob May, with costume design by Nikki Webster, set design by Bob May, with the following cast:

The Steward—Jacob Fluech
King—Brady Ness
Queen—Lesley Allen
Candide—Karen Owings
Miettes—Erin Anson
Lilac—F. E. Mosby
Carabosse—Darren White
Guards—Jay Barber, Clay Stubs
Aurora at Eight—Abby Shourd
Philamund at Ten—Joe Coker
Aurora at Thirteen—Ellie Halloran
Philamund at Fifteen—Sam Coker
Aurora at Sixteen—Katie Barber
Philamund at Eighteen—Ben Scheuter
Eldeen—Matt Audibert
Jimi—Dylan Barber

Janice—Miki Brewington
Lords and Ladies of the Court: Jay Barber, Miki Brewinton, Joe Coker, Sam Coker, Hollan Donham, Ellie Holloran, Maddie Moss, Caroline Osborn, Abby Shourd, Caitlin Straw, Clay Stubbs

SCENE ONE

(AT RISE: The Great Hall is crowded with the LORDS and LADIES of the court in celebration. The atmosphere is festive. SOUND: A fanfare is heard. STEWARD enters.)

STEWARD: Attention. Attention, Lords and Ladies of the court. The guests of honor have arrived. Please welcome your very own King Florestan, Queen Willameana, and Princess Aurora.

(The KING and QUEEN enter. The QUEEN holds a one-year-old baby in her arms. The LORDS and LADIES applaud and cheer.)

KING: We thank you, my subjects, for your continued devotion to the royal family.

STEWARD: On the occasion of our Princess Aurora's first birthday, we are gathered for her christening. Princess Aurora, named after the dawn... the dawn of a new day... the beginning of a new era.

KING: For too many years our great kingdom didn't have an heir or a future, but now the queen holds your future in her hands. (*The QUEEN holds the baby high and the LORDS and LADIES cheer.*) This celebration reflects the mood of our kingdom... positive. (*The LORDS and LADIES applaud and cheer.*) With the war among the fairies over, our kingdom... prospers. (*The LORDS and LADIES applaud and cheer.*) The good fairies will look after our kingdom... proudly. (*The LORDS and LADIES applaud and cheer.*)

QUEEN: But what about the fairy, Carabosse?

KING: The bad fairy has no... power. (*The LORDS and LADIES applaud and cheer.*)

QUEEN: Are you sure?

STEWARD: You need not worry about her, madam. The war among the fairies put her in her place and now the good fairies out number her, three to one. The kingdom is safe from Carabosse. And as is tradition, on her sixteenth birthday the good fairies will recommend a prince for Princess Aurora to marry; further assuring the continued future of the kingdom.

(*The LORDS and LADIES applaud and cheer.*)

KING: Oh, and Sir Steward, doesn't your son share the same birthday with the princess?

STEWARD: Yes, your Majesty, our baby boy, Philamund, is three today. He is at home with his mother. (*A fanfare is heard.*) Your majesty, the three good fairies have arrived and are ready to christen and honor the princess with their own special wishes.

KING: Enter, good fairies, with my blessing. (*Two of the three good fairies, MIETTES and LILAC, enter.*) And let it be known to all my subjects, that from this day forth these three good fairies are godmothers to the princess. Steward, please introduce the fairy godmothers to the members of court.

STEWARD: Fairy number one, Candide, the Kind.

LILAC: Oh goodness, Candide is not here. She is always late. Let me go get her.

(*LILAC exits. CANDIDE enters on the run.*)

CANDIDE: I'm here. I'm here. So sorry. Sorry, I am late. I'm late, but I'm here now. Here I am. I'm here.

STEWARD: Candide, the Kind, fairy number one.

(*CANDIDE moves to the QUEEN.*)

CANDIDE: Congratulations, King Florestan and Queen Willameana. Congratulations, Sir King and Madam Queen. I happily christen Princess Aurora. Yes, I christen the princess, I do. And I grant upon the princess the gift of kindness. Being Candide, the Kind, I wish kindness upon the princess. (*She casts a spell. A SOUND is heard.*)

KING: You are most gracious, Candide.

STEWARD: And number two is the merry fairy Miettes.

(*MIETTES moves to the QUEEN. She is giggling nervously as she talks.*)

MIETTES: I grant upon the princess the gift of merriment. (*She casts a spell. A SOUND is heard. She begins to cry. She cries over almost everything. It's not a sad cry, or a wailing cry; remember her name is Miettes, the merry fairy.*)

QUEEN: Bless you, Miettes. But why do you cry?

MIETTES: Yes, I am usually merry, but christenings always make me cry. I just love them.

(*MIETTES cries loudly. CANDIDE pulls MIETTES to her.*)

CANDIDE: Come on, you big happy crybaby. Come on.
STEWARD: And the third fairy godmother is...
(CARABOSSE *bursts upon the scene with* SOUND: *a thunderclap, and a flash pot.*)
CARABOSSE: How about the fourth fairy? Don't I count?
STEWARD: It's the evil fairy Carabosse, the Cruel.
(*The* LORDS *and* LADIES *scream and cower.*)
CARABOSSE: I am very offended, King Florestan, that I was not invited to the christening.
CANDIDE: Your evilness was the reason you were not invited. Yes, your evilness equals no invitation.
CARABOSSE: Candide, I don't waste words on you. I was talking to the king. (CARABOSSE *flicks her wrist at* CANDIDE. *A spell* SOUND *is heard.* CANDIDE *stumbles backward and is dazed.* MIETTES *runs to help* CANDIDE *to her feet.*) Did you hear me, King Florestan. I am talking to you.
CANDIDE: Obviously she isn't abiding... no, she's not... by the rules... rules of the fairy war treaty. She is breaking the treaty.
KING: I concur with Candide about your evilness, Carabosse.
CARABOSSE: I'm not so evil... just ask your beautiful queen.
KING: What does she mean, my dear?
QUEEN: I don't know.
CARABOSSE: Let me refresh your memory, Madam Queen. If it weren't for me... you would never have given birth to Princess Aurora.
QUEEN: That's not true.

CARABOSSE: And in exchange, the queen promised me…
QUEEN: Nothing. I promised her nothing.
CARABOSSE: …she promised, on the first birthday of the princess, I would be recognized as the number one fairy in the kingdom.
QUEEN: Dearest Husband, please have the guards remove this creature from this celebration.
CARABOSSE: My dear Queen, one gets back what one gives.
KING: Guards, please escort this unwelcome guest from the premises.
(*Two GUARDS move toward CARABOSSE. She zaps them with a spell; a SOUND is heard.*)
CARABOSSE: Freeze. (*The guards fall down.*) I'll not leave before I grant my christening gift upon the princess.
QUEEN: Please don't hurt my baby.
CARABOSSE: Oh, I won't hurt her.
QUEEN: Thank you.
CARABOSSE: No, I won't hurt the princess.
QUEEN: Candide, can't you make Carabosse the number one fairy?
CARABOSSE: I won't hurt Aurora, she will hurt herself. My christening gift is… before her sixteenth birthday, she will prick her finger on a sewing needle and soon after… die. (*She casts a spell. A SOUND is heard.*)
QUEEN: No!! You can't do this!
CARABOSSE: But I can, Madam Queen, and I did. Now for the next fifteen years, you, the king, the entire kingdom will always be thinking, it

can happen at any time... tomorrow, next week, month, year, in two years, six... will your pretty baby make it to her sixteenth birthday? And all this was really so unnecessary. Oh and thank you, I got what I needed from you. (*She cackles as she exits.*)

KING: My dear, what have you done? You promised things we cannot deliver.

QUEEN: Yes, I did. I did it for us... so we could have a baby.

CANDIDE: Without consulting... consulting any of the other... other good fairies or me? Me or the others?

QUEEN: I'm sorry, I was only thinking about the future of the kingdom.

MIETTES: And now the kingdom doesn't have any future. (*She cries.*) The princess could prick her finger on a needle at any time and die. (*She cries a bit more and then sniffles.*)

CANDIDE: Madam Queen, my Queen, Carabosse knew... yes, she knew... you couldn't deliver... never deliver... on the promise of making her the number one fairy. Being number one fairy was not in her future. She used you... yes, she used you for something else. Something?

MIETTES: She did say... she got what she needed. Oh, no. (*She cries.*) Yes, she did, but what? What did she get?

QUEEN: I didn't give her anything.

KING: Candide, I demand that you or Miettes stop this horrendous deed from happening.

MIETTES: I'm sorry, my dear King, we cannot. (*She cries.*)

CANDIDE: We've already granted… granted our wishes upon the princess. The princess has received our wishes. And we only get one. Just one.
(*LILAC enters. She speaks calmly, a bit on the shy side.*)
LILAC: Excuse me; I might be able to help.
KING: Who are you?
STEWARD: The third fairy, Lilac, the Little.
CANDIDE: Where have you been? You've been where?
LILAC: Once Carabosse entered, I hid. Just in case.
CANDIDE: Smart move, Lilac. So meek and very smart. Lilac the Little, Lilac the meek. Little and meek.
QUEEN: How can you help? The curse has already been set.
LILAC: Yes, it has. But you see, I've not granted my wish upon the princess yet. I might be able to alter Carabosse's spell. I can try.
KING: Speak up and do it. This is no time to be meek. I demand that you do it now. Please stop this evil deed from happening.
MIETTES: But overturning another fairy's curse will be very hard to do.
CANDIDE: Especially a wish… yes, a wish from Carabosse. Her evil power… power is very strong. Very strong.
QUEEN: Princess Aurora was too long in the making. You must do something.
CANDIDE: Why… why should we… we fairies… help you, my dear Queen? Dearest Queen?
MIETTES: You made a pact with Carabosse against us.

CANDIDE: Let the evil fairy deal with you. You deal with the evil fairy.

QUEEN: The king and I were desperate for a child. She tricked me.

CANDIDE: Yes, she did. She did do that. I just wish... oh, I wish I knew what she gained from it. What did she gain?

QUEEN: Please help us. (*The KING holds the QUEEN.*)

KING: Please, Lilac. Do something.

LILAC: Well, I was going to wish upon the princess, wisdom. It seems we all can use that now.

KING: You are very wise for your young age.

LILAC: Thank you, your majesty. But as the wise Miettes said, reversing a curse cast by Carabosse will not be easy.

QUEEN: Whatever you can do is better than doing nothing.

LILAC: Let me see. I will try. (*She concentrates.*) I'm sorry, I'm afraid I can't stop the princess from pricking her finger on a needle...

KING: No, this can't happen.

LILAC: ... but I will try my best to prevent her from dying... if that deed happens.

QUEEN: Bless you.

LILAC: Instead, I wish that the princess will...

(*CARABOSSE enters with a big SOUND. A thunderclap.*)

CARABOSSE: What is going on here? Lilac, what do you think you are doing?

LILAC: Undoing what should have never been done.

(*The following is like a sword fight with words. SOUND should accompany this. LILAC and CARABOSSE wave their hands as they speak. Each fairy reacts to some words*

like they are being punched or hit by each word. Lilac uses strength in her voice she never knew she had.)
CARABOSSE: You think… you can stop… the princess… from dying?
LILAC: Yes… I do. She… will… not… die.
CARABOSSE: Who are you… you young upstart… you are too meek to try and change… what I have wished?
LILAC: Yes, I am Lilac, the Little, the meek. But I am the youth and future of fairies… just as Aurora is the youth… and future of this kingdom. And she… will not die. (*She moves to the QUEEN who is holding the princess.*) My wish is that, if Princess Aurora pricks her finger on a needle, she will not die (*LILAC makes a big gesture to the baby. A SOUND effect is heard. She then faces off with CARABOSSE again.*) The princess will not die. And you can't reverse that. (*She gestures toward CARABOSSE. CARABOSSE stumbles. LILAC wins this round. The war of words begins again.*)
CARABOSSE: Touché, my young fairy. Well, played. The princess won't die. At least right away. Instead, she will sleep… for two… hundred years.
LILAC: No… fifty.
CARABOSSE: One… hundred… years… and then… she will die. You can't reverse that.
(*CARABOSSE casts a spell. A SOUND is heard. LILAC falls down.*)
KING: One hundred years? And then die?
(*LILAC jumps up.*)
LILAC: No! She'll sleep, yes… sleep for one hundred years… but she will not die! I have wished that and

you can't change my wish. And after she sleeps for one hundred years, she will wake and she will not have aged a minute. (*She casts a spell. A SOUND is heard.*)

CARABOSSE: (*One last thrust.*) Once she is awake, a prince must kiss her. And the prince who gives her that first kiss will own her. (*CARABOSSE casts a spell. A SOUND is heard.*) You cannot change that. (*She casts another spell and gestures toward LILAC. Another SOUND is heard. LILAC falls to the ground, spent. CARABOSSE exits, laughing. MIETTES runs to LILAC.*)

MIETTES: Little Lilac, are you all right? (*LILAC doesn't respond or move. MIETTES begins to cry.*) Oh no! (*CANDIDE runs to LILAC.*)

CANDIDE: What's wrong? Wrong? Alive? Is she alive? (*Pause and then LILAC wakes up.*)

LILAC: What? I'm all right. Miettes, why are you crying?

MIETTES: You fought so bravely. You are meek no more. (*She cries as she embraces LILAC.*)

KING: So, sometime between now and Aurora's sixteenth birthday, she will still prick her finger on a sewing needle?

CANDIDE: Yes, I'm afraid so, yes. But at least she won't die. She won't die.

KING: No, she'll just sleep for one hundred years?

CANDIDE: Correct. It is so.

KING: And sometime in those one hundred sleep-filled years, the queen and I will be the ones who die. So Carabosse has won. And we lose. We won't get to see the princess grow up, marry, and make us grandparents. I can't believe that three good fairies can't reverse the curse that one evil fairy has declared.

CANDIDE: He's right. Yes, he is. Maybe if we join together… together we join… we can stop this. Stop this! (*The three fairies huddle. They all bounce and hum for a few beats.*)

MIETTES: Carabosse's magic is very powerful. We can't do anything. (*She sniffles.*)

CANDIDE: No, we can't. No.

LILAC: Wait, I can alter my spell slightly. (*She casts a spell.*) If she pricks her finger… the entire royal family and all the Lords and Ladies of the court will sleep with the princess…all frozen in time… until she is the kissed by a prince, and then you, dear King and Queen, and the others will awaken. No one will have aged. (*LILAC claps her hands. A spell SOUND is heard. LILAC falls to the ground, spent. CANDIDE and MIETTES run to LILAC and help her to her feet.*) That's the best I can do.

QUEEN: Thank you.

CANDIDE: King Florestan, we will be leaving now. We are leaving. We will return on the princess's sixteenth birthday… her sixteenth birthday… if she makes it to that day… to recommend a prince for her to marry. Recommend a prince.

QUEEN: You can't desert us now. What about Carabosse?

CANDIDE: As her actions have shown… they have shown… her wings flutter to a different purpose than ours. Very different. (*CANDIDE and MIETTES help LILAC as all three exit. There is a beat.*)

KING: No, I won't accept this. The fairies' best is not good enough. We can beat Carabosse's curse ourselves and prevent this horrendous deed from ever happening. Steward.
STEWARD: Yes, your Majesty.
KING: Make a declaration throughout the kingdom that...
STEWARD: ... from this day forth... all spinning wheels and sewing needles must be destroyed. (*The LORDS and LADIES cheer in support.*)
KING: All clothing will be imported from this day forth. On pain of death, I decree that sewing of any kind is forbidden throughout the kingdom. The Princess Aurora's fate is...
STEWARD: ...in the hands of all that love her and care about the future of the kingdom. (*The LORDS and LADIES cheer in support. The KING and QUEEN exit.*) Thank you all for destroying your spinning wheels... and doing without any other sharp instruments that might even look like a needle. Seven years have passed without incident, and Princess Aurora has grown from a baby to a sweet young eight-year-old girl.
(*The STEWARD, LORDS, and LADIES exit. AURORA at EIGHT years old enters playing a game.*)
AURORA @ EIGHT: Ready or not, here I come.
(*PHILAMUND @ TEN years old enters.*)
PHILAMUND @ TEN: Here I am.
AURORA @ EIGHT: Philamund, why aren't you hiding?
PHILAMUND @ TEN: I wanted you to find me.
AURORA @ EIGHT: Philamund, stop acting silly.

PHILAMUND @ TEN: You're right, it is silly. Go hide. I'll be "it."
AURORA @ EIGHT: You'll never find me. (*She runs off.*)
PHILAMUND @ TEN: Oh, yes, I will. (*He runs off after her. The STEWARD enters.*)
STEWARD: Lords and Ladies, through your continued sacrifices, five more years have passed. The princess still lives, and the silliness between Philamund and Aurora has developed into love.
(*A thirteen-year-old AURORA and fifteen-year-old PHILAMUND enter.*)
AURORA @ THIRTEEN: So you found me again?
PHILAMUND @ FIFTEEN: I think it's you now who doesn't hide from me.
AURORA @ THIRTEEN: Philamund, do you ever dream?
PHILAMUND @ FIFTEEN: Yes, I had a nightmare last night.
AURORA @ THIRTEEN: No, I mean, do you dream about what your future has in store for you?
PHILAMUND @ FIFTEEN: That's what my nightmare was about. My future didn't look very good. You pricked your finger on a spinning wheel needle and died in my arms.
AURORA @ THIRTEEN: Oh, you still don't believe in that old Carabosse fairy nonsense, do you?
PHILAMUND @ FIFTEEN: I suppose not. It has been twelve years since the kingdom has seen any fairies and the evil curse was cast.
AURORA @ THIRTEEN: Father thinks that all the fairies died years ago. He says, "otherwise,

Carabosse would have acted before now, if she were alive."

PHILAMUND @ FIFTEEN: Does that mean the fairies won't have a prince to recommend for you to marry on your sixteenth birthday?

AURORA @ THIRTEEN: Why?

(*PHILAMUND avoids the question.*)

PHILAMUND @ FIFTEEN: So what do you dream about?

AURORA @ THIRTEEN: I dream about our future, you and me, together, of course, and how rapidly things around us are changing. Do you think man will ever be able to fly like a bird?

PHILAMUND @ FIFTEEN: That would really be something.

AURORA @ THIRTEEN: If it were true we could fly to the moon to get away from here.

PHILAMUND @ FIFTEEN: Since we can't fly there now… do you want to run to our secret spot?

AURORA @ THIRTEEN: I'll beat you there. (*She runs off stage.*)

PHILAMUND @ FIFTEEN: Oh, no you won't. (*PHILAMUND @ FIFTEEN runs after AURORA @ THIRTEEN. The STEWARD enters.*)

STEWARD: The secret spot they referred to wasn't far from the castle, but it seemed as far away as the moon to Aurora and Philamund. Why would the two young lovers want to separate themselves from the eyes of the kingdom? (*The KING enters.*)

KING: Excuse me, Steward.

STEWARD: Your majesty. (*He bows.*)

KING: It seems our children have developed a fondness for one another.

STEWARD: Yes, they are inseparable.

KING: Philamund is a fine young boy, however, we must keep the kingdom's future in mind. The princess can't have a relationship with a common citizen. She must marry a prince recommended by the fairies.

STEWARD: Do the fairies still play a part in the kingdom's future?

KING: It's tradition and I must believe in it. Your son is not a prince and has no chance of being recommended by the fairies. Do you understand.

STEWARD: I understand, sire.

KING: As I knew you would.

STEWARD: I will speak to Philamund.

KING: Thank you. Give my best to your wife. (*He exits.*)

STEWARD: I must speak with Philamund. (*PHILAMUND @ FIFTEEN enters.*)

PHILAMUND @ FIFTEEN: No, Father, I will not stop seeing Aurora.

STEWARD: Then be careful. Keep your Secret Spot, secret.

PHILAMUND @ FIFTEEN: Thank you, Father. (*He exits.*)

STEWARD: Lords and Ladies, three more years have passed and Princess Aurora has blossomed into a beautiful young woman, soon to be sixteen years old. Carabosse's evil curse will soon be over. In fact, it looks like it isn't even going to happen.

(*The LIGHTS fade to black.*)

SCENE TWO

(AT RISE: The scene is The Secret Spot, played in front of a forest drop. An eighteen-year-old PHILAMUND and a sixteen-year-old AURORA enter.)

PHILAMUND: Aurora, my love, it is time we stop hiding our love from the kingdom.
AURORA: I wish we could. But you know we can't because of my father.
PHILAMUND: Then I think it's time to ask your father the big question.
AURORA: And what is the big question?
PHILAMUND: May I have your hand in marriage?
AURORA: Don't you think you ought to ask me first?
PHILAMUND: Oh, stop. We've talked about this.
AURORA: Do you still have Carabosse nightmares?
PHILAMUND: With only two days before your sixteenth birthday… Carabosse is not our problem anymore. No, I think you're safe from her. Your dad is our problem now.
AURORA: You know Daddy is planning a big celebration for my birthday and will have a prince there for me to marry.
PHILAMUND: Didn't the fairies die?
AURORA: The good fairies didn't.
PHILAMUND: Do they have a prince picked for you?
AURORA: I've not heard.
PHILAMUND: Then it's time we break tradition. I will ask your father… in front of the entire kingdom… if I can marry you.

AURORA: Let's just get married right now.
PHILAMUND: I wish we could.
AURORA: If we get married before my sixteenth birthday, I can't marry anyone else.
PHILAMUND: How do we get married?
AURORA: My Godmothers can do it.
PHILAMUND: Do you know how to contact them?
AURORA: Who do you think keeps us safe when we're here at our Secret Spot? (*She closes her eyes and waves her arms.*) Come to me, my Godmothers.
(*SOUND is heard and LILAC enters. She has aged.*)
LILAC: Is there a problem, my dear?
AURORA: Where are Candide and Miettes?
LILAC: Their health is failing. What can I do for you?
AURORA: Philamund and I wish to get married.
LILAC: Oh! I think they better be here for that.
(*She does a mental telepathy thing. SOUND is heard. CANDIDE and MIETTES enter. They have aged.*)
CANDIDE: Is there a problem? A problem, do you have?
LILAC: Aurora wants to break from the wedding tradition.
AURORA: Do you have a prince for me?
LILAC: We were hoping love would take its true course.
AURORA: Love has hit the mark.
MIETTES: Oh! (*She cries.*)
AURORA: Candide, will you do the honors?
CANDIDE: Gladly, my child. Gladly. I see no reason... no reason we can't get a jump on things. Jump. And then on your birthday... sixteenth birthday... I will recommend... recommend to your father...

recommend to the king that Philamund be your husband. Your husband. Line them up, Miettes and Lilac. Put them in a wedding line.

(*MIETTES pulls PHILAMUND to her and LILAC pulls AURORA to her. The lovers stand together between the fairies. CANDIDE is upstage of them.*)

MIETTES: Weddings make me cry.

LILAC: Everything makes you cry.

CANDIDE: It is an honor… honor… for me not only as a fairy… fairy… of the kingdom, but also as a godmother to Aurora… godmother to the princess… to perform this marriage ceremony. I will gladly marry you. (*MIETTES begins to cry.*)

LILAC: Miettes, they're not married yet.

MIETTES: It's the anticipation of it all.

CANDIDE: Do you, Philamund, take the princess, Princess Aurora, as your one true love and bride? True love and bride.

PHILAMUND: I do, gladly. (*MIETTES wails.*)

CANDIDE: Do you, Princess Aurora, take Philamund… Philamund… as your one true love and groom? True love and groom.

AURORA: Yes, I do. (*MIETTES wails.*)

CANDIDE: I now pronounce… I pronounce you husband and wife, princess and prince.

(*MIETTES wails.*)

LILAC: Prince?

CANDIDE: Philamund became a prince… yes, a prince… as soon as he married Aurora. Once they were married.

MIETTES: (*Crying.*) How romantic.

CANDIDE: The prince may kiss the princess. The princess may kiss the prince.
(*PHILAMUND and AURORA kiss.*)
MIETTES: (*Crying.*) We now have a prince to recommend to the king. (*CANDIDE coughs.*)
LILAC: I must get these two back home. We'll see you in two days at your birthday celebration.
(*All embrace one another.*)
AURORA: Thank you.
CANDIDE: I'm happy for you. Happy. True love is a blessing. A blessing is true love.
MIETTES: (*Crying.*) Yes, it is.
PHILAMUND: Before you go. I must know... is Carabosse still alive?
CANDIDE: We've not seen... not seen... that evil fairy... evil... since the day of the christening, fifteen years ago. Fifteen years.
LILAC: We still wonder what it was she gained from helping the queen?
CANDIDE: She was older... much older... than Miettes and me... both of us... so her health can't be any better than ours. Health no better.
(*The LIGHTS fade on that scene.*)

SCENE THREE

(*The scene is the Great Hall once again. AT RISE: The LORDS and LADIES are discovered. PHILAMUND is among them. The STEWARD enters and speaks.*)

STEWARD: Lords and Ladies, today we celebrate the sixteenth birthday of our Princess Aurora. It's

not every day that a princess turns sweet sixteen, rids herself of an evil curse, and meets her future husband. And rumor has it… that the fairies have a prince to recommend. (*SOUND: A fanfare is heard.*) Please welcome King Florestan, Queen Willameana, and Princess Aurora.
(*All cheer as the KING, QUEEN, and AURORA enter.*)
KING: Thank you, my subjects, for coming. You all know what this day means to the kingdom. Happy birthday to the princess. (*The crowd cheers.*) When the clock strikes seven o'clock, the time the princess was born, she will turn sixteen and the needle curse will finally be over. (*The crowd cheers.*) And I proudly announce that the fairies have recommended a handsome prince for the princess. (*The crowd cheers. AURORA and PHILAMUND share a smile.*)
STEWARD: The princess will now accept all birthday and wedding gifts.
AURORA: Father, where are the fairies? (*A MAN moves to AURORA.*)
MAN: Blessings to you, beautiful princess, on these three wonderful occasions. This sword was given to me after the great war of the fairies. It will protect you from the evils of the kingdom.
AURORA: Thank you. (*To the KING.*) Father, has Candide told you about the marriage?
KING: Yes, I have received the recommendation of the fairies.
PHILAMUND: Thank you, your majesty, father, for accepting this marriage.
KING: Excuse me?

PHILAMUND: My marriage to your daughter.
QUEEN: Oh dear, this sounds like trouble.
KING: Impossible. My daughter will soon be marrying Prince Eldeen to further secure the future of our kingdom.
AURORA: Prince who? What are you talking about?
KING: You shall marry the Prince Eldeen recommended by the fairies. (*He calls to the STEWARD.*) Steward.
STEWARD: Lords and Ladies of the Court… please welcome Prince Eldeen.
(*SOUND: A fanfare is heard. ELDEEN, a handsome young man enters and moves to AURORA.*)
ELDEEN: It's an honor, Princess Aurora. (*He kisses her hand.*)
AURORA: OUCH! (*She shakes her hand.*)
ELDEEN: You are more beautiful than the fairies described.
AURORA: But, Father.
(*SOUND: A clock begins to strike seven o'clock.*)
KING: As the clock strikes seven, punctuating your birth sixteen years ago… I am pleased to say the fairy Candide has recommended that Prince Eldeen be your husband and marry you tonight.
PHILAMUND: (*To AURORA.*) Why would Candide change her mind?
AURORA: (*To PHILAMUND.*) She wouldn't. (*To the KING.*) But, father, I don't love Prince Eldeen.
KING: You will grow to love him. Your mother and I had a marriage arranged by the fairies and we are very happy. The fairies know what they're doing.

AURORA: Father, there is something very wrong about this recommendation.
KING: Stop clinging to Philamund. Come stand next to Eldeen.
AURORA: No, I refuse to do this.
KING: What?
PHILAMUND: She refuses because she's already married.
KING: Guards, take that boy away. (*Two GUARDS move to PHILAMUND and grab him.*)
AURORA: Father, please stop this. The fairy Candide has given her blessing on my marriage to Philamund.
KING: That is not the word I received from her this morning.
AURORA: Just ask her.
KING: Where is she?
AURORA: You know she is always late to everything.
KING: (*To ELDEEN.*) I'm sorry Eldeen.
ELDEEN: Think nothing of it.
KING: Aurora, it is your responsibility to stand next to Prince Eldeen... if you care at all about the future of this kingdom.
AURORA: I can care about the future in a different way.
KING: (*To ELDEEN.*) She's usually not like this.
ELDEEN: It doesn't matter. The deed has been done upon the beauty.
KING: Deed?
ELDEEN: Carabosse's curse upon the princess. Aurora will soon be a sleeping beauty.

KING: If you have a sewing needle… you better leave at once. Guards!
(*With a loud SOUND, CARABOSSE enters. The COURT screams and cowers.*)
CARABOSSE: You are a fool, King Florestan. Eldeen doesn't have a sewing needle. He is the sewing needle.
KING: What nonsense are you talking about?
PHILAMUND: It doesn't matter what she says… a needle can't hurt her now… the clock has just struck seven and the princess was born at seven… she is sixteen now and it is too late for the curse to happen.
ELDEEN: But I kissed her hand before the clock tolled.
KING: What does kissing her hand have to do with anything?
CARABOSSE: It will take time for the curse to take effect.
AURORA: I feel fine.
(*With a loud SOUND, CANDIDE, MIETTES, and LILAC enter.*)
CANDIDE: Carabosse stalled us… we were stalled… watch out for her. Be careful of the evil fairy. King Florestan, we… I and the other good fairies… recommend Philamund to marry the princess. Philamund is our recommendation.
CARABOSSE: You're too late. I made your recommendation for you.
MIETTES: What have you done?
CARABOSSE: I've not done anything… my son has.
LILAC: Your son?

CARABOSSE: Eldeen, let me introduce you to your aunts.
LILAC: Oh no, Eldeen! Aurora, has he touched you yet?
AURORA: He kissed my hand, but it felt more like a bite.
KING: He doesn't have a needle.
LILAC: No, he is the needle. Spell Eldeen backward.
PHILAMUND: N - E - E - D - L - E.
CARABOSSE: And in anyone's dictionary that spells… Needle!
QUEEN: Please say it hasn't happened.
KING: I demand that you both leave this Great Hall this instance.
ELDEEN: Once the princess falls asleep… we will. (*AURORA falls down.*)
AURORA: Father?
QUEEN: My baby. (*She runs toward AURORA, but falls.*)
KING: You will pay for this. (*He moves toward ELDEEN, but falls down.*) What is happening?
QUEEN: I am so sleepy.
AURORA: Philamund?
PHILAMUND: My wife.
AURORA: Save me.
(*CANDIDE and MIETTES move toward CARABOSSE.*)
CANDIDE: You've had this planned… planned for sixteen years, haven't you? Sixteen years. (*She falls down.*)
MIETTES: And now we know what you gained by helping the Queen. (*She falls down.*)

CARABOSSE: Yes, the Queen got a daughter. And I got a son… Eldeen! The spell only works when two babies are created.
ELDEEN: Carabosse's curse has come true. The princess will sleep for one hundred years.
PHILAMUND: And you shall die for what you've done. (*PHILAMUND takes the sword that was given to AURORA. He and ELDEEN have a sword fight.*)
LILAC: You stay put.

(*LILAC holds CARABOSSE. PHILAMUND wounds ELDEEN. ELDEEN moves away from PHILAMUND holding the wound.*)

ELDEEN: You will pay for this, Philamund.
(*CARABOSSE breaks free and runs to ELDEEN.*)
CARABOSSE: This little scratch means nothing, Philamund. We still win. You will never see your princess-wife again. Sleep well, everyone.

(*CARABOSSE helps ELDEEN off. PHILAMUND runs to AURORA. LILAC runs to CANDIDE and MIETTES.*)

PHILAMUND: Aurora, are you all right?
LILAC: You two must fight this.
AURORA: Philamund, I'm afraid.
CANDIDE: We're in your hands, Lilac. Your… (*She falls asleep.*)
MIETTES: Fix this mess. (*She falls asleep.*)
PHILAMUND: Aurora, please don't go to sleep.
KING: I'm sorry I doubted you, Philamund.
(*KING, QUEEN, LORDS and LADIES fall asleep.*)
AURORA: I love you. (*AURORA falls asleep. PHILAMUND stands.*)
PHILAMUND: (*Screaming.*) NOOO!
LILAC: Yes, yes. Calm down.

PHILAMUND: Why didn't the curse affect you and me?

LILAC: I guess because we weren't present when Carabosse cast her original spell. You were a baby at home with your mother, and I hid as soon as I saw that evil fairy enter the Great Hall.

PHILAMUND: The evil fairy has won. If a prince kisses Aurora, it won't be me. I can't live for one hundred years. (*He screams in frustration and then speaks.*) Goodbye, Lilac. (*He starts to exit.*)

LILAC: Time travel. (*PHILAMUND stops and turns to LILAC.*)

PHILAMUND: Excuse me?

LILAC: Time travel. We travel forward in time, find them all, Aurora wakes up, you kiss her, everyone else wakes up, and we all live happily ever after.

PHILAMUND: That is the craziest thing I've ever heard. We can't travel forward in time. (*He starts to exit.*)

LILAC: I've been thinking about how to do it for quite a while.

PHILAMUND: Wouldn't we age? If we got there I'd be over a hundred years old.

LILAC: I don't think that would happen.

PHILAMUND: You don't think? So, what you're saying is, you've never done this time traveling before?

LILAC: Well, no.

PHILAMUND: It'll never work. Goodbye.

LILAC: We have to do something… or Carabosse is right, you'll never see your wife again.

PHILAMUND: Okay… How do we do it?

LILAC: First let's put the princess on a table.
(*PHILAMUND moves a table center stage and then he and LILAC pick up AURORA and put her on it.*) Now we stand next to the table and the princess, so when we get to her in the future we'll know exactly where to find her.
(*They both move to the left of LILAC and the table.*)
PHILAMUND: Now what?
LILAC: Hold my hands, and as we spin clockwise, we must chant "jartolken" over and over.
PHILAMUND: Jartolken?
LILAC: It means believe in fairy talk. The centrifugal force we create as we spin should shoot us into any year we set.
PHILAMUND: The year now is 1768.
LILAC: Correct, and we want to go to 1868, just before seven o'clock. Are you ready?
PHILAMUND: As ready as I'll ever be.
LILAC: Give me your hands. (*They take each other's hands.*) Here we go.
(*They start chanting "jartolken" and spin clockwise. All exit but PHILAMUND and LILAC. SOUND and LIGHTS accompany this.*)

SCENE FOUR

(*AT RISE: PHILAMUND and LILAC are discovered in the Great Hall, but it is weathered with time. They are still spinning and chanting "jartolken." They stop.*)

PHILAMUND: Did we make it? Did your time traveling spell work?

LILAC: I'm sure it did. At least we're still in the Great Hall. And here's the table we put Aurora on.
PHILAMUND: What happened to her and the others?
LILAC: I don't know about the others, but there's Aurora. (*She points to a body lying on the floor.*)
PHILAMUND: Aurora! (*He runs to her and turns her body to face him. JIMI wakes up. He has the same color hair as AURORA.*)
JIMI: I'm awake. I'm awake. Chill out. Did you find the room?
PHILAMUND: I sorry, I beg your pardon. I thought you were someone else.
JIMI: That's cool, dude. I thought you were my old lady, Janis. We traveled a long way to find these digs. I was, like, catching some zees. The name's Jimi. Love and peace, bro. (*He flashes a peace sign.*) Far out clothes, dude. You too, sister. Like, whoa, man, who sews your threads? They're really groovy.
PHILAMUND: Have you seen any other people around here?
JIMI: No, man, this castle's been empty for hundreds of years. Isn't it out-a-site? Janice is checking it out for just the right room. We're gonna get hitched here.
PHILAMUND: We're looking for a princess.
JIMI: Well, dude, you've come to the right place – Janice, my main squeeze, is a princess.
(*JANIS enters and moves to JIMI.*)
JANIS: What's chillin', Jimi?
JIMI: This is my old lady, Janis.
LILAC: She doesn't look that old.

JIMI: Did you find the Great Hall?
JANIS: Solid, I think this is the Great Hall.
PHILAMUND: This is the Great Hall. We're looking for a princess named Aurora.
JIMI: Cool. Far out name, huh? We're hip to that name. It's the name of the last chick who was hitched here.
PHILAMUND: Aurora! Where is she?
JIMI: Peace, dude. You are so uptight.
JANIS: Yea, like, mellow out. That gig took place many moons ago.
LILAC: Excuse me, what language are you two speaking?
PHILAMUND: Can you tell us what year is it?
JIMI: The year of the youth: 1968. The year of the hippie. It's the dawning of the Age of Aquarius.
LILAC: I guess we over jumped our target date by one hundred years.
PHILAMUND: Can we jartolken backward a hundred years?
LILAC: We should be able to, if we spin counterclockwise, the opposite way we did to get here.
JIMI: Wow, you two are tripping me out. What are you bogarting?
PHILAMUND: Do you know what time it is?
JIMI: Does anyone really care what time it is?
LILAC: We need to get back to 1868 before seven o'clock.
JANIS: Don't freak out, you got a few minutes. But that's a long way to boogie in such a short amount of time.

LILAC: Give me your hands.

(*PHILAMUND holds LILAC's hands. They spin counterclockwise and chant "jartolken." Mad LIGHTS and SOUND accompany this. JIMI and JANIS exit. LORDS, LADIES, KING, QUEEN, STEWARD, and AURORA all enter and go to the positions they were in at the end of Scene Three.*)

SCENE FIVE

(*AT RISE: PHILAMUND and LILAC are still spinning and chanting "jartolken." They stop spinning and chanting, and see AURORA lying on the table.*)

LILAC: There's the princess. (*They move to AURORA.*)
PHILAMUND: Let me kiss her.
LILAC: Not yet. It has to happen after she has slept for one hundred years. She was bitten by Eldeen at seven o'clock. She'll wake up at seven and then you need to be the first to kiss her. If you're the first, then she will love you. (*ELDEEN and CARABOSSE enter.*)
ELDEEN: Unless I kiss her first.
LILAC: How did the two of you get here?
CARABOSSE: Lilac, you're not the only fairy who knows how to time travel. Eldeen and I have been jumping all around the world these past one hundred years. In 1773, Eldeen was a leader in the Boston Tea Party; 1775, we both were responsible for starting the Revolutionary War; Eldeen witnessed the duel between Aaron Burr and

Alexander Hamilton in 1804; I started the War of 1812; and not to be outdone, in 1861, Eldeen was instrumental in starting the Civil War. That ugly mess is just winding down. That brings us to the present, 1868.

ELDEEN: Our next adventure, starting a revolution in Spain, involves Princess Aurora, right after she wakes up and I kiss her.

PHILAMUND: Over my dead body.

ELDEEN: That can be arranged. (*He draws his sword.*)

PHILAMUND: I beat you once, I can do it again. (*He draws his sword.*)

ELDEEN: Yes, you did, and I promised you would pay for that.

(*SOUND: A clock begins to strike seven times.*)

CARABOSSE: The clock tolls. The one hundred years are up.

ELDEEN: Excuse me while I kiss the princess.

PHILAMUND: Stay away from her. (*PHILAMUND and ELDEEN begin sword fight.*)

CARABOSSE: (*To LILAC.*) You stay out of this.

LILAC: And you heed your own words.

(*The sword fight continues. ELDEEN takes control. PHILAMUND trips and falls backward. ELDEEN stands over PHILAMUND with his sword touching PHILAMUND's chest.*)

ELDEEN: Any last words before you can speak no more?

(*LILAC runs toward ELDEEN.*)

LILAC: You'll have to go through me first.

(*CARABOSSE steps forward and casts a spell on LILAC.*)

CARABOSSE: Freeze.

(*LILAC freezes. The clock has tolled seven times. AURORA wakes and sits up on the table.*)
AURORA: Where am I?
CARABOSSE: (*To ELDEEN.*) Finish him off. And kiss the princess.
(*JIMI and JANIS enter on the run. JIMI tackles ELDEEN. JANIS runs to AURORA.*)
JIMI and JANIS: AHHH!
JIMI: Grab the chick, Janice. And run. Come on, dude, run! Everyone, this way.
(*JIMI leads JANIS, AURORA, and PHILAMUND into the audience for a chase through the seats. ELDEEN and CARABOSSE are after them. They run back onstage. CARABOSSE stops them as she stands at stage right. ELDEEN has them cornered as he stands stage left.*)
ELDEEN: What now, mummy?
CARABOSSE: Take the girl and kiss her.
LILAC: (*Although frozen, she can still talk.*) Philamund, she's standing right next to you... kiss her.
(*PHILAMUND kisses AURORA. SOUND and LIGHTS irrupt and a few beats later, the KING, QUEEN, CANDIDE, MIETTES, STEWARD, LORDS, and LADIES wake up. LILAC unfreezes. LIGHTS fade to black.*)

SCENE SIX

(*AT RISE: All are discovered in a wedding tableau with AURORA and PHILAMUND at center, still kissing. CANDIDE is standing upstage of them. PHILAMUND and AURORA break kiss.*)

CANDIDE: And with that kiss...

(*MIETTES cries. ELDEEN and CARABOSSE are down left, away from the tableau.*)
CARABOSSE and ELDEEN: NOOO!
CANDIDE: You're too late, Carabosse. Too late. A prince who truly loves Aurora... Philamund loves Aurora and has kissed her, securing... securing... the future of the kingdom. Our kingdom has a future.
KING: Guards, arrest those two.
(*The GUARDS move to ELDEEN and CARABOSSE.*)
CARABOSSE: Freeze. (*She casts a spell. The GUARDS freeze.*) Come on, Eldeen. Mummy's bored. Let's go raise some havoc in Spain.
(*CARABOSSE and ELDEEN exit. The LORDS and LADIES cheer.*)
PHILAMUND: (*To JIMI and JANIS.*) How did you two follow us?
JIMI: We were stowaways on your jartolken trip.
JANIS: What a gas.
PHILAMUND: (*To JIMI.*) Thank you, my brother.
JIMI: Anything for you and your foxy lady.
LILAC: We need to get the two of you back to the future and the rest of us to the future in the past.
(*The LORDS and LADIES cheer as the LIGHTS fade to black.*)

END

A Collection from a Career in Theatre

The True Story of the Pied Piper

by

Bob May

© 2017 by Bob May

All rights reserved

CAST OF CHARACTERS

TOWNSPEOPLE and CHILDREN OF HAMELIN
MAYOR
WIFE of the Mayor
LOTHAR, their sixteen-year-old son
VALDA
BERTA, Valda's twelve-year-old daughter
KARLINA
GRETEL, Karlina's fifteen-year-old daughter
RATSO
RATSO'S RAT PACK (*In squeaking order*)
MR. SQUEAKS
SNEAKY
WHISKERS
SQUEAKS A LOT
STINKY
LITTLE NIBBLER
THE PIED PIPER

SYNOPSIS OF SCENES

Scene One: The Hamelin, Germany Town Square
Scene Two: The Town Square
Scene Three: The Town Square
Scene Four: The banks of the River Weser with the mouth of a cave in the mountains
Scene Five: The Town Square
Scene Six: The banks of the River Weser with the mouth of a cave in the mountains

The play is written to flow without major breaks between scenes.

The premiere of *The True Story of the Pied Piper* (*originally titled The Pied Piper*) was presented by Children's Theatre To Go, Inc. at the Reynolds Performance Hall in Conway, Arkansas, on August 5, 2005, under the direction of Bob May, choreography by Lacy Dunn, with set design by Joe Meils, costume design by Nikki Webster, under the stage management of Andi Schultes, with the following cast:

Doc—Kelsie Craig (*cut from 2017 draft*)
The Pied Piper—Tiffany Sledge
Mayor—Chad Bradford
Wife of the Mayor—Erin Lewter
Lothar—A. J. Spiridigliozzi (*MICKEY in 2005 draft*)
Valda—Sarah Hoelzeman (*POOR PEARL in 2005 draft*)
Berta—Madeline Welhite (*RUBY in 2005 draft*)
Karlina—Karen Owings (*MS. BIZ in 2005 draft*)
Gretel—Kayte Reder (*MINNIE in 2005 draft*)
Ratso—Patsy L. Paul

Mother of the Twins—Adrieanna Hutson (*cut from 2017 draft*)
Ratso's Rat Pack:
Mr. Squeaks—Brooke McCollum
Sneaky—Katie Oslica
Whiskers—Jasmine Paulie
Squeaks-a-Lot—Hannah Eaton
Stinky—Elijah Paulie
Little Nibbler—Hayley Hicks
Children of Hamelin: Alyssa Anderson, Abby Hicks, Hannah Lewter, Sarah Lewter, Sara Rickman, Colton Schott, Libby Speck

The 2017 draft had a workshop reading by The Young Players at The Royal Players in Benton, AR, in March 2017.

SCENE ONE

(The scene is a town square. Hills and a river are seen in the background. AT RISE: The TOWNSPEOPLE are discovered.)

TOWNSPEOPLE: (*Chanting.*) Rid the town of the rats. Rid the town of the rats. Rid the town of the rats. (*The MAYOR and his WIFE enter.*)

MAYOR: Welcome good citizens of Hamelin to our annual Fall Festival feast.

KARLINA: Herr Mayor, with your reelection looming, is this a good time for you to ignore the rat problem in our town?

MAYOR: I am not ignoring it, Frau Karlina. Poison has been spread throughout the wealthy side of the town. (*The TOWNSPEOPLE cheer.*)

KARLINA: Is that enough?

MAYOR: The apothecary guaranteed me that it will work.

KARLINA: It had better work. You need the vote of the people, and I need my customers to feel safe when they enter my shops. And I wouldn't want anything to happen to my darling Gretel.

(*KARLINA hugs GRETEL who stands by her.*)

GRETEL: Mother!

MAYOR: Let's not spoil the Fall Festival with talk of rats. My wife and I are excited to see so many familiar faces.

WIFE: I've made my special bratkartoffeln. And I can't wait to see what others have brought for our harvest celebration feast.

LOTHAR: Father, may I speak?

MAYOR: Lothar, please don't ruin this joyous occasion. Enjoy the feast and the prosperous times we are living in. Stop trying to cause trouble.

LOTHAR: Everyone is not enjoying "prosperous times" in our hamlet. What about the poor?

MAYOR: The poor are taken care of.

LOTHAR: We could do more for them, especially during festival time. The rich have much more than we need.

MAYOR: Nonsense. (*VALDA steps out of the crowd. BERTA stands next to her.*)

VALDA: Your son speaks the truth.

MAYOR: Frau Valda, why do you always interfere with our celebrations?

VALDA: I fight with your son for the rights of the poor.

MAYOR: Go home where you belong, with the poor.
LOTHAR: The rich of Hamelin are all so greedy. We should not exclude the poor from the Fall Festival. Frau Valda and the rest of the poor should be celebrating with us.
BERTA: You tell 'em, Lothar.
MAYOR: Frau Valda, please keep your daughter under control.
LOTHAR: This greed will prove to be the downfall of this town.
(*The TOWNSPEOPLE laugh at LOTHAR.*)
MAYOR: Good citizens, I once again apologize for my son's behavior.
KARLINA: Herr Mayor, why can't you control your child? You'll notice how obedient my Gretel is.
GRETEL: Mother!
KARLINA: I guess he can't taste the silver spoon hanging from his mouth.
WIFE: Please, let's all just go to the feast.
MAYOR: My wife is right; we are here to celebrate the harvest.
(*RATSO enters and sniffs around two children. They scream.*)
CHILD: It's a rat.
(*The TOWNSPEOPLE scream and scurry for cover. They clump in groups around the stage. VALDA and BERTA stand-alone center stage.*)
KARLINA: Well, Herr Mayor, so much for your poison guarantee.
(*RATSO sniffs and circles VALDA and BERTA. Mother holds daughter tightly.*)
BERTA: Mama, don't let it hurt me.

VALDA: Just be calm, my Berta.
WIFE: (*To MAYOR.*) My dear, do something.
MAYOR: Frau Valda and Fraulein Berta are used to rats in their part of town. They can fend for themselves.
GRETEL: Mother, help them.
KARLINA: Do I look like an exterminator? (*LOTHAR steps toward RATSO.*)
LOTHAR: What do you want?
RATSO: Ah, youth, the future of Hamelin. Learn to think on your own, or you won't have a future. (*He moves to two children.*) Boogidy-boo! (*The CHILDREN scream and RATSO scurries off.*)
WIFE: That sounded like a threat against our children?
KARLINA: Yes, it did. The rats of Hamelin are getting very brave. Herr Mayor, what are you going to do?
TOWNSPEOPLE: Rid the town of the rats. Rid the town of the rats.
KARLINA: We must protect our children. (*The TOWNSPEOPLE ad-lib their agreement.*)
VALDA: We face this problem every day in the poor part of town. Our children have to live with the fear of rats all the time.
MAYOR: Would someone please escort Frau Valda and her daughter back to their part of town?
BERTA: We don't need any help.
VALDA: We know our place in this town. (*VALDA and BERTA move to exit.*)
LOTHAR: I'm sorry, Frau Valda. (*VALDA and BERTA exit.*) Father, you can't continue to treat the poor as

you do. We are all Germans and they should have the same rights as the wealthy.

MAYOR: The poor can fend for themselves.

KARLINA: You need to do something about these rats.

MAYOR: Relax, Frau Karlina, it just takes time for the poison to work.

WIFE: I've heard stories about a Pied Piper who can help us.

KARINA: I know what a Piper is… someone who plays a flute-like musical instrument. But what is a "pied" Piper?

WIFE: Pied means "having patches of two or more colors."

KARINA: I know the definition of pied.

WIFE: I assume the Pied Piper is a piper dressed in a multicolored costume. The legend is, the Piper is sort of a musical Jack-of-all-trades.

MAYOR: I promise I will look into this Pied Piper. Meanwhile, let us get on with our Fall Festival.

WIFE: Yes, let us go to the Great Hall and celebrate.

LOTHAR: Father, I would like to ask all the young to stay behind for a bit.

MAYOR: Any children who want to stay and listen to another one of my son's sermons are free to do so. Otherwise… the feast waits.

WIFE: Please, let's go. (*The ADULTS exit.*)

KARLINA: Gretel, do as I told you.

GRETEL: I will honor your wishes, Mother.
(*KARLINA exits.*)

LOTHAR: Thank you for staying. You know, as the youth Hamelin, just as the rat said, we are its future. (*BERTA runs in.*)
BERTA: Yes, we are.
LOTHAR: Berta, I can handle this alone. If we fight together, we can get justice for all.
GRETEL: Can't you see that this tomboy is the only supporter you have?
(*CHILDREN ad-lib their agreement.*)
LOTHAR: All the children stayed, didn't they?
GRETEL: They stayed because I asked them to. I didn't want to be alone with you.
LOTHAR: What's wrong, Gretel? You were once on my side.
GRETEL: This is the end of you and me.
LOTHAR: What?
GRETEL: Here is the charm you gave me. (*GRETEL unfastens a necklace and hands it to LOTHAR.*)
LOTHAR: What has happened to you, Gretel?
GRETEL: Nothing has happened to me.
BERTA: What has happened to her is her mother.
LOTHAR: Gretel, you were once embarrassed by your mother's actions.
BERTA: Her mama threatened to send her away if she doesn't stop being your girlfriend.
LOTHAR: Is this true?
GRETEL: Come on, everyone, we're missing the feast. Let's leave this dreamer in his own world. (*All the children, but BERTA, ad-lib as they exit.*)
BERTA: By acting like that, she'll still be in town and she can at least see you.

LOTHAR: Berta, I appreciate your support; but please just leave me alone right now.

(*BERTA exits. LOTHAR paces. RATSO enters when LOTHAR's back is to him.*)

RATSO: It's tough when no one will listen to you.

(*LOTHAR spins around. There is a moment between the two. LOTHAR speaks with friendship in his voice.*)

LOTHAR: Hey, Ratso.

RATSO: My friend, Lothar, how did I do? (*RATSO and LOTHAR do a special handshake.*)

LOTHAR: You were great. (*VALDA enters.*)

VALDA: He was more than great, he was fantastic. He had everyone scared to death.

RATSO: Especially Frau Karlina.

LOTHAR: My father sure was aghast.

VALDA: That's cause he's in denial that rats are in his rich part of town.

LOTHAR: The "youth of the city is its future" was a great line. (*The three laugh.*)

RATSO: I got it from you. But does this stunt prove anything? My rats and the poor are still starving as the smell of festival bratkartoffeln and sauerbraten hang over the rich part of town like a well-fed cloud.

VALDA: The greedier the rich become, the less they give to the poor, and in turn, we leave less for the rats to eat.

LOTHAR: I'll continue to get food for everyone. Ratso, you and your rats just continue to make appearances here on the rich side of town and show my father and the rest of the rich that the greedy wall they have built around themselves is falling down.

RATSO: Let's pledge our cooperation. (*The three shake hands.*)

LOTHAR: Come, let's have our own harvest celebration. Ratso, call your rats.

RATSO: Come, my rat pack. (*The RATS enter. They scurry around the stage and end behind RATSO in a formation. BERTA enters too and moves to her mother.*) Fraulein Berta, have you met all my rat pack?

BERTA: No. (*As RATSO introduces each RAT, they step to BERTA, do their own special salute, and then scurry back behind RATSO.*)

RATSO: First, this is my Second, Mr. Squeaks… then there's Whiskers… Sneaky… Squeaks-a-lot… Stinky, my sewer rat… and this is Little Nibbler. (*A very small child should play LITTLE NIBBLER.*) Praise to Lothar.

RAT PACK: Praise to Lothar.

LOTHAR: I promise to fight for the rights of the rats and the poor. And to feed you all. During the harvest, there is always an abundance of food. Now, go and make your presence known throughout this side of town. And be careful of the poison my father has put all around.

(*The LIGHTS fade to black.*)

SCENE TWO

(*AT RISE: The MAYOR and TOWNSPEOPLE are discovered in the town square.*)

MAYOR: Welcome, good citizens of Hamelin, I sense a problem.

KARLINA: Herr Mayor, have you noticed the increase in rat activity in our part of this fair town? Your poison hasn't worked.

WIFE: There are rats everywhere. (*TOWNSPEOPLE agree with KARLINA and the WIFE.*)

MAYOR: Not to worry. I have sent for this Pied Piper. Meanwhile, keep your houses clean of food crumbs and the rats will go back to the poor side of town where they belong.

(*RATSO and the RAT PACK enter. Two groups are formed. The RATS on one side of the stage, the TOWNSPEOPLE on the other.*)

RATSO: You'll never defeat us.

(*The RAT PACK shouts their agreement. LOTHAR and VALDA enter and stand with the RATS.*)

LOTHAR: Father, these rats are my friends. They are only working with Frau Valda and me to right the wrongs in Hamelin.

MAYOR: Son, you can never trust a rat.

VALDA: Your son preaches a good sermon. We must all coexist in this world if any of us are going to survive.

MAYOR: Frau Valda, are you on the side of these rats?

VALDA: Your son and these rats offer my people and me more hope than you do.

MAYOR: Valda, if you stand by us... I promise to improve your living conditions.

VALDA: You swear you will do this?

MAYOR: You have my word.

LOTHAR: Don't trust him. He's only saying that to get even with me.
VALDA: But, Lothar, this is what we've been fighting for.
(*VALDA begins to move from one group to the other. BERTA stops her with a shout.*)
BERTA: But, Mama, what about Ratso and the rats?
(*VALDA moves to BERTA and pulls her to the TOWNSPEOPLE side of the stage.*)
VALDA: It's not everything we fought for, but one must take what one is given.
RATSO: Herr Mayor, we all are sensitive to feeling included or excluded. Why do you now include Valda and her kind? Does that make you feel better? And yet, you exclude my rat pack and me. How do you think that makes us feel? Got any promises for us?
(*The RAT PACK adlib their support of RATSO.*)
MAYOR: Now that all the citizens of Hamelin... poor and rich alike... are united, I promise we will defeat your kind, Ratso.
RATSO: Up to now, Herr Mayor, my rats and I have been playing along with your son's agenda. But from now on, we vow to make your cozy lives... rich and poor... miserable.
LOTHAR: This was not supposed to happen. Father, stop this. Ratso.
RATSO: Sorry kid, your way isn't working, we must fight for our rights.
(*RATSO and his RATS exit ad-libbing like a mob. BERTA runs after them, but does not exit.*)
BERTA: Rasto!

LOTHAR: Father, stop this fighting.
MAYOR: Citizens of Hamelin, I give you my word, the Pied Piper will exterminate all rats.
(*The MAYOR leads all the TOWNSPEOPLE off as they adlib like a mob. This leaves VALDA on one side of the stage and BERTA on the other.*)
VALDA: Come, Berta.
BERTA: Mama, you're a traitor. (*VALDA moves to BERTA.*)
VALDA: Tell me that when your stomach is full and your bedroom is rat free. (*VALDA grabs BERTA by the arm and they exit the same way the MAYOR did.*)
LOTHAR: This was not supposed to happen. (*PIED PIPER enters.*)
PIPER: You look like you can use my services.
LOTHAR: What? Who are you?
PIPER: One who believes in righting the wrongs in the world.
LOTHAR: Are you the Pied Piper?
PIPER: I answer to no other name.
LOTHAR: It's my father that wants your help, not me.
PIPER: Are you sure? For one thousand silver kreutzer pieces, I can make you Hamelin's hero.
LOTHAR: I would gladly pay you ten times that fee to save Hamelin's future.
PIPER: You can pay me once the job is done.
LOTHAR: I don't have that kind of money.
PIPER: Do you have anything of value?
LOTHAR: All I have is this charm. It's worthless.
PIPER: It must have some worth to you.
LOTHAR: It once had more value than anything else in the world.

PIPER: Then I would hold on to it if I were you.
LOTHAR: You can have it. (*He hands the charm to the PIPER.*) I don't need your help. There's no hope for the people of Hamelin. I am leaving this sorry place.
(*LOTHAR exits as the LIGHTS fade to black.*)

SCENE THREE

(*The scene is the town square. AR RISE: RATSO is discovered with his RAT PACK.*)

RATSO: Mr. Squeaks? (*MR. SQUEAKS steps forward and salutes RATSO.*)
MR. SQUEAKS: Yes, sir!
RATSO: Round up all of the rats in the surrounding countryside and bring them here to Hamelin.
MR. SQUEAKS: Yes, sir! (*MR. SQUEAKS salutes RATSO and scurries away.*)
RATSO: Come here, Little Nibbler. (*LITTLE NIBBLER enters. RATSO bends down to speak to her.*) The townsfolk think that bolted doors can keep us out. You are small enough to squeeze under them and then open the latches. Will you do that for us?
LITTLE NIBBLER: Yes, Papa. (*RATSO hugs the little rat.*)
RATSO: My dear, Little Nibbler, you're a chip off the old block of cheese. (*To the other RATS.*) Go forth, my minions! Go forth and feast at this great banquet called Hamelin! Leave not a crumb uneaten nor a glass not drunk!

(*The RATS exit. The LIGHTS crossfade to a LIGHT special down left. WIFE is discovered.*)
WIFE: Good night, honey. Aren't you going to kiss me good night? (*SQUEAKS-A-LOT enters.*)
SQUEAKS-A-LOT: I'd love to. Kiss, kiss! Goodnight. Kiss, kiss!
(*WIFE screams as SQUEAKS-A-LOT chases her off. The down left LIGHT special fades. In a LIGHT special down right KARLINA is discovered with a couple of TOWNSPEOPLE.*)
KARLINA: Everything in the shop is half price today.
(*TOWNSPEOPLE react favorably. SNEAKY runs in.*)
SNEAKY: And you get a free rat with every purchase.
(*TOWNSPEOPLE scream as SNEAKY chases them off. The down right LIGHT special fades. A down left LIGHT special comes up to reveal a line of children playing.*)
CHILDREN: Red rover, red rover... Send Gretel right over.
(*STINKY and WHISKERS run into the scene.*)
WHISKERS: Gretel's all tied up.
STINKY: Will we do?
(*The KIDS scream and WHISKERS and STINKY chase them off stage. The down right LIGHT special fades and the full stage is flooded with LIGHT as all the TOWNSPEOPLE enter.*)
KARLINA: Herr Mayor, you promised you would exterminate all the rats.
(*The TOWNSPEOPLE shout their agreement.*)
VALDA: Herr Mayor, the poor never had much to eat; but since you said you would provide for us... we have even less.
WIFE: I'm afraid it's true, my dear, the rats are beginning to eat everything. They are not only

eating the food, they are eating pillows, books, buttons, chairs, and tables.

CHILD: The rats are everywhere.

CHILD: In our beds.

CHILD: We can't sleep.

KARLINA: The rats have even chased off the cats. Where is this Pied Piper?

MAYOR: Trust me. I've sent for the Pied Piper. He will be here soon.

GRETEL: Where is Lothar? He could stop this.

(*The TOWNSPEOPLE shout for something to be done. The PIED PIPER enters, pipe in hand, and stands next to the MAYOR.*)

MAYOR: Who are you?

PIPER: I am the Pied Piper. You sent for me.

MAYOR: We need you to rid Hamelin of the rats. Can you do it?

PIPER: My pipe and I are here to help you.

MAYOR: What can you do with a pipe? Don't you have a weapon?

PIPER: My musical pipe is magical; and when I play the right tune, all the rats will follow me out of town. To put it simply… I can rid your town of the rat problem for one thousand silver kreutzer pieces.

KARLINA: That's a lot of kreutzers, let us hear you play your pipe.

(*The PIPER plays her pipe, and it hurts the ears of all who hear it.*)

WIFE: Please stop.

KARLINA: I agree, wholeheartedly.

MAYOR: How will those sour notes rid our town of the rats?
(*RATSO and the RAT PACK enter.*)
RATSO: They won't. (*The TOWNSPEOPLE run to the opposite side of the stage from where the RATS entered.*) I think it's time for the rats to completely take over this town. Get 'em, Rat Pack! And I want a prisoner.
(*RATSO and the RAT PACK begin to chase the TOWNSPEOPLE around. SOUND: Music should accompany a chase that begins on stage, some chase in the audience, and all end back on stage as RATSO takes GRETEL hostage. The PIPER sits throughout all of this and watches.*)
GRETEL: Help me.
KARLINA: Herr Mayor, do something. Piper, save my daughter.
(*RATSO holds GRETEL in front of him and puts his tale to her throat like a knife.*)
RATSO: Don't anyone move or the kid gets it and the rest of your children will end up our slaves.
BERTA: Ratso, you wouldn't hurt Gretel.
RATSO: We all do strange things when faced with survival. Just ask your mother.
MAYOR: What do you want?
RATSO: Food and safe lodging for my rats.
MAYOR: You've been eating better than we have this harvest season, thanks to my son.
RATSO: Lothar is gone now. I want a guarantee that we will always have food. And in return, we promise not to hurt Gretel or any of your other children.
MAYOR: We will not give in to the demands of rats.

KARLINA: Herr Mayor, are you crazy?

MAYOR: No, you all want the rats destroyed, so that is what I am going to do.

RATSO: What you're doing is saying goodbye to your children and Hamelin's future. (*To the RATS.*) Rat pack, scatter and separate. Surround this town square. Await my signal. Be on alert.

(*The RATS exit at various points around the stage. RATSO pulls GRETEL off.*)

GRETEL: (*Yells as she is being pulled off.*) Berta, go find Lothar. He can stop this from happening.

BERTA: Okay. (*She runs off.*)

KARLINA: So, now, Herr Mayor, what are you going to do?

(*The TOWNSPEOPLE agree with KARLINA.*)

MAYOR: (*To the PIPER.*) Why didn't you do anything? You said you could rid the town of these rats?

PIPER: Yes, I did, for the cheap price of one thousand silver kreutzer pieces. But we hadn't agreed on the deal.

VALDA: Give Herr Piper what he wants.

PIPER: It's not Herr, and I'm not just Piper; I am the Pied Piper.

VALDA: I always assumed that the Pied Piper was a male.

PIPER: Prehistoric fairy-tale propaganda. Nope, I'm a female. Do we have a deal?

MAYOR: That sounds like a very reasonable fee.

KARLINA: I'll pay you ten times what you want. Just save my daughter.

PIPER: I'm an honest Pied Piper and will do it for the one thousand silver kreutzer pieces I've requested. Will you shake on it?
KARLINA: Of course we will. (*KARLINA shakes PIPER's hand.*)
MAYOR: Yes. (*MAYOR shakes PIPER's hand.*)
VALDA: I'll shake on it too. (*VALDA pushes MAYOR out of the way, and shakes PIPER's hand.*)
KARLINA: You better not let anything happen to my daughter.
PIPER: I'll rid this town of the rats. Your daughter is not one of them. Mr. Mayor, please ask everyone to leave; I don't want to hurt any innocent people with my magic.
MAYOR: You heard the Pied Piper.

(*All the TOWNSPEOPLE exit. The PIPER begins to play her pipe and dance around the stage. RATS begin to pop into view from behind various set pieces and form a line as they dance merrily behind the PIPER. RATSO is the last in line. The scene is shifted as the PIPER plays on and dances the RATS into the audience right aisle on their way to the river. They all exit back of the audience. SOUND: Music (with flute) should accompany all this.*)

SCENE FOUR

(*The action is continuous. The scene is now the river. A mouth of a cave can be seen on the up stage bank of the river. The PIPER and the RATS enter the back of the audience and the PIPER leads the RATS down the left aisle and back onto the stage as soon as the shift is completed. Two cut out strips of water/waves are manipulated back and forth in opposite directions to create a river/water effect. The RATS dance behind the waves and exit. LOTHAR and BERTA run in.)*

LOTHAR: How could you do this?
PIPER: For one thousand silver kreutzer pieces.
LOTHAR: Does money really mean so much to you?
PIPER: I only do what the masses want. Now out of my way. If you have a problem with my actions, talk to your father. Life goes on, son. And by the way, go save your girlfriend.
   (*PIPER exits. The LIGHTS shift to a special down left. GRETEL is discovered in the light, bound and gagged. LOTHAR and BERTA run to her. The scene is shifted back to the Town Square during this scene. LOTHAR takes the gag from GRETEL's mouth and unties her.)*
LOTHAR: Are you all right?
GRETEL: The rats wouldn't have harmed me.
LOTHAR: I know.
GRETEL: I'm sorry for doubting you.
LOTHAR: I knew you didn't mean it. It was your mother. (*GRETEL embraces LOTHAR.*)
BERTA: I think I'll take a walk.
GRETEL: Sorry, Berta.
LOTHAR: Me too. Thanks, kiddo. (*BERTA exits.*)
GRETEL: What's going on?
LOTHAR: Our parents just aren't thinking with harmony in mind.
GRETEL: I'm scared.
LOTHAR: I won't let anything happen to you. (*They embrace.*) We better get home. May the rats rest in peace.

GRETEL: Shouldn't we do something in honor of
   Ratso and the other rats?
(BERTA enters and joins LOTHAR and GRETEL as the three go to their knees in prayer. After a beat the LIGHT special fades.)

SCENE FIVE

(The scene is the Town Square. AT RISE: The TOWNSPEOPLE are celebrating.)

KARLINA: Thank you, Herr Mayor, you have finally
   spent our tax money wisely. The rats are gone. And
   you will probably get reelected.
MAYOR: The Pied Piper is hereby named a heroine
   in Hamelin.
(The TOWNSPEOPLE cheer in support of the Pied Piper. LOTHAR, GRETEL, and BERTA walk into the crowded town square.)
WIFE: Look it's Lothar. He and Berta have saved
   Gretel.
KARLINA: Oh, thank you, Lothar. My Gretel is
   safe. *(KARLINA pulls GRETEL from LOTHAR and embraces her).*
A TOWNSPERSON: Three cheers for Lothar.
ALL: Hip, hip, hooray. Hip, hip, hooray. Hip, hip,
   hooray! *(The TOWNSPEOPLE surround LOTHAR.)*
LOTHAR: Come on, Berta, Gretel, let's get out
   of here. I don't want anything to do with this
   celebration. *(LOTHAR, BERTA, and GRETEL exit.)*
VALDA: Thank you, Herr Mayor, for making the
   poor part of the Hamelin family.

KARLINA: Yes, this is the beginning of a brand new life for all of us.

MAYOR: We will always live as one. (*The TOWNSPEOPLE shout their approval. The PIPER enters.*) And here is our heroine. (*The TOWNSPEOPLE shout for joy.*)

PIPER: I have rid your town of the rats. May I have my one thousand silver kreutzer pieces?

MAYOR: Our savior speaks. (*The TOWNSPEOPLE cheer.*)

KARLINA: Thank you, Pied Piper, for not letting anything happen to my Gretel.

WIFE: Please join us in our celebration.

PIPER: I'll be on my way as soon as I collect my fee.

MAYOR: Let us dance. (*SOUND: Music is heard and the TOWNSPEOPLE begin to dance.*)

PIPER: May I have my fee?

VALDA: The rats are gone; join in the celebration.

MAYOR: Gretel's safe return should be enough payment for anyone.

PIPER: Do you refuse to pay?

KARLINA: If the woman wants a reference for playing the pipe… I think we can back her on that. (*ALL laugh and continue to celebrate.*)

PIPER: I will get my revenge. (*PIPER plays a few short blasts on her pipe.*) Sleep. All adults sleep, except Herr Mayor. (*PIPER plays a few more short blasts. All the adults, except the MAYOR fall to the ground as if dead. All the children become zombies.*) Herr Mayor, I want you to witness this.

MAYOR: What are you doing?

PIPER: The children of this town shall join the rats. Their parents don't really seem to care a whole lot about them. And they need to learn a lesson in honesty.
MAYOR: You wouldn't take our children to the river?
PIPER: Follow me, children of Hamelin.
(*The PIPER begins to play her pipe. The children dance after her. The MAYOR runs around the stage trying to stop the children from following the PIPER.*)
MAYOR: Stop! Don't follow her! You can't do this! Not the children! Stop! Please. Stop! (*The PIPER dances around the stage, then through the audience and they exit at the back of the audience. The MAYOR stays onstage. He runs to the adults, trying to wake them up.*) Wake up, everyone. Our children are in danger. We must stop the Piper. Wake up!
(*LOTHAR, GRETEL, and BERTA run on stage.*)
LOTHAR: What's happening, Father?
MAYOR: The Piper is leading the children to the river. Rich and poor, all the children are following her just like the rats did. Come, we must stop her.
LOTHAR: No, you stay here and care for mother and the others.
(*LOTHAR, GRETEL, and BERTA move into the audience and ask the audience children if they know which way the PIPER went, as the scene is shifted to the river bank and the mouth of the cave.*)

SCENE SIX

(*The scene is now the river. A mouth of a cave can be seen on the up stage bank of the river. AT RISE: The PIPER enters with the children following behind. They stop at the river and pause at the water's edge... it looks like the children are going to join the rats. LOTHAR, GRETEL, and BERTA run on stage.)*

LOTHAR: Frau Piper... Pied Piper, stop.
GRETEL: What are you doing?
BERTA: You can't do this.
PIPER: You're too late.
LOTHAR: I will get you your money.
PIPER: It's no longer about the money.
LOTHAR: Do you really plan to lead the children into the river like you did the rats?
PIPER: Maybe I'll seal them all up in this cave.
BERTA: Forever.
GRETEL: You can't!
LOTHAR: Why?
PIPER: So every time the wind blows from these mountains, their parents will hear the laughter of the children they once had and will remember how greedy they were.
LOTHAR: So, do your evil deed. What are you waiting for?
PIPER: For the three of you to join the other children.
BERTA: No way.
GRETEL: Do something, Lothar.
LOTHAR: I refuse to accept this outcome. And I will stop you.
   (LOTHAR advances on the PIPER. RATSO enters from the cave.)

RATSO: Hold on there, Lothar. The Pied Piper is just testing you. Where have you been? It's about time the three of you got here.

LOTHAR: Is that you, Ratso?

RATSO: None other. (*RATSO and LOTHAR do their special shake.*)

GRETEL: I thought you and your rats drowned?

RATSO: No, we didn't drown. The Pied Piper had other plans for us. We entered the water and found our way to the other side of the River Weser, to this cave. Come, my Rat Pack, welcome the children. (*The RATS enter and greet the CHILDREN.*)

PIPER: At the back of the cave, there is an entrance to this wonderful new world without prejudice, where all are equal. (*The CHILDREN cheer.*)

GRETEL: You mean we can all start over?

RATSO: That seems to have been the Pied Piper's plan all along. Yes, we all have a second chance now. Rats and kids, poor and rich alike can live together in peace and harmony.

BERTA: And we won't make the same mistakes our parents did. (*ALL ad-lib their agreement.*)

GRETEL: What a great world.

RATSO: (*Jokingly.*) I'm sure Lothar will find problems with our new world.

PIPER: Oh, Lothar, you might want this back. (*PIPER gives LOTHAR the charm.*)

LOTHAR: You're not only a musician, but a magician too. (*LOTHAR puts the charm necklace around GRETEL's neck and embraces her.*)

ALL: Ahhh.

PIPER: Enjoy your new world.

(LOTHAR, GRETEL, BERTA, RATSO, the RAT PACK, and CHILDREN begin to dance in celebration as the LIGHTS fade to black.)

END

A Collection from a Career in Theatre

The White Cat with the Crystal-Blue Eyes

a play

by

Bob May

suggested by the tale *The White Cat*

by

Madame d'Aulnoy

© 2009/2017 by Bob May

All rights reserved

CAST OF CHARACTERS

MARCELLUS
KING AUGUSTAN
ADAM
BEN
CLAY
RAT
THE WHITE CAT
CATS IN PORTRAITS
CAT SERVANTS

RAT
WARRIORS
EVE
BEAUTY
FATHER
MOTHER

SYNOPSIS OF SCENES

Scene One: The Great Hall in the castle of King Augustan, February.
Scene Two: The Forest, not far from the King's Castle, not long after. And Manmar Forest.
Scene Three: The Interior of the White Cat's Chateau, immediately following.
Scene Four: The Interior of the White Cat's Chateau, immediately following.
Scene Five: The Great Hall in the King's Castle, March 21.
Scene Six: Manmar Forest, a day later.
Scene Seven: The Great Hall in the King's Castle, Easter.
Scene Eight: The Interior of the White Cat's Chateau, right after Easter.
Scene Nine: The Great Hall in the King's Palace, June 1st.

The premiere of *The White Cat With Crystal-Blue Eyes* was presented by Young Players at the Royal Theatre in Benton, Arkansas, August 2008, under the direction of Dapane Shoppach.

SCENE ONE

(AT RISE: MARCELLUS is discovered in the Great Hall of the King's Castle. He speaks his lines to the audience.)

MARCELLUS: This is a tale of power and marriage. Land equals power, and beauty equals marriage. It all began not so very long ago in a kingdom not so very far from here. A King... *(KING appears.)*... King Augustan had asked his three sons to meet him in the Great Hall of the castle. *(The three sons enter.)*

ADAM: Father, will this take long? I have swordsmanship practice in half an hour.

BEN: Says the macho-man.

ADAM: Go read a book, Ben.

BEN: Thank you. I am currently reading several.

KING: My sons, I have had a long and prosperous life as King, and it's time I step down. I no longer want to rule. I wish to turn over my crown to one of you and retire to my estate in the country.

ADAM: As the oldest son...

MARCELLUS: *(To the audience.)* And some say, the greatest warrior in all the kingdom.

ADAM: ...am I not the one to inherit the throne?

MARCELLUS: But he was all muscle and not much brain.

KING: You are correct, Adam, but that is only in the case of my death. I'm not dead. I am going to choose one of you to transfer the Kingship over to.

BEN: As your middle son, I believe I am the one you want.

MARCELLUS: Ben was usually quiet…
BEN: You've always said I was the most stable of the three princes.
MARCELLUS: …quiet, but very cunning.
KING: Indeed, I have, Ben.
BEN: Then I'm your man.
ADAM: You're not half the man I am. (*ADAM pushes BEN.*)
BEN: Being half the man you are is not hard to do. (*ADAM and BEN wrestle.*)
KING: Enough, you two. (*ADAM and BEN stop their wrestling.*)
MARCELLUS: The King turned to, not only the youngest son, but the most handsome and the smartest of the three sons.
KING: How goes the memorial, Clay?
CLAY: Just put the finishing touches on it this morning. It is ready for your viewing.
KING: I look forward to seeing it. I'm sure you've done your mother proud. (*Beat*) Do you have an opinion on this issue?
CLAY: Why do you want to retire, dear father? You are still in good health.
KING: Since we lost your mother I've realized there is more to life than ruling a kingdom.
CLAY: I'd be honored to follow in your footsteps and will do so proudly if you chose me.
ADAM: I really object to this. As the oldest, I am the rightful heir to the throne and want that tradition to be recognized.
BEN: This kingdom needs brains, not brawn. (*Looks to CLAY.*) Or beauty.

KING: To help me decide who I should turn my crown over to, I have decided that when I retire to my country estate, I want a pretty little dog to keep me company. Whichever of you brings me the prettiest little dog shall be the new King.

ADAM: A pretty little dog is going to decide who the next King is? Let us fight for the crown.

BEN: Give us an exam. Why a dog?

CLAY: (*To the KING.*) I understand, father. Mother loved little dogs. It will help you remember her.

KING: You all have one month to bring me the cutest little dog in the kingdom.

MARCELLUS: Each Prince kissed the King's hand...

CLAY: (*As he kisses the KING's hand.*) Dear Father, I will find a dog to keep you company.

KING: I am looking forward to seeing your mother's memorial.

ADAM: (*As he kisses the KING's hand.*) This is the most ridiculous thing I've ever heard.

BEN: (*As he kisses the KING's hand.*) Keep the throne warm for me, Father.

KING: Be back here on the first day of Spring, March 21st.

MARCELLUS: ...and each prince set forth on a journey to find the prettiest little dog in the kingdom. (*The three sons exit.*)

KING: I have done as you suggested, Marcellus.

MARCELLUS: (*To the audience.*) That is my name, Marcellus. I am the spiritual advisor to the great king. (*He moves to the KING and bows.*) Yes, you have, my king. Remember, this is all for a better future for your kingdom.

KING: Please, excuse me. (*The KING exits. as the LIGHTS fade to black.*
(*MARCELLUS moves to a LIGHT special and speaks as the scene is shifted.*)
MARCELLUS: The three princes left the castle at different times but ended up in the same area of the forest, not far from the castle.
(*The LIGHT special fades to black.*)

SCENE TWO

(*AT RISE: The scene is a forest. CLAY is discovered stage right. ADAM and BEN are stage left.*)

ADAM: You can't search here. I was here first.
BEN: Actually, I was just leaving. (*BEN exits. ADAM follows.*)
CLAY: What fools. They search the same area.
(*MARCELLUS enters and moves to CLAY.*)
MARCELLUS: I agree with you… your brothers' tactics are not very smart. I suggest you venture away from the castle.
CLAY: Why do you help me? You are my father's advisor.
MARCELLUS: And you are your father's favorite son.
CLAY: I don't need your advice to know that I shouldn't do what my brothers do.
MARCELLUS: I hear there are very small dogs in the lands beyond Manmar Forest.
CLAY: Manmar Forest is haunted. Getting through it will not be easy. And the lands beyond it do not belong to my father. I may not be welcome there.

MARCELLUS: Do as you wish. Just some friendly advice.
CLAY: Thank you. I might head in that direction. (*He exits.*)
MARCELLUS: Clay made his way in the direction of the haunted forest. But didn't find any dogs he thought suited his father's request. Adam meanwhile bought a new dog every day and sold it as soon as he found a prettier one. (*ADAM is discovered in a LIGHT special holding a small dog.*)
ADAM: I am Prince Adam, the rightful heir to the throne, and I want your dog. Pay for it? Why, no. Here you can have this one. (*LIGHT special out.*)
MARCELLUS: Ben used his brains and logged all the dogs he came across.
(*BEN is discovered in a LIGHT special writing in a small notebook.*)
BEN: The poodle was at the West End and the schnauzer was near the Northern border. (*LIGHT special out.*)
MARCELLUS: By the time Clay reached the haunted forest, he still hadn't seen any dogs he thought would fit the bill and soon found himself in... (*CLAY enters.*)
CLAY: Manmar Forest. It doesn't seem so spooky.
MARCELLUS: How's this for spooky? (*MARCELLUS waves his hand and a spell SOUND is heard. A RAT enters in battle armor.*)
RAT: Halt. You are not welcome in our forest.
CLAY: I didn't realize that this forest belonged to rats.
RAT: I don't like the way you said that.

CLAY: Look, I'm sorry. I didn't mean to offend you. I would like to pass through your forest on my quest to find a tiny dog.
RAT: Our enemy lies on the other side of this forest and it's not a dog.
CLAY: Who is your enemy?
RAT: You will never know because to get through this forest you must pass through me. (*He draws a sword.*)
CLAY: I'm going to walk away from this.
RAT: No, you're not.
(*There is a sword fight between CLAY and the RAT. CLAY pins the RAT.*)
CLAY: I wish you no harm. You may leave with your life and I will pass through your forest.
(*The RAT runs off. CLAY and MARCELLUS move down stage in LIGHT specials at opposite ends of the stage as the scene is shifted.*)
MARCELLUS: Suddenly a terrifying thunderstorm came up. (*He waves his hand and SOUND: Thunder is heard.*) Rain fell like cats and the little dogs he was looking for.
CLAY: That's odd, a thunderstorm in winter? I must find some shelter.
MARCELLUS: He saw a bright red light shining through the trees.
CLAY: I see a place to rest, but can I get to it? (*He struggles as he moves across the stage.*)
MARCELLUS: After a struggle, he finally found himself at the entrance to an eerie looking chateau. (*MARCELLUS gestures, SOUND: Thunder clap, and a*

door flies in. Or one of the cat servants can hold a door, with a cat's face painted on it, to her right side.)
CLAY: A door in the middle of nowhere?
MARCELLUS: At the door, a gold cat's paw hung from a chain of diamonds.
CLAY: What an odd doorbell.
MARCELLUS: The prince pulled the chain and heard… not the ringing of a bell.
(*SOUND: A cat's meow.*)
CLAY: A cat's meow?
MARCELLUS: A moment later the door opened…
(*The LIGHTS fade to the next scene as the door flies out. Or as CLAY enters, the cat holding the door turns in a clockwise circle, CLAY follows with the door ending behind him. LIGHTING can help show he is now inside the chateau.*)

SCENE THREE

(*The action is continuous. The LIGHTS fade up to reveal the interior of a chateau.*)

MARCELLUS: … but there was no one there.
CLAY: Hello? (*Pause.*) Is anyone here? (*He pulls his sword from its sheath and moves into the room.*) Hello?
MARCELLUS: On the walls hung portraits of famous cats: Puss in Boots, Cleopatra's cat, the Cheshire cat, and others the prince didn't recognize. (*Actors dressed as the cats mentioned above stand in oversized wooden picture frames. The cats in the frames reacted to the following action.*)
CLAY: For a prince looking for a beautiful small dog, it seems I've entered the wrong chateau.

(*After another pause. SOUND: A voice is heard.*)
VOICE: Do not be afraid.
MARCELLUS: Oh, but be aware. (*He laughs.*)
VOICE: You are welcome here. (*MARCELLUS exits laughing.*)
CLAY: Who said that? (*The WHITE CAT enters.*)
WHITE: Friend or foe?
CLAY: I am Prince Clay, Mistress Cat. I only seek shelter from the storm.
WHITE: Ah, King Augustan's son. You are a long way from home. It is my pleasure to welcome you to my feline chateau.
CLAY: Thank you.
WHITE: You are indeed brave to pass through Manmar Forest alone.
CLAY: I met the rats of the forest.
WHITE: Oh, yes, just one of my several enemies.
CLAY: Several?
WHITE: Not to worry. My castle is a peaceful one.
CLAY: I thank you. Do you have a name?
WHITE: Just call me, the White Cat.
CLAY: The White Cat with crystal-blue eyes.
WHITE: Excuse me?
CLAY: Your eyes are the most beautiful blue I have ever seen.
WHITE: Thank you.
CLAY: Surely you are no ordinary cat, with your gift of speech and your splendid chateau? And all the jewels. The doorbell with diamonds, and your bracelet. It must be very special.
WHITE: This bracelet is my good-luck charm. It protects me or anyone who wears it.

CLAY: (*Looking at the bracelet.*) How fitting... a silver cat's paw with tiny diamond claws. (*Beat*)
WHITE: I was just about to sit down to dinner. Are you hungry?
CLAY: Indeed I am. I can't remember the last time I ate.
WHITE: Please join me. (*She shouts.*) Servants, please set another place at the table for our guest. (*There is a choreographed dance as the servants bring in a table, two chairs, and food. CLAY and WHITE sit and eat.*)
CLAY: How is it I've never heard about you or your beautiful chateau?
WHITE: You are a long way from your father's castle and his lands.
CLAY: How long have you lived here?
WHITE: The chateau has been in my family for generations.
CLAY: Are your parents still living on the premises?
WHITE: You are so full of questions. Let us enjoy our meal.
CLAY: I'm sorry. I do appreciate your generosity. (*Pause as they eat.*)
WHITE: Tell me about the lands on the other side of Manmar Forest.
CLAY: Around my father's castle, things look a lot like they do here, lovely rolling hills, with many lakes and streams. I especially love the outdoors, so I spend a lot of time in nature. In the west, my father's land rises many thousand feet with the peaks of the Randmae Mountains on the edge of the great Catlauria Ocean. I'd love to share it all with you.

WHITE: Maybe one day you can do that. (*Beat*) What brings you so far from home?
CLAY: I am in search of a beautiful tiny dog.
WHITE: Why a tiny dog?
CLAY: It's a long story.
WHITE: Well, even a small dog wouldn't be welcome at a chateau full of cats.
CLAY: Exactly what I said. (*CLAY and WHITE laugh and talk as music plays. We don't hear the conversation. LIGHTING suggests the passage of time.*)
WHITE: The dinner was lovely and the evening has been wonderful. Thank you.
CLAY: It is I that should be thanking you. I've not enjoyed myself this much since my mother passed on.
WHITE: It's been some time since I've had a dinner guest or, for that matter, any company as charming as you.
CLAY: The life I lead back home can't compare to the joy I've found here tonight. How is it a cat can talk and be as beautiful as you?
WHITE: Let my servants show you the way to a comfortable bedroom and a good night's sleep.
(*WHITE exits as the LIGHTS cross fade to a special on MARCELLUS. He speaks to the audience as the scene is shifted.*)
MARCELLUS: Clay didn't sleep like a prince that night… he slept like a king that night and for twenty-eight more nights. He and the White Cat filled that month of days with many activities. They walked in the rolling hills surrounding the chateau.

SCENE FOUR

(AT RISE: The scene is still the interior of the WHITE cat's chateau. CLAY and WHITE are sitting at the table. The dishes have been struck.)

MARCELLUS: They played chess...
WHITE: Checkmate.
MARCELLUS: ...drank milk punch...
CLAY: Delicious.
MARCELLUS: ...listened to the palace musicians...
   (SOUND: Music plays under the following.)
MARCELLUS: ...but mostly talked.
CLAY: We have talked so much, but you have managed to avoid things about your personal life. You are hiding something.
WHITE: All cats are mysterious.
MARCELLUS: And before long, the month was almost over.
CLAY: I must return home before March 21. That only gives me a few days to find the pretty little dog my father has asked for. My whole future depends on it. I don't want to go. What shall I do?
WHITE: Your duty is to your father.
CLAY: Adam, my brother can be king.
WHITE: No, you shall be king. *(She pulls from a pouch that is part of her costume an acorn.)* Here take this.
CLAY: An acorn?
WHITE: Yes, an acorn. It contains the loveliest little dog in all the world.
CLAY: A dog in an acorn?
WHITE: I speak the truth.

CLAY: And I believe you.
WHITE: You must promise, you will open the acorn only in the presence of your father. Let no one else have it.
CLAY: I am overjoyed, and you have my word I will not open it until I am with my father.
WHITE: I give you this in return for your friendship and good company.
CLAY: Thank you, a thousand times.
(*The LIGHTS fade to black.*)

SCENE FIVE

(*AT RISE: CLAY is discovered in the Great Hall of the King's Castle. The KING and MARCELLUS enter. MARCELLUS moves to the background.*)

KING: Welcome home, Clay, my son. It's March 21 and you are the first to arrive back home.
CLAY: Are you well, Father? I worry about you.
KING: Thank you. I am ready to retire to the country. Do you have a dog?
(*ADAM enters with a dog in his arms.*)
ADAM: Greetings, Father. Here is the most beautiful dog in all of my soon to be kingdom.
KING: Indeed, it is. (*BEN enters with a dog in arms.*)
BEN: Father, put that ugly dog down and hold the winner of this contest.
KING: Very impressive. I don't know which to choose.
ADAM: Why, Clay, don't you have a dog for Father?

CLAY: I only have this acorn. (*ADAM and BEN laugh at CLAY.*)
BEN: Father wanted a dog, not a seed.
CLAY: There is a dog inside this acorn.
ADAM: And there are two sane princes inside this room. (*ADAM and BEN laugh.*)
BEN: Father, since Clay doesn't have a dog, you must choose between Adam's dog or mine.
KING: Yes, you are correct.
MARCELLUS: Excuse me, your majesty, I suggest you let the boy open his acorn.
KING: Very well. Open the acorn, Clay. (*CLAY cracks open the acorn and a small dog emerges. The KING begins to laugh.*) Why it's so small it could jump through my ring. I am charmed, and I declare Clay the winner. He has brought me the most beautiful little dog in the kingdom. He is the new king.
ADAM: This is not fair.
BEN: For once, I agree with my older brother. The dog is so small it's hard to even see it.
ADAM: This is silly, what do small, beautiful dogs have to do with deciding the next king?
MARCELLUS: Give them test two. (*MARCELLUS gestures toward the KING. The KING reacts like he was hit by something.*)
KING: Stop grumbling. All right. I will give you another test. You all have one month to find a piece of...
MARCELLUS: Linen.
KING: ...linen so fine that it...
MARCELLUS: ...that it can pass through the eye of the thinnest needle.

KING: Return with the linen on the first day of Passover. Whichever of you that has the finest linen will become the king.
ADAM: This gets crazier with each task. (*He exits.*)
BEN: Why linen, Father, why not silk? (*He exits.*)
CLAY: Father, are you all right?
KING: I'm fine.
CLAY: I know when you're hiding something.
KING: I really just miss your mother and want this transfer of power to be over.
CLAY: Then let Adam be the king. He is the firstborn son and rightful heir to the throne.
KING: Go find the linen I ask for and you'll be the king.
CLAY: I only do what you wish. (*CLAY embraces the KING and exits.*)
MARCELLUS: You are doing wonderfully, your Majesty.
KING: As Clay just said… "I only do what you wish."
MARCELLUS: Sire, may I have the little dog Clay brought to you?
KING: You can have all three of them.
MARCELLUS: I only want the one. Trust me, your Majesty, things will work out in your favor.

(*The LIGHTS fade to black. MARCELLUS moves to a LIGHT special and speaks as the scene change takes place.*)
The three brothers set out, each in a different direction. Adam bought and sold linen each day as he did with the dogs. Ben logged in his journal all the places the finest linen was manufactured. Clay journeyed once again toward the chateau of the White Cat. But he never made it. He met the crystal-blue-eyed cat in Manmar Forest.

SCENE SIX

(AT RISE: CLAY meets WHITE in Manmar Forest.)

CLAY: What are you doing in this eerie Manmar Forest? And why are you dressed for battle?

WHITE: Clay, I am so happy that you have returned. I have missed you.

CLAY: And I have missed you too. Please tell me what is going on.

(WHITE raises a horn and blows on it. An army of soldier CATS enter in formation ready to fight.)

WHITE: We are at war with the horrible rats that live in Manmar Forest. Since you were here last, they have been pillaging my lands and driving my subjects from their homes.

CLAY: Why didn't you send for me?

WHITE: You have your own problems. But now that you're here, will you help us?

CLAY: I will gladly fight by your side.

MARCELLUS: The cats, led by Prince Clay and the White Cat marched into battle. The battle was long and ferocious. *(An army of RATS runs in and there is a battle between them and the cats. CLAY and the RAT from the earlier scene have a sword fight downstage of the others. CLAY and RAT fight in regular speed, the others behind fight in slow motion.)* After a day of hard fighting, the White Cat, with Prince Clay by her side, defeated the rats, pushed them out of Manmar Forest, and sent them scurrying for a new home. *(The RATS run offstage.)* For weeks, there was one victory celebration after another. (*WHITE, CLAY, and the other CATS dance in celebration of their victory.*) And soon, the month was over and Passover approached. (*MARCELLUS and CATS exit.*)

CLAY: It saddens me that I must once again leave you, my beloved White Cat. Know that I would rather stay here with you than become king. Besides, I've not found the piece of fine linen that my father has asked for. (*WHITE pulls from her pouch a walnut.*)

WHITE: Here, take this walnut.

CLAY: A walnut?

WHITE: You must return to your father. It is your duty, and if you don't hurry, you could be late.

CLAY: Are you trying to get rid of me?

WHITE: Open this walnut only when you are in the presence of your father. Make sure no one else gets it. The walnut will satisfy his wish.

CLAY: Linen in a walnut?

WHITE: Trust me.

CLAY: I do.

WHITE: You will soon be king. (*CLAY kisses her paw.*)

CLAY: Goodbye, my feline friend. (*CLAY exits as the LIGHTS fade to black.*)

SCENE SEVEN

(*AT RISE: ADAM, BEN, and the KING are discovered in the Great Hall. MARCELLUS stands behind the KING.*)

KING: Welcome, my sons. Happy Easter.

ADAM: Father, I hold in my hand the finest linen you will find in the entire kingdom. (*ADAM holds old a length of linen. The KING and MARCELLUS feel the fabric.)*

KING: Ah, very fine. What do you think, Marcellus?

MARCELLUS: Yes, indeed, it is very fine.

BEN: Not as fine as this. (*BEN holds out a length of linen. The KING and MARCELLUS feel the fabric.*)

MARCELLUS: Oh, yes. Very fine too.

KING: It's tough to decide between the two.

MARCELLUS: But will either pass the needle test?

KING: Marcellus, take a thread from each piece of linen and see if it will go through the eye of the needle. (*MARCELLUS takes a treat from each piece of linen.*)

MARCELLUS: First. Let us try Prince Adam's thread. (*MARCELLUS attempts to thread the needle, but he can't do it.*)

KING: I'm sorry, Adam.

ADAM: Give it to me. Let me try. (*ADAM takes the needle and thread and tries to put the thread through the needle without any success.*)

BEN: You lose, Adam. Try mine now, Marcellus. (*MARCELLUS takes the needle from ADAM and attempts to thread the needle with BEN's thread without success.*)

KING: I'm sorry, Ben.

ADAM: You will just have to skip that step and choose the finest linen on texture and appearance.

MARCELLUS: Remember, your Majesty, your youngest son hasn't returned yet.

ADAM: He's late. He should be disqualified.

KING: The day is not over yet. He may still appear.

BEN: He couldn't possibly find a better linen than mine.
(*CLAY runs into the room.*)
CLAY: I'm sorry it took me so long to get here. I hold in my hand the finest linen you have ever seen. (*CLAY holds up the walnut.*)
ADAM: You hold in your hand a walnut.
CLAY: Yes, but inside the walnut is the linen.
BEN: What is it with you and these nuts? First you bring an acorn for the dog, and now a walnut for the linen.
ADAM: Father, Ben and I have brought the linen you requested. Not a nut like our brother the nut. You must choose between what is before your eyes.
MARCELLUS: Please, your Grace, let the boy open his walnut.
KING: Crack open your walnut, Prince Clay.
(*All of this action is accented with musical chords. CLAY cracks the walnut open and pulls out.*)
ADAM: Ha, ha, a hazelnut.
MARCELLUS: Continue. (*CLAY cracks the hazelnut open and finds...*)
BEN: A cheery pit?
ADAM: He mocks you, Father.
KING: Is this a joke, my son?
CLAY: No, Father.
ADAM: You asked for linen and he produces seeds.
MARCELLUS: Please let him continue.
KING: All right. Proceed, Clay. (*CLAY breaks open the cheery pit and finds...*)
ADAM: A piece of wheat?

BEN: He's making a fool of himself. A piece of linen can't be inside a grain of wheat.
(*The brothers laugh at CLAY.*)
CLAY: Father, I have what you want.
KING: Then, where is it? (*CLAY opens the grain of wheat and finds...*)
CLAY: A mustard seed. White Cat, have you played a joke on me?
(*SOUND: A whisper is heard.*)
WHITE: Have you so little faith in your friend? Open the mustard seed.
(*CLAY opens the mustard seed.*)
CLAY: Here it is at last. (*CLAY begins to pull out yards of the finest linen. Having CLAY behind a table or box can create this effect. After he breaks the seed, he pulls the cloth out of the table just like tissue out of a box. The KING touches the cloth.*)
KING: The linen is very fine. And look, it is painted with birds, animals, and fish, as well as trees, shrubs, fruit, and the sun, moon, and stars.
MARCELLUS: Are there any portraits of people?
KING: Why yes, there seems to be a king and queen.
MARCELLUS: Excellent. (*ADAM and BEN look at the linen.*)
ADAM: What is this?
BEN: It's a picture of a white cat that seems to be guarding the king and queen.
KING: This is indeed the finest linen I've ever seen.
ADAM: Yes, but will it pass the needle test?
MARCELLUS: (*To the audience.*) It did indeed pass the test. A thread from the cloth was passed three times through the eye of the thinnest needle. (*To

the KING.) I will keep this linen safe for you, your majesty.

KING: Thank you, Marcellus. (*Announcing.*) I proclaim the winner and new king to be —

ADAM: No, this isn't fair.

BEN: I quite agree.

ADAM: The fate of the kingdom should not be decided by a piece of cloth.

BEN: Or a little dog.

CLAY: But mother loved fine linen.

(*MARCELLUS gestures toward the KING. The KING reacts like he was hit by something.*)

KING: Yes, how simpleminded of me. A king can't be without a queen. There should be one final test. Go forth and travel for another month. Whichever of you brings home the most beautiful young lady shall marry her, and the two of you will be crowned king and queen. But mark my words: this time my decision will be final. Return on the first day of Spring. (*The KING exits with MARCELLUS.*)

BEN: Father, may I have a word with you? (*BEN runs after the KING and exits.*)

CLAY: I've been cheated out of the throne twice. And I don't even want it.

ADAM: Then go back to your White Cat, and never let me see your face again.

CLAY: How do you know about the White Cat?

ADAM: All that matters is that I do know about her and she has supplied you with the magic nuts that produce just what father wants. How is that? Have you ever thought about how it is she has each of the items father has asked for? Well, she can't be your beautiful woman because she's not a woman, she's a cat.

CLAY: I hope you'll be happy with the kingdom.

ADAM: I will. (*CLAY exits. ADAM shouts.*) Where did you say I could find my beautiful woman? (*MARCELLUS enters.*)

MARCELLUS: Prince Adam, keep your voice down. I am here to serve you. (*He bows.*) I promise, you will have the most beautiful woman in the kingdom.

ADAM: Where do I find her?

MARCELLUS: Here. She's right here. (*He claps his hands, a spell SOUND is heard, and EVE enters.*) Adam, meet your Eve. (*EVE embraces ADAM.*)

ADAM: She is indeed a beauty. I trust with your help I will be the next king?

MARCELLUS: Doesn't Eve prove that I am in your service? Trust me. Now, go talk to your father. Let him know that Ben doesn't really love him, and Clay has won the last two contests because he is consorting with a white cat who knows black magic. And then take your Eve away from the castle for a month. I'll see you come Spring. (*ADAM and EVE exit. MARCELLUS moves to a LIGHT special and speaks as the set is shifted to the new scene.*) Ben logged the beautiful woman just like he had done with the dogs and linen. Of course, Clay set out on the long, familiar road back to his beloved White Cat.

SCENE EIGHT

(*AT RISE: CLAY enters the WHITE CAT's chateau.*)

CLAY: Hello, I'm back. Mistress White Cat? (*WHITE enters.*)
WHITE: Hello, my friend.
CLAY: Where is everyone?
WHITE: I have sent them away.
CLAY: Why?
WHITE: That can wait. Have you come back as the new king?
CLAY: I will never be king.
WHITE: I'm sorry...
CLAY: Why did you send everyone away?
WHITE: ...I thought I helped you become king.
CLAY: You did. I won both contests with your acorn and walnut. (*Beat*) Where did you send everyone?
WHITE: To safety. Do you have the dog and linen?
CLAY: They are safe with my father. (*Beat*) Please stop ignoring my questions.
WHITE: I'm not ignoring your questions.
CLAY: There is sadness in your eyes, and I don't think it's because I am not king. Have the rats come back?
WHITE: No, the rats have not bothered us since you helped us drive them away.
CLAY: Then what troubles you?
WHITE: Nothing, I am fine. I long for Spring to arrive.
CLAY: You have been hiding something from me since the day we met.
WHITE: That's absurd.
CLAY: No more absurd than my carrying on a conversation with a cat with the most beautiful crystal-blue eyes I have ever seen.

(*They almost kiss. WHITE walks away from CLAY. There is a pause; she turns to CLAY.*)
WHITE: Today my life ends.
CLAY: What? Don't talk such nonsense.
WHITE: It's true. Today the Manmar Forest Wizard arrives to ask for my hand in marriage.
CLAY: A wizard? Marriage?
WHITE: He gave me one year to agree to his proposal.
CLAY: Just tell him no.
WHITE: I've done that, and when I said no, he transformed my parents.
CLAY: Transformed?
WHITE: Yes, he turned my father into a tiny dog and mother into fine linen.
CLAY: What?
WHITE: I've been hiding them from him in the acorn and walnut. Please take care of them. When he finds that I will not marry him, he will destroy me. But at least my parents are safe.
CLAY: No, we will fight him with your troops? And defeat him like we did the rats. Call your troops back.
WHITE: No, he has cast a spell over all my lands and all who call it home… no one who lives here can defeat him. No one. But my heart remains my own. I would rather die than marry him.
CLAY: I don't live here. I will challenge him for you.
WHITE: No, he is too powerful.
CLAY: After all you have done for me… it's the least I can do for you.

WHITE: I beg you to change your mind. For the sake of my parents.
CLAY: All right, then come with me back to my home. My father has an advisor who might be able to help us.
WHITE: We don't have time to escape.
CLAY: Then it looks like I will be challenging this Manmar Forest Wizard. I will not let anything happen to you. (*CLAY pulls his sword from its sheath.*)
WHITE: Here, take this. (*She takes off her bracelet.*)
CLAY: I've never seen you without this on your wrist.
WHITE: Remember, it's my good-luck charm. Perhaps it will protect you from the wizard's power.
CLAY: I will gladly wear it on a chain around my neck so it will be next to my heart. (*CLAY sheaths his sword. WHITE and CLAY embrace. MARCELLUS bursts into the room.*)
MARCELLUS: How touching.
WHITE: That's him. The Manmar Wizard.
CLAY: Marcellus? It's you? Stand back. (*CLAY pulls his sword from its sheath and puts it at MARCELLUS's throat.*)
MARCELLUS: Prince Clay, I don't know what she has told you, but I am on your side. I followed you here to save you. She's using you to gain control of your father's kingdom.
(*CLAY looks to WHITE.*)
WHITE: Why would I want your father's kingdom?
MARCELLUS: Don't you find it odd that she had the tiny dog and the linen? The rats in Manmar Forest

were trying to keep her from spreading her evil
power into your father's kingdom.

WHITE: He's using us both to gain control of my
lands and your father's.

CLAY: I don't know who to believe.

MARCELLUS: Clay, I am totally devoted to your
father.

WHITE: Clay, are my eyes lying? (*WHITE and CLAY look at one another.*)

CLAY: (*To MARCELLUS.*) What is my mother's name?

MARCELLUS: Your mother is no longer with us.

CLAY: I know, and if you are so devoted to my father you would know my mother's name.

(*MARCELLUS maneuvers away from CLAY's sword.*)

MARCELLUS: Got me. (*He moves to WHITE.*) You know, Miss White Cat, my feline friend, you can stop all that is about to happen. Just say "yes" to becoming my bride.

CLAY: She would rather die.

MARCELLUS: And that's just what will happen to her if she says no.

CLAY: Not if I destroy you first.

MARCELLUS: How touching. (*MARCELLUS gestures with his wand and a charge is sent toward CLAY. This is illustrated through SOUND. CLAY falls back to the ground as if hit with something. WHITE rushes to CLAY.*)

WHITE: Are you hurt?

CLAY: (*As he stands.*) I'm fine, but I'm afraid your bracelet is a bit fried. (*He shows the charred bracelet, and then slashes his sword in the air.*) Remember,

I am not from her feline chateau. I can hurt you.
(*MARCELLUS holds his wand like a sword.*)
MARCELLUS: You hurt me and the princess perishes.
CLAY: Princess? (*MARCELLUS attacks. A sword/wand fight ensues. CLAY wins. When CLAY pushes his sword into MARCELLUS, he vanishes with great SOUND effects. CLAY turns to WHITE.*) That's the end of him.
WHITE: And the end of me. Goodbye. (*WHITE disappears with SOUND effects. A piece of rock crystal is discovered lying on the floor where WHITE stood.*)
CLAY: What have I done? By slaying the evil wizard, I've destroyed my beloved friend. (*He cries out.*) Where have you gone, my White Cat with crystal-blue eyes?
VOICE: You will never see the White Cat again. But take the crystal and present it to your father.
(*The LIGHTS fade to black.*)

SCENE NINE

(*AT RISE: ADAM, EVE, and KING are discovered in the Great Hall of the KING's palace.*)

ADAM: Father, meet my Eve. The most beautiful woman in our kingdom.
(*BEN and BEAUTY enter.*)
BEN: Until he rests his eyes on my beauty.
BEAUTY: I have a name.
KING: It would be very difficult choosing a winner from these two. They both are very gorgeous.

ADAM: Then, I think the decision should go back to the fact that I am the eldest and the rightful heir.
KING: The rightful heir that is full of wrong.
ADAM: Excuse me?
KING: Ben, did you know your brother told me that you didn't love me.
BEN: Father, you know that is not true.
KING: It's more true than false. (*Beat*) I wonder where Clay is?
ADAM: I don't think he'll be returning.
KING: Why do you say that?
ADAM: Marcellus told me.
KING: I wonder were Marcellus is? I've not seen him in several days. (*CLAY enters.*)
CLAY: Marcellus won't be coming back. He was an evil wizard, and I have destroyed him.
ADAM: He's not evil, he promised me the kingdom.
KING: Are you sure you destroyed him?
CLAY: Yes.
KING: How?
BEN: He probably threw magic nuts at him. Father, can we get on with the choosing a new king? I never liked Marcellus anyway. Glad to see him gone.
ADAM: Clay, have you brought a beautiful woman?
CLAY: All I have is this beautiful crystal. (*The brothers laugh at him.*)
BEN: Nuts, and now crystals. He doesn't have a woman. Unless he's going to pull her from the crystal. Father, you must choose between Eve and Beauty.

KING: Don't you get it? It doesn't matter anymore who has the smallest dog or the finest linen.
ADAM: I know, because I have the most beautiful woman.
KING: She doesn't matter either. I was only doing this stupid search for Marcellus.
CLAY: What do you mean?
KING: He told me if I got him a tiny dog, the finest linen, and the most beautiful lady in the kingdom, he would bring back your mother and I could retire with her.
CLAY: Did you truly think he could bring back mother?
KING: I missed her so much I wanted to believe it. But you're right, he was evil. And I am no longer giving up my throne.
BEN: What?
ADAM: You can't do this. I want to be king.
KING: I've been a fool to wish for things I cannot have.
ADAM: Marcellus told me if this happened all I had to do was to kiss my beautiful Eve, and I would be crowned king.
KING: Go ahead and kiss her. At least that will keep you from talking.
ADAM: I'll show you— I'll be a great King. (*ADAM kisses EVE. SOUND erupts and EVE turns into MARCELLUS.*)
MARCELLUS: Thank you, Adam.
ADAM: What? (*He starts spitting.*)
CLAY: You had everything perfectly planned out, didn't you?

MARCELLUS: I wasn't sure where the princess, the White Cat, was hiding her parents, the King and Queen, once I turned them into the dog and linen. But now I own her father, the acorn tiny dog, and her mother, the walnut linen. And as soon as I wrap my hands around that crystal, I'll own the princess. Mom, dad, and daughter... equal all their lands. And it will all be mine. May I have the crystal?

CLAY: You will have to pry this crystal from my lifeless hands.

MARCELLUS: That can be arranged. (*To CLAY.*) You know Clay, there's one thing I didn't plan on. You weren't supposed to fall in love with the White Cat. I only wanted you to bring her to me. Now, for the last time... give me the crystal.

CLAY: Never.

KING: You will not hurt my son. (*KING rushes toward MARCELLUS.*)

MARCELLUS: Freeze. (*MARCELLUS makes a gesture, a spell SOUND is heard. The KING freezes.*)

ADAM: What have you done to my Eve?

MARCELLUS: And you wanted to be king? (*MARCELLUS makes a gesture, a spell SOUND is heard, and ADAM freezes.*)

BEN: I think my beauty and I will take our leave. (*BEN and BEAUTY start to exit.*)

MARCELLUS: The two of you are going nowhere. (*MARCELLUS makes a gesture, a spell SOUND is heard, and BEN and BEAUTY freeze.*) It's just you and me, Clay.

CLAY: Why don't you flip your wrist and turn me into one of your pawns?
MARCELLUS: I want that crystal.
CLAY: I'd rather break it into a million pieces than give it to you.
MARCELLUS: I can destroy you and get the crystal. And then I would own not only the White Cat's land but your father's kingdom too. But I'll be happy with just the White Cat's land. You can be the new king here and own this kingdom. Now give me that crystal.
CLAY: I don't want you as a neighbor.
MARCELLUS: AHHH! (*MARCELLUS reaches for the crystal. There is a struggle. CLAY throws the crystal to the floor and it shatters. SOUND erupts. LIGHTS flash. A beautiful lady appears, with golden hair, wearing a white linen gown decorated with embroidered cats.*)
CLAY: My White Cat. I would recognize those crystal-blue eyes anywhere.
MARCELLUS: Say goodbye to those eyes.
WHITE: Use the bracelet.
CLAY: What?
WHITE: It's why you've not been frozen.
MARCELLUS: You talk too much. (*MARCELLUS grabs WHITE.*)
CLAY: Let her go.
WHITE: Break the bracelet.
(*CLAY snaps the bracelet in half and MARCELLUS screams as he melts into the floor.*)
MARCELLUS: Oh, you wicked, wicked children. (*MARCELLUS is gone.*)
CLAY: So, this is what you've been hiding?

WHITE: When I said, "no," to Marcellus's marriage proposal he turned me into the White Cat. He never figured that anyone would fall in love with a cat.

CLAY: What do we do about my family and yours?

WHITE: True love will triumph. Kiss me and we'll free them all.

CLAY: Gladly. (*CLAY kisses WHITE. KING, ADAM, BEN, and BEAUTY come to life.*)

KING: I believe that Clay has the most beautiful woman in the kingdom.

ADAM: Indeed, he does and he can be the next king.

BEN: I have no problem with that. Do you, my beauty?

BEAUTY: None.

KING: Then I declare Clay and his crystal-blue-eyed lady the new king and queen. And I can retire.

CLAY: Father, if you want to retire, I will support that. But I don't want to be King—at least not of this kingdom. Let Adam be the king.

BEN: What about me?

WHITE: Manmar Forest needs the rule of someone with your smarts. You and Beauty may be king and queen of Manmar Forest.

BEN: Beauty and I accept your offer. (*WHITE's parents enter.*)

FATHER: What about us?

WHITE: Mom and Dad. (*WHITE runs to embrace them.*)

MOTHER: Let's have a wedding before your father and I retire to the country.

(There is a wedding tableau with CLAY and WHITE as the center focus. The LIGHTS fade to black.)

END

A Collection from a Career in Theatre

The Wizard of Bamboozlement

a play

by

Bob May

© 2009/2017 by Bob May

All rights reserved

CAST OF CHARACTERS

GIDGET
FIGURE/WJ
THE QUEEN
CANDY
THE WICKED WITCH OF THE WEST
BEANIE: CLASSMATE A
CLASSMATE B
CLASSMATE C
B. J.
DOROTHY
HANSEL: GRETEL
SNOW WHITE
DEWIE DECIMAL
LEWIE DECIMAL
CHRIS
VOICE/HEWIE DECIMAL
PROFESSOR LIBRUM

SYNOPSIS OF SCENES

Scene One: Gidget's office in the Boren Home, late evening.
Scene Two: The same; immediately following.
Scene Three: The garage behind the Boren Home; immediately following.
Scene Four: Someplace in Bookworld; the next morning; 6 a.m.
Scene Five: A crossroad in Bookworld; 7 a.m.
Scene Six: Another location in Bookworld; 8 a.m.
Scene Seven: Another location in Bookworld; 10 a.m.
Scene Eight: At the main library of Bookworld; 11 a.m.
Scene Nine: Librum's Lair; immediately following.
Scene Ten: Outside the Wicked Witch of the West's castle; immediately following.
Scene Eleven: Inside the Wicked Witch of the West's castle; just before 12 noon.
Scene Twelve: Librum's Lair; not long after.

The premiere of *The Wizard of Bamboozlement* was presented by Children's Theatre To Go, Inc. at the Reynolds Performance Hall in Conway, Arkansas, on May 13, 2009, under the direction of Bob May, with set design by Bob May, costume design by Nikki Webster, with the following cast:

Gidget—Niki Moss
Figure/WJ—Katie Crawford
The Queen—Katie Oslica
Candy—Susy Webb
The Wicked Witch of the West—Karen Owings
Beanie—Cris Tibbetts
Classmate A—Sam Coker
Classmate B—Jacob Webb
Classmate C—Miki Brewington
BJ—Jacob Fluech
Dorothy—Maddie Moss
Hansel—Joe Coker
Gretel—Skyler Hale
Snow White—Katie Barber
Dewie Decimal—Ben Schueter
Lewie Decimal—Ashley Jones
Chris—Chris Webster
Voice/Hewie Decimal—Daisy Owings
Professor Librum—Matt Forrester

SCENE ONE

(AT RISE: GIDGET is discovered sitting at a desk in her office at home. She speaks as she types on a computer keyboard.)

GIDGET: Chapter Thirteen. Winter had shown its ugly face about the middle of October and it looked like it was going to hang around like an unwanted house guest for the remainder of the season. Each night after the sun said, "goodbye," the mercury fell well below freezing. So I was surprised to find the temperature on this Halloween night as warm as a witch's caldron. There wasn't any mention of the warm-up in the weather forecast. I unzipped my coat... (*She stands, unzips her coat, and acts the following out.*) and proceeded to cautiously walk toward a very spooky-looking castle. A full moon helped cast shadows on the fortress making it appear even eerier as I got nearer. Bats flew in the semidarkened sky all around me like flies devouring the carcass of a dead animal. I paused and pondered, "Why does this structure standing in front of me looked so familiar?" It gave me the creeps. I stood frozen like a deer in a bright light as I remembered how this bizarre investigation had begun two days earlier with a phone call. (*The SOUND of a phone ringing is heard. GIDGET sits at the desk and answers a phone.*) We Know Witches. Gidget Mae Brown-Boren speaking.

(*A FIGURE stands in the shadows - LIGHT special - talking on a cell phone.*)

FIGURE: How well?

GIDGET: Excuse me?

FIGURE: How well do you know witches?

GIDGET: Halloween always brings out the crank calls. Goodbye.

FIGURE: Don't hang up. This is not a crank call. So, how well do you know witches?

GIDGET: My husband and I have dealt with—

FIGURE: Is your husband the famous Beanie Boren?

GIDGET: Yes, Beanie and I have dealt with some of the most famous witches in literary history. The queen witch from Snow White...

FIGURE: ...ah yes... the queen who hated Snow White's beauty. (*The QUEEN appears in a LIGHT special.*)

QUEEN: Mirror, mirror in my hand. Who's the fairest in all the land? (*LIGHT special out on QUEEN.*)

GIDGET: And the witch from Hansel and Gretel.

FIGURE: Candy was her name, and she lured children to her house made of candy and gingerbread cookies so she could eat them. (*CANDY appears in a LIGHT special.*)

CANDY: Nibble, nibble, like a mouse... who is nibbling on my house? (*LIGHT special out on CANDY as she cackles.*)

GIDGET: You know your witches well.

FIGURE: How about the Wicked Witch of the West? (*WEST appears in a LIGHT special.*)

WEST: I'll get you yet, my pretty. And your little dog too. (*LIGHT special out on WEST as she cackles.*)

GIDGET: Yes, we especially know the Wicked Witch of the West from The Wizard of Oz. Is there a point to all your questions?

FIGURE: I know a new witch, and she wants to meet you.

GIDGET: Oh, yeah, what's her name?

FIGURE: You can meet her at a haunted castle with reflections from your past—just like the one you described in your book.

GIDGET: How do you know what is in my book? No one has read my book.

FIGURE: Be in front of the castle at midnight on Halloween night. I will call your cell phone. (*The LIGHT special fades on FIGURE. GIDGET hangs up the phone and moves to another area on the stage.*)

GIDGET: So, there I stood on this freakishly warm Halloween night at midnight in front of a haunted castle. Why did the structure look so familiar? Reflections from my past? Waiting for a cell phone to ring is like waiting for a pot of water to boil. It never seems to happen. And then it hit me. Water! The fortress that loomed before me looked exactly like what the Wicked Witch of the West called home. At any moment, I expected the green-faced witch to greet me with a "I'll get you yet, my pretty," but she didn't, nor did any other witch. But I wasn't waiting for a witch to greet me. I was waiting for a phone call from a witch. After what seemed like a lifetime I cried out, "Are you here?" The only answer I received was the echo of my own voice. (*SOUND: "Are you here?" is heard in an echo.*) My stomach growled what my mind screamed… "turn back; this is one witch investigation you don't want to get into." When the phone rang… I screamed. (*SOUND: A phone rings. GIDGET screams and then answers her cell phone.*) Hello. (*Pause.*) Hello. (*Pause.*) WHO IS THIS? (*The phone continues to ring. She realizes it is not her cell phone that is ringing but the phone on her desk. She sits at the desk and answers the phone.*) Hello? (*BEANIE is discovered in a LIGHT special on his cell phone.*)

BEANIE: Hey, Gidge, it's me, how's the writing going?

GIDGET: Oh, Beanie, your call scared me.
BEANIE: Sorry, kiddo, are you all right?
GIDGET: Yeah, I'm fine. I guess I'm just scaring myself. It's like the characters in my book are coming to life in my office tonight.
BEANIE: Then staying home to write was worth it?
GIDGET: I guess so. How was the movie?
BEANIE: There's a new witch you should meet.
GIDGET: What? Did you say a new witch?
BEANIE: Yes, the witches in Harry Potter are not like any of the witches we knew when we were young.
GIDGET: Just like in my book. All witches are not bad. Did you sneak a peek at my book?
BEANIE: No, and when are you going to let your husband sneak a peek?
GIDGET: Not till I'm finished. Hurry home, honey.
BEANIE: We'll be there soon, and BJ might need some cheering up. Some of his classmates were at the movie theatre and they were making fun of him.
(*CLASSMATES A, B, and C are discovered in a LIGHT special, heckling BJ.*)
B: BJ, buddy, how Bookworld?
A: Hey, Bennie Junior, has your daddy introduced you to any witches lately?
C: Hey, classmates, I wonder if they know Harry Potter. (*The LIGHT fades on the CLASSMATES as they laugh.*)
GIDGET: I look forward to seeing you both.
BEANIE: Love you.
GIDGET: Same here. (*The LIGHT fades on BEANIE. GIDGET gets back to her book. She begins to type and*

talk.) The phone call was a wrong number. I looked at my watch and oddly it still read midnight. But that couldn't be. I knew I had been at the castle for over an hour. As I was tapping my watch to see if it was broken, a figure stepped out of the shadows and spoke to me.

(*The FIGURE enters. She is a miniature/younger version of The Wicked Witch of the West from the book, The Wizard of Oz, complete with a green face. She speaks in a coarse, high-pitched voice.*)

WJ: I'll get you yet, my pretty. And your little dog too.

(*WJ cackles and GIDGET screams.*)

GIDGET: How did you get in my house?

WJ: I told you I'd meet you at midnight.

GIDGET: No, you were going to call me at midnight.

WJ: I changed my mind.

GIDGET: You can't do that. You're not even real.

(*WJ claps her hands and flicks her wrist toward GIDGET. A flash of lightning strikes next to GIDGET and the SOUND of a crack of thunder is heard.*)

WJ: Is that real enough for you?

GIDGET: What do you want?

WJ: As my creator, you should know what I want.

GIDGET: You seem to be doing the writing now.

WJ: That's right, but you're the professional and you're going to compose a list of my demands. Come, you are my prisoner until this world gives me what I want. (*Beat*) Do I have a name?

GIDGET: You look just like your mother, the Wicked Witch of the West, so let's call you WJ?

WJ: WJ?

GIDGET: West Junior.

WJ: I like it. Now come on, my pretty.

(WJ grabs GIDGET's arm, twists it behind her back, and pushes her off stage, cackling as the LIGHTS fade to black. Music bridges the gap between scenes.)

SCENE TWO

(AT RISE: The office is empty. BEANIE and BJ enter.)

BEANIE: Gidget, we're home. (*To BJ.*) BJ, I'm sorry your classmates continue to make fun of you. And I know the teasing gets worse every Halloween because of the witches. It never used to bother you. Why is this year so different?

BJ: Come on, Dad, Bookworld? The entire story is really hard to believe.

BEANIE: But it's true, there is a Bookworld, a place in a galaxy far, far away where—

BJ: Yeah, yeah, where all storybook characters live.

BEANIE: We met some very good characters.

BJ: I know... Dorothy from The Wizard of Oz. And Hansel and Gretel, and Snow White.

BEANIE: Don't forget Professor Librum and the three Decimals.

BJ: Dad, this story was fun when I was younger.

BEANIE: You're still just a boy.

BJ: I'm eleven years old.

BEANIE: (*Calling*) Gidget, where are you? (*To BJ.*) You've seen the book reading machine.

(BJ acts very nervously when he says the following.)

BJ: That twenty-year-old hunk of junk metal gathering dust in the garage?
BEANIE: I won my school Science Fair two years in a row with that hunk of junk metal.
BJ: So, you've always been a computer nerd.
BEANIE: My being a computer nerd has afforded us the comfortable life we have and you enjoy with us.
BJ: (*Still nervous.*) All right, but you won the Science Fair because the machine could read books, not because it made the characters from those books come to life. That's the part that is hard to swallow.
BEANIE: I guess the Bookworld story is hard to believe. (*Beat*) I wonder where your mother is?
BJ: Her computer is still on. And look, here's her cell phone. She can't be far. She never goes anywhere without her phone.
BEANIE: (*Calling.*) GIDGET? (*To BJ.*) Her car was out front.
BJ: What's this?
BEANIE: What?
BJ: A note. (*Picks up a note off the desk.*)
BEANIE: Read it to me.
BJ: What?
BEANIE: What does it say?
BJ: I… ah…
BEANIE: What's wrong, can't you read?
BJ: Of course I can read. But it's addressed to you. Here. (*BJ hands BEANIE the note.*)
BEANIE: (*Reading.*) Dear Mr. Beanie. Your wife is my prisoner. Gidget tells me that I need to talk to a Professor Librum to obtain what I want. And she also tells me that you can make this happen.

It is now midnight. I'll give you until twelve noon tomorrow—twelve hours—to set up a meeting between Librum and me. Otherwise, Gidget, your lovely wife, may never finish writing her book. I will be in touch. This note will self-destruct as soon as you read it. (*Beat*) It's signed by... WJ. Who is WJ? (*The note in BEANIE's hand goes up in flames.*)

BJ: Is this some kind of spooky Halloween prank for my benefit?

BEANIE: What's the last thing your mom wrote on her computer? (*Reading from her computer.*) "The phone call was a wrong number. I looked at my watch and oddly it still read midnight. That couldn't be. I knew I had been at the castle for over an hour. Just as I was about to say "goodbye," a figure stepped out of the shadows and spoke to me."

BJ: Maybe we should call the police?

BEANIE: The police can't help.

BJ: Stop it, Dad.

BEANIE: This mess has Bookworld written all over it.

BJ: Okay, fine, I play your game. How do we get in touch with this Professor Librum in your Bookworld?

BEANIE: He always just showed up when I used my book-reading machine and things went bad.

BJ: Then we better fire up the machine.

BEANIE: The machine's been idle for twenty years; since I destroyed it. It doesn't work.

BJ: Sure, it does. I repaired it and have been using it to read for me.

BEANIE: Read for you?

BJ: Dad, I have trouble reading, so I've been using your book-reading machine to help me.
BEANIE: If my machine has been reading books once again, we have really big problems. Come on, we need to get to the machine.
(*The LIGHTS fade to black. Music bridges the gap between scenes.*)

SCENE THREE

(*AT RISE: BEANIE and BJ are discovered in the garage, standing next to an object covered with a tarp.*)

BEANIE: Why didn't you tell me you were having trouble reading?
BJ: How could I? You and Mom were Book-It Reading Champions. I was embarrassed that I couldn't live up to your expectations.
BEANIE: Help me with this. (*They pull the tarp off the machine, revealing an enormous object with a monitor, typing keyboard, and other science fiction-looking buttons and levers.*) How did you get this old thing to work again?
BJ: I guess I inherited some of your smarts.
BEANIE: Having a reading disorder doesn't make you stupid. Some very smart people have trouble learning to read. (*He looks at the machine.*) Oh, my, seeing this old thing brings back so many memories. (*A beanie cap sits on the machine. He puts it on and says what he said when he was younger at the Science Fair.*) "I have combined an Apple Z-28 computer and a Sony Mini-Video-Cam...

in conjunction with a contraption of my own design… to create a machine that will read any book in a matter of moments."

BJ: You could read three books at one time.

BEANIE: (*As he puts the beanie cap on BJ.*) Yes, with the handy-dandy, super-duper, deluxe solar power converter… three books at once. But that's when the problems began.

(*The QUEEN, CANDY, and WEST appear in a LIGHT special.*)

WEST: Don't you realize what has happened? This Beanie kid and his machine have freed us. We aren't in our books anymore… or for that matter… we're not in Bookworld.

WEST, CANDY, and QUEEN: We're free. (*The LIGHT special fades on the three witches as they cackle.*)

BEANIE: This machine has caused more problems than good.

BJ: It's been good to me. It's helped me with my reading problems.

BEANIE: There are other solutions to your reading problems that don't include using this bamboozling book-reading machine. And we'll deal with that, but right now I think your bringing the machine back to life is responsible for your mother's disappearance.

BJ: But how?

BEANIE: What books has the machine read for you?

BJ: I've mostly used it to read my textbooks so I could complete my homework assignments. And I used the voice-to-text printer to write for me.

BEANIE: Textbooks aren't the problem. How did you get this old thing to turn on?

BJ: I made an adapter for my new MacBookMark and plugged it into the machine's super-duper solar converter link. After it read all the old Apple files without a problem, I downloaded all the new MacBookMark files to the machine. I guess my laptop is the next generation bamboozling reading machine. It's all saved on my jump drive.

BEANIE: Have you read any books other than textbooks lately?

BJ: Yeah, I began with the three books that were left in the machine's reading slots. Here, I'll plug in my jump drive and let the machine's monitor remind you of what they were. (*BJ pulls a jump drive from his pocket and plugs it into the machine. The machine turns on. LIGHTS flash. The machine hums.*)

BEANIE: I remember what they were.

(*SOUND erupts. DOROTHY pops out of the machine, clicking the heels of her ruby slippers together.*)

DOROTHY: There's no place like home. There's no place like home.

BEANIE: Dorothy?

DOROTHY: Oh, my goodness, how did I get here? I was on my way back to my Auntie Em in Kansas. Who are you?

BEANIE: It's me, Beanie.

DOROTHY: Beanie? It can't be. You've aged so.

BEANIE: I may not look the same on the outside, but inside I am the same.

DOROTHY: Good and kind. (*DOROTHY embraces BEANIE.*)

BEANIE: (*To BJ.*) The Wizard of Oz was one of the books.
(*More SOUNDS. HANSEL and GRETEL pop out of the machine.*)
HANSEL: Whoever you are, don't mess with me or my little sister, or you'll be sorry.
GRETEL: Ya, dear bruder. Where are we?
DOROTHY: Relax, Gretel. You too, Hansel. It's just Beanie and his bamboozling book machine in action once again. (*HANSEL walks up to BJ and hugs him.*)
HANSEL: Beanie, you've not changed a bit.
BJ: I'm not Beanie.
BEANIE: Hi, Hansel.
HANSEL: Beanie?
BEANIE: Yes, it's me. You just embraced my son, BJ, Beanie Junior.
HANSEL: But you are an adult.
BEANIE: I'm not a storybook character; real people age as their childhood heroes remain the same. (*HANSEL hugs BEANIE.*)
HANSEL: Beanie, brother, you will always be my friend.
GRETEL: Ya, mine, too, dear Beanie. (*GRETEL embraces BEANIE.*)
HANSEL: Are the witches causing you harm again? I'll take care of those rascals.
BEANIE: I'm not sure what is going on. (*To BJ.*) And Hansel and Gretel was book two.
BJ: Yes. (*More SOUNDS. SNOW WHITE pops out of the machine.*)
SNOW: Help me. Why, what's going on?

BEANIE: Snow White. (*BEANIE sighs in love.*)
SNOW: Beanie, my prince. (*She sighs in love.*) I would recognize those beautiful eyes in a crowd of people. (*She embraces BEANIE.*) Has your machine begun another adventure?
BEANIE: (*To BJ.*) Slot three was Snow White.
BJ: Yes, the same three books you read to demonstrate your machine when you won the Science Fair. But this can't be real.
BEANIE: It's real, and it means… just like these characters have done… the witches from those stories have once again escaped from their books and taken your mom prisoner.
BJ: But which witch has her? The note was signed WJ.
(*The SOUND of the Space Rider landing outside the garage is heard.*)
BEANIE: We're about to find out. I will never forget that sound. Professor Librum's space rider has landed.
(*DEWIE DECIMAL enters. DEWIE is an android. SNOW, DOROTHY, HANSEL, and GRETEL begin to ad-lib to him about what is going on.*)
DEWIE: Calm down, Bookworld characters. Please. All calm down.
BEANIE: Help us, Gidget is missing.
DEWIE: Beanie Boren… please calm down as all have been requested to do. My memory chips remind me that book-reading machine was destroyed twenty years ago.
BJ: Is this Professor Librum?
BEANIE: You must do something.

DEWIE: (*To BJ.*) Dewie Decimal at your service. Professor Librum has retired. I am head librarian of Bookworld now.
BJ: Along with your brother and sister, Hewie and Lewie?
DEWIE: Since Dewey Decimal System has been replaced with the Library of Congress system, there's not much work for three Decimals. Brother and sister are managers of Starbucks in Bookworld library. (*To BEANIE.*) Why firing bamboozling book machine up?
BEANIE: Because of a reading problem... my son has been using it to read for him. But we have—
(*DEWIE uses his hand to do a scan of BJ's head and body. SOUND accompanies this.*)
DEWIE: Reading problem detected in Beanie son. In most humans, brain able to connect abstract symbols—letters—into a sound, but BJ brain not able to do this—malfunctioning. For example, letter D doesn't make sense to him—nor do other letters. Condition called dyslexia. Person can learn to cope with condition with much work and by using strategies.
HANSEL: I don't believe BJ's dyslexia is the reason why we're all standing in this garage right now.
GRETEL: Ya, dear bruder.
BEANIE: That's what I've been trying to tell you. We have a bigger problem. It's Gidget. She's been kidnapped by one of the witches, along with someone called WJ.

DEWIE: Scan of Bookworld library checkout records has three evil witches from these stories accounted for.
BEANIE: What? It has to be one of those witches. Those are the books BJ read with the machine.
DEWIE: Initial speedy scan of Bookworld card catalogue is negative on any character with name WJ.
BEANIE: The kidnapper demands to meet Professor Librum.
DEWIE: I am number one now. Kidnapper must deal with Dewie.

(*There is an explosion. All scream. WJ appears before them.*)

WJ: Lizard guts and bat wings! Listen, you overgrown pile of tin, circuits, and wires. What part of my request don't you understand?
DOROTHY: Look out! It's the Wicked Witch of the West!
DEWIE: Negative, not Wicked Witch of the West.
WJ: I don't want to deal with you, Dewie. I want Librum.
DEWIE: Whom shall I say wants to see him?
WJ: Tell him my name is WJ.
DEWIE: Why do you want to see Librum?
WJ: When I meet with him, I will tell him.
DEWIE: Be reasonable, young lady.
WJ: I know what you're doing, Dewie Decimal. You're trying to get a character analysis reading on me. Let me save you the trouble. I am no one in your new Library of Congress filing system or Librum's old system named after you. You will not find me

in any informational system. The clock is ticking. Let me remind you who I have as my prisoner. (*WJ claps her hands. A SOUND is heard. GIDGET is seen in a LIGHT special, next to an hourglass.*)

GIDGET: Don't give in to her. I refuse to be manipulated by a character I gave birth to. (*To WJ.*) You're not even real.

WJ: Oh, but I am now. (*WJ claps her hands and the LIGHT goes out on GIDGET. SOUND illustrates this.*)

DEWIE: Has Book Machine read Gidget's new book?

BJ: Yes, I read it.

DEWIE: WJ is new witch, escaped from Gidget book.

BJ: Listen, you little witch, you better not hurt my mother.

WJ: Silence, kid. I demand to see Librum. And your time is running out. (*WJ casts a spell. All stand like zombies and sway to her words.*)

You've already wasted an hour
Not a smart move I must confess
It's time I show you my power
Give me justice and nothing less.
Back to Bookworld you all go
via a twister that blows and blows.

(*WJ claps her hands, a spell SOUND is heard, and then the SOUND of a tornado/ wind is heard. WJ exits cackling. All shout as they spin off stage.*)

SNOW: What is happening?

DEWIE: I believe in Kansas this action called tornado.

DOROTHY: It sure sounds like one.

BEANIE: Can't you stop this, Dewie?

DEWIE: This WJ witch is very powerful.

HANSEL: Hold my hand, dear sister.

GRETEL: Ya, dear bruder.
DEWIE: Try to meet up, back in Bookworld.
BJ: Dad?
BEANIE: BJ.
SNOW: Beanie!
DOROTHY: Auntie Em!

(*ALL spin off. The LIGHTS fade to black. The tornado wind SOUND bridges the gap between scenes.*)

SCENE FOUR

(*AT RISE: BJ is discovered lying unconscious on the ground in the middle of Bookworld. BJ wakes up.*)

BJ: Dad? (*The SOUND of laughter is heard.*) Dad, where did you go? Dewie? Dorothy? Anyone? (*The SOUND of laughter is heard.*) I don't think I'm in the garage anymore.

(*A bright ball of LIGHT floats all around the auditorium and then heads toward BJ. The ball of light becomes LEWIE DECIMAL, another android.*)

LEWIE: Oh, BJ, what have you done now?
BJ: Who are you?
LEWIE: I am Lewie Decimal.
BJ: Sister to Dewie? I thought you were selling coffee?
LEWIE: Yes, Dewie sister. Am bistro at Starbucks. It keeps memory chips active. White chocolate caramel macchiato? (*Beat*) Hewie and I received Dewie distress signal and been on lookout for you and others.
BJ: Where am I?

LEWIE: BJ in retired book region of Bookworld. (*The SOUND of laughter is heard.*)
BJ: Who keeps laughing at me?
LEWIE: Fellow classmates. Come out, come out wherever you are. (*CLASSMATES A, B, and C enter.*)
B: BJ, buddy, how's Bookworld?
A: Hey, Bennie Junior, has your daddy introduced you to any witches lately?
C: Hey, classmates, I wonder if they know Harry Potter. (*The CLASSMATES laugh.*)
BJ: Lewie, I must save my mother. How do I find this Professor Librum?
LEWIE: Professor has retired. Dewie in charge now.
BJ: I know all that. Dewie won't do. It must be Professor Librum. He holds the key to my mom's freedom. Where is he?
LEWIE: At central section of Bookworld main library. (*There is an eruption of SOUND. The CLASSMATES scatter and hide offstage. WJ enters.*)
WJ: I see, sweet, sweet Lewie, that you are playing the good Decimal once again.
LEWIE: Who addresses me? Character not in Library of Congress files.
WJ: Chill, you overheated android, don't blow a circuit trying to figure this out.
BJ: She's a new witch in the book my mother is writing.
WJ: Hey, BJ, you have something I want when I meet with Librum.
BJ: What?
WJ: Your jump drive.

LEWIE: No, Little Beanie, hold on to it. Whatever is on that jump drive must be very powerful. Don't let her have it.
WJ: I will get it from you, you little sprout. Meanwhile, time is slipping away for your mother. Check the time. (*WJ exits cackling.*)
BJ: What time is it? We only have until noon.
LEWIE: You lost much time in twister. Now, six in the morning.
BJ: Will you take me to the main library?
LEWIE: You must find own way by following the Yellowed Pages Trail of the retired books through Bookworld.
BJ: Where do I find this trail?
LEWIE: Read and follow signs posted along trail.
BJ: Haven't you heard… I've been diagnosed with dyslexia by Dewie.
(*LEWIE does a scan of BJ with her hand. SOUND accompanies this.*)
LEWIE: Lewie concur with Brother Dewie's findings.
BJ: So, can you point me in the right direction?
LEWIE: I am machine, but not book-reading machine. I can't read for you. You must read for self.
BJ: Now is not the time to be teaching me a lesson. I need a little help here.
LEWIE: All humans possess defects, and all strive to overcome defects—often by focusing and using strengths. BJ intelligence, motivation, and education have gotten you this far. Focus.

(*LEWIE disappears as a ball of LIGHT. CLASSMATES enter to say "goodbye." They carry big poster boards with letters drawn on them.*)

BJ: Defects! Focus! I don't even know where to begin. (*To CLASSMATES.*) Will you help me?

A: Maybe one of the…

B: …witches from the books…

C: …the machine read will help you?

BJ: Stop making fun of me. Just show me the way to the central section of the main library.

A: All right. (*The three CLASSMATES laugh.*)

B: We're holding letters… just read them.

BJ: Letters don't make sense to me when I try to read.

A, B, and C: You do have a problem. (*They laugh.*)

A: Am I an A… (*Holds up the poster board with letter A.*)… or an E? (*Flips to the poster board around to a letter E. Flips poster board back and forth several times.*) A? E? A? E? A? E? (*Beat*) You better know or you won't find your wa-ay.

B: To be… (*Holds up the letter B.*)… or not a be? (*Flips poster board to a 3.*)

C: See you. (*C holds poster board to look like a C and then turns it to look like a U. He flips between a C and a U, several times.*) C – U. C – U. C – U.

A, B, and C: Bye bye. (*The CLASSMATES laugh.*)

BJ: Which way do I go?

A: Didn't Lewie tell you…

B: …to follow the…

C: …Yellow Brick Road.

BJ: Very funny. No, she said, "Follow the Yellowed Pages Trail."

A: It is A… (*Shows letter A.*)

B: ...direction to go.
C: When you can't C... (*Shows letter C.*)
B: ...any other direction to go.
BJ: What are you babbling about?
B: Follow the arrow. (*B walks to A and turns the letter A he/she is holding to look like an arrow ->.*)
BJ: That way? (*BJ points in the direction the arrow is pointing.*)
A, B, and C: What a loser. (*The CLASSMATES exit laughing.*)
BJ: I guess I should go this way. (*BJ starts walking off as the LIGHTS fade to black. Music bridges the gap between scenes.*)

SCENE FIVE

(*AT RISE: BJ is discovered at a crossroads. There are two signs that read gibberish, or what BJ sees when he looks at words. The first sign says, "cnetarl Sektoin Boolworkd mian Libanry," with an arrow pointing to stage right. The other sign says, "The Uesd Baak Sektoin," with an arrow pointing stage left.*)

BJ: Oh great, this way or that? (*CLASSMATES enter and do a short dance to the Jackson Five's "ABC-123."*) Stop. (*The CLASSMATES stop dancing.*) Please, just tell me which way to go.
A: Okay, it's this way. (*CLASSMATE A stands behind one of the two gibberish signs and points the same direction as the arrow on the sign.*)

B: No, it's this way (*CLASSMATE B stands behind the other gibberish sign and points in the same direction as the arrow on the sign.*)
BJ: What do they say? (*CLASSMATE C laughs at BJ.*)
C: Ha, ha, when you have trouble "decoding" letters, they might as well be written in a foreign language. (*BJ holds out his jump drive.*)
BJ: This jump drive could read those signs.
C: But wouldn't you like to stop hiding your secret?
B: Stop making excuses when asked to read in class?
C: Remember, you read from left to right.
A: Or maybe you just belong in the slow learners' part of the class?
(*CLASSMATES start laughing. HANSEL and GRETEL enter.*)
HANSEL: Back off, you aggressive classmate letters before I twist you into numbers.
GRETEL: Ya, bad letters, you better do as my bruder says. Go away.
(*The CLASSMATES back away, huddle, but don't leave the stage.*)
BJ: Thanks. It sure is good to see someone I know.
HANSEL: Yea, glad to see you're all right after the twister. Where in Bookworld are we?
BJ: I'm not sure... I'm working my way along the Yellow Pages Trail to the central section of the main library and Professor Librum.
HANSEL: We should probably get there too. And we better get there soon.
GRETEL: Yah, tis seven o'clock in da morning. Five hours before da noon deadline.

BJ: I don't know which way to go… I can't read these road signs.
GRETEL: We can help. Bruder Hansel and I know our ABCs.
HANSEL: Sure, you betcha, sister is right. We know how to read.
A: Oh yeah, what does this spell? (*The CLASSMATES hold up letters to spell the word CAT.*)
HANSEL: We know how to sound out the letters.
GRETEL: C is a kah, kah, kah sound. Say it, BJ.
BJ: Kah.
HANSEL: A is an aah sound like an old dog groaning when he sleeps. (*HANSEL groans like an old dog.*)
BJ: AAH.
GRETEL: And da T is easy. Tah. Say it.
BJ: Tah.
HANSEL: Put them all together and it is… kah… aah… tah.
GRETEL: Now you put them all together, Little Beanie… Kah.
HANSEL: Aah.
GRETEL: Tah.
BJ: Kah… aah… tah… Kah… aah… tah…
  (*If anywhere in this sequence the kids in the audience shout out the word, GRETEL can say, "Shhh, no, let BJ figure it out."*)
HANSEL: Say them faster.
BJ: Kah— aah— tah— Kah— aah— tah…
GRETEL: …and that word spells…
BJ: Kah— aah— tah… It spells cat.
(*WJ enters accompanied by an explosion of SOUND.*)

WJ: Bravo, to the German brother and sister duo. Reading lessons on the run. Education to go. Let's say the cat in question is a black cat and it just crossed your path. That's bad luck. (*She produces a flame. HANSEL and GRETEL jump back in fear.*) Does this fire remind you of the oven you both will soon cook in? (*GRETEL screams.*)

HANSEL: Stand behind me, sister. You too, BJ. I will protect you from this evil.

GRETEL: Ya, dear bruder.

WJ: Give me that jump drive, BJ.

BJ: Never.

WJ: Do you ever want to see your mother again?

BJ: We're working our way to see Professor Librum. I thought you wanted to meet him?

WJ: I want that jump drive in my hands before I see him.

HANSEL: Hold tight to that jump drive, BJ.

WJ: Do you like candy?

BJ: What?

WJ: Maybe the witch from the Hansel and Gretel story, Candy, can convince you to give me the jump drive. (*WJ exits laughing. CANDY enters.*)

CANDY: Nibble, nibble, like a mouse... who is nibbling on my house?

HANSEL: This bamboozlement just keeps getting worse.

GRETEL: Ya, dear bruder.

CANDY: Oh, my sweet Hansel and Gretel. Who's your new friend? Let me show him all the delicious things I cook in my special oven.

BJ: I thought Dewie said the witches from your books were safe back in Bookworld?
HANSEL: Remember, we are back in Bookworld. Back in their world.
BJ: We have to get past her to continue our journey to the central section of the main library.
HANSEL: I know we do, my friend. Be careful. She has lots of magical powers.
CANDY: (*She licks her lips and says...*) Oh, lovely children. (*Very sweet and innocent.*) Would you like a gingerbread cookie? I baked it myself in my own special oven.
GRETEL: Dear bruder, we need to do as we always do and trick her into an oven and be done with her.
CANDY: I heard what you said, my sweet Gretel.
BJ: Well, the element of surprise is gone. And besides, I don't see an oven.
GRETEL: We have da letters... so let us build one.
BJ: There are only three letters here.
HANSEL: An A, B, and a C to be exact.
CANDY: Humor me. I need a good laugh before I devour the three of you.
GRETEL: Come here, C. (*CLASSMATE C enters with a poster board with a C written on it. GRETEL acts out what she says.*) We turn the C around and draw another one to join it and we have an O.
HANSEL: Oh, I "see," little sister.
GRETEL: A, get over here.
(*CLASSMATE A enters with a poster board with the letter A written on it.*)
A: There isn't an A in the word oven.
GRETEL: Turn your A upside down and be quiet.

(*CLASSMATE A flips his sign upside down.*) Now we erase this from the A. (*GRETEL removes the line that connects the two sides of the upside down A. It now looks like a V.*)
HANSEL: That's great. But where are you going to get an E?
GRETEL: Hey, B, I need an E. Can you help?
(*CLASSMATE B enters with a poster board with the letter B written on it.*)
B: Sorry, I'm just a B.
GRETEL: Oh, no imagination. You won't be a B if I take a little bit away from you. (*GRETEL erases the two round parts of the B to make an E.*)
CANDY: You still need an N to make an oven.
GRETEL: Oh, but we do have one.
CANDY: Where? I don't see one.
GRETEL: Look in…side.
CANDY: What?
GRETEL: Once you're in…side we will have our N.
(*CANDY looks closely at the letters O-V-E and the three kids push CANDY N-side the oven. The CLASSMATES surround CANDY, and they exit with CANDY. A SOUND of a burp is heard, and the letter N is thrown on stage. GRETEL holds up the letter N. HANSEL, GRETEL, and BJ celebrate by dancing and cheering.*)
HANSEL: Very clever, sister, dear.
GRETEL: Ya, dear bruder.
HANSEL: I need to use my mind more effectively like you when lost in the woods. Maybe the Professor can help me do that?
BJ: Need I remind you both that time is slipping bye-bye.

GRETEL: Yah, da noon deadline is nearing. The Professor, he can help us all.

BJ: You know, I understand about sounding out letters. But letters just don't look the same to me as they do to you. So, I can't relate a sound to a letter. CAT might as well be DOG in my mind.

GRETEL: Oh, dear. Do not be discouraged, BJ, my friend. We will help you.

BJ: So, which way do we go?

HANSEL: Meow. CAT way. (*HANSEL points in the direction the arrow on the "cnetarl Sektoin Boolworkd mian Libanry," points. They all laugh.*)

BJ: Come on, let's run. We can't be that far away.

(*They run off as the LIGHTS fade to black. Music bridges the gap between scenes.*)

SCENE SIX

(*AT RISE: HANSEL, GRETEL, and BJ enter running. They are still in the outlands of Bookworld.*)

GRETEL: Stop. Stop. (*HANSEL, GRETEL, and BJ stop running.*)

HANSEL: What is wrong, my little sister, are you tired?

GRETEL: No, dear bruder.

BJ: We have been running for over an hour.

GRETEL: Look. (*She points at something across the stage.*)

HANSEL: What is it?

BJ: It could be a trap.

HANSEL: You two stay here. I will check it out. (*He moves to the object.*)
BJ: Be careful.
(*HANSEL gets to the object and discovers SNOW WHITE lying asleep on a table.*)
HANSEL: It is not a danger. It is Snow White. Come, look.
(*BJ and GRETEL move to HANSEL. As soon as they get there the QUEEN enters with a cackle. The three kids jump back in a huddle.*)
QUEEN: Mirror, mirror in my hand... who is the fairest in the land? It is I. You awful kids must give up trying to get to the professor and give WJ the jump drive... or you'll end up just like Snow White. (*QUEEN exits laughing. BJ looks at SNOW.*)
BJ: What's wrong with her?
GRETEL: Look, she must have taken a bite of an apple. (*She holds up an apple with a bite taken out of it.*)
BJ: Yes, she's in a poison-apple-induced sleep. A kiss from a prince is the only thing that can wake her up.
HANSEL: Don't look my way. We know from past experience I'm not a prince.
GRETEL: Then it is up to BJ.
BJ: I'm not a prince either.
GRETEL: A prince must be true at heart, and honest.
BJ: That description doesn't fit me.
GRETEL: Beanie woke Fraulein Snow White with a kiss once. Aren't you like your papa?
BJ: Not much. I'm a big disappointment to my dad.

HANSEL: You're a coward because you have never kissed a fraulein before.

BJ: Yes, I have.

GRETEL: Then, please, Young BJ, you must do it again.

(*BJ bends over to kiss her, but can't do it. HANSEL and GRETEL urge him on. He finally gives SNOW a peck on the lips. The three wait for something to happen, nothing does.*)

BJ: See, I told you, I am not a prince. Come on, once we get to the professor we can send someone back to get her.

HANSEL: You didn't kiss her long enough.

GRETEL: Ya, dear bruder.

BJ: What?

HANSEL: Your lips were not on hers for long enough.

BJ: Yes, they were.

GRETEL: You must do it again. And this time… kiss the beauty like a true prince. (*GRETEL and HANSEL urge him on once again. BJ kisses SNOW. GRETEL holds BJ's head down as he kisses SNOW. BJ struggles. When GRETEL lets up, BJ jumps back. Nothing happens.*)

HANSEL: Come, we will send the Decimals back for her. (*Just as the three are about to walk away, SNOW wakes up.*)

SNOW: My prince has come at last.

HANSEL: You're the man, BJ. (*HANSEL holds out his hands for BJ to slap, which he does.*)

SNOW: Thank you, Master BJ. Oh, I am so confused. So many princes to choose from. My heart is twisted in many directions.

GRETEL: Hey, Fraulein Snowie, come with us. The professor can set your heart in the right direction.

SNOW: Yes, my heart is in search of the right Prince Charming. (*The QUEEN enters.*)

QUEEN: Nice kiss, String Beanie. Now, give me that jump drive or you'll never kiss again.

BJ: Isn't this where the red-hot iron dancing shoes take over?

QUEEN: Don't have them? Oh, I'm so sorry, for I do love to dance.

BJ: Then dance to this. Hey, Classmates, sing your song.

(*CLASSMATES enter and sing the chorus to the Jackson Five song, "ABC-123." QUEEN begins to dance.*)

QUEEN: What is happening? (*She dances off stage wildly. CLASSMATES follow her off.*)

HANSEL: All this is very odd. What is this all about? A brain and a heart? Why does this all sound so familiar?

GRETEL: Ya, dear bruder.

BJ: The professor can answer all our questions. Come on, we only have four hours left.

(*The four run off as the LIGHTS fade to black. Music bridges the gap between scenes.*)

SCENE SEVEN

(*AT RISE: DOROTHY is discovered somewhere in Bookworld clicking her shoe heels together.*)

DOROTHY: There's no place like home. There's no place like home.

(*SNOW, HANSEL, GRETEL, and BJ enter.*)
HANSEL: Hey, Dot, it's us. (*DOROTHY screams.*)
GRETEL: We've scared her.
DOROTHY: Yes, you scared me. Ever since that Wicked Witch look-a-like blew us all back to Bookworld, I've been lost and I'm wondering if I really have the courage to deal with something I'm not familiar with. Clicking my heels is not getting me home.
BJ: Brain, heart, and courage. Dorothy, I think this WJ is making us all experience some twisted version of your story.
HANSEL: The Wizard of Bamboozlement.
DOROTHY: But why?
BJ: She's trying to scare us, so I will give her the jump drive. Your stories are the only thing she knows. When I read my mom's book with the machine, she became familiar with your stories, and now she's making us act out what she knows.
DOROTHY: But why does she want your jump drive?
SNOW: Stop talking; the Professor will know what to do.
BJ: How much time do we have?
HANSEL: Only two hours.
HANSEL, GRETEL, SNOW, and DOROTHY: Show us the way, BJ.
(*WJ appears in a LIGHT special and casts a spell.*)
WJ: Apostrophes, exclamation points, questions marks,
Periods, commas, colons, and quotations marks
Invade their world and confuse the children.
I need that jump drive so a new chapter can begin.

(*WJ claps her hands, and a spell SOUND is heard. Punctuation symbols flood the stage. CLASSMATES enter carrying punctuation symbols as they circle the group.*)
HANSEL: Vat does it all mean?
GRETEL: Ya, dear bruder.
DOROTHY: It's just punctuation marks.
SNOW: What do they mean? Which way do we go, Prince BJ?
(*LEWIE appears in a LIGHT special.*)
LEWIE: Get past the punctuation. See the letters, the words. Sound them out. Find your way.
(*LIGHT special out on LEWIE.*)
BJ: The central section of the Bookworld main library is straight ahead.
HANSEL: Are you sure, BJ, my bruder?
BJ: I'm positive; punctuation doesn't confuse me.
SNOW: I trust my Prince Beanie J.
BJ: This way.
(*HANSEL, GRETEL, SNOW, DOROTHY, and BJ run off as the LIGHTS fade to black. Music bridges the gap between scenes.*)

SCENE EIGHT

(*AT RISE: HANSEL, GRETEL, SNOW, DOROTHY, and BJ are discovered at the main entrance to the central section of the Bookworld Library.*)

HANSEL: Here we are... the main entrance to the central section of the Bookworld Library.
GRETEL: Ya, dear bruder.

BJ: How much time do we have?

SNOW: Only an hour, my Sweet Prince.

BJ: How do we find the professor? (*CHRIS enters in a motorized wheelchair. In the original production, CHRIS was played by an actor who had cerebral palsy.*) Are you Professor Librum?

CHRIS: No.

HANSEL: That's Chris, the bookkeeper. Give me five, Chris. (*HANSEL and CHRIS do a high five. GRETEL, SNOW, and DOROTHY ad-lib "hello" to CHRIS.*)

DOROTHY: All books are checked out through Master Chris.

BJ: We don't need to check out any books. Master Chris, do you know where can we find the professor?

CHRIS: Yes.

BJ: You do, then please take us to him.

CHRIS: First read this. (*CHRIS hands BJ a note.*)

BJ: Read this? Very funny. I can't read. I'm handicapped.

CHRIS: Handicapable.

BJ: Handicapable? What does that mean? Handicapable?

CHRIS: Stop feeling sorry for yourself.

BJ: I'm not feeling sorry for myself.

CHRIS: Look at the note. (*BJ looks at the note.*)

BJ: Fine, I'll look at the note. Oh, it's from my father. I recognize the handwriting. Where is he?

CHRIS: I'll call him.

BJ: Yes, please, call him. (*CHRIS rings a bell. BEANIE and DEWIE enter.*)

BEANIE: BJ.

BJ: Dad. (*BJ runs to BEANIE and they embrace.*)
DEWIE: Thank you, Chris. You may go. (*CHRIS exits.*)
BEANIE: I knew you'd find your way here.
BJ: My new friends not only helped me get here but taught me some things about reading too.
DEWIE: Never be ashamed about reading problem. There's no help in hiding.
BJ: I see that now, thanks, Dewie. Do you know where Mom is?
BEANIE: Unfortunately, not.
GRETEL: We'll find her BJ, bruder.
BJ: Have you set up a meeting between Professor Librum and WJ? There's not much time left.
DEWIE: The professor says he will see us. And he knows how to rescue your mother.
BJ: Do you know who this WJ is?
BEANIE: After reading what your mom wrote, we know...
DEWIE: ...Gidget created a new Oz character.
DOROTHY: A new character in my story? Who?
BEANIE: The daughter of the Wicked Witch of the West: WJ, West Junior.
DOROTHY: The Wicked Witch didn't have any children.
DEWIE: In Gidget's book, she does.
BJ: Who is the father?
BEANIE: Your mom hasn't revealed that yet.
BJ: What?
BEANIE: She hasn't written that chapter yet.
DEWIE: Priority... to figure out why WJ wants to see the professor.

BJ: She wants my jump drive more than a meeting with the professor.
HANSEL: Hey, we now have less than an hour.
BEANIE: Dewie, I think it's time to see the professor.
DEWIE: Follow me.

(*BJ, BEANIE, DOROTHY, SNOW, HANSEL, GRETEL, and DEWIE run off as the LIGHTS fade to black. Music bridges the gap between scenes.*)

SCENE NINE

(*AT RISE: BJ, BEANIE, DOROTHY, SNOW, HANSEL, GRETEL, and DEWIE are discovered in LIBRUM's lair.*)

BJ: Where does Professor Librum live?
DEWIE: Deep in the heart of the library. He's sort of like the core of a computer.
BEANIE: I'm looking forward to seeing him again.
DEWIE: Librum now only sees characters via his spirit.
DOROTHY: Since when has the professor been so unavailable?

(*A VOICE is heard, along with visual effects on a screen. Just like in The Wizard of Oz.*)

VOICE: To answer your question, Dorothy of Kansas, I am unavailable since I retired. Dewie, I'm not happy that you could not deal with this problem on your own.
BEANIE: Professor, it's me, Beanie.
VOICE: I know who you are.
BJ: This is the great Professor Librum?

VOICE: Silence, boy. We wouldn't have this problem if you had left your father's book machine alone.
HANSEL: Hey, Librum, cut the kid some slack. He needed some help with his reading.
VOICE: Watch how you talk to me, book character.
BJ: I'm sorry, Professor. I take full responsibility for causing this problem. I know my mom needs help, but so do these characters and I hope you can help them too. Hansel and Gretel would like more intelligence. Snow White's heart is unsure of which prince is her Prince Charming.
DOROTHY: And I could use some more courage as I face new dilemmas.
HANSEL: Thank you, BJ, but your mother is the most important problem facing us and we are getting very close to the noon deadline.
BJ: Professor, will you please meet with this witch, WJ, before noon today?
VOICE: We don't need to worry about this deadline. Gidget is being held prisoner at The Wicked Witch of the West's castle. You must go there and destroy this WJ.
BEANIE: How do we do that?
VOICE: Use water. Just like her mother, she will melt. You don't need much.
DEWIE: Will a vial do?
VOICE: Yes. Throw some water on this Wicked Witch WJ. Then bring the broom of this evil one to me. Now leave.
(There is an explosion of SOUND and the special effects and the VOICE stops.)

BJ: Wait a minute. I've never seen this daughter of the Wicked Witch with a broom. Have any of you?
DEWIE: The great and powerful Professor Librum has spoken. And that's that!
BJ: How do we get to the Wicked Witch of the West's castle?
BEANIE: Gidget's book reads… (*He reads from a piece of paper.*) "I proceeded to walk toward a spooky-looking castle. A full moon cast shadows on the fortress making it eerier as I got nearer. Bats flew in the darkened sky all around me. The fortress that loomed before me looked exactly like what the Wicked Witch of the West called home. At any moment, I expected the green faced witch to greet me with a "I'll get you yet, my pretty."
DEWIE: Wicked Witch's castle located in fantasy adventure section of library.
DOROTHY: Once we get there, I will know how to find the castle and get in.
SNOW: Look at us. We are seven strong. Just like the seven dwarves in my story.
BJ: Let's hope we are as strong as those brave little fellows were.
BEANIE: Think positive.
DEWIE: We can take space rider. Follow me.

(*The seven run off and the LIGHTS fade to black as the theme from The Mod Squad TV show is heard, and then the SOUND of the space rider taking off is heard.*)

SCENE TEN

(AT RISE: BJ, BEANIE, DOROTHY, SNOW, HANSEL, GRETEL, and DEWIE are discovered outside the Wicked Witch of the West's castle.)

DEWIE: We made it. This is Fantasy Adventure Land.
SNOW: And my blue eyes are focused on an eerie looking castle with bats flying around it.
DOROTHY: I would recognize this castle in my sleep. It reeks of the Wicked Witch of the West.
BJ: Boy, the Bookworld library is gigantic.
DEWIE: Big as all authors' imaginations combined. Dorothy, is vial of water in your possession?
DOROTHY: It's concealed close to my heart.
HANSEL: Come on, let's go get that witch.
GRETEL: Ya, dear bruder.
DOROTHY: As soon as I see her I'll throw the water on her.
SNOW: Oh, *(She giggles.)* I'm so happy that I can be a part of this rescue. I'm usually in a poison-apple-induced sleep during all the action in my story.
BEANIE: Come, son, if anyone can save your mother, it's this motley crew.
BJ: Motley?
DEWIE: "Exhibiting diversity of elements." Let us enter.
DOROTHY: Follow me.

(BJ, BEANIE, DOROTHY, SNOW, HANSEL, GRETEL, and DEWIE exit as the LIGHTS fade to black. Music bridges the gap between scenes.)

SCENE ELEVEN

(*AT RISE: WJ is discovered standing over the body of GIDGET, who lies on a table, inside the castle. WJ is touching GIDGET's lips as she speaks.*)

WJ: Oh, Gidget, my creator, it seems my noon meeting with the professor is not going to happen. Nor do I have the jump drive. What will become of you? (*She exits.*)
(*BJ, BEANIE, DOROTHY, SNOW, HANSEL, GRETEL, and DEWIE enter.*)
HANSEL: Look. There. (*They all run to GIDGET.*)
BJ: Mom?
BEANIE: Gidge?
DOROTHY: What's wrong with her?
(*DEWIE picks up an apple that is lying next to GIDGET.*)
DEWIE: Look, an apple.
SNOW: Oh, goodness, she is in a poison-apple-induced sleep. A prince must kiss her to wake her up.
BJ: Dad, you're her prince. Kiss Mom and wake her up so we can get out of here.
DEWIE: BJ is correct, my friend.
BEANIE: Wait. This rescue is all much too easy.
DEWIE: Just do it. (*BEANIE kisses GIDGET. Nothing happens.*)
HANSEL: You must have lost your touch, my old pal, Beanie. (*They all laugh.*)

GRETEL: Do it again, but this time keep your lips on hers longer. Right, BJ. (*They all laugh again. A beat later BEANIE stumbles.*)
DEWIE: Is there problem, Beanie?
BEANIE: I think I've been poisoned. (*He falls down.*)
BJ: Dad. (*He runs to BEANIE.*) Is he dead?
(*DEWIE does a scan of BEANIE's body with his hand. SOUND accompanies this.*)
DEWIE: Beanie not dead. Just in deep sleep like wife, Gidget. WJ planted sleep potion on Gidget's lips.
DOROTHY: What is Gidget holding in her hand?
(*DOROTHY takes a small device from GIDGET's hand.*)
HANSEL: Let me see. (*DOROTHY hands device to HANSEL.*) Some sort of remote control device.
BJ: What does it do? (*HANSEL pushes a button on the device.*)
DEWIE: NOOO, do not push button. (*As he malfunctions, SOUND is heard.*) Device planted to fry my circuits. (*DEWIE freezes. WJ enters.*)
WJ: Ah, look. How sad. All the adults and androids are in a deep sleep.
HANSEL: Your evilness must be stopped. (*He charges WJ.*) AHHH!
WJ: Freeze. (*She holds up a hand, a spell SOUND effect accompanies this, and HANSEL freezes.*) Jump drive or not, I'm disappointed, BJ, that you didn't set up a meeting between Librum and me?
DOROTHY: Why should we? We've come here to destroy you. And this water should do the trick. (*She throws the vial of water on WJ. WJ falls to the floor as she speaks.*)

WJ: AHHH!! Water! You cursed brat… Look what you've done! I'm melting… I'm melting. Oh, what a world… my world. Who would have thought a good little girl like you could destroy my beautiful wickedness? (*HANSEL unfreezes. The kids walk over to WJ and look. After a beat WJ pops up and yells.*) AHHH! (*All scream. WJ stands up and laughs.*) Just playing with you. Water doesn't make me melt like it does my mother. In fact, thanks to your mother, BJ, I shower each day just like you do. There's nothing worse than a smelly child, especially a kid who's a witch.

GRETEL: WJ, please, come back to the main library with us. I'm sure Professor Librum will see you and give you what you vant.

WJ: I've decided I really don't need to see Professor Librum. All I want is BJ's jump drive.

BJ: Why do you want my jump drive so badly?

WJ: It can make me legitimate.

DOROTHY: The professor can do that.

WJ: I need to see what is written about me.

SNOW: Just read Gidget's book. (*BJ understands her problem.*)

BJ: You don't know how to read.

WJ: What? No, I can read.

BJ: If you can… what does this say? (*HANSEL, GRETEL, SNOW, and DOROTHY hold up letters… O-T-A-C. BJ puts them in order to spell "cat." It takes him a bit, but he gets it done, discarding the O letter.*) What does that spell?

WJ: I know "spells"… and I think I'll cast a wicked spell right now to stop you from talking your evil garbage.
BJ: I'm sorry for picking on you. (*WJ is not so tough anymore.*)
WJ: Yes, I know spells… I just don't know how to spell. I'm a witch that can't read. I need your jump drive so I can use the book machine to read about my mother. I've never known her.
BJ: Come with us back to the central section of the main library. Professor Librum is going to help all of us and I bet he can help you too. You shouldn't be embarrassed that you can't read.
(*WJ points to the word CAT.*)
WJ: What does that spell?
BJ: Cat. And I just learned how to spell it and so can you.
(*The WICKED WITCH of the WEST enters.*)
WEST: What is all this racket going on in my castle? (*All scream, and huddle across the stage from her.*)
WJ: Who's that?
BJ: I think that is your mother.
DOROTHY: That's her. The Wicked Witch of the West.
WEST: I am the mother to no one. Dorothy, my little pretty, who are all these strangers with you?
WJ: Do I look like her?
HANSEL: Not as ugly.
WEST: Watch your mouth, young lad. (*WEST flicks her wrist. A spell SOUND is heard, and HANSEL tumbles across the stage.*)
GRETEL: Bruder. (*GRETEL runs to HANSEL.*)

WJ: I'm not sure I want to be like her.
SNOW: You don't have to be.
DOROTHY: WJ, come with us back to see Professor Librum.
WEST: Librum? Ha! None of you will ever make it out of my castle. (*WEST begins to cackle and dance.*)
WJ: (*Speaks in a stage whisper.*) Follow me. I know a secret way out of here.
BJ: What about my mom, dad, and Dewie?
DOROTHY: We can come back for them. Right now, without any water to protect us, I think we better leave.
WJ: Come. (*WJ leads others and they exit.*)
WEST: (*Shouts*) You'll never make it out of my castle.
(*WEST cackles as the LIGHTS fade to black. Music bridges the gap between scenes.*)

SCENE TWELVE

(*AT RISE: BJ, HANSEL, GRETEL, SNOW, DOROTHY, and WJ run into LIBRUM's lair.*)

VOICE: Who dares enter Librum's lair uninvited?
BJ: It's us, Professor, BJ.
DOROTHY: And Dorothy and the other kids.
VOICE: I only see book characters by appointment.
BJ: We have brought you the young witch, WJ; just as you asked us to do.
VOICE: You were instructed to throw water on this new witch, WJ, and bring me her broomstick.
WJ: I have never owned a broomstick.

BJ: Dewie and my parents are trapped in the Wicked Witch's castle.
VOICE: I have asked for the broomstick. Why haven't you brought it to me?
(HANSEL *reveals HEWIE behind a curtain with a microphone in hand.*)
HANSEL: Who are you?
HEWIE: I am the great and powerful Professor Librum.
GRETEL: No, you're not.
SNOW: That's Hewie Decimal.
HEWIE: Oh, hi. Would you like cup of coffee?
BJ: Where's Professor Librum?
HEWIE: We Decimals don't want to bother him... because... (*Hangs his head.*)... we can solve this problem.
BJ: You were afraid to ask for his help. Just like I was afraid to do with my dyslexia problem.
HEWIE: This all Dewie's idea. Wish he or Lewie were here to help me.
(WEST *enters, cackling. All the kids scream and huddle together on the opposite side of the stage from across* WEST.)
WEST: I knew Librum wasn't in control of things anymore.
HEWIE: Danger. Danger. Wicked Witch is present. Danger.
WEST: Beanie Junior, rumor has it that you, my little sprout, have a jump drive that can change storybook history. I want that device.
BJ: I'll give it to you if you don't hurt my parents.
WEST: You want your parents? I figured you would say that. Fine, here they are. (WEST *claps her hands.*

A spell SOUND is heard. GIDGET and BEANIE enter, walking as zombies, and fall down, once again asleep.) I'll even throw in the irritating Decimal, Dewie. (*WEST snaps her fingers. A spell sound is heard. DEWIE enters, walking as a zombie, and freezes.*) Now, drop that jump drive into my beautiful green hand.

(*WEST holds out one of her hands. BJ is just about to give the jump drive to WEST when LEWIE enters.*)

LEWIE: Not so fast, West.

WEST: Call me Mae.

WJ: Mother, why do you have to be so wicked?

WEST: You're not my child. You're too weak.

HEWIE: Lewie, my sister, please put situation back to order.

LEWIE: Yep, I possess the solution to situation.

WEST: Don't make me laugh, there is no solution to this bamboozlement.

LEWIE: Yes, there is… it is called…water. (*She produces a vial of water.*)

WEST: WATER! NO! (*WEST runs into the audience as all the others chase her throughout the audience. They end up back on stage and have WEST surrounded. WEST has WJ in her grasp.*) Throw that water and you destroy the young witch too.

LEWIE: No, Lewie can't do that.

BJ: Don't worry, water doesn't hurt WJ. Give it to me. I can do it. (*BJ grabs the vial and throws it on WEST and WJ. Both scream as they melt into the floor.*)

WEST and WJ: AHHH!! Water! You cursed brat…

WEST: Look what you've done! I'm melting…

WJ: I'm melting. Oh, what a world…

WEST: My world.
WJ: Who would have thought...
WEST: ...a good little boy...
WJ: ...like you could destroy...
WEST and WJ: ...our beautiful wickedness. (*WEST and WJ are gone.*)
BJ: What have I done?
(*LEWIE does a scan with his hand of the area WEST and WJ melted into.*)
LEWIE: Water affected WJ because West was holding little witch. (*The mood is solemn.*)
BJ: WJ wanted to be a good witch.
LEWIE: Are there really any good witches?
HEWIE: You have done well, BJ. By throwing water, you saved parents and Dewie.
BJ: Did I? Look at them. Lifeless. What do we do about them?

(*The bodies of BEANIE and GIDGET are carried and placed up center. DEWIE is moved near them. ALL then sit dejectedly. CHRIS enters in his motorized wheelchair. LIBRUM is standing/riding on the back of it.*)

CHRIS: Special delivery.
LIBRUM: Yes, special delivery. Thanks for the ride, Chris. (*To the others.*) Will I really ever be able to retire?
HEWIE: Decimals sorry, Professor; we thought we could handle situation.
LIBRUM: (*He laughs.*) "Bring me the broom of this witch WJ?" What were you thinking, Hewie?
HEWIE: That's all I could think to say. Just like Wizard demanded in The Wizard of Oz.

LIBRUM: Never be afraid to ask for help if you have a problem.
BJ: Are you Professor Librum?
LIBRUM: At your service. And you must be Master BJ?
BJ: I've caused one big mess. See what I've done to my mom and dad. And Dewie.
LIBRUM: We can deal with the three of them in just a bit. I think it's important to note that your wanting to read is a positive sign.
BJ: Just a slow brain.
LIBRUM: You have a brain full intelligence.
BJ: I know Hansel and Gretel would like to increase their brainpower.
LIBRUM: They've always had the power to do that. What letter does brain begin with, BJ?
BJ: Brain? Bah, bah… a B… just like my name.
LIBRUM: Correct, so here's a B for Hansel and Gretel. (*CLASSMATE B enters.*)
B: I'm just a B. (*HANSEL and GRETEL move to B.*)
HANSEL: The sum of the square root for cooking Candy, the witch, is equal in all ovens.
GRETEL: How very true, dearest brother.
SNOW: Professor, will my heart once again belong to the real Prince Charming?
LIBRUM: As long as you want it to. BJ, with your intelligence, you must know what the biggest part of the heart is?
BJ: It's the aorta.
LIBRUM: And aorta begins with what letter?
BJ: That's easy… an A.

LIBRUM: Enter A. (*CLASSMATE A enters doing the Fonz, "Aay!" and moves to SNOW. He is PRINCE CHARMING.*)

A/PRINCE: Princess Snow White, I am your Prince Charming and my heart is yours. (*PRINCE kisses SNOW.*)

SNOW: My heart is once again whole.

LIBRUM: And Dorothy wants more courage. Having courage doesn't mean that you don't have fear. Your courage just wins out over your fear. BJ, what letter does courage begin with?

BJ: Courage? Ca, ca… C.

PROFESSOR: And here's a C. (*CLASSMATE C enters and moves to DOROTHY.*)

DOROTHY: BJ, because of you, I found my courage and will face any situation fearlessly, but cautiously.

LIBRUM: And you, BJ, have proved you're on your way to dealing with your dyslexia.

(*CLASSMATES walk over to BJ and hoist him up on their shoulders ala a football hero. Everyone cheers.*)

BJ: All isn't so great. Yes, Hansel now has an intelligent brain, Snow a loving heart, and Dorothy strong courage. But what about my mom, dad, and Dewie? There aren't any letters left to help me save them. (*CLASSMATES put BJ down.*)

LIBRUM: Oh, Dewie just needs a jumpstart from his brother and sister.

(*HEWIE and LEWIE touch DEWIE and with SOUND effects DEWIE jumps to life.*)

DEWIE: Beep, beep, knick, knick, knick. Varoom. All circuits back to normal operating mode.

LIBRUM: And you, BJ, should know what to do about your mom and dad?

BJ: I don't know.

LIBRUM: Some of my best authors were dyslexic. Walt Disney, Albert Einstein. And they were anything but dumb. They found other things they were good at.

BJ: Snow White needs to kiss my dad, wake him up, and then he can kiss his one true love, my mom.

LIBRUM: Let's see if that works. Miss White, please do the honors. (*SNOW kisses BEANIE. He pops to life.*)

BEANIE: I'll never forget those lips. Thank you, Snow White. But my lips belong to Gidget.

(*BEANIE kisses GIDGET and she pops to life.*)

GIDGET: Chapter fourteen… I knew my prince and son would save me.

BJ: Dad, I'm sorry I ever doubted that Bookworld was real. And, Mom, it's sad that we lost WJ.

GIDGET: No, love, I don't think we have. (*Beat*) Dewie, do you have a laptop. (*DEWIE produces a small laptop computer or just a keyboard. DEWIE holds it so GIDGET can type. GIDGET says what she types.*) "My captor was the spitting image of the Wicked Witch of the West, but her personality wasn't anything like the evil witch. She used this Halloween night to show people that not all witches are bad." (*She stops typing.*) Now, BJ, plug your jump drive into this laptop.

(*BJ plugs his jump drive into the computer, SOUND is heard, and WJ crawls out of the hole she and WEST melted into earlier.*)

WJ: Melting into the floor is not much fun.
GIDGET: (*Continuing to type.*) "I knew the daughter of the Wicked Witch was good because I was married to her father."
WJ: Beanie is my father?
ALL: Beanie?
BEANIE: Gidget?
GIDGET: Oh, no, not her real father. The chapter telling who her real father is has not been written. So, Beanie and I would like to adopt you, then he would become your father.
BEANIE: Yes, we can do that.
LIBRUM: And I think I can arrange that the Bookworld birth records reflect that fact.
WJ: Then you'd have two children who can't read.
BJ: No, no, enough of this bamboozlement.
WJ: Bamboozle?
DEWIE: "To deceive by trickery."
BEANIE: We will get you both some help for your dyslexia.
LIBRUM: And remember if any of you ever have a problem... the key is to persist in working at it, doing the best you can do, and never give up.
BJ: Yes, we can do that. As Chris said... we are all...
CHRIS: ...handicapable.
ALL: Handicapable.
WJ: Yes, we are.
BJ: Now, you're thinking, sister. Help me spell out that this bamboozlement is over. (*BJ and WJ move the twelve other characters around to spell out "THE END." DEWIE is the "T" - LEWIE and HEWIE make the "H" - HANSEL and GRETEL form an "E" - SNOW and*

DOROTHY make another "E" - A, B, and C are an "N" - and GIDGET and BEANIE are the "D." CHRIS holds up an exclamation point. The Jackson Five song, "ABC-123" plays as they move. LIBRUM looks at the message.)
LIBRUM: The end.
(The LIGHTS fade to black. The song continues playing under the curtain call.)

END

A Collection from a Career in Theatre

Two Old Men

a play

by

Bob May

© 2017 by Bob May

All rights reserved

CAST OF CHARACTERS

TERRY
BOB
JACKSON
REBECCA
CINDY
SANTANA

SYNOPSIS OF SCENES

ACT ONE
Scene one: A park in Miami, Florida, fall 2016
Scene Two: The park, fall 2018
ACT TWO
Scene One: The park, fall 2020
Scene Two: The park, immediately following

Two Old Men was first presented as a reading at The Lantern Theatre in Conway, Arkansas, on June 24, 2017, under the direction of Shua Miller, with the following cast:

Terry—Terry Wright
Bob—Bob May
Jackson—Tavares Pilgrim
Rebecca—Heather Hooten
Cindy—Ruthann Curry
Santana—Augustine Nguyen

ACT ONE

SCENE ONE

(AT RISE: TERRY is sitting on a bench in a park. He is holding a gun semi-secretly. After a beat, he puts the gun in his jacket pocket. A beat later, BOB enters and moves to the park bench. The conversation begins awkwardly. They don't know what to say.)

BOB: Sorry, I'm late.
TERRY: Where ya been?
BOB: Waiting for my daughter to drive me here. She forgot.
TERRY: You could have called.
BOB: You don't have a phone.
TERRY: Not me, your daughter.
BOB: I did, that's how she remembered I needed a ride. She was getting the U-Haul. She's going to pick me up in an hour. *(Beat)*
TERRY: Well, you're here now. So, say it.

BOB: Say what?
TERRY: Goodbye. Isn't that why we're meeting here today? (*Pause*)
BOB: How long have we been coming to this park? (*Pause*)
TERRY: Are you really going to go through with this?
BOB: I don't have any choice.
TERRY: You always have a choice. (*Pause*)
BOB: Maggie died this morning.
TERRY: This morning?
BOB: Well, sometime overnight. I found her this morning.
TERRY: I'm sorry; I know how close you were to that dog. What did you do with her?
BOB: Nothing yet. I didn't want to be late meeting you.
TERRY: But you were late.
BOB: Only because Rebecca was picking up the U-Haul. (*Beat*)
TERRY: Did she hire anyone to load it?
BOB: Load what?
TERRY: Your stuff.
BOB: The U-Haul is for her stuff. She sold most of my stuff when I moved in with her. You know that.
TERRY: Yeah, I guess I did. I forgot. (*Beat*) Enough with the small talk. Just say it. (*Pause*)
BOB: Some guys she worked with are going to load the U-Haul. They're doing it as we speak.
TERRY: Is it a truck or trailer?
BOB: It's a trailer. We're going to pull it with her car.
TERRY: She got a bonus for taking the new job, didn't she?

BOB: A hefty one, and they're paying to ship all the big items.
TERRY: Rebecca's a talented young woman. (*Pause*)
BOB: Why don't you move too, come with us?
TERRY: Who would I live with?
BOB: With me. We can get a place together.
TERRY: We can do that here. I already got a place.
BOB: You're being evicted.
TERRY: If you stayed and moved in with me, I'd have enough money to pay what I owe. I thought we were always going to look after one another.
BOB: Rebecca won't let me stay.
TERRY: Last time I checked, you were the parent and she was the child.
BOB: Since Shelia died, and my health issues, the roles have reversed.
TERRY: Reverse them back.
BOB: It's cheaper for us to get a place together in Ohio than it is to live together here.
TERRY: I don't want to leave Miami. I like the beach. All the chicks in bikinis.
BOB: When's the last time you were at the beach?
TERRY: Knowing that I can go anytime I want to is comforting. (*Beat*) We promised to stick together. Take care of one another. Just be together. (*Pause*)
BOB: Do you remember, we promised we would try to surf again when we turned seventy?
TERRY: I got it.
BOB: What, a surfboard?
TERRY: No, you know… a gun.
BOB: You did?
TERRY: Yea, I did.

BOB: Do you have it with you?
TERRY: Yes.
BOB: Let me see it. (*TERRY pulls the gun out. The conversation is flowing now.*) Jesus, put that damn thing away.
TERRY: Relax. It's cool. There's really no one around. This place is always so deserted. It never used to be.
BOB: Let me hold it. (*TERRY hands BOB the gun.*) It's not very big.
TERRY: It's a Beretta .380. And I'm told it'll do the trick.
BOB: Do you know how to use it?
TERRY: It can't be that difficult. Point and shoot. Are you with me?
BOB: No, I told you, I can't do it. (*BOB hands TERRY the gun. TERRY puts the gun back into his pocket.*)
TERRY: Come on, I got everything all worked out.
BOB: And I still think it's the craziest scheme I've ever heard.
TERRY: It's foolproof.
BOB: No, we'd be the fools if we did it.
TERRY: If we did it, we'd have enough money to pay for a place here in Miami together. On the beach. And I could get a headstone for Allison. (*Pause*)
BOB: No sane crack dealers are going to just hand over their stash to us.
TERRY: We don't want their stash. Just all the money that's always lying around on the coffee table. Every time I see a bust on TV there is hundreds of thousands just lying there for the taking. They can keep their stash.

BOB: If we don't take the stash, they'll know it's not a real bust.
TERRY: Okay, we'll take the stash and dump it in the Intracoastal.
BOB: Where are we going to get the jackets?
TERRY: I had them made already. (*From a bag, he pulls out a brown windbreaker jacket that reads DEA in big yellow letters on the back. He puts it on and models it.*) Here's one for you. (*He throws a jacket to BOB.*)
BOB: It's crazy. They're going have guns and they will shoot us.
TERRY: We'll have the element of surprise. We bust in yelling, with guns drawn.
BOB: Gun drawn. We only have one gun.
TERRY: I'm working on another.
BOB: Let's say it works.
TERRY: It'll work. I 've been rehearsing my badass agent voice. "DEA! This is a bust. Hands up." And our long hair works to our advantage. We look like undercover agents.
BOB: This isn't the sixties Mod Squad times. We just look like the two old hippies we are. They will turn us in.
TERRY: To who? The cops? What do they tell them, two old hippie DEA agents just stole all our drug money?
BOB: How do we find a crack house?
TERRY: Every other house in South Beach is probably a crack house. Or we ask one the pimps or drug dealers stealing our park from us where one is. (*BOB throws the jacket back to TERRY.*)
BOB: Old hippies?

TERRY: What?
BOB: We just called ourselves... old hippies. (*Pause.*)
TERRY: Dammit, Bob, I don't want you to leave.
BOB: You know I'd stay if I could.
TERRY: What are you going to do in Ohio?
BOB: Cleveland. And we can go to the Rock 'n' Roll Hall of Fame. Indians games. (*Pause*)
TERRY: We've been coming to this park for almost fifty years.
BOB: Excuse me?
TERRY: You asked how long we've been coming to this park. Almost fifty years... 1969. Since the first time you abandoned me. You took off for Woodstock with the gang from Toad Hall.
BOB: I didn't abandon you. You got the job at the high school and that prevented you from going.
TERRY: Damn those start-of-school-year meetings. I'm still jealous I didn't get to go.
BOB: Joni Mitchell felt the same way...
TERRY: (*Mockingly*) I've heard it before... Joni couldn't go because she had to do the Dick Cavett show...
BOB: That's right. And Crosby, Stills, and Nash got to go, and Joni was jealous.
TERRY: (*Serious again*) But Joni immortalized the event with her song... all I did was teach tenth graders poetry.
BOB: It was all meant to be. I met Sheila at the festival; you met Allison at the school. And because of you, I got the teaching gig at the high school too.
TERRY: Do you miss her?
BOB: Shelia?

TERRY: Yeah.
BOB: After forty-two years of marriage, hell yes.
TERRY: It's been over four years since she…
BOB: Passed. The emptiness is still in my heart. Having you has helped me adjust.
TERRY: And just like Woodstock, you're abandoning me when I need you. I don't know if I can continue. God, I miss Allison.
BOB: Give it some time. It's only been a few months for you. The living gets easier, the emptiness just lingers. (*Beat*) And you know I'd stay if I could. (*Pause*)
TERRY: Lewy body dementia?
BOB: Rebecca told you, didn't she?
TERRY: I knew something was wrong when our park meetings became sporadic.
BOB: And Parkinson's. They usually go hand in hand.
TERRY: You seem fine to me.
BOB: I am, until I go on one of my trips.
TERRY: The hippie is still taking trips.
BOB: I wish it were the same. These trips are not enlightening. I don't even remember them. I just know when I get back. Rebecca says when I'm on one, I talk like I'm back at the high school directing a show, barking out commands. (*He barks out some commands*) I said move down right not down left… your right, not the audience's right. How many times do I have to tell you? (*Beat*) They're happening with more frequency.
TERRY: Why haven't you talked to me about it?
BOB: I didn't want to burden you.
TERRY: You're my best friend.

BOB: Brothers with different mothers.
TERRY: We were going to change the world.
BOB: You'd gone through enough with Allison.
TERRY: How long do these trips last?
BOB: Could be a few minutes or a few days.
TERRY: If that's why you don't want to stay, I could handle it. It can't be any harder than dealing with Allison's cancer toward the end. You can't leave. We were always going to be together.
BOB: Rebecca says I get violent sometimes.
TERRY: I'm not worried. I've always been able to kick your butt.
BOB: In your dreams. (*They wrestle briefly.*)
TERRY: Do you take anything for it?
BOB: A colorful assortment of pills.
TERRY: The hippie is still taking pills. Any good ones you want to share?
BOB: There's no cure.
TERRY: Then why all the pills?
BOB: They treat all the side effects, lack of sleep, Parkinson movement problems.
TERRY: Can we talk about something more positive? Like raiding a crack house.
BOB: Getting old is a pain in the butt.
TERRY: It's not for pussies.
BOB: Can you believe that dumbass, Trump, thinks he can grab any woman he wants cause he's a celebrity?
TERRY: That's talking about something positive?
BOB: Just a reality in this very weird election cycle.
TERRY: There's no way that narcissist can be the president.

BOB: No, he's not qualified. And he's said too many things that a politician can't say and be elected.

TERRY: That's what was being said throughout the primary. And he won the nomination.

BOB: The Republicans have never been on the side of the average wage earner. There's nothing to worry about; the polls have Hillary ahead... bigly!

TERRY: I could use some of his money. But... sad!

BOB: Does he really have any money?

TERRY: His tax returns would answer lots of questions.

BOB: Haven't you received Allison's life insurance money yet?

TERRY: Again, not a very positive subject.

BOB: Is there anything positive we can talk about at our age?

TERRY: All the chicks on the beach in bikinis.

BOB: Hey, and we can now take a cruise ship to Cuba.

TERRY: If we had the money. (*Pause*) I had to borrow money on Allison's insurance policy to pay for her treatments.

BOB: One would think after a lifetime of teaching, this country would treat its educators with more respect.

TERRY: All its seniors.

BOB: I heard that, bro.

TERRY: You got life insurance money when Sheila died, right?

BOB: She only had five thousand... and most of that went for the funeral. We put a lot on me because we thought I'd be the first to go. I'm worth a lot more dead than alive.

TERRY: Dead don't help the situation now.
BOB: Have you thought about getting married again? Marry a rich snowbird widow.
TERRY: You and I could get married. It's legal now, thanks to Obama. We could say we were gay and get married now. Two can live cheaper than one.
BOB: We don't need to be married to live together.
TERRY: I only wanted your life insurance money.
BOB: Okay, I'll do it.
TERRY: I was just kidding, I don't really want to marry you.
BOB: No, let's raid the crack house. You need the money.
TERRY: All right, now you're talking. (*TERRY grabs the DEA jacket and throws it to BOB. BOB puts it on.*)
BOB: We need another gun. Each DEA agent in a raid would have their own gun. Where did you get the one you have? (*He sees something off in the distance.*) Did you see that? (*He yells off in the distance.*) Hey dumbass, pick up that soda can. (*To TERRY.*) Where did you get the gun?
TERRY: From the pimp you just called a dumbass.
(*JACKSON enters, talking on his cell phone.*)
JACKSON: Yea, yea, I be here. Bidness as usual. I gots to go. (*He puts his cell phone in his upper, inside coat pocket, and then talks to BOB.*) Yo, old man. Who you calling a dumbass?
BOB: You, you dumbass. The reason the city placed trash cans throughout this park is so the people who use the park won't litter. Now, pick up the soda can you just threw on the ground and put it in its proper place.

TERRY: Hey, Jackson, dude, please excuse my friend, Bob, he's angry that he's being forced to leave his home.

BOB: Don't make up excuses for me, Terry. I want him to pick up the damn can.

JACKSON: Bob, is that yo name? Bob. Well, Bob, I guess you don't know that the city don't own this park no mo, I do. This be my office. And I've been letting you and Terry use my park because you don't never cause no trouble. So, I'll tell you what… you want that soda can picked up so bad, you do it or get the fuck out of my office.

BOB: Did anyone ever tell you that your grammar is horrible?

TERRY: I'll pick up the can.

BOB: Don't move, Terry. Jackson thinks we "don't never cause no trouble," well, "he gots" another think coming. Now, Jackson, I'm going to ask you one more time, nicely, to pick up that can and dispose of it properly.

JACKSON: Fuck you, old man.

(*BOB starts to growl like a dog as he reaches into TERRY's coat pocket and grabs the gun. He turns and points the gun in JACKSON's face.*)

BOB: Is not picking up that can worth dying for?

JACKSON: Be careful with that thing, old man.

BOB: Stop calling me, old man.

TERRY: Bob, put the gun down.

JACKSON: Yeah, Bob, put the gun down.

BOB: Or what?

JACKSON: Or I might just shoot yo dumbass before you hurt yo-self. (*JACKSON pulls a gun out and points it at BOB.*)

TERRY: Okay, holy shit. Both of you... put the guns down. (*TERRY moves in between BOB and JACKSON. He now has both guns pointed at him.*)

BOB: That was a stupid move, Terry.

TERRY: I can see that, Bob.

JACKSON: Yo, Terry, I ain't got no beef with you. It's the hippie behind you, I want. Now get out of my way.

TERRY: Listen, Jackson, can we talk this over.

JACKSON: I will shoot yo ass first and then the old hippie if you don't get the fuck out of my way.

BOB: Who are you calling an old hippie?

JACKSON: You, you old-man-hippie. Get yo haircut.

BOB: You pull up your pants.

(*JACKSON grabs TERRY and puts one arm around TERRY and pulls TERRY into his chest, then puts the gun to TERRY's head.*)

JACKSON: Drop the gun, Bob, or I'll put a bullet in this hippie's head.

BOB: Go ahead, shoot him... he won't move with me, so I don't care what happens to him.

TERRY: You don't mean that.

BOB: Maybe I do.

TERRY: You're the one deserting me.

BOB: Goodbye, Terry. There, I said it... you wanted me to say it. I said it. Goodbye.

TERRY: Jackson, you have my permission to shoot that old man.

JACKSON: Both of ya'll... shut the fuck up.

(*When JACKSON says that last line, he moves the gun away from TERRY's head. TERRY smashes his elbow into JACKSON's gut causing JACKSON to bend over gasping for air. TERRY snatches the gun from JACKSON and moves to the opposite side of JACKSON of where BOB stands. BOB and TERRY are now on both sides of JACKSON with guns pointed at him.*)

BOB: Wow, Terry, for an old man, you still got the moves.

TERRY: That's what the chicks say.

BOB: Well, we now have that second gun we wanted.

JACKSON: Okay, I'll pick up the damn can.

BOB: How much money do you have, Jackson?

JACKSON: What?

BOB: You're a drug dealer in our park. I'm a DEA agent, read my jacket. Now, how much money have you made today?

JACKSON: I ain't made no money today, you old dirty bastard.

BOB: Empty your pockets.

JACKSON: It's been a slow day.

TERRY: You heard Agent Bob... empty your pockets.

JACKSON: Terry, I thought you was my friend.

(*BOB pushes the gun closer into JACKSON's face.*)

BOB: I said empty your goddamn pockets.

JACKSON: Okay, here, take it. (*JACKSON pulls out a big wad of cash.*) I will get it back before you leave my park.

BOB: Jackson, you lied to me. Look at all that money. I should just shoot your ass for lying to me.

JACKSON: You better shoot me, cause if you don't, you is a fucking dead man. Both of you.

BOB: Give the money to my DEA partner. Check out his jacket.
JACKSON: You both ain't no DEA. That there is the gun I sold to Terry.
BOB: Then you know it works and how much it will hurt if I shoot you. Now give him the money.
JACKSON: Bob, you is one sick fuck.
BOB: That's right, Jackson, I am sick. Very sick. I am a very sick old man. Ain't that right, Terry? Tell this dumbass how sick I am.
TERRY: He's not lying. He is sick. You better give me the money. (*JACKSON hands the wad of cash to TERRY.*)
BOB: There, Terry, that looks like enough to get you out of debt with your living arrangements. And buy a headstone for Allison. (*To JACKSON*) Empty the rest of your pockets.
JACKSON: You got it all.
BOB: Jackson, forgive me if I don't believe you.
JACKSON: I ain't lying. (*JACKSON turns his pants pockets and coat pockets inside-out. From one pocket, he takes a set of car keys.*)
BOB: Look at that. You lied again.
JACKSON: It's just my car keys.
BOB: Throw them to me.
JACKSON: The car ain't here. I left it at home.
BOB: I don't believe you. Now throw me the keys.
  (*JACKSON throws BOB the keys.*)
JACKSON: I walked.
  (*BOB holds the keys in the air and pushes the door lock button. The sound of a car horn beep is heard from offstage.*)

BOB: Will you look at that shiny new Mustang convertible? Jackson, you lied to me again.
JACKSON: I thought I walked. Are we finished here?
BOB: Almost.
JACKSON: What now?
BOB: What about your inside coat pocket? And don't lie again.
JACKSON: You got everything I have.
BOB: (*Forcefully*) Stop lying to me. (*BOB fires the gun in the ground by JACKSON's feet.*)
JACKSON: All right, Jesus. It's my cell phone.
BOB: Take it out slowly.
JACKSON: Not my phone. It's got all my contacts.
BOB: Do I look like I care?
JACKSON: If I give it to you, will you let me go?
BOB: You have my word.
TERRY: I don't think we can let him go. He'll hunt us down.
BOB: No, he won't. He'll be the laughing stock with his drug dealer friends if it gets out two "old men" robbed his sorry ass.
JACKSON: You right. Here. (*He reaches into his inside coat pocket and takes his phone out.*)
BOB: Give it to Terry. (*TERRY walks up to JACKSON and takes the phone.*) Look, Terry, now you have a cell phone.
JACKSON: That's it. You got everything. Can I go?
BOB: I don't know, can you?
JACKSON: What the fuck is you asking me for?
BOB: Are all drug dealers as dumb as you?
JACKSON: You gave me your word.
BOB: Yes, I did. But maybe I lied.

JACKSON: So, can I go?
BOB: After I shoot you in the foot.
JACKSON: What?
BOB: Are you deaf as well as dumb? I said... (*He shouts it as though JACKSON is deaf.*) after I shoot you in the foot. (*BOB shoots JACKSON in the foot. JACKSON yells in pain.*)
JACKSON: Ahh... son of a bitch!
TERRY: What did you do that for?
BOB: So he can't chase us when we run.
TERRY: He'll just find us later.
BOB: I'll be gone.
TERRY: Well, I won't.
BOB: Then I guess you'll have to move with me.
(*Pause*)
TERRY: Can we rob a crack house in Ohio?
BOB: Well, we do have two guns now.
TERRY: And a convertible. We'll be just like Thelma and Louise.
BOB: I prefer Butch Cassidy and the Sundance Kid.
TERRY: I get to be Sundance.
BOB: No, I'm Sundance. You're Butch.
TERRY: I don't want to be Butch. I want to be Sundance.
(*BOB and TERRY continue to bicker over who is going to be Sundance. JACKSON interrupts them.*)
JACKSON: It don't matter. I saw that movie and they both end up fucking dead. (*Beat*)
BOB: Run, Terry, run.
(*BOB and TERRY run offstage. The SOUND of a souped-up Mustang is heard starting, engine revving, and tires squealing as the LIGHTS fade to black.*)

SCENE TWO

(The scene is the park, two years later. There is a new park bench with a trash can sitting near it. AT RISE: TERRY and REBECCA enter. TERRY carries an urn for cremation ashes.)

REBECCA: So, this is the infamous park that you and my dad call your own? In all the years I lived in Miami, I never once came here. It was always known for pimps and drug dealers.
TERRY: Your dad and I fit right in.
REBECCA: Were you pimps or drug dealers?
TERRY: DEA. Mod Squad.
REBECCA: More like the Odd Squad.
TERRY: Just two old hippies doing their thing. *(Pause)* The city put in the new bench.
REBECCA: And the dedication plaque to Dad looks very nice. It was a wonderful idea.
TERRY: It'll serve as his headstone after we sprinkle his ashes about.
REBECCA: Are you nervous about being here? *(Playfully, she doesn't really believe it.)* Isn't this the scene of the crime where Dad says he shot the drug dealer in the foot?
TERRY: My sources say the drug dealer is serving time at the Dade Correctional Institution.
REBECCA: Thanks for being there for Dad in the end. And for the past two years.

TERRY: I didn't think I'd like Cleveland, but it grew on me. I'm not fond of winter and snow, but the summers were great... especially all the chicks in bikinis at the beach in Edgewater Park on Lake Erie.

REBECCA: The two of you were a sight trying to surf on the small lake waves.

TERRY: I know every inch of every floor at the Rock 'n' Roll Hall of Fame.

REBECCA: Dad loved that place.

TERRY: Especially the Woodstock exhibition.

REBECCA: It reminded him of Mom.

TERRY: I loved all the Major League Baseball stadiums close to Cleveland. What a treat. Besides the Indians, we made games in Detroit, Pittsburg, and Cincinnati... Philadelphia and St. Louis were on the tour schedule for this summer.

REBECCA: Thanks for taking him on all those trips. I know he enjoyed each one of them.

TERRY: I didn't want him to be the only one taking trips.

REBECCA: His trips got pretty bad in the end. I couldn't have dealt with it all by myself. It was so painful when he didn't recognize me.

TERRY: He didn't recognize me either.

REBECCA: But he never asked you to leave. I always knew he was in safe hands with you. And just like you promised, you were there for him.

TERRY: You're the saint for putting up with the two of us. Two old men. We never did get our own place like we planned.

REBECCA: Two old… judgmental men, scrutinizing every guy I went out with. That did cramp my dating retention.
TERRY: It didn't stop you from ending up with a great guy.
REBECCA: You know, you can continue to live with us. Steve doesn't mind.
TERRY: I appreciate that. But I want to move back to Miami. It's my home.
REBECCA: Plus the chicks in bikinis are on the beach all year round.
TERRY: There is that. And I can afford it now with Bob's life insurance money. I don't need it all. You need to take some.
REBECCA: He wanted you to have it. And Steve and I have plenty. We're doing just fine.
TERRY: I still need to buy a headstone for Allison.
REBECCA: And a place on the beach.
TERRY: With a big picture window so I can check out all those chicks in bikinis. (*Pause*)
REBECCA: Are you sure you don't mind if I leave you here for an hour or two?
TERRY: No, you go see your old coworkers. I don't mind. I'll be fine. The game doesn't start until two. (*He holds up the urn.*) It'll be just like old times, just Bob and me sitting on the bench in our park.
REBECCA: All right. Call me if you need me. You have your cell phone?
TERRY: Got it. Don't worry. I want some alone time before I sprinkle the ashes. I can wait to do it till you get back.

REBECCA: No, you do it. I've said my goodbye. (*She kisses TERRY on the cheek.*) I'll be back in a couple of hours.
TERRY: Have fun.
REBECCA: You have my cell phone number?
TERRY: Yes, Rebecca. I'll be fine. Go.

(*REBECCA exits. TERRY sits on the park bench and puts the urn next to him on the bench. He speaks out, occasionally turning to speak to the urn.*)

TERRY: Well, here we are again, Bob. You and me... just sitting on the park bench. Home sweet home. The park looks good. And the beach is full of bikini-clad chicks. (*Beat*) Thanks, my man, for the money. You're a lifesaver. I live because of your death. (*Beat*) Hey, I got tickets to see the Marlins play the Indians this afternoon. I still don't like inner league play. It takes the specialness out of the World Series. (*Beat*) You went and abandoned me again. Damn you. I miss you, you old hippie. (*He sees something off in the distance. He stands and moves to the far-left side of the stage and yells off.*) Hey you, pick up that soda can and put it in the trash can. (*Beat*) Thank you.

(*CINDY enters, moves to the bench and sits. TERRY turns and starts back to the bench.*)

TERRY: Oh. Hello there.
CINDY: Good morning.
TERRY: Where did you come from?
CINDY: I'm originally from Georgia, but I've been living in Minnesota for the past fifty years.

TERRY: No, I meant, I was sitting there just a second ago… I turned my back briefly and then, poof, there you are. (*CINDY stands up.*)
CINDY: I'm sorry. Here, if you had the bench first, sit down.
TERRY: We can share.
CINDY: You look harmless. (*CINDY sits on the bench.*)
TERRY: Do I? Then I need to do some work on my image. (*He sits on the bench. Beat*) Do you always offer so much information about yourself to strangers? You're from Georgia… you now live in Minnesota… for the past fifty years.
CINDY: It's a southern thing. I can buy something at a garage sale and the seller ends up knowing my life story.
TERRY: I don't mind. (*CINDY points to the urn in TERRY's hands.*)
CINDY: Friend of yours?
TERRY: You're sitting on his bench. (*CINDY reads the plaque on the bench.*)
CINDY: Bob?
TERRY: The one and only.
CINDY: I'm sorry for your loss.
TERRY: It's just part of getting older. And the older one gets, the more they deal with death. Family… friends.
CINDY: You utter the painful truth.
TERRY: Bob and I were going to live forever.
CINDY: Change the world.
TERRY: Love and peace.
CINDY: Rock and roll.
TERRY: Mary Jane.

CINDY: Pop festivals.
TERRY: Bob was at Woodstock.
CINDY: I was on my way but never made it.
TERRY: Oh, so you're a member of the Joni Mitchell club too.
CINDY: Damn Dick Cavett. (*TERRY sings the chorus to "Woodstock."*)
(*CINDY joins TERRY in singing.*)
CINDY: The Atlanta Pop Festival was in July, a few weeks before Woodstock. I was there with a bunch of my Georgia friends. When it was over, about half of them went on to New York. The other half of us made it as far north as Blowing Rock, North Carolina.
TERRY: What stopped you?
CINDY: Too many pitchers of beer. You?
TERRY: Prep for the beginning of the school year.
CINDY: Student?
TERRY: Teacher.
CINDY: Me too. Thirty-seven years.
TERRY: Forty-five.
CINDY: I was pop festivaled out.
TERRY: Pop festivals made you quit teaching?
CINDY: No, the reason I didn't continue on to Woodstock. I was fried after Atlanta.
TERRY: Are you sorry you didn't make it?
CINDY: Hindsight is twenty-twenty. Had I known it was going to be the event of a generation, none of us would have let Blowing Rock stop us.
TERRY: Bob told me about it so much… I feel like I was there. And we've seen the film zillions of times.

CINDY: My husband was there.
TERRY: Oh, you're married?
CINDY: He died a year ago.
TERRY: Here in Miami?
CINDY: Back in Minneapolis. We've come to Miami every winter for the past twenty years. Ever since our son moved here.
TERRY: You're a snowbird widow?
CINDY: I guess I am. A snowbird widow on a mission.
TERRY: This sounds serious.
CINDY: I'm looking for a gun.
TERRY: This is serious.
CINDY: I was told I could get one in this park.
TERRY: Maybe. Why do you need a gun?
CINDY: What does one usually do with a gun?
TERRY: I raided crack houses.
CINDY: I want one to shoot a crack dealer.
TERRY: Jackson?
CINDY: Who?
TERRY: I once knew a crack dealer named Jackson.
CINDY: Where can I find him? Any crack dealer will do.
TERRY: You need to sit down and mellow out.
CINDY: I'll have plenty of time to do that in jail… once I rid the world of one less crack dealer.
TERRY: Do you drink?
CINDY: Not since all the pitchers of beer back in Blowing Rock. (*TERRY pulls out a flask.*)
TERRY: Here, you need to start again.
CINDY: No, thanks. (*TERRY puts the flask back in his pocket.*) Do you have a gun?

TERRY: I used to have two, but one of them ended up in the wrong hands and it was responsible for my leaving Miami.
CINDY: Where are they now?
TERRY: Bob and I traded them both in for baseball gloves.
CINDY: I love baseball. Go Twins.
TERRY: Do you want to go to a Marlins' game this afternoon? I have two tickets.
CINDY: Who are they playing?
TERRY: The Indians.
CINDY: American League Central, Twins' rivals. I've never cared for inner league play. It takes the specialness out of the World Series.
TERRY: Did you really just say that?
CINDY: They should do away with inner league play.
TERRY: Let's trade your search for a crack dealer for the crack of a bat.
CINDY: My son wasted away because of crack. He hid it from his wife for years. When she found out, he couldn't quit. She left him a year ago. And within six months he was gone.
TERRY: Killing a random crack dealer won't bring him back.
CINDY: Two deaths in six months are too much.
TERRY: I've been there, well, halfway there. Living will get easier.
CINDY: I didn't come here for counseling. I've had plenty of it. I was told to face my pain, so that's why I'm here… to find a gun and shoot a drug dealer.

TERRY: Have you ever thought of channeling that energy in another way?
CINDY: I've tried yoga and tai chi. It didn't give me any satisfaction.
TERRY: How about raiding a crack house?
CINDY: I like it. There's usually guns and lots of cash lying on the coffee table in the crack house raids I see on TV.
TERRY: I know, that's what I told Bob for years.
CINDY: We could steal the money and take the guns.
TERRY: We'd have to take the stash too or they would know it wasn't a real raid.
CINDY: I don't want the stash.
TERRY: We can just dump it in the Intracoastal.
CINDY: I don't really want the cash either. I just want one of the guns. And since it's a crack house, there would be a dealer there, so I could just shoot him.
TERRY: I don't want to be involved with any killing.
CINDY: Then I'll search for another partner to do it with.
TERRY: Wait a minute. It was my idea. You were my partner, not the other way around.
CINDY: Forget it. We don't have DEA jackets.
TERRY: Have I got a surprise for you.
CINDY: This just keeps getting better.
TERRY: Listen to this. I've been practicing for years. (*He does his DEA voice.*) DEA. This is a bust. Hands in the air.
CINDY: That's very convincing.
TERRY: And my long hair fits the part too.
CINDY: We're two-thirds of the Mod Squad. All we need is a black dude.

TERRY: Butch Cassidy and the Sundance Kid.
CINDY: Bonnie and Clyde.
TERRY: Bob always thought it was a crazy idea.
CINDY: It is a crazy idea. The dealers are going to have guns in hand... not on the coffee table... and they will shoot us.
TERRY: We'll have the element of surprise.
CINDY: Finding a dealer outside his element is more of a surprise.
TERRY: So, the crack house raid is out.
CINDY: You'll have to find another partner, Butch.
TERRY: I'm Sundance, Bob was Butch.
CINDY: Sorry, Sundance, no crack house raid for this Etta.
TERRY: Etta?
CINDY: Sundance's woman, the Katharine Ross character.
TERRY: That's right! Well, Etta, the invite to the baseball game is still an option for you.
CINDY: If I can find a gun before the game starts, I'd love to join you. The crack dealer shooting can wait until after the game. (*Pause*)
TERRY: How did your husband pass away?
CINDY: Alzheimer's disease.
TERRY: I was there with Bob though his dementia.
CINDY: Kevin technically died of malnutrition. He wouldn't eat and we had to feed him and then finally his body didn't know how to eat or swallow. By then he was just skin and bones. He was no longer able to talk, and he didn't know me anymore. He had also broken both hips and had both replaced. It was very sad.

TERRY: Bob didn't recognize me in the end either. He contracted C-diff, we think from a visit to the emergency room. Dehydration set in, along with severe diarrhea, which led to a significant loss of fluids and electrolytes. That caused his blood pressure to drop to dangerously low levels so quickly that his kidney functions rapidly deteriorated and eventually failed.

CINDY: I'll spare you the details of my son's death. (*Pause*)

TERRY: Looking at something positive… Donald Trump was impeached.

CINDY: I voted for him.

TERRY: And I thought we had a lot in common. You can forget going to the game with me.

CINDY: Hold on, it didn't take me long to discover the mistake I made. I really thought he was the change that Washington needed.

TERRY: He and co-president Bannon changed Washington all right… and the country. All the undoing of the good Obama accomplished.

CINDY: Instead of draining the swamp, he flooded it. Reading the… (*She uses her hands to show air quotes.*) "fake news" each day almost made me start drinking again.

TERRY: It's not too late. (*TERRY pulls out his flask and hands it to CINDY. She takes a small sip.*)

CINDY: Whoa, what do you have in there, kerosene? (*Beat*) Trump's cabinet picks were the beginning of the end. (*CINDY takes another sip from the flask.*)

TERRY: His pick to run the EPA hated the EPA.

CINDY: You just earned a drink. (*CINDY hands TERRY the flask. He takes a drink.*) His labor secretary hated laborers.
TERRY: Another drink for you. (*TERRY hands CINDY the flask. She takes a drink.*) I guess we do have a lot in common. Give me that flask. (*CINDY hands TERRY the flask. He puts it in his pocket.*) You're still invited to the baseball game.
CINDY: Let's get me a gun first.
TERRY: I thought we were past that.
CINDY: I don't know anything about you. I don't even know your name. As far as I know, you could be a drug dealer. You look like one with your long hair.
TERRY: You're living in the sixties. Today's drug dealers don't look like they used to.
CINDY: And how would you know?
TERRY: Let's just say that, I've had my run-ins with some drug dealers.
CINDY: Now were talking. Introduce me to one.
TERRY: Let me introduce myself first. My name is Terry. I taught creative writing at North Miami High School since I graduated from FSU in 1969 through retiring in 2013. I have several poetry books published that no one ever buys. My wife died two years, four months, and seventeen days ago. I just spent the past two years in Ohio caring for my best friend, Bob, and I'm in this park to spread his ashes in the place we both have loved since Woodstock.
CINDY: Hi, Terry, my name is Cindy. I taught algebra at North Minneapolis High School since

I graduated from the University of Minnesota in 1972, until my husband got ill in 2007. I don't have any books published, but I am impressed that you do. Kevin died last winter and my son died six months ago. I am in this park to purchase a…

TERRY: Yea, yea, I know all that.

CINDY: It's nice to meet you, Terry. Now if you can't help me find a gun and introduce me to one of the drug dealers you say you know, I'll be moving on.

TERRY: Mellow out, Cindy. You've come to the right park. It's just a bit too early for the pimps and drug dealers to be here. Those are nocturnal occupations.

CINDY: Give me another drink from your flask.

TERRY: I'd hate to be the reason for you to start drinking again.

CINDY: You are the reason. Just give me the flask. (*TERRY gives CINDY the flask. She takes a drink.*) Smooth!

TERRY: Was your husband a teacher too?

CINDY: Trump's Secretary of Education didn't know public schools.

TERRY: You earned another swig. (*CINDY takes another drink and hands the flask to TERRY.*) I've not earned it yet.

CINDY: Have a swig. I hate to drink alone. (*TERRY drinks from the flask.*) My husband sold insurance. That's one good thing about his death. He left me with more money than I need. And I'm worth a fortune dead.

TERRY: Any other children?

CINDY: Just the dead crack addict. (*She takes the flask from TERRY and takes another swig.*)
TERRY: You mention he was married.
CINDY: I'm staying with her and my granddaughter in Ft. Lauderdale. Did you have children?
TERRY: We weren't able. Our students were our kids.
CINDY: What did your wife teach?
TERRY: You're not going to believe me.
CINDY: Try me.
TERRY: Algebra.
CINDY: You're right, I don't believe you.
TERRY: I swear.
CINDY: You're just saying this to talk me out of my mission. Next, you'll probably say she had Alzheimer's.
TERRY: No, ovarian cancer.
CINDY: I'm sorry. If dementia doesn't get us old folks, cancer will.
TERRY: Prostate for me.
CINDY: Breast for me.
TERRY: You do remind me of my Allison.
CINDY: All us math nerds are the same.
TERRY: She didn't vote for Trump.
CINDY: Ouch! I really was behind Bernie.
TERRY: Oh, a socialist.
CINDY: I think he could have beaten Trump.
TERRY: We'll never know. The entire election was a farce.
CINDY: Rick Perry heading the same Energy Department he wanted to eliminate was a farce.
TERRY: Touché. Drink. (*CINDY takes a swig from the flask.*)

CINDY: The Attorney General was a racist.
TERRY: Bigly. (*Both CINDY and TERRY begin to giggle.*)
CINDY: We both get to drink for that. (*CINDY takes a drink and then hands the flask to TERRY. He drinks.*)
TERRY: Oh, to turn back time.
CINDY: Yes, I could have done something about my son.
TERRY: It's not your fault.
CINDY: His drug problem began so innocently. He hurt his back on the job. He worked for Florida Power and Light. He was prescribed an opioid-based pain medication and that soon led to the needle and heroin.
TERRY: Shouldn't you be looking for a heroin dealer and not a crack dealer?
CINDY: He started mixing, doing both.
TERRY: We should get going if we're going to get to the game on time.
CINDY: You're right… I can always complete my mission tomorrow. A good ballpark hotdog will cheer me up.
TERRY: And a couple of Budweisers.
CINDY: I told you, I don't drink.
TERRY: You've been doing a good job with my flask.
CINDY: I've earned it all.
TERRY: Yes, you did.
CINDY: Unlike Trump who spent all the promised infrastructure money on his stupid wall.
TERRY: That the Mexicans kept blowing up. (*CINDY and TERRY laugh again.*)

CINDY: Another double drink. (*TERRY takes a swig and then hands the flask to CINDY. She takes a swig.*)
TERRY: Did you drive?
CINDY: I parked over there. I am in the Rogue, right next to the Mustang convertible. (*She points off.*)
TERRY: Mustang convertible?
CINDY: No, the Rogue.
TERRY: Uh oh.
CINDY: What's wrong?
TERRY: I think we should get to the baseball game. (*CINDY is laughing now.*)
CINDY: And what about the bromance?
TERRY: Not now, come on, let's go.
CINDY: Trump and Putin was the final straw. Cover-up. Worse than Watergate. Treason. (*CINDY takes a swig from the flask. JACKSON enters. He is walking with a cane because of a limp. CINDY speaks to JACKSON*) Cheers.
JACKSON: Are you two lovebirds enjoying my park? (*TERRY moves upstage so he can hide his face from JACKSON.*)
CINDY: Your park?
JACKSON: Ain't nothin gone down in this here park wid-out me knowin bout it.
CINDY: Is that so?
JACKSON: You can take dat to da bank.
CINDY: Do you know where I can buy a gun?
JACKSON: The best place be the gun store.
CINDY: I don't want to wait. I need it now.
JACKSON: What if I did know… how do I know you ain't a cop?
CINDY: Do I look like a cop?

JACKSON: No mo than yo hippie-ass friend do. Do he gots a problem with me? Keeping his back to us.
CINDY: I guess he doesn't approve of me trying to buy a gun.
JACKSON: Do you gots the cash?
CINDY: Do you have a gun?
JACKSON: Why do you need a gun?
CINDY: I'm going to shoot a drug dealer.
JACKSON: I tell you what I'm gone do fo you, old lady.
CINDY: Who are you calling old?
(*JACKSON pulls his gun out and points it at CINDY.*)
JACKSON: You. You is dumb and old. Coming into my park wit enough cash to buy a gun. And you gone shoot a drug dealer. That ain't very nice of you. I tell you want you gone do. You gone hand me yo purse, and if you do, I might not shoot yo ass.
CINDY: Just let me buy that gun you have pointed at me, and I will leave your park.
JACKSON: Oh, you gone leave my park a'ight, but it ain't gone be with no gun or purse. Now hand it over. (*TERRY turns around and has his gun out and points it at JACKSON.*)
TERRY: Leave the lady's purse alone, Jackson.
JACKSON: Terry, is that you?
TERRY: Yeah, it's me. We don't want any trouble.
JACKSON: I thought I recognized that long gray ponytail.
CINDY: Terry, you had a gun all along? You lied to me.
TERRY: No, I didn't lie. I just didn't tell you I had one.

CINDY: Do you know this fool?
TERRY: Meet the new face of America.
CINDY: Please, shoot him.
TERRY: I don't want blood on my gun.
CINDY: Then what good does it do to point it at this lowlife?
JACKSON: Hey, I ain't no lowlife, but, Terry, she do got a point. If you ain't gone shoot me, why point it at me? Listen, old lady, I'm gone give you a break. I ain't got no beef wid you. You take yo purse and leave. My beef be with Terry.
TERRY: Go on, Cindy. Leave.
JACKSON: You heard the old hippie, Cindy. Leave. Unless you want to watch me shoot this old man in the foot. Where's Bob? I'm gone kill his ass.
TERRY: You're too late. He's dead already. Say hello to your old friend, Bob.
(*He holds up the urn.*)
JACKSON: Damn, for two years I've been looking forward to making that bitch suffer.
CINDY: Are you two going to stand there and flap your mouths all morning? (*She moves to TERRY.*) Shoot him, Terry.
TERRY: Will you just leave, while you can?
CINDY: Give me the damn gun, I'll shoot him.
(*CINDY grabs TERRY's gun out of his hand and moves to JACKSON and points the gun at his face.*)
TERRY: Cindy!
CINDY: Now, Jackson, Terry might not want blood on his gun, but I don't give a shit. I'll wipe it off.
JACKSON: I will shoot yo old lady ass.

CINDY: I'm betting you won't. You don't want blood on your gun any more than Terry does.

TERRY: Come on, Cindy.

CINDY: Shut the fuck up, Terry. (*To JACKSON.*) I'm going to ask you some questions... and depending on the answers... I may or may not shoot your dumb ass.

JACKSON: I ain't afraid to shoot you.

CINDY: Then do it. I'm ready to die.

JACKSON: Goddamn, Terry, does you only hang out with crazy fuckin' people?

CINDY: Are you a drug dealer?

JACKSON: Not this again. I don't gots no money wid me today.

CINDY: Did you sell my son, Steve, the drugs that killed him?

JACKSON: How the hell am I post to know if I sold yo son any drugs? I have lots of customers and we ain't on no goddamn first-name basis. They gots the money, I gives em the dope they wants.

(*CINDY pulls out a photo from a pocket and puts it in JACKSON's face.*)

CINDY: This is him. Take a long look.

JACKSON: He don't look familiar to me.

CINDY: He worked for the electric company.

JACKSON: The electric company?

CINDY: Yes.

JACKSON: Let me look at the picture again.

(*CINDY holds up the photo for JACKSON. JACKSON hits her with his cane, then drops his cane, and grabs the gun CINDY is holding.*)

TERRY: Cindy! Are you, all right?

(*JACKSON holds a gun in each hand and points them at TERRY and CINDY.*)

JACKSON: Both of you, go sit on the bench. (*TERRY and CINDY sit on the bench.*)

TERRY: Are you okay?

CINDY: I'm fine.

TERRY: Boy, that was a dumb move.

CINDY: Tell me something I don't know. Give me another pull on that flask of yours. (*TERRY gives the flask to CINDY. She takes a swig and then hands it back to TERRY.*)

TERRY: Jackson, you want a snort?

JACKSON: That be real nice of you, Terry, but my hands are full.

TERRY: I see that.

JACKSON: Now, listen to me, old lady, I might not wanna get blood on my gun, but I don't give a shit about Terry's.

TERRY: Are you sure? Remember, that gun used to be yours.

CINDY: Go ahead and shoot. I told you, I'm ready to die.

JACKSON: I'm not gone kill you. But you shoulda left when I gave you yo chance. Terry, tell her what I'm gone do.

CINDY: Yeah, Terry, go ahead and tell me.

TERRY: He's going to shoot us in the foot.

CINDY: If you don't mind, I'd rather just die.

JACKSON: Terry, does she ever shut up? How the hell can you stand to be with her?

CINDY: We are not together.

JACKSON: What's wrong? Ain't he good enough fo you?
CINDY: I just met him.
JACKSON: What was your first impression of him? Mine is usually right about the people I meet.
CINDY: All the people you meet fit into the same mold... drug addicts.
JACKSON: I just met you. Are you a drug addict?
CINDY: I don't drink or do drugs?
JACKSON: Who you think you fooling? You smell like a cheap hoe at a bar on a Saturday night.
(*CINDY points to the flask.*)
CINDY: I think Terry is trying to take advantage of me.
JACKSON: Damn, Terry, you still got it in ya. Hot damn.
TERRY: That's what the chicks say.
CINDY: So, what was your first impression of me?
JACKSON: I done said it already... you two was lovebirds.
CINDY: I am a grieving widow and mother.
JACKSON: Widows and mothers love. I know this for a fact.
TERRY: What do you say, Jackson... just let us go?
JACKSON: You see that there cane? It be part of my life now... fo the past two years.
TERRY: I didn't shoot you... Bob did. Remember, I tried to stop him.
JACKSON: You stole my Mustang.
TERRY: You got it back. I talked Bob into leaving it where the cops would find it. I even left your cell phone in it.

JACKSON: But not my money.
TERRY: Well, we needed that. Two out of three ain't bad.
JACKSON: Two out a four. You took my gun too.
TERRY: You got it back now. Three out of four.
JACKSON: I needed that money, especially after going to the urgent care to get my foot fixed.
CINDY: Didn't you have Obamacare?
JACKSON: Shit no, I never needed no care. But after my foot injury, I gots me the Affordable Care Acts insurance. It be better than Obamacare... especially since it been took away. Obamacare. If I'da had it, I wouldn't have no insurance now.
CINDY: It was the same damn insurance. And you don't have "no" insurance now. You would think after eight years of repeal and replace, the damn Republicans would have come up with something better.
TERRY: Damn, that was good, Cindy. That earns you another drink.
CINDY: That was good. (*She takes a drink from the flask.*) And not keeping their promise will cost the Republicans in the midterms. Did you vote, Jackson?
JACKSON: You is making fun of me right now, just like that damn Bob did.
TERRY: What do say, Jackson, let's let bygones be bygones?
JACKSON: I have no idea what just came out of yo mouth.
TERRY: Why don't you just let us go?
CINDY: Don't grovel to this dumbass.

JACKSON: You calling me a dumbass is really bringing back bad memories of that damn Bob. I'm gone shoot you in both yo damn feet.
CINDY: Stop flapping your damn mouth and just do it, if you got the guts.
JACKSON: Give me yo purse.
CINDY: You said I could keep it.
JACKSON: I lied.
TERRY: Just give him your purse.
CINDY: If he wants the purse, he'll have to pry it from the cold hands of my dead body.
JACKSON: I said give me the goddamn purse.
(*JACKSON shoots the gun into the ground at CINDY's feet.*)
CINDY: You missed… both feet.
JACKSON: I won't miss the next time.
CINDY: There won't be a next time.
(*CINDY starts to scream and she charges JACKSON, beating him with her purse. She knocks one of the guns—JACKSON's gun—out of his hand. JACKSON still holds TERRY's gun. She continues to scream and beat JACKSON. TERRY picks up the gun that was dropped. JACKSON finally corrals CINDY, holding her with one arm around her as he pulls her into his chest. He puts the gun to her head. TERRY points the gun at JACKSON.*)
TERRY: Let her go, Jackson.
JACKSON: Or what, you gone shoot me? You don't want blood on yo gun.
TERRY: This ain't my gun, it's yours.
JACKSON: You wouldn't shoot me with my own gun, would you?
TERRY: Just let her go.

JACKSON: I'm gone keep the purse.
TERRY: You can have it.
CINDY: No, he can't.
TERRY: Yes, he can.
CINDY: It's my purse.
JACKSON: This is why I ain't never got married.
TERRY: You have my word, Jackson.
JACKSON: How do I know you ain't lying?
TERRY: Here, I'm putting the gun down. (*He puts the gun on the ground.*) All I have is Bob in my hands now.
JACKSON: I really wanted to shoot his ass.
TERRY: Let Cindy go.
JACKSON: Tell her to give me the purse.
CINDY: I said you couldn't have my damn purse. (*CINDY stomps on JACKSON's foot. JACKSON screams as he releases CINDY.*)
JACKSON: Son of a bitch! (*JACKSON and CINDY are having a tug-of-war over the purse.*)
TERRY: Let it go, Cindy, let's go.
CINDY: He can't have my purse.
JACKSON: Say hello to my little friend.
TERRY: No, you say hello to my old friend, Bob. (*TERRY tosses BOB's ashes from the urn into JACKSON's face. JACKSON screams.*)
JACKSON: Motherfucker! I can't see! I'm blind!
TERRY: Come on, Cindy.
CINDY: Grab the guns. (*CINDY takes the gun out of JACKSON's hand. TERRY picks up the one off the ground.*)
JACKSON: You both is dead.
TERRY: I think we can still make the game.

CINDY: He's a drug dealer. I need to take my shot.
TERRY: He's lame and blind. I think he's suffered enough.
JACKSON: You better shoot me, bitch. Cause I'm gone shoot yo ass if I ever sees you again.
CINDY: You're right. He's clubfoot and blind. He's suffered enough. Just like Oedipus.
JACKSON: I ain't no puss. I'll find you this time, Terry. And your wife.
CINDY: Come on, Clyde, take this Bonnie to the game.
TERRY: Run, Bonnie, run! (*TERRY and CINDY run offstage laughing as the LIGHTS fade to black.*)
END ACT ONE

ACT TWO

SCENE ONE

(*The scene is still the park, two years later. Things don't look very good. There is trash scattered about the area. The trash can is turned over. AT RISE: REBECCA and CINDY enter and move to the bench. CINDY carries an urn for cremation ashes. REBECCA carries a picnic basket and a blanket.*)

CINDY: This place doesn't look too good. (*She places the urn on the bench and then sets the trash can back up.*) I guess because Bob and Terry aren't here to keep it clean.
REBECCA: Or to stop the graffiti. This bench is now dedicated to Boob.
CINDY: What?

REBECCA: Someone added an O to my dad's name. (*She spells it out.*) B-O-O-B. I guess he's been called worse.
CINDY: A lot can happen in two years. Wow, has it really been two years since I met Terry sitting on this bench?
REBECCA: Yes, just over two years since boob passed.
CINDY: That old plaque will go away when the city puts the new one on the bench.
REBECCA: Let's just simplify it to read "Two Old Men."
CINDY: Sounds good to me.
(*REBECCA places the basket and blanket on the bench. They both begin to pick up the trash on the ground and put it in the trash can.*)
CINDY: I really wish I could have met your father. Terry couldn't say enough good about him.
REBECCA: They've been there for each other for a long time.
CINDY: Thanks for sharing the photo albums you had of their childhood. The teen surfing pictures were fun. They were both such hotties.
REBECCA: They loved this park. It would bother them to see it now.
CINDY: I have an emotional attachment to this place too.
REBECCA: Do you think Jackson will show?
CINDY: I hope so. I've spread the word around the area that I'm looking for him. It's tough to find someone when you don't know their last name. I said I'd be here at eleven o'clock.

REBECCA: I can't believe you didn't run into him with all the looking you did.
CINDY: I've been to the park every day since the memorial service and there have been no sightings. The park has a different vibe to it now.
REBECCA: Do drug dealers take vacations?
CINDY: When I lived in Minnesota, I recall there was a city in South Dakota named Blunt. Maybe they go there.
REBECCA: My company ships product to Weed, California.
CINDY: In Georgia, I lived near Boozeville. (*Beat as they laugh.*) Remind me when you're making the move? I know you've told me, but my mind has been elsewhere lately.
REBECCA: I fly back to Cleveland next week to oversee the loading of the moving van. I can't believe the house sold as quickly as it did.
CINDY: Do you feel like you're moving backward?
REBECCA: It's not been the same living there since Dad died and Terry left. And then with Steve's passing, it was very lonely. Miami kept calling. And I'm not getting any younger. I was lucky the old company wanted me back.
CINDY: And I gained a roommate. The house we bought is too big for me alone.
REBECCA: I've always wanted to live on the beach.
CINDY: Two single chicks surfside.
REBECCA: Thelma and Louise.
CINDY: Together at last.
REBECCA: And with the spreading of Terry's ashes, the two old men will finally be back together too.

CINDY: Butch and Sundance.
REBECCA: You and Terry were?
CINDY: Bonnie and Clyde. How about you and Steve?
REBECCA: Nothing as badass as you and Terry or Terry and Dad.
CINDY: Tell me.
REBECCA: Steve-3-P-O and R-2-D-2. The "R" was for Rebecca.
CINDY: I got it.
REBECCA: We both loved Star Wars.
CINDY: I would never have guessed. Did he have any history of heart problems?
REBECCA: He was forced to stop working because of arrhythmia. His heart would flutter… just beat too fast. The doctor tied eating chocolate to the arrhythmia. He loved Chips Ahoy chocolate chip cookies, but he had to give them up because every time he ate them, his heart rate would increase. The chocolate was stimulating his heart. He was in the hospital a couple of weeks before the incident and he was getting along just fine.
CINDY: He was putting up mini-blinds?
REBECCA: And eating Chips Ahoy. The paramedics said he was probably dead before he hit the floor.
CINDY: Welcome to the front pew at the church. It's just you and me sitting alone together. (*They have finished picking up the trash.*)
REBECCA: There, the place looks a little better. I'll leave you to sprinkle the ashes.
CINDY: You are more than welcome to stay.
REBECCA: I know, but you need to do it alone. I have to get some paperwork signed at the office.

CINDY: At least eat some of my fried chicken.
REBECCA: The chicken is your peace offering for Jackson.
CINDY: Don't worry about coming back to pick me up, I'll call a taxi.
REBECCA: I'll pick up something for dinner.
CINDY: Thanks, Rebecca.
REBECCA: You have my cell number?
CINDY: Terry mentioned how the roles between you and your father had reversed. I'm not that far gone yet, you don't have to mother me.
REBECCA: Just watching out for my roomy.
CINDY: You're the only family I have left.
REBECCA: Things still aren't good between you and the ex-daughter-in-law?
CINDY: It hurts my granddaughter, Cassie, the most. Her mom says I remind Cassie of her father too much. Truth is, my daughter-in-law never really liked me.
REBECCA: Well, you're my only family now too. (*They embrace.*) Call me if you need anything.
CINDY: Ten–four, R-2-D-2.
REBECCA: Call me, Thelma.
CINDY: Run, Thelma, run. (*REBECCA exits. CINDY sits on the bench and talks to the urn.*) Once again, I am sitting on your bench. You turn your back and here I am. (*Beat*) In the end, dementia or cancer didn't get you. A stroke did. Watching too many chicks in bikinis on the beach from the front porch did you in. (*Beat*) Had I been home, I could have gotten you to the hospital. (*Beat*) But the daughter-in-law granted me some time with Cassie.

(*JACKSON enters, but it doesn't look like JACKSON. He is wearing dark glasses like he is blind. He even has a red-tipped cane that the blind use. He doesn't have the walking cane that he used in the second scene of act one. He is wearing a suit and a tie. His hair is neatly trimmed. He even talks properly. He taps his way with the cane to the bench. The cane hits the picnic basket.*)

JACKSON: I'm sorry, is someone sitting here?

(*CINDY moves the basket and blanket from the bench.*)

CINDY: I am, but just let me move this and you can sit with me.

JACKSON: Thank you, ma'am, that's very kind of you.

CINDY: No problem. Okay, you can sit now.

JACKSON: I know I can, but may I?

CINDY: Yes, you may. (*JACKSON uses his hands to feel the bench and he sits.*) I'm waiting for someone to join me.

JACKSON: Oh, I can find another bench to sit on.

CINDY: No, you're fine.

JACKSON: Thank you. I just really like this bench. I've been coming to this park and sitting here for years.

CINDY: My husband liked this bench too.

JACKSON: When he gets here, I can move.

CINDY: I'm not meeting my husband.

JACKSON: I've had many encounters on and around this bench.

CINDY: No, it's not like that. I'm not even sure if whom I'm waiting for is even going to show up.

JACKSON: Oh, this sounds serious.

CINDY: Oh no, it's just a friend.

JACKSON: A friend?
CINDY: More like an acquaintance. I've not seen him in a couple of years.
JACKSON: What makes you think he won't show up?
CINDY: Here I go again, my husband has tried to break me of the habit of telling my life story to complete strangers.
JACKSON: I'm sorry, where are my manners? My name is Terry.
CINDY: That's my husband's name.
JACKSON: Really, I'd like to meet your husband. It's too bad he won't be joining you at the park? Or will he? (*Beat*)
CINDY: Have we met before?
JACKSON: I don't think so.
CINDY: Your voice sounds familiar.
JACKSON: You know what they say; all black people sound the same to white people. We look alike too.
CINDY: How do you know I'm white?
JACKSON: I just assumed.
CINDY: From what, the sound of my voice?
JACKSON: You got me. I'm guilty. I'm sorry, can we start again? (*JACKSON sticks out his hand for CINDY to shake.*) Hi, my name is Terry; it's nice to meet you, Cindy, and thank you for sharing the park bench with me. (*There is a beat before CINDY shakes JACKSON's hand.*)
CINDY: Are you sure we don't know one another?
JACKSON: When I could see, I never forgot a face. And now that I can't, I never forget a voice.
CINDY: For me, it's the hands.
JACKSON: Excuse me?

CINDY: A person's hands. I never forget someone's hands. And I'll never forget your hands; one pulling on my purse strap while the other pointed a gun at my face.

JACKSON: I don't know what you're talking about.

CINDY: How did you know my name? I never said it to you.

JACKSON: Sure, you did. Right after I told you my name.

CINDY: What game are you playing, Jackson? (*The charade is over.*)

JACKSON: When's Terry going to get here?

CINDY: He's already here. (*JACKSON jumps up and looks around.*)

JACKSON: Is this a trap? Where is he? I don't see him.

CINDY: I thought you were blind.

JACKSON: I should be after he threw Bob's ashes in my face.

CINDY: That's why I invited you to meet me here. (*JACKSON points to the urn.*)

JACKSON: Oh, I see. Terry's dead, so now you want to throw him in my face too.

CINDY: Yes, this is Terry, but I don't want to throw him in your face.

JACKSON: Then what do you want? I'm crippled and half-blind because of those two old men.

CINDY: I'll get to what I wanted to see you for in a bit. But first tell me about yourself. You look good.

JACKSON: What is this... white guilt? I should run as fast as I can away from you. Every time I run into Terry, something bad happens to me.

CINDY: I promise you nothing bad is going to happen to you.
JACKSON: I can't promise you the same.
CINDY: What are you going to do, shoot me in the foot?
JACKSON: No, not the foot. I'm just going to shoot you. It's been boiling inside me for two years. I have to do it. It's the only reason I even came here today. I was hoping to get two birds with one stone.
CINDY: I guess I don't blame you for feeling that way. I'm really sorry about all the pain Bob, Terry, and I have caused you.
JACKSON: Forgive me if I don't believe you.
CINDY: Are you hungry?
JACKSON: Am I hungry?
CINDY: Yes, I brought a picnic for us. Fried chicken.
JACKSON: Do you have watermelon too? (*CINDY gets the basket and blanket.*)
CINDY: Come on, help me spread this blanket.
(*JACKSON and CINDY spread the blanket on the ground. They both sit on the blanket.*)
JACKSON: Food is God's love language.
CINDY: Jackson, do I detect a new man in you?
JACKSON: I am a different person. But that doesn't change what I have to do to you.
CINDY: If you must do it, get it over with. Do you have your gun?
(*JACKSON pats his breast pocket.*)
JACKSON: Right here. (*Pause*)
CINDY: Is there anything really wrong with your eyesight?

(*JACKSON takes off the dark sunglasses.*)
JACKSON: For the longest time, after Bob was thrown into my eyes, I thought there was. But in reality, Bob actually opened my eyes.
CINDY: From what Terry told me about Bob, he had that effect on many lives.
JACKSON: Are we going to eat that chicken or just stare at it?
CINDY: I thought you were going to shoot me.
JACKSON: I don't like to shoot people on an empty stomach.
(*CINDY fixes a plate with chicken and potato salad.*)
CINDY: Talk to me.
JACKSON: Jewel.
CINDY: As in jewelry?
JACKSON: As in woman.
CINDY: Like the singer, Jewel, who sang "Foolish Games"?
JACKSON: I hear you.
CINDY: Tell me about your Jewel.
JACKSON: She's a nurse. I first met her after Bob shot me in the foot four years ago. She works at the Urgent Care across from the park.
(*CINDY gives JACKSON the plate and begins to fix another one for herself.*)
CINDY: Here, for you. (*JACKSON takes the plate.*)
JACKSON: Do you have any hot sauce?
CINDY: Hot sauce?
JACKSON: Louisiana Hot Sauce… for the chicken.
CINDY: My fried chicken doesn't need hot sauce.
JACKSON: All fried chicken needs hot sauce.
CINDY: Tell me more about Jewel.

JACKSON: She treated my foot.
CINDY: I suppose she reported it to the police.
JACKSON: What for?
CINDY: All gunshot wounds have to be reported to the police.
JACKSON: It wasn't that bad. It was just a flesh wound. Bob almost missed my foot.
CINDY: The last time I saw you, you were using a cane to hobble around here like poor little Tiny Tim.
JACKSON: That was all an act. After word got out I was robbed and shot, I played the cripple card. And it worked. I got lots of sympathy. My sales skyrocketed, so I just kept it up. The cane really sold it.
CINDY: Do you want sweet tea or water?
JACKSON: What, no booze?
CINDY: I haven't had a drink since the last time we were in this park together.
JACKSON: Sweet tea. (*CINDY hands JACKSON a bottle of sweet tea.*)
CINDY: So, Jewel.
JACKSON: I ran into her again after Terry tossed Bob into my eyes. I stumbled to the clinic barely able to see. She fixed me up. I asked her out. She said she couldn't date a drug dealer. I said the heck with her and left.
CINDY: You said, "the heck with her."
JACKSON: I probably used different words.
CINDY: I'm sure you did.
JACKSON: But I couldn't get her out of my mind, so I went back to see her. I pretended my eyes were

still bothering me. She once again said she wouldn't date a drug dealer.

CINDY: So, you gave up dealing for her?

JACKSON: I sure did and I enrolled at the community college.

CINDY: You look very good and you talk like a new person.

JACKSON: I can't give all the credit for that to the community college. My poor grammar and diction were also part of my act. Who wants to buy drugs from a proper gentleman? I was playing the part. (*He puts on his ghetto voice.*) It "gots" me whats I needed. And I ain't gots no regrets. (*Back to regular voice.*) Jewel didn't like my ghetto talk and I couldn't deal drugs for the rest of my life, not if I wanted to share it with Jewel. Plus the young Hispanics were invading my park and stealing my clients. Oh, and she set me straight about Obama Care and the Affordable Care Act.

CINDY: Damn Republicans never could figure out a better health care program.

(*JACKSON gestures air quotes with his hands.*)

JACKSON: Obama "done good" for a "brother."

CINDY: I think we can take back the White House this year.

JACKSON: Bernie, two-point-oh.

CINDY: I'd like to meet Jewel.

JACKSON: I'm sure you will. She's probably watching us—just to make sure I don't shoot you.

CINDY: Before you do that, I need to give you something. (*CINDY gets her purse and pulls out a checkbook and a pen.*) What's your last name?

JACKSON: My last name?
CINDY: I want to give you a check.
JACKSON: Now, this really is white guilt.
CINDY: Call it what you want. Terry always wanted to pay you back the money he and Bob took from you.
JACKSON: I don't even know how much they got.
CINDY: Terry said it was two thousand, one hundred and seventy-eight dollars.
JACKSON: Plus pain and suffering. Make it out for five thousand.
CINDY: I was thinking twenty.
JACKSON: Grand?
CINDY: Do you want more?
JACKSON: I'm still going to shoot you.
CINDY: Let me sign the check first.
JACKSON: I don't want your white guilt money. Just give me what he stole from me.
CINDY: I received lots of insurance money when my first husband died. And then when Terry died, I got more. I'm a rich old lady.
JACKSON: So, you and Terry did get married?
CINDY: Yes.
JACKSON: I told you… my first impressions are always right.
CINDY: Lovebirds.
JACKSON: Jewel and I are going to get married.
CINDY: Congratulations. Think of this money as a wedding gift.
JACKSON: We have our eyes on this house not far from the clinic. And the money sure would help.

CINDY: Give me your last name and I can fill in the blank on the check.

(*SANTANA enters. He wears a Hawaiian shirt, khakis, and sandals. He speaks with a Spanish accent.*)

SANTANA: What's this, a picnic in my park?

(*JACKSON puts on his ghetto voice.*)

JACKSON: Yo, Bro, we don't wants no trouble.

SANTANA: First off, I ain't your Bro, and, second, I don't respond to ghetto, especially from a well-dressed dude like yourself.

JACKSON: My mistake. We don't want any trouble.

SANTANA: There won't be no trouble if you pay the picnic fee.

CINDY: This is a city park; there are no fees to picnic here.

SANTANA: The rules changed when I took over the park.

CINDY: This damn park sure changes ownership a lot.

JACKSON: The new demographics of America.

SANTANA: Now, about my fee.

CINDY: Your park is a mess. I just cleaned up this area, so you owe me a fee for my work.

JACKSON: What is the fee? How much do you want?

SANTANA: It was twenty bucks, but because of this old lady's mouth, the fee has gone up.

CINDY: We're not paying him anything.

JACKSON: How much has the fee gone up?

SANTANA: I want the bitch's purse.

JACKSON: You just said the wrong thing.

SANTANA: What, bitch?

JACKSON: No, purse. You don't know how much this lady loves her purse.
SANTANA: Is it worth dying over?
CINDY: I guess you'll find out. Come on, Jackson, help me pack up. We're leaving this dump.
(*CINDY takes the plates and puts them into the trash can. She packs the basket and folds the blanket as they talk.*)
SANTANA: Dude, my man, are you "the" Jackson that used to own this park?
JACKSON: That's me.
SANTANA: Jackson Brown?
JACKSON: The one and only.
CINDY: Brown? Your last name is Brown?
JACKSON: That's it, Jackson Brown.
CINDY: He's one of my favorite singers. "The Pretender."
JACKSON: He spells his last name differently than I do. (*To SANTANA.*) So, my reputation precedes me.
SANTANA: Reputation, shit. You went soft. Two old fucks robbed your ass twice, and now you hanging with this old bitch.
CINDY: That is the second time you've called me a bitch.
SANTANA: Have I reached my quota?
JACKSON: We don't want any trouble. Just tell us what the fee is now.
SANTANA: The fee has gone up again because of her sassy mouth. It's now going to cost you your wallet, along with her purse.
CINDY: Come on, Jackson. Let's just leave.
JACKSON: You may have a death wish, but I want to marry Jewel.

CINDY: This fool won't do anything to us. What's he going to do, shoot us?

SANTANA: The name is Santana and I will shoot you. (*He pulls out a gun.*)

CINDY: How appropriate… "Soul Sacrifice."

JACKSON: What are you talking about?

CINDY: Carlos Santana… "Soul Sacrifice." It's is one of my favorite Santana songs… and one of the highlights of the Woodstock film.

SANTANA: His last name is Santana. Santana is my first name.

CINDY: Jackson, now that he has his gun out, aren't you going to stand up to this dumbass?

JACKSON: Look out, Santana, she called you a dumbass. It is my experience that things get bad when "dumbass" is used.

CINDY: If you won't pull your gun out and stand up to him, give it to me.

SANTANA: Are you packing heat, Jackson?

JACKSON: Who me, no, I'm cool, cool as a cucumber.

CINDY: Jackson is hot, and he isn't afraid to get blood on his gun.

SANTANA: Shut the fuck up and give me your purse.

CINDY: Are you a drug dealer?

SANTANA: I provide a service to those in need.

JACKSON: Believe me, Santana, you don't want to go down that road with this lady.

SANTANA: She's going to be sorry she drove anywhere near my park.

CINDY: How long have you been providing your services?

SANTANA: Since before I took this park from Jackson.
JACKSON: You didn't take anything from me.
CINDY: Would you say three years or so?
SANTANA: 'bout that.
CINDY: You... you sorry ass shit. You killed my son. Shoot his ass, Jackson.
SANTANA: I never killed nobody.
CINDY: Your goddamn drugs kill people all the time. And my son died from your drugs.
SANTANA: Damn, Jackson, where'd you find this crazy bitch?
CINDY: That's number three. Don't call me that again.
JACKSON: Santana, you haven't seen anything yet. If I were you, I'd leave while you can still walk and see.
SANTANA: It's the two of you that's going to be leaving the park and only after you give me the purse and wallet. Now, you can walk out or ride out on a stretcher, which one that will be is up to you. You can leave the fried chicken too.
JACKSON: She doesn't have any hot sauce.
SANTANA: No hot sauce for chicken?
JACKSON: That's exactly what I said.
CINDY: My fried chicken doesn't need any damn hot sauce.
SANTANA: Cool down, bitch.
CINDY: That's it. (*She moves toward JACKSON.*) Give me your gun, Jackson. (*CINDY reaches in JACKSON's coat and pulls out his gun and points it at SANTANA.*)

SANTANA: What are you going to do with that, you psycho bitch?
CINDY: This bitch is going to make you as dead as my son is.
SANTANA: What? Are you going to drown me?
CINDY: I'm not afraid to shoot you.
SANTANA: Look at the gun. (*CINDY looks at the gun and realizes it is a water gun. She speaks to JACKSON.*)
CINDY: WTF, Jackson?
JACKSON: It was Jewel's idea. Since I still felt the urge to shoot you, she said I should symbolically do it with a water gun. It would be like cleansing your soul.
SANTANA: Give me your wallet. (*JACKSON throws SANTANA his wallet.*)
JACKSON: Here, now let us go. (*SANTANA looks in the wallet.*)
SANTANA: There ain't no money in it. (*He throws the wallet down.*)
JACKSON: I could have told you that, but you didn't ask. You just said you wanted my wallet.
SANTANA: Don't get smart with me.
CINDY: Jackson is smart. He is very smart. He used to be a dumbass like you. But he's attending the community college now and making a better life for himself. You should do the same thing. Because you won't be young forever. And you can't sell drugs forever.
SANTANA: Shut up and give me your purse.
CINDY: How did you make it over Trump's wall?
SANTANA: I'm Cuban, not Mexican, and I'm a third generation American. Now, give me that damn

purse. (*SANTANA grabs CINDY's purse strap. She won't let it go and there is a tug-of-war over the purse.*)

CINDY: You'll never get this purse.

SANTANA: When I shoot your bitch-ass, I will pull it from your dead hands.

CINDY: I don't think you'll shoot me. All you men talk tough, but when it comes down to it, none of you got the balls to do it. Well, I'm not afraid to use my gun and I will. (*CINDY starts spraying SANTANA in the face with the water gun.*)

SANTANA: Knock it off.

CINDY: Jackson, go get Terry for some help.

JACKSON: Get Terry?

CINDY: Yes, Terry. On the bench.

(*JACKSON runs to the bench and gets the urn. He runs back to CINDY and SANTANA and throws the ashes in SANTANA's face.*)

SANTANA: Son of a bitch. I'm blind. (*SANTANA lets go of the purse strap and drops his gun.*)

CINDY: Grab his gun, Linc. I'll get your wallet.

(*JACKSON picks up the gun. CINDY gets the wallet.*)

JACKSON: Linc?

CINDY: The Mod Squad. Pete, Julie, and Linc. One black, one white, and one blonde. Terry and I were two-thirds of that hip team. All we needed was a black dude to complete the trio.

JACKSON: I say… you and I are more like Harold and Maude.

SANTANA: I'll find you both and you'll be DOA.

JACKSON: Don't forget the chicken.

CINDY: I thought it needed hot sauce.

JACKSON: We can buy some.

CINDY: I'll not have you mess up my chicken with hot sauce.

JACKSON: Okay, just get it. I'll keep him covered.

(*CINDY gets the picnic basket. She takes out a piece of chicken and gives it to SANTANA.*)

CINDY: You'll see, Santana, my fried chicken doesn't need hot sauce because I put habanero peppers in the batter. (*She moves to JACKSON.*) I want to meet Jewel.

JACKSON: She has the getaway car running.

CINDY: You still got the Mustang.

JACKSON: Yes, now run, Cindy, run.

(*JACKSON and CINDY run off and SANTANA screams in frustration. The SOUND of an engine revving and tires squealing are heard as the LIGHTS fade to black.*)

ACT TWO

SCENE TWO

(*The scene is still the park, immediately following the previous scene. AT RISE: The park is empty. There is a glow to everything in the park. After a beat, SANTANA's voice can be heard.*)

SANTANA: Son of a bitch. I'm blind. (*CINDY's voice is heard.*)

CINDY: The Mod Squad. Pete, Julie, and Linc. One black, one white, and one blonde. Terry and I were two-thirds of that hip team. All we needed was a black dude to complete the trio.

(*The SOUND of an engine revving and tires squealing is heard. A beat after that SOUND is over, a SOUND of something squeezing in between two balloons, followed by a popping SOUND. On that popping sound TERRY stumbles on as if projected into the scene.*)

TERRY: Wow, what a crazy trip. (*He yells off in the direction that CINDY and JACKSON exited.*) Cindy. Come back, Cindy. (*Beat*) I guess it's true. I must be dead. (*Beat*) But where am I? Where the hell am I? (*Beat*) Hell? Could it be? (*He looks around*) No, it looks like the park. It is the park. And there's our bench. (*He sees a note.*) What's this? (*He picks up the note and reads it.*) Mr. Godot told me to tell you he won't come this evening but surely tomorrow. (*Beat*) This has to be a joke. Hello? Is anybody here? (*Pause*) Oh great! Alone! (*He sits on the bench.*) Nothing to be done. (*He takes a shoe off and looks for something on the inside of it. Long pause*) Eternity is a long time. (*He puts his shoe back on. Pause. BOB enters on the run.*)

BOB: Sorry, I'm late.

TERRY: Where ya been?

BOB: Waiting for my…

TERRY: (*Shouting*) Stop! Stop this right now.

BOB: Stop what?

TERRY: This… this Déjà vu… or whatever you want to call it. You're about to tell me you were waiting for your daughter to pick you up because she was getting the U-Haul and you're here to say goodbye.

BOB: No, I wasn't. I was about to say I was… waiting for my best friend to get here so I could say welcome.

TERRY: You weren't.
BOB: I wasn't, what?
TERRY: Waiting for me. When I got here. The place was empty.
BOB: Yeah, I'm sorry. I should have been here. I was checking on something.
TERRY: Checking on what?
BOB: It's a surprise. Come on, I'll show you. (*Beat*)
TERRY: Where the hell... are we... you know... are we... in... hell?
BOB: Don't be silly.
TERRY: You and I did some bad shit in our lives toward the end. You shot Jackson. We stole money from him. I lusted after chicks in bikinis.
BOB: You made all that Jackson bad shit good when Cindy gave Jackson a check. As for the lusting, you're safe on that one. There is no foul in lusting.
TERRY: Well, I just assumed we were in hell. I don't see any wings on you.
BOB: Do you see any horns?
TERRY: No.
BOB: I'm working on my wings. But don't expect to see big, birdlike appendages with feathers coming out of my back. It's more like the wings a pilot gets after passing aviation school.
TERRY: Then where are we?
BOB: I stopped questioning that not long after I got here. It's just the park.
TERRY: Who's in charge?
BOB: Didn't you get my note? I left it on the bench.
TERRY: Godot? Not funny.

BOB: I thought it was. A little theatre humor. Would it be funnier if the note were from Ferlinghetti? I'm sorry. Come on, I want to take you somewhere.
TERRY: You've been here two years and you don't know where we are or who's in charge?
BOB: Nope. Every day, I expect someone to tell me what's going on and no one ever shows up.
TERRY: Well, I need to talk to someone. I still have a lot of living to do. I think I got here too early. There has to be more to life than I had. My bucket list is half-empty. I never got to raid a crack house.
BOB: Just cause you're here doesn't mean that life stops. After all, it's called life after death.
TERRY: How do you know all this, if you're still waiting for someone to tell you what's going on?
BOB: Some things just come to me. It's like osmosis. And some is common knowledge, passed down by loved ones.
TERRY: Who told you?
BOB: Allison and Sheila.
TERRY: Are they here?
BOB: Where else would they be?
TERRY: I don't know, because I don't know where we are.
BOB: Maggie is here too.
TERRY: Where is she?
BOB: At home. There are no dogs allowed in the park.
TERRY: Where are Allison and Shelia? I want to see them.
BOB: They're not here at the moment.
TERRY: Where are they?

BOB: I know you're full of questions, but try to relax. They're just shopping.
TERRY: Shopping?
BOB: Yes, at J. C. Penny.
TERRY: I bet the J. C. takes on special meaning here?
BOB: Yes, when you think the alternative is shopping at Kohl's (*coals*). I hear it's really hot there.
TERRY: I still want to talk to whoever is in charge.
BOB: Pick a number. Chill out; it's common to feel the way you do. I'm here to help you make the leap, the transition.
TERRY: Why would you do that?
BOB: If I recall accurately, you are my best friend and we promised to always be there for each other.
TERRY: What do you personally get out of helping me?
BOB: Okay, I get my wings when you accept your fate, but I'd do it because you are my friend. You haven't forgotten that, have you?
TERRY: I was pretty damn angry with you when you left me, again. Just like Woodstock.
BOB: I don't think you can compare my dying to my going to Woodstock. I didn't have a choice with death.
TERRY: You didn't have to go to Woodstock.
BOB: You told me to go.
TERRY: I didn't think you would.
BOB: Why haven't you ever told me this?
TERRY: I thought you knew.
BOB: What, that you've been mad at me for fifty years because I went to Woodstock.

TERRY: I learned to live with it. The feeling just resurfaced when you died.
BOB: Well, maybe you don't even want to be here if you're so mad.
TERRY: Haven't you heard anything I've said? No… hell no, I don't want to be here. That's what I've been telling you.
BOB: Sorry, you're kind of stuck here since you're dead.
TERRY: I refuse to believe there is no way out.
BOB: There is alternative routing, but it is not an option for you.
TERRY: How do you know I can't go back?
BOB: Look, I don't have all the answers. I'm new to this death thing too.
TERRY: You just want your wings.
BOB: I really just want the two of us to be there for each other, the way we used to be. Please trust me. Come on, I know how I can ease your crossover pain. (*Pause*)
TERRY: I thought this place would be a lot more crowded. When one considers all the deaths there have been since the Garden, this place should be standing room only, like China.
BOB: It depends on where you go. Some places are crowded. Like the Catholic-burbs. Now, that cloud is crowded. But you're thinking space as in size. You know, the room is this big or the country that big. Think universe. Look out there. There is no end to it; there are no walls or boundaries. It's endless. It goes on forever. That's a lot of room for all of us.

TERRY: How do you find your way around? Is there a map?
BOB: All categorized by names, events, or year in a massive telepathic computer. And travel anywhere is timeless. (*Beat*)
TERRY: Does Allison know I'm here?
BOB: She's been waiting for you longer than I have.
TERRY: Then why wasn't she here to greet me?
BOB: She thought it would be better if I did.
TERRY: She's probably mad at me for meeting and marrying Cindy.
BOB: Who do you think was instrumental in sending Cindy your way?
TERRY: Allison?
BOB: Cindy was practically Allison's twin.
TERRY: All but the voting for Trump.
BOB: How do you know Allison wouldn't have voted for Trump?
TERRY: I was married to her for forty-five years, I just know.
BOB: Glad to see you still have your mind.
TERRY: It was my ticker that gave out, not my thinker.
BOB: Good, you'll be happy to learn that the history books are reporting that Trump was the worst president in US history. Russian history sees it differently. (*Beat*)
TERRY: What's going to happen when Cindy gets here?
BOB: If you don't know what to do with two women who love you, all that talk about chicks in bikinis was just that... talk.

TERRY: I doubt Cindy and Allison would... you know...
BOB: Loosen up; I'm just playing with you. That messy part of relationships doesn't play a big role in the formula in this life. It makes things much easier. And don't forget, Cindy will have her first husband here too.
TERRY: This place sounds like one big orgy.
BOB: I suppose if that's what you want, it can be arranged.
TERRY: Getting back to Cindy is what I want arranged. We were going to open up an after-school tutoring center in algebra and writing.
BOB: She's done that with Jackson.
TERRY: In what... algebra and crack?
BOB: Jackson went on to get a degree in counseling and social work from Florida Atlantic University.
TERRY: No one is that quick a study. I've only been here ten minutes.
BOB: Time is not measured the same way up here. When you have eternity, why look at it in years, months, days, hours, or minutes. It is just always now.
TERRY: How did you fill your now? The past two years?
BOB: I supervised the sculpting of this park for your arrival.
TERRY: It looks very realistic.
BOB: All my theatre training paid off. I'm hoping I can help with the new theme park proposed for Cloud Nine.
TERRY: I like the glow the park gives off.

BOB: I call it sparkle.
TERRY: Like the vampires in the Twilight series?
BOB: You got it.
TERRY: You've said things like "up here," "J. C.," and "Cloud Nine." That suggests that we are up, so doesn't that mean we're in heaven?
BOB: Call it what you want. No one has really told me what it's called. I know that nothing bad happens to me here. I am never hungry. Or tired. If I want to work, I can. Shelia and I never fight. If I want to read all day, I do.
TERRY: (*Sarcastically, he wants out.*) I want to read Heaven Can Wait, so there has to be someone to talk to about that.
BOB: Access to the library card catalogue files are in the telepathic computer. Drones will deliver the book directly to you. Both your books are available.
TERRY: Reading was a metaphor.
BOB: Didn't you hear anything I just said? You can do whatever you want to here. It's better than retirement.
TERRY: Anything?
BOB: Anything. (*Beat.*) But leave.
TERRY: Okay, I want to raid a crack house.
BOB: I figured you'd say that, Sundance.
TERRY: Oh, so now I'm Sundance?
BOB: I relinquish the title to you.
TERRY: Do you get extra points in earning your wings for being nice to the new arrival?
BOB: See that box by the bench?
TERRY: Yeah.

BOB: The DEA jackets are in it. (*TERRY runs to the box and pulls out the jackets.*)
TERRY: Damn, these are better than the ones I had made. (*He puts one of the jackets on.*)
BOB: Remember where you are. We have the best of the best here. I think Betsy Ross stitched those letters on the back.
TERRY: This is better than Westworld.
BOB: That's the idea behind the Cloud Nine Theme Park, but more spiritual. (*TERRY is looking in the box.*)
TERRY: Where are the guns?
BOB: There are strict gun laws here. We don't need them. Nothing bad will happen.
TERRY: Shit, that takes the danger aspect out of the raid.
BOB: At least we're back together. Even without a concept of time, I've missed you. (*Beat*)
TERRY: I suppose you know that you saved Cindy and me from Jackson?
BOB: Yeah, I might not have been alive, but I wasn't dead.
TERRY: I wanted to spread you more evenly throughout the park.
BOB: I was just glad I could help my friend.
TERRY: But of course, you were the first to do it.
BOB: To do what?
TERRY: Having your ashes thrown in someone's face to save a life. By the time I did it, it wasn't even fashionable.

BOB: You were mixed with all that water from the squirt gun. Things got pretty gummy. It looked like Santana was wearing a facial scrub mask.
TERRY: (*Forcefully*) My life had no meaning. Let me go back and help Cindy with the after-school tutoring program.
BOB: Your life had plenty of meaning. You were voted one of the top ten teachers of all time at the high school.
TERRY: Really. Did you make the list?
BOB: No, but the new theatre was named in my honor.
TERRY: Always one step better than me.
BOB: Without the poet, there is no theatre. We all are reliant on one another, throughout history. Lennon and McCartney couldn't have been a team without Bach or Elvis. Many in life don't know that basic fact. You and I were a team. And now, I need you to fill my eternity.
TERRY: You have Shelia.
BOB: She's a big part of my eternity, but without you, it has a big black hole.
TERRY: (*He says this angrily.*) Careful, people will think we're gay.
BOB: Well, you did get my life insurance money. And you didn't have to marry me.
TERRY: Look, I'll be back. I'll join you up here in your make-believe park later. It's just not my time. Not now. (*TERRY starts to exit.*)
BOB: Where are you going to go?
TERRY: To find whoever is in charge.

BOB: I know you're hearing me. You're just not listening. No one knows how to find this person.

(*The following crescendos to TERRY punching BOB.*)

TERRY: Goddamn it, I'm frustrated. I'm angry. I've been angry since you died. I had just lost Allison and then you.

BOB: I was angry, too, when I lost Shelia. And then the Lewy body took over my life. I took it out on poor Jackson. I can't believe I shot him in the foot.

TERRY: I wanted to die. And then I met Cindy and found life again. Now, I don't want to die.

BOB: You're not the first person to feel that way.

TERRY: I don't care about anyone but me.

BOB: Fine, then be by yourself. I give up. Good luck trying to find your way back. (*BOB starts to walk away.*)

TERRY: Yeah, walk away, you hypocrite. Where are you going?

BOB: I'm leaving you to wallow in your own self-pity.

TERRY: That's right. Leave me again. You're good at doing that.

BOB: I am tired of you throwing that in my face. (*TERRY gets right in BOB's face.*)

TERRY: You want in your face, okay, here's in your face. (*BOB pushes TERRY forcefully.*)

BOB: Fuck you.

TERRY: No, fuck you. (*TERRY punches BOB in the face.*)

BOB: Ah! Damn, dude, what the fuck.

TERRY: You just kept pushing me, didn't you? You just couldn't let it go. (*TERRY pushes BOB.*)

BOB: Okay, you made your point. So much for my theory that nothing bad happens up here. Damn, that hurt.
TERRY: I'm scared, Bob. I don't want to die and have no one remember me. (*Beat*)
BOB: Thank you for caring for me in Cleveland. It got pretty messy.
TERRY: I never had to change any children's diapers, but I got plenty of practice with you.
BOB: It takes a true friend to do that.
TERRY: There were times I questioned my promise.
BOB: I wouldn't know who you were at times, but I trusted you.
TERRY: It was that promise to always be there for one another that kept me going.
BOB: Exactly, have you gone back on your word now? (*Pause*)
TERRY: By the way, you missed his foot.
BOB: Missed whose foot?
TERRY: Jackson. When you shot his foot, you only grazed it.
BOB: Yeah, I heard. How did you know? You were dead when that information was revealed to Cindy.
TERRY: I don't know; it just came to me.
BOB: Like osmosis?
TERRY: Sort of.
BOB: This place is beginning to work on you.
TERRY: No way.
BOB: Missing his foot just proves that I could never be Sundance. He was a sharp shooter. (*Pause*)
TERRY: What ever happened to Santana? I hope he got shingles.

BOB: A car hit him as he stumbled blindly across the street trying to get to the Urgent Care and he died.
TERRY: Ouch, that's worse than shingles. (*SANTANA enters with a popping SOUND.*)
SANTANA: What the fuck? Wow, what a trip. (*He looks around.*) Thank you, Jesus, I am back at the park. (*He sees BOB and TERRY.*) What the fuck is your problem?
BOB: It wasn't me. It was him... he was in your eyes.
TERRY: Thanks for ratting on me, Bob.
BOB: But I wouldn't say anything to him right now if I were you. He's not happy at the moment.
SANTANA: Join the fucking club.
BOB: I'm not even sure how you got here. You should have turned south at the crossroads, not north. You know, Robert Johnson, going down to the crossroads.
SANTANA: No, not Johnson. I'm looking for a black dude named Jackson.
BOB: He's not here yet.
SANTANA: He threw some shit into my eyes.
TERRY: Didn't you hear what Bob just said, that shit was me.
SANTANA: Wait a minute. Where the fuck am I?
TERRY: For Christ's sake, Bob, does anyone know where there are when they get here? I think that is a problem that needs to be addressed with management.
BOB: He doesn't belong here.
TERRY: Neither do I. Hey, Santana, maybe we can work together to get out of this place.
BOB: I don't think you want to go where he is going.

SANTANA: I ain't going nowhere. It's you two old dudes that is leaving my park.
TERRY: This park sure is popular among its inhabitants. Everyone thinks they own it.
SANTANA: I ain't never seen you two old dudes in my park.
TERRY: We used to own it, until Jackson took it from us.
SANTANA: So, you know Jackson?
TERRY: Bob was a fleck of dust in his eyes years ago.
SANTANA: You say you want to work with me, fine. Let's find that shit and the bitch that was with him.
TERRY: What bitch is that?
BOB: I think he is referring to Cindy.
SANTANA: Yeah, that's the bitch's name. I want her too.
TERRY: This is where we have to part company. That woman is not a bitch, she is my wife.
SANTANA: If I can't find either one of them, and your wife is the bitch, then you will die in her place.
BOB: The city cops really need to patrol this park more. There are an awful lot of death threats here since we lost our park, Terry.
SANTANA: Just the bitch and the black dude.
TERRY: I would really like it if you would stop referring to my wife as a bitch.
SANTANA: Your mouth is just as smart-ass as hers is.
TERRY: We have a lot in common.
SANTANA: Yeah, you both don't shut up.

BOB: I hate to break up this intellectual, stimulating conversation, but Santana, you're going to have to find an exit portal.
SANTANA: Exit portal?
TERRY: What? Exit portal? Why didn't you tell me about these exit portals?
BOB: I told you about the alternate routing.
TERRY: But not about any damn exit portals.
BOB: You say tomato (*to-may-toe*), I say tomato (*to-mah-toe*).
SANTANA: We ain't at the vegetable market.
TERRY: Or a diction class.
BOB: Terry, you don't want to exit via an exit portal.
TERRY: Why not?
SANTANA: What he said?
BOB: They only go one way and that is straight south, nonstop!
SANTANA: You mean to Key West. I ain't going there, it's too gay.
BOB: Is this really the next generation? Did we leave the world in these hands?
TERRY: Not guilty. The generation after us is responsible for his kind.
SANTANA: I'm through trying to talk to you. You don't make any sense. Now, get out of my park before I charge you a loitering fee.
TERRY: You don't get it, do you, Santana?
SANTANA: I get you ain't moving fast enough.
TERRY: What is the last thing you remember before seeing us in the park?
SANTANA: That damn Jackson threw a vase full of white powder in my face. At first I thought I was

Al Pacino in Scarface, cocaine heaven. But it tasted like shit.

TERRY: Hey, I resent that.

BOB: Do you remember anything after that?

SANTANA: I couldn't see. My eyes were burning; they were on fire. I had to get to the Urgent Care across the street. Right over there. (*He points off.*) Hey, where is it?

BOB: And then what?

SANTANA: I was in the middle of the street and I heard a car coming toward me. I squinted through the pain and saw a car coming right toward me. (*Realization*) I was hit by a car. You mean, I'm fucking dead.

TERRY: Bingo.

SANTANA: If I'm dead, what am I doing back in the park?

BOB: That is the million-dollar question.

TERRY: Someone thought the park was paradise.

BOB: (*To TERRY*) I thought you would like it.

TERRY: If I have to be stuck somewhere, I can think of better places than a crack-infested park. Did you ever think I might like a beach filled with bikini-clad chicks more than this?

SANTANA: If you dudes ain't gonna leave my park, I'm gonna have to charge you the loitering fee to stay.

TERRY: We're not back to that bullshit again, are we?

SANTANA: Just when I was forgetting that you were married to the bitch with Jackson, you go and insult me.

TERRY: You want insult? How about this… I didn't think you were intelligent enough to understand what an insult was. (*SANTANA pulls out his gun.*)
SANTANA: Are you intelligent enough to understand what I have pointed at you?
TERRY: I thought you said there were no guns up here.
BOB: First off, I don't know where he got it from. Jackson picked his gun up after he dropped it. And, second, how he got it past TSA and the metal detectors.
TERRY: There are TSA screeners working heaven's gate?
BOB: There invisible, but they're here.
SANTANA: And so am I. Stop acting like I ain't here. Have you forgotten I have a gun pointed at both of you?
BOB: Your gun won't hurt anyone up here.
TERRY: Uh, Bob, we established with my punch to your face that people can get hurt up here.
BOB: You do have a point, Terry.
TERRY: By the way, are we still called people, or are we angels?
SANTANA: Dammit, you guys piss me off when you ignore me.
BOB: Santana, although I think it will hurt if you shoot us, I hate to inform you that you can't kill us because we are already dead.
TERRY: You can shoot me, Santana.
BOB: Terry, stop playing around.
SANTANA: Don't think I won't, you dumb old man.

TERRY: I want you to. I have a theory... if I am shot and die in heaven, maybe then I return to my life on the beach in Miami with Cindy. You know, things just get reversed.
BOB: Do you know how ridiculous that sounds?
TERRY: No more ridiculous than if I told you... we were being held hostage by a drug dealer in heaven... who is pointing a gun at you and me... demanding a loitering fee from us... so we can stay in a park... that he thinks he owns... that isn't even real.
BOB: Well, when you put it that way... the beach with chicks in bikinis does sound better.
SANTANA: Both of you give me your wallets.
BOB: There is no need for wallets up here because there is no need for money because everything is free.
SANTANA: Goddamn it... shut the fuck up.
BOB: You probably shouldn't have said that up here.
SANTANA: What, fuck?
TERRY: No, the damning God part.
SANTANA: Have you two been smoking pot?
TERRY: No, but if you have some.
SANTANA: What of value do either of you have?
BOB: Another dead end, Santana. I think I should show you the exit portal.
SANTANA: I know what you value more than anything.
TERRY: What's that?
SANTANA: Each other. (*SANTANA grabs BOB and pulls him into his chest, then puts the gun to BOB's head.*)

TERRY: Damn, Bob, this park sure has gotten violent. The last time you and I were together in it, this same thing happened. The only difference was, we had a gun and I was in your situation.
BOB: Well, what are you going to do about this? (*Beat*)
TERRY: Probably nothing.
BOB: Thanks a lot.
TERRY: I want to test out my theory. If he shoots you, I can see if you die and stay here or die and return to Miami. If you end up in Miami, I'll force him to shoot me too.
SANTANA: Give me your DEA jacket.
TERRY: No, you can't have my jacket.
SANTANA: Then say goodbye to your friend.
TERRY: Dammit, Santana, you're right. He is my friend. He and I go way back. And what kind of friend would I be if I didn't do anything to save him? (*TERRY charges SANTANA and manages to free BOB. BOB backs away from SANTANA. SANTANA fires the gun and hits BOB in the gut.*)
BOB: Ouch, he got me.
   (*A lot of blood appears from BOB's gut. BOB falls to the ground. TERRY runs to BOB. TERRY then screams a continuous yell as charges SANTANA and punches him in the face. SANTANA falls to the ground out cold. TERRY runs back to BOB.*)
TERRY: Bob! Bob, are you there? (*There is no response from BOB. TERRY shouts to the heavens.*) I defy you, Godot! (*Beat. BOB stirs and wakes up.*)
BOB: Help me, I've fallen and I can't get up.
TERRY: Damn, I thought you were...

BOB: Dead?
TERRY: Yeah.
BOB: No, I'm already dead. I'm fine. (*He examines his blood-soaked shirt.*) It looks a lot worse than it is.
TERRY: Did you make it back to Miami?
BOB: Sorry, no chicks in bikinis to report.
TERRY: Well, that theory didn't work out, but my punch still packs a wallop. Santana's ready for a transfer south. Where's the exit portal?
BOB: If I show you, you won't try anything stupid?
TERRY: No, I've accepted my fate. I'm ready to cross over, make the leap. One can't go backward in life.
BOB: Or in death. (*TERRY embraces BOB.*) The portal is right over there. (*He points off. TERRY crosses to SANTANA and starts to drag him offstage.*) Take his gun too.
TERRY: We'll need it to raid crack houses.
BOB: He'll need it more where he is going.

(*TERRY goes back and picks up the gun. He moves back to SANTANA and drags him offstage. The SOUND of the Star Trek transporter is heard. There is a flash of LIGHT from offstage. TERRY reenters and moves to BOB.*)

TERRY: What's this big surprise you have for me?
BOB: We're going to Woodstock.
TERRY: That's cool, to visit the site?
BOB: No, bro, we are going back to 1969… and you and I are going to Woodstock together.
TERRY: Run, Bob, run.

(*BOB and TERRY run off stage as the Crosby, Stills, and Nash cover of "Woodstock" fills the heavens. After the guitar opening and as the singing begins, the LIGHTS slowly fade to black. The song continues under the curtain call and as the audience exits.)*

END

About the Author

Bob May began writing plays in 1971 while he was earning a BA in theatre with the emphasis in directing at St. Cloud (*MN*) State University. After graduating in 1972, Bob began a directing career that spanned the next fifty years, and he guided over 450 shows around the country to opening night. All the while, he continued to write, and in 1994 he earned an MFA in Playwriting from the University of Nevada, Las Vegas. Twenty-five of his plays, including *Beanie and the Bamboozling Book Machine*, *The Great Santa Claus Reindeer Roundup*, *A Different Kind of Nutcracker*, *Jack and Bella: From Beanstalk to Broadway*, and *Elson, the First Christmas Elf*, are published by Samuel French, Playscripts, Dramatic Publishing, Heuer, Broadway Publishing, and others. His books *Scriptwriting Structure: To the Point Pointers* and *The Process of Play Directing: From Concept to Curtain* are published by Skye Bridge Publishing. Dominion Publications publishes his acting book *Postcard Pointers to the Performer*. He has taught in higher education for the past thirty-three years and currently teaches playwriting and screenwriting at the University of Central Arkansas.

Contact Bob May at bobmay1049@gmail.com.

Published Works

BOOKS

Postcard Pointers to the Performer. Published by Dominion Publications, Cedar Rapids, IA

Scriptwriting Structure: To-the-Point Pointers. Published by Skye Bridge Publishing, Asheville. NC

The Process of Play Directing: From Concept to Curtain. Published by Skye Bridge Publishing, Asheville, NC

NONFICTION

"Home Run Heroes" published in the online literary journal *Hobart*, April 19, 2018 - http://www.hobartpulp.com/web_features/home-run-heroes

PLAYS

Beanie and the Bamboozling Book Machine - a fantasy-adventure published by Samuel French, Inc., New York, NY

Beanie and the Bamboozling Horror Machine - a sequel - published by Samuel French, Inc.

Beanie and the Bamboozling Adventure Machine - a second sequel –published by Samuel French, Inc.

The Andrew is Dead Story - a play in one act - published by I. E. Clark, Inc., Schelenburg, TX

9th Inning Wedding - a play in one act - published by I. E. Clark, Inc.

9th Inning Wedding – also published in the textbook, *The Golden Stage: Dramatic Activities for Older Adults* by Ann McDonough, Ph.D. Kendall/Hunt, publisher.

Broadway Memories - a musical revue – published in *The Golden Stage*

A Collection from a Career in Theatre

Concerned Citizens - a short play - published in the collection *Short Stuff: 10- to 20- Minute Plays for Mature Actors*, Dramatic Publishing, Chicago, IL

Cinderella and the Fairy Godfather - published by Playscripts, Inc., New York, NY

Alice and Wonderland - published by Playscripts, Inc.

Snow White and the Magic Mirror - published by Playscripts, Inc.

Gidget's Gadget to Bamboozle Beanie - published by Playscripts, Inc.

Snowmen, Elves, and Nutcrackers: Three Christmas Plays
Crystal and the Christmas Snowman
Elson, The First Christmas Elf

A Different Kind of Nutcracker published by Baker's Plays, New York, NY

Hocus Pocus Horticulture - published by Playscripts, Inc., New York, NY

Go To ... a ten-minute absurdist play, published in *Exquisite Corpse Literary Journal,* Jan 2009, and also published by Heuer Publishing, Cedar Rapids, IA

Jack and Bella: From Beanstalk to Broadway – a musical – published by Heuer Publishing, Cedar Rapids, IA

The Great Santa Claus Reindeer Roundup – published by Brooklyn Publishers, Cedar Rapids, IA

The Three Little Pigs – published by Heuer Publishing, Cedar Rapids, IA

Two Old Men (one-act version) – published by *Cave Region Review Journal,* North Arkansas College, Harrison, AR

www.ingramcontent.com/pod-product-compliance
Lightning Source LLC
Chambersburg PA
CBHW051932290426
44110CB00015B/1945